By BEN MADDOW

A Sunday between Wars

The Course of American Life
from 1865 to 1917

W · W · NORTON & COMPANY · *NEW YORK* · *LONDON*

First Edition

PERMISSIONS GRANTED BY:

Houghton Mifflin (Boston, 1950), *A Diary From Dixie*, Mary Boykin Chestnut, ed. Ben Ames Williams.
University of Oklahoma Press (1976), *Great Plains Command*, Marvin Kroeker.
Manuscripts and Archives Division, The New York Public Library, Astor, Lenox and Tilden Foundations, *Reminiscences and Experiences of a Union Soldier of the 79th New York Regiment at Platte Bridge.*
University of Oklahoma Press (1966), *Up and Down California*, William H. Brewer.
Arno Press (New York, 1969), *Annals of the Great Strike*, J. A. Dacus.
Arno Press (New York, 1969), *The Steel Workers*, John A. Fitch.
Arno Press (New York, 1971), *Workers Speak, Self Portraits*, eds. Leon Stein and Philip Taft.
Crown Publishers, Inc., *Workin' on the Railroad*, © 1970 by Richard Reinhardt.
Dover Publications (1973), *Favorite Songs of the Nineties*, R. A. Fremont.
Caxton Printers, *Gold Rushes and Mining Camps*, Vardis Fisher and O. L. Holmes.
Talisman Press, *Letters of the Pikes Peak Gold Rush*, Libeus Barney.
Ward Ritchie Press, *Six Months in the Gold Mines*, E. G. Buffum.
Archives of Industrial Society, University of Pittsburgh Libraries, *History of the Jones and Laughlin Steel Corp.*, Thomas L. Lloyd.
Archives of Industrial Society, University of Pittsburgh Libraries, *Diary of Benjamin Franklin Jones.*
University of Washington, Master's thesis 1973, *Logging with Steam in the Pacific Northwest*, Father Andrew M. Prouty.
Oklahoma Historical Society, *Diary of L. F. Carroll.*
Cornell University Press, *Autobiography of a Farm Boy*, Isaac P. Roberts.
Robinson-Shattuck Papers, Schlesinger Library, Radcliffe College, Allis R. Wolfe, *Labor History* Vol. 17, No. 1, Letters of a Lowell Mill Girl and Friends."
Crown Publishers, Inc., *A Pictorial History of American Labor*, © 1972 by William Cahn.
Margaret McDowd for the *Memoirs* of her great-grandfather, J. C. Kuner.
Arno Press (New York), *The City Worker's World in America*, Mary K. Simkhovitch
Little, Brown & Company, *An American Saga*, Carl Jensen.
University of Oklahoma Press © 1971, *Flashes of Merriment: A Century of Humorous Songs in America 1805–1905.*
Executive Committee for the Publication of Issei (1973), *Issei: A History of Japanese Immigrants in North America*, Kazuo Ito.
Ethel Ginsberg for use of taped interview with author.
Arno Press (New York), *Homestead: The Households of A Mill Town*, Margaret F. Byington.
Arno Press (New York), *The Autobiography of Mother Jones.*
Arno Press (New York), *Massacre at Ludlow.*
Arno Press (New York), *The Accused and the Accusers*, Dyer D. Lunn.
Arno Press (New York), *The Pullman Strike.*
Arizona Historical Society, *Diary of George Berrell.*
Manuscripts and Archives Division, The New York Public Library, Astor Lenox and Tilden Foundations, *Diary of Eulalie Matthews Ashmore.*
Knox College Archives, Galesburg, Illinois, *The Dunneville Journal*, Edwin Dunn.
Arno Press (New York), *Children in Bondage*, Markham, Lindsly and Creel.
Sherbourne Press (1963), *Sportin' Life*, Stephen Longstreet.
Montana Historical Society, *Diary of John W. Grannis.*

Library of Congress Cataloging in Publication Data

Maddow, Ben, 1909–

  A Sunday between wars.

  Bibliography: p.

    1. United States—History—1865–1921.   2. United States—Economic conditions—1865–1918.   3. United States—Social conditions—1865–1918.   I. Title.

E661.M2   1979   973.8   78–24098

ISBN 0 393 05698 8

1 2 3 4 5 6 7 8 9 0

Contents

Acknowledgments

THE DEMERITS of this study are entirely the author's, since he is biased, and must always be, by the experiences of his generation.

The merits are due, in large part, to the special help and encouragement of the following institutions; to these, my earnest thanks: Library of Congress, particularly the staff of the MSS and Archives Division; Wyoming State Archives and History Department; Nebraska State Historical Society; Oklahoma Historical Society; Research Library, University of California at Los Angeles; Alderman Library, University of Virginia; Tamiment Foundation Research Library, New York University; Montana Historical Society; New York Public Library, Manuscript and Archives Division; Archives of Industrial Society, University of Pittsburgh Libraries; Department of MSS and University Archives, Cornell University; Idaho State Library; Western History MSS Collection, University of Missouri; Illinois State Historical Society; Special Collections, University of Nevada Library; Edison Archives, Edison National Historical Site; Library Archives, Knox College, Galesburg, Illinois; Archives and MSS Division, Rutgers University; Wyoming State Historical Research and Publication Division.

And particular thanks to the following individuals: Mary Millard; Mrs. Margaret McDowd; Mrs. Ethel Ginsberg; Kazuo Ito; Father Andrew M. Prouty; Mrs. Eulalie Ashmore Scull.

A Sunday between Wars

1

Looking Backward: A Note in Warning

THERE is no end to the nineteenth century. Its depth and luxury of detail frustrate the analyst. Even if, as in this book, one focuses only on America, and in particular on the double generation between the Civil War and World War I, and even then on a few selected topics, the materials are overwhelming in their generosity of fact and contradiction. Here, for example, was an entry in the diary of an upper-class Southern woman on July 12, 1862: "Our small colonel, Paul Hayne's son, came into my room. To amuse the child I gave him a photograph album to look over. 'You have Lincoln in your book! I am astonished at you! I hate him!' And he placed the book on the floor and struck old Abe in the face with his fist."[1] She hated and despised Lincoln as much as her nephew—but she had his photo in her album.

Many histories tell us all, and often tell it well, but fail to tell us the real thing, only the gist of it; it is like eating the label and not the bread. What follows is an attempt to remedy that hunger; it is in this effort that the pages are full of quotation. The reader will find great chunks of raw narrative, sometimes ungrammatical, by people who were there, who, with all their prejudices, were rarely conscious enough to be liars. They illustrate, for one thing, that the view from the bottom was a lot different than the view from the top. Here was an account of a Civil War battle, by a Major Williams, an aide to General Sherman:

"The sun was now fast going down behind a grove of water-oaks and as his last rays gilded the earth, all eyes once more turned toward the Rebel fort. Suddenly white puffs of smoke shot out from the thick woods surrounding the line of works. Hazen was closing in . . . General Sherman . . . said: 'Signal General Hazen that he must carry the fort by assault, tonight if possible.'

"The little flag waved and fluttered in the evening air, and the answer came, 'I am ready, and will assault at once!'

"The words had hardly passed when from out the encircling woods there came a long line of blue coats and bright bayonets, and the dear old flag was there, waving proudly in the breeze . . . Sherman stood watching

with anxious air, awaiting the decisive moment . . . 'They have been re-
pulsed!' said one of the group of officers who watched the fight.

" 'No, by Heaven!' said another; 'There is not a man in retreat—not a
straggler in all the glorious line!'

"The firing ceased . . . Victory! The fort was won. Then all of us who
had witnessed the strife and exulted in the triumph, grasped each the other's
hand, embraced, and were glad, and some of us found the water in our
eyes . . ."[2]

This was the view from above, colored red, white, and blue, of a Civil
War that killed 618,000 men out of a total in both armies of 3,000,000—a
death rate of one in five. In mortality, amputation, epidemic, and disloca-
tion, the U.S. suffered the four-year shock of more than 6,000 battles. Here
was another view of such engagements, not by a major with field glasses, but
by an anonymous private with his feet in the bloody grass:

". . . The day was terribly hot, and the troops suffered from lack of
water, which was hard to get, and was mostly obtained from stagnant pools,
and that mixed with blood of the dead or dying soldiers and horses. All we
had to eat was blackberries picked upon the battlefield . . . Now that the
conflict was over . . . perhaps a thousand soldiers lay cold in death—the blue
and the gray side by side—while hundreds lay wounded, unable to aid themselves, pleading for help and almost famished from lack of water. Many with
an arm or leg shattered, and weak from loss of blood and suffering intense
agony, begged to be put out of their misery . . .

"There were broken caissons, gun carriages, ammunition wagons, mus-
kets and small arms scattered over the field. There were also wounded
horses groaning in agony, and others that had escaped galloping about in
frantic terror, trampling the wounded soldiers in their mad flight across the
fields . . ."[3]

It is of such experience that this book is mostly composed: the views of
the ordinary person—those without names or with names that matter to nobody anymore. They are the units of our statistics. But it is important to
remember and read them in the very particulars of their anonymity.

The events that followed the Civil War, in the last third of the century,
and the first decade and a half of the twentieth, were not as serene as, at a
textbook distance, they first appear. The major crisis was the hectic growth
of industry. The Jeffersonian ideal, expressed so marvelously and so falsely
in Whitman's 1856 *Leaves of Grass*, of a nation of independent men each
standing in the doorway of his own shop or in a furrow of his own acres, was
altered, where not destroyed, by the sheer force of industrial expansion.

One of the sad victims of this uncomfortable fact was the American Indian. But he was not the only one. Millions of men, both foreign and native-
born, powered the gears of this machine. This book is for better or worse,
their view of our history—from below. It will therefore be full of theoretical
gaps and absent of many things abridged or neglected; but perhaps too it will
hold, as it held to the writer, some greatly exciting rush of the truth.

2

Whites Like Insects
Too Many to Kill

I N THE Omaha Public Library, there is a black-haired
slice of scalp preserved under glass. It was the property of a railway repairman, William Thompson, who
survived an Indian attack, brought his severed scalp back in a pail of water,
and tried to restore it to his head—without success. It was one of the sacrifices of the common man to the glories of the transcontinental railway.

On May 7, 1869, only four years after the end of the Civil War, the iron
tracks of the Union Pacific Railroad joined those of the Central Pacific at
Promontory, Utah. General Dodge, who was in charge of the civilian teams
on one side, made one of several high-flown speeches: "Gentlemen, the
great Benton proposed that some day a giant statue of Columbus be erected
on the highest peak of the Rocky Mountains, pointing westward, denoting
that as the great route across the continent. You have made that prophecy
today a fact. This is the way to India."[1] He also sent a telegram to General
J. D. Cox, secretary of the interior under President (and formerly, of course,
General) Grant: "The Final connection of Rail was made today at Promontory—summit one thousand and eighty-six (1086) miles from Missouri River
and six hundred and ninety (690) miles from Sacramento—It enables the
Millions of China to find an outlet eastwardly and eventually they will be cul-
tivating the cotton fields of the South."[2] This prophecy was gloriously unful-
filled, but the enthusiasm of the American people for this project has remained undiminished.

There were some authentic native-born Americans, however, who
hated and fought the railroads. These were the hunting tribes west of the
Missouri, whose land the railroads had cut open with the raw edge of steel.
The Sioux and the Cheyenne hated the Iron Horse, from whose moving plat-
forms, vacationing sportsmen would shoot buffalo, elk, and deer without
bothering even to pick up the heads for mounting. This double-iron ribbon
was the brand of possession, and neither the whites nor the Indians had any
doubt of that. So the young men of these hunting tribes fought as their ancestors had fought—by sudden, swift attack, for the booty and the honor
which were not always distinguishable from one another.

In Nebraska, in August of 1867, a group of young Cheyenne bloods—having learned that simply tearing out two lengths of rail meant that the repair was swift and easy—pried up and stacked a block of ties, secured it with lengths of wire cut from the telegraph lines above, and set it afire. The heat curled up and twisted the red-hot rails; General Sherman, devastating the Confederate rear in the 1864 Georgia campaign, had used a similar strategy. It worked. The next freight train was derailed into a spectacular show. The engine overturned and the following cars burst open and burned gloriously: " 'Plunder was scattered all over the prairie for half a mile. It looked as if a big cyclone had picked up a general merchandise store and sifted its contents over half the country. They [the Indians] cut the tops out of hats and the seats out of trousers and cut the arms off of coats. They cut the feet off the boots, threw them away and wore the legs. They wanted plenty of ventilation. They had tied the end of a bolt of cloth to a horse's tail and rode around with it streaming behind them . . .' "[3] This Cheyenne band was pursued by United States troops accompanied by a detachment of Pawnee scouts. In the fight among the nearby hills, several Cheyenne were killed, some of the prizes recaptured, and a Cheyenne woman and boy kidnapped. The railroad was, it appeared, an irresistible and evil monster.

But it was in the very belly of this dragon that a party of twenty-one important Indians went to Washington voluntarily just about three years later, on May 27, 1870. This delegation of Oglala Sioux was headed by forty-eight-year-old Red Cloud, accompanied by sixteen minor chiefs, chosen by him and by four women whose husbands had refused to travel without them—or possibly vice-versa: "Not one of these Indians had ever seen a town or railroad."[4] The hatred and fear by the whites of these "Wild people" was by no means universal in America. The Cherokee, for example, had recruited a whole regiment to the Confederacy, as did some other southern tribes. And there was a considerable, somewhat contemptuously named "Peace Party" in the Northeast, made up of people morally concerned with the broken treaties and the revengeful expeditions of the past century. But these "Indian-lovers" were hardly to be found in the West, on the frontier farms and raw wood settlements. Here self-interest dictated that the Indian must, like slavery, be abolished by force. So the Sioux delegation, proceeding on horse from Laramie, was advised to bypass rough, one-year-old Cheyenne, Wyoming, and board the Union Pacific train at Pine Bluff, forty miles east.

They had a special car to Washington and were provided with the dark and constricting civilized clothes of that period, to wear if they liked, and many of them did. They were also furnished with two white interpreters, and, at Red Cloud's special request, two other whites whom he considered his friends: the trader Jules Ecoffey and the half-breed John Richard, Jr., who was eager to be in Washington to secure a pardon (well in advance of either an indictment or a trial) for killing a soldier who was courting the same lady he was. So the railway car held twenty-four persons, for one of the chiefs, Man-Afraid-Of-His-Horses (the actual name was somewhat longer: Man-Whose-Enemies-Are-Even-Afraid-Of-His-Horses), fell ill—or took fright—and didn't go. The windows of the special car were a thin and fragile separation of two worlds. The train would slow down when it passed through the small, crude stations along the Platte River, and hundreds of white faces would peer with that intense yet expressionless curiosity that is particularly American. The Brule and the Oglala also, these fenceless and nomadic peoples, looked out of the same windows at the strange white settlements, at the wooden or turf cabins with their square sides, at the cattle and pigs and even horses enclosed by wooden fencing, and the square lots and the regular green of the corn and wheat fields rooting in the mildness of early June.

The train stopped at Omaha, junction of the railroad and the Missouri River. In a town founded only sixteen years before by eight crazy speculators—for the place had no particular advantages as to site or transportation—there were now buildings that were five times the height of a man. Dangerous, secret, and powerful was the medicine of the whites, and his numbers were unbelievably great. The telegraph lines that were strung from pole to pole along the right-of-way were quite obviously an example of this magic, for no sane man could believe that a message might go the distance of a hundred days' journey in the clap of a hand. Maybe it was a lie. The whites were notorious in this respect. Sitting Bull, another chief of one of the Sioux tribes, when invited to give a speech at a railway ceremony, spoke in his own tongue, and was not translated: "I hate all whites. They are liars and thieves."

Omaha was exciting and novel, but Chicago was terrifying, with its streets as thick with white faces as a sky full of grasshoppers. They were, as the Chief said on another occasion, "too many to kill." And they passed through forests cut down on both sides as if by a tornado, and saw engines in the fields breathing fire and steam, or twenty horses strapped together, pulling a great harrow of curved iron knives over the face of the land. At night, they saw from the train the glare of huge fires in Ohio and Indiana— blast furnaces changing metal into water and back again into metal. Of the locomotive itself, one Indian said:

". . . We regarded them as *wakan* (mysterious), a race whose power bordered upon the supernatural. I learned that they had made a 'fire-boat.' I could not understand how they could unite two elements which cannot exist together. I thought the water would put out the fire, and the fire would consume the boat if it had the shadow of a chance. This was to me a preposterous thing! But when I was told that the Big Knives had created a 'fire-boat-walks-on-mountains' (a locomotive) it was too much to believe.

" 'Why,' declared my informant, 'those who saw this monster move said that it flew from mountain to mountain when it seemed to be excited. They said also that they believed it carried a thunder-bird, for they frequently heard his usual war-whoop as the creature sped along!' "[5]

2

The fascinating and ironic thing about this conflict of mutually incomprehensible cultures is that they were not as contradictory as each chose to believe of the other. Americans of the first decade after the Civil War were largely Protestant; the Irish and Italian Catholic immigrants were still a minority. The practice of talking directly and uniquely to the Supernatural, without a necessary intervening priesthood, was a practice common both to the homesteader and to the Indian. Also, Indian and American had a great love for rhetoric. It was for both groups a form of folk theatre, and they shared the corresponding—if contradictory—belief that words can change reality. The Plains Indian (but not the Hopi, for example) placed great value on the exploit of the individual, on reckless, gallant bravery; on its corollary, the uncomplaining endurance of physical suffering; and on its consequence: that any individual character, sufficiently unique, colorful, strong, and finally enigmatic, would be famous and admired. And this was just as true of the American culture as it was of the Indian.

Rough rude humor, a dry turn of phrase about onself sometimes disguised as boastfulness, and an acid humor about others—this was also common to both Indian and American. The Sioux, in particular, were famous for their practical jokes. But Plains Indian humor could sometimes be hardly distinguished from sadism, particularly if the odds favored them, as the following story makes clear:

"I remember one morning when we were all at breakfast. It was an early, 6:00 o'clock breakfast too, and no one seemed very talkative. There was to be a busy day ahead, so we were eating a big breakfast of biscuits, potatoes, steak and coffee. Suddenly a rider came tearing into the yard. His horse was covered with lather. It was a neighbor . . .

"In the middle of the night he had been awakened by a rider who came to his and Curley's cabin on the Upper Piney, bringing a tragic story . . . He and his trapper partner had been trapping on Snake River, just above Gray's River. Fur was plentiful. They had built a crude cabin, planning on a fall and winter of lots of furs and a small amount of comfort . . .

"One morning the horses had strayed farther than usual, and [as] . . . the trapper who . . . left the cabin to catch [them] . . . climbed the hill, he paused to look back at the cabin. Smoke was curling from the chimney. It was their home! Then, as he looked a second longer, he discerned a large group of riders and horses coming toward their cabin. They were Indians! There were squaws behind the bucks. He could even see the travois poles sticking up from the horses. He stood and watched them, thinking they were just going past. He felt no fear because the bucks, when they had the squaws with them, were generally peaceful, if not friendly. Furthermore, neither he nor his trapper friend had ever had the slightest trouble with any Indians. Being rather tired, he kept on watching, and as he did, he could see Jack, his partner, come out of the cabin. Jack's hat was on the back of his head, a sign of western nonchalance.

"Some Indians pushed ahead of the others, but talk was difficult, and as they were trying to convey ideas, other Indians gathered closer. Suddenly he could see one of the bucks wave his arms, and on a high lope, he and his horse tore completely around the cabin. This seemed strange. Then as the racing Indian came back to his comrades, he knocked Jack's hat to the ground. At this the Indians seemed to be readying their horses, and he could hear their weird voices. Jack seemed to try to get back into the cabin.

"Then suddenly one buck rode up to him and grabbed Jack around the neck. Partly dragging and partly pulling, the Indian started toward the rest of the group. Another buck grabbed Jack's legs and in some way they threw him across the front of a horse . . . He could see them go straight to the river, and as they neared it they hurried faster. The rider carrying Jack led the group but stopped his horse at the bank of the stream. Several bucks then arrived and yelling, jumped from their horses and grabbed Jack. Then they threw him into the river. The amazed watcher could not believe what he saw. Before he could move, one buck jumped into the river, grabbed Jack as he came up, and dragged him to the bank . . . Ten or more of them were still at the cabin. Then with a big yell the Indians at the bank again seized Jack and threw him into the river. One big fellow jumped in, and as Jack came to the surface, this buck pushed him in again . . . He thought, or really tried to think, that this was just a game—an Indian way of having fun . . ."[6]

Poor Jack was killed in this game. A posse of eight white men rode out to take revenge, but found the cavalry from Ft. Washakie had preceded them. One witness recalled:

"When we got there a grizzly sight met our eyes. There on the ground, scattered about, lay twenty dead Indians and many dead horses. There were also about eight or nine dead papooses—all shot by the soldiers who had beaten us there by twenty minutes. Thus was avenged the unwarranted murder of the white trapper.

"We took what we wanted from the dead Indians, and headed home. I took some buckskin, some blankets, and an Indian packsaddle. This had a large, odd horn in front and back. I also took a needle gun. It was a single-shot four-inch shell, breech load, pulled back like a bolt action, had a firing pin. I prized this gun highly. . . ."[7]

A passion for souvenirs was obviously a trait shared by white and red.

Another quality in common, though scarcely credited by the Americans of that day, was the closeness of family feeling universal in every Indian culture: of parents for children and of children for parents; of fraternal love that extended into the circle of cousins; and of spouses for one another. Nothing is more common, and less true, than the universal belief that people of another race, region, persuasion, or culture, somehow do not suffer the long pain of mourning. The Indians may well have been stoic in battle, though even that is more an appearance than a reality, but they mourned their dead with a dramatic show of feeling. The corpse was exposed on a high platform, even in the treeless plains; these hunters felt that since man ate the flesh of animals, it was only fair to return the gift. After a year, the bones were then buried ceremonially, and food was brought periodically to the grave, when the living were expected to tell the family news to the dead.

Though the richer and more famous among them had several wives, the intimacies of marriage, when they were broken, provoked a dramatic outburst of emotion. In 1906, J. W. Schultz wrote an autobiographical account of his stay with the Blackfoot as a very young man. He relates the death from tuberculosis of the wife of a friend, Four Horns. In the effort to die of the same disease, her husband drank of her final hemorrhage. This gesture, one must admit, is scarcely in the Anglo-Saxon tradition.

Both whites and reds, in the nineteenth century, found religion, in the sense of the reality of spirit and of a single, powerful God, to be a daily necessity. And once one was outside the cities and towns, there was not all that difference in the simple articles of ordinary life: iron knives, kettles, needles, and guns.

More surprising, because of our own misapprehension of the various Indian cultures, was another character held in common: the economics of getting and holding property, and its corollary—the creation of hierarchies and classes. These were invented and reinforced by tribal war. War, in both white and red society, had the same purpose: prestige and loot, in that order—yet often they intertwined so strongly that they were indistinguishable. As the anthropologist Robert Lowie noted, ". . . Why did a Crow risk his neck to cut loose a picketed horse in the midst of a hostile camp when he could easily have driven off a whole herd from the outskirts? . . ."[8] One answer was given by George Grinnell in his classic study of another Plains tribe, the Cheyenne: "The most daring and acquisitive men would go into the center of an enemy's camp to cut the horses tied before the tipi. Undoubtedly this was a more daring deed but at the same time a more profitable one, because a man's best horse was tied to a stake inside the camp."[9] This is scarcely the invented Indian, the ideal primitive created by the whites of our own generation—perhaps for want of a better paradigm.

The analysis by Bernard Mishkin, based on the history of the Kiowa, the Cheyenne, the Comanche, the Crow, the Pawnee, and the various Sioux, is particularly apt and subtle on this point:

"Stressing the economic character of warfare does not imply total rejection of the game aspect in Plains warfare. Rank goes with successful participation in war and war is principally economic. Yet . . . within the economic framework of war there functioned a system of warrior etiquette and formal accomplishment the successful performance of which was essential to rank . . .

"Prestige, status and property control are almost universally associated.

Even stratified social groups, which are essentially noneconomic, seem generally to be linked with property factors. In the case of the Plains, rank distinctions similarly involve economic differentiation. Because war, above all, yielded property returns, the men who achieved formal military status also accumulated wealth. . . .

"The wealthy class could afford to set their offspring on the path of military careers while the poor, for the most part, were compelled to specialize in the prosaic activities, hunting, camp duties, etc. The propertied group could advance the interests of their descendants because they controlled the channels of publicity. Finally, the achievement of great war reknown [sic] and the winning of leadership in war opened the way to further wealth accumulation . . ."[10]

And like all such castes, whether Hindu or English, these were self-perpetuating. Thus, as Mishkin concludes, ". . . In Plains society, the horse, rank, and warfare are inextricably interwoven."

Cruelty in warfare is the permanent character of one's enemy. Yet it's perfectly true that scalping, for example, whether Indian or French in origin, was certainly a tangible proof of one's valor, and therefore a badge of one's rank; this trophy could be, and was, sewn onto a special shirt. It had a religious rationalization, too, because among the Plains people one mutilated the corpse of one's enemy (often it was done by bereaved women after a battle) in order to cripple the spirit of the dead man and prevent him from returning to this world for revenge. The whites were horrified—and did the same thing, though for less spooky reasons.

The notorious Colonel Chivington, for example, said, "Damn any man who sympathizes with Indians! I have come to kill Indians, and believe it is right and honorable to use any means under God's heaven to kill Indians."[11] He massacred 105 women and children and 28 men at Sand Creek in 1864. Robert Bent, a half-white, half-Cheyenne, who rode with Colonel Chivington that morning, reported: "The squaws offered no resistance. Every one I saw dead was scalped. I saw one squaw cut open with an unborn child, as I thought, lying by her side. Captain Soule afterwards told me that such was the fact. I saw the body of White Antelope with the privates cut off, and I heard a soldier say he was going to make a tobacco pouch out of them. I saw one squaw whose privates had been cut out . . ."[12] Lieutenant James Connor, who participated, unwillingly, in Colonel Chivington's ambush, testified that he had heard of "numerous instances in which men had cut out the private parts of females and stretched them over the saddle-bows and wore them over their hats while riding in the ranks."[13]

The difference between the Anglo culture of the mid-nineteenth century and that of the Plains Indian, was, above anything else, a difference of form, not of motive. The whites held, fenced, and cultivated a fixed piece of land. But the Plains Indian saw no sense to sitting imprisoned on 140 acres of soil, worked by hard labor to produce energy for that same labor, plus a little cash for the surplus. The Sioux wanted land—not in terms of acres but of square miles—because a hunting economy was based on flesh, not wheat. And this flesh, mostly in the form of herds of massive beasts, had to be followed from one pasture to another in order to be gathered and killed and eaten. Now there is nothing more admirable in a culture based on the consumption of buffalo, than the cultivation of cereal and the fattening of pigs and the delactation of cows, even though Indian rhetoric, quite naturally, would tend to think it so: "It is a sin to wound or cut, to tear or scratch our common mother by working at agriculture . . . You ask me to dig in the earth? Am I to take a knife and plunge it into the breast of my mother? But then, when I die, she will not gather me again to her bosom. You tell me to dig up and take away the stones. Must I mutilate her flesh so as to get at her bones? Then I can never again enter into her body and be born again. You ask me to cut the grass and the corn and sell them, to get rich like the white man. But how dare I crop the hair of my mother?"[14]

These words, quoted so often and with such admiration, were spoken about mid-century by a member of a fishing tribe of the Nez Perce on the Columbia River, the religious visionary Smohalla, who also declared, "My young men shall never work. Men who work cannot dream, and wisdom comes to us in dreams."—a sentiment that would not have been out of place among the young people of the 1960's. But the real, not the rhetorical, reason for the resistance of the hunting cultures to the practice of farming was the plain fact that agriculture had been the role, for many generations, of women, not men. In spite of the complex and even powerful position of Indian women, they were held to be inferior. No man but a *berdache*—a declared homosexual—would plant and weed and harvest and cook. Hunting, war, and medicine were the only possible occupations for a man. Needless to say, neither whites nor Indians understood the peculiar ways of the other.

Ironically, the high, splendid, prosperous culture of the Plains tribes was not that of their ancestors. They had hunted the dangerous buffalo on foot, disguised in buffalo skin and head, armed with stone, not steel, at the tips of their arrows. Their knives had been made of bone or rock. The women had planted and cultivated around the villages to supplement their food; and the only domestic animal was the dog hitched to the travois, two poles that dragged on the earth. Now they had a breed of hardy, fast, small horses, progeny of the old herds that had drifted north and east from the Spanish colonies, supplemented by the nearly universal practice of armed acquisition. And they had guns bartered from the white settlers, and metal ammunition for those guns. The horses they could breed. But guns and bullets are sterile, and they had to trade to get them. Nor should we, in our ignorance of the discomforts and anxieties of nomadic life, underrate the merit of iron tools. Or, as time went on, of ready-made flour, sugar—and alcohol.

So these two things—trade, and room to hunt—were absolute necessities for the Sioux, the Cheyenne, the Blackfoot, the Pawnee, and the Crow. The whites, exploding westward and outward after their Civil War, were willing enough to trade. As to the land, however, there was no compromise possible between farmers and hunters. The conflict between Indian and white was thus irreconcilable from the beginning. Each needed what he needed, not to become rich (although that was possible in either culture), but simply to survive. Of course, by the very laws of the whites, the land belonged to the Sioux. But force is a higher court than any other. If any proof were needed, one has only to realize that the Sioux had expelled the Crow by force from these very territories.

By our civilized standards, there never truly was an Indian War, but rather a series of small battles or skirmishes; and the end was predictable, simply because the army of the whites outnumbered the Indians by a ratio too absurd even to calculate. Nevertheless, in the wild Territory of Wyoming in 1868 and 1869, the Indians managed to win several times—mostly because of the bold, clever leadership of an Oglala Sioux, Red Cloud.

3

On September 20, 1822, when the Oglala Sioux were still hunting on their old lands near the Minnesota River, a meteorite flamed across the night sky. It has long been noted as a universal of Indian culture—indeed, of most cultures except for the most advanced—that natural phenomena are regarded as entirely personal: a tiny cloud in the sky is a message for a particular person or a particular group. So the meteorite, too, had a powerful, but vague meaning to the tribes that saw it. It was splendid and menacing. Many named their children after this heavenly omen, and Red Cloud was one of these favorites.

He was the son of the Brule chief Lone-Man and Walks-As-She-Thinks, who both died with Red Cloud was three. He was adopted by his uncle, and was involved in a tribal murder when he was nineteen. The upper hierarchy in these tribes could and did afford polygamy; according to one of his daughters, Red Cloud had six wives before he was twenty-four. There is some question whether he was truly a chief, except in the eyes of the U.S. government, who thought in Anglo terms and wanted someone who could sign a treaty and bind his people to it. There were no secret elections, corrupt or otherwise, among the Plains peoples; power was determined by heredity, valor, and the magnetic force of character. The structure of the Plains tribes, in particular, was simply irrelevant to a treaty arrangement; if members of the tribe found the agreement unbearable, they simply moved away from the jurisdiction of the chief who had signed it. Still, it is ironic that the violations of the treaties with the Indians, of every tribe and culture, were made by the much more formal and restricted government of the United States.

Red Cloud, in 1870, was a man of great prestige and influence. He had, in his youth, been a reckless and dashing warrior. There was, for example, ". . . a raid on the Pawnees in which Red Cloud killed four men with his own hand . . . Another time, when they were out against the Utes, [a Ute,] crossing a stream on a wounded horse, was about to drown. Red Cloud rode out, grabbed the man by the hair and brought him to shore. When they reached the shore, he took off his knife, slashed off the Ute's scalp, and let him fall to the ground . . . Cruelty was one of his marked characteristics."[15]

Red Cloud had refused to sign the current peace pact with Washington. It provided that the federal government had the right to build forts and roads in the Sioux hunting preserves. The Treaty Commissioners claimed nine signatures to their proposal, but these were Teton Sioux from villages to the east along the Missouri, not from the wilder country further west where the Brule and the Oglala (not to reckon the Cheyenne) numbered upward of 18,000. Still, the chief of the Brule, Spotted Tail, had "touched the pen" for quite naturally none of the Indians were literate in the Anglo sense. Indeed, they had to have the terms of the treaty explained to them through an interpreter whose notion of what it really said was governed by his wish to see it consummated. But Spotted Tail had a sick daughter and wanted a white Army doctor to cure her; sadly, she died on the journey to Fort Laramie.

Spotted Tail wanted her burial platform put up in the military cemetery, and the commander of the fort gave his permission. Spotted Tail was in that state of melancholy kindness that sometimes follows upon a personal loss. When Col, Maynadier urged him to sign the peace treaty, he said, "This must be a dream for me to be in such a fine room and surrounded by such as you. Have I been asleep during the last four years of hardship and trial and am dreaming that all is to be well again, or is this real? Yes, I see that it is; the beautiful day, the sky blue, without a cloud, the wind calm and still to suit the errand I come on and remind me that you have offered me peace. We think we have been much wronged and are entitled to compensation for the damages and distress caused by making so many roads through our country, and driving off and destroying the buffalo and game. My heart is very sad and I cannot talk on business; I will wait and see the counsellors the Great Father will send."[16]

He stayed near the fort, though, till Red Cloud appeared. The latter was torn between despair for the present and concern for the future. The bands that looked to him for leadership had suffered a bad winter; the buffalo were becoming scarce, and their robes and clothes were inadequate, and their food scarce and poor. So Red Cloud, in return for ammunition, food, and blankets, was willing to talk peace. But not at the cost of losing the western herds of the Powder River to the invasion of the swarming whites and their voracious cattle.

This was March 12, 1866, and thousands of discharged soldiers, both Union and Confederate, already uprooted by the war—not only physically, but morally and socially—were heading west to find gold as others had once found it in California. Or failing a quick fortune, they would start life again on fresh, unplowed soil. The fact that this ground didn't belong to them never troubled their consciences; they were simply trying to get along, get married, raise children, and build a house and a church. The fact that by such action they were committing genocide against another group would have been simply incomprehensible.

Red Cloud was not unaware of the tragic history of these encounters, but he was caught between the means to resist and the temptations of diplomacy. So, while Red Cloud hedged, delayed, and parlayed, the whites sent Col. Carrington up toward the Platte River country with a train of wagons, horses, soldiers, and guns. Rumors of their purpose reached the two thousand Indians camped with Red Cloud near the Fort, so when Carrington was introduced at the Treaty Council next morning, he was greeted as the messenger and symbol of deceit. Charles Eastmen, a full-blooded Sioux, reported long afterward, from information he had gathered from very old men, the words of Red Cloud's speech to his fellow Indians on the Council: "Hear ye, Dakotas! When the Great Father at Washington sent us his chief soldier [Major General William S. Harney] to ask for a path through our hunting grounds, a way for his iron road to the mountains and the western sea, we were told that they wished merely to pass through our country, not to tarry among us, but to seek for gold in the far west. Our old chiefs thought to show their friendship and good will, when they allowed this dangerous snake in our midst. . . . Yet before the ashes of the council fire are cold, the Great Father is building his forts among us. You have heard the sound of the white soldier's axe upon the Little Piney. His presence here is an insult and a threat. It is an insult to the spirits of our ancestors. Are we then to give up their sacred graves to be plowed for corn? Dakotas, I am for war!"[17]

The words are undoubtedly apocryphal; Eastman is notorious for his disregard for precise facts and dates; the sense, though, is accurate enough. Red Cloud quit the Council. Spotted Tail did not; he signed the treaty. After all, the Brule Sioux did not hunt north of the Platte, as Red Cloud's warriors did, so there were no interests vital to the Brule that he must defend. Besides, his group stood to get $75,000 a year from Washington. It is stupidly easy for us to call this an act of betrayal to the Indian cause; the truth is a little more complicated.

We have, for more than five thousand years, since the earliest towns and probably since the Babylonian epic *Gilgamesh*, made semi-divine heroes out of our misconception of the forest-dwelling primitive man: pure, defiant, ignorant, hairy, and immensely strong. The late–twentieth—century version of this myth is the glorification of the Indian as the secular martyr of our history. But by elevating the Indian cultures to the sacred status of a violated paradise, we demean them as well. For we deny the Indian his common humanity—the right to be as short-sighted, murderous, and confused as the rest of us.

Let us consider, for a moment, the great difference between tribes. In the Plains hunting culture, for example, prestige was based on personal coups, of which the highest was striking the enemy with a harmless stick. In the agricultural Hopi culture, on the other hand, open egotism was thought to be funny. In such cases, we have disregarded the particulars of Indian culture and projected upon them the illusion that man is somehow perfectable; when we discovered that the Indians were not, our rage and fear was immense. Nevertheless, the Indians, in their contacts with the whites, did not have the obverse illusion; they were realistic and practical, but they suffered from the consequent fault: they only saw the immediate, tangible fact.

For Red Cloud, the tactical situation was such that he felt he could resist the U.S. Army, thin and extended as it was over hundreds of miles; and, what is more, he thought he could win. For several years, he turned out to be right.

4

Red Cloud, by his defiance of the white negotiating team and by his refusal to accept presents or sign the treaty to which they were a prelude, had become the acknowledged leader of the Powder River bands of the Sioux. His courage had attracted allies from the Cheyenne and from a smaller tribe, the Arapaho. All summer and autumn they had mounted a series of skirmishes, decoys, and ambushes. Young Crazy Horse was prominent in the small but exciting actions. He was only twenty-two. Red Cloud was twice that age and was not expected to fight, but to lead and advise. But Indian victories didn't prevent the use of the Army forts along that disputed road to the mines of Montana. Casualties on both sides were small—indeed, on the Civil Was scale, so minute as to deserve historical oblivion. In any case, they had decided nothing, although to the individual Indian or white soldier, a small battle like the one described below might be the end of the visible world:

"A detail of twenty-five men from I and K companies under Sergeant Hankammer, including the mail party under Corporal Gimm, was ordered to go to the relief of Sergt. Custard. Lieut. Caspar Collins, Eleventh Ohio, who had just arrived with Grimm's mail party volunteered to take command of the detachment. They crossed the bridge to the north side of the river and at full speed made their way toward the hills. They had proceeded about half a mile when from behind the hills and out of the ravines came swooping down upon them hundreds of Indians, yelling, whooping, shooting arrows and rifles, and riding in circles about them like so many fiends, while a large body of them coming down from the bluffs, attempted to get between them and the bridge. Capt. Greer, Company I, seeing the peril threatening the brave boys under Collins, charged, crossed the bridge with the balance of his company and poured a deadly fire into the howling savages, driving them back, and thus opening a way of retreat for Collins and his men, if they suc-

ceeded in making their way through the hundreds of savages that surrounded them. Collins, finding that more than half of his men were killed or
wounded, gave command for everyone to make for the bridge. It was a race
for life. Nehring, a private of company K, Eleventh Kansas, not understanding the order, dismounted to fight from a deep washout in the road.
Grimm looking around, yelled to him in German: 'To the bridge.' That was
the last that was seen of poor Nehring. Camp, also of Company K, Eleventh
Kansas, lost his horse and then ran for dear life, but when within a few rods
of safety was overtaken and tomahawked. Sergeant Hankammer's horse was
wounded, but carried him safely to the bridge and there dropped.

"A wounded soldier fell from his horse and called out to his comrades:
'Don't leave me; don't leave me.' Collins turned and rode back to the man
and thus lost all possibility of saving his own life. The brave lieutenant was
mounted on a magnificent horse and might have escaped had he not gone
back on this errand of mercy. . . . Our soldiers held the bridge and stockade,
although the Indians crossed the river above and below the bridge and
fought desperately, harassing our forces on every side throughout that day
and a part of the next. On the evening of the 26th two men came out of the
chaparral in a bend of the river on the south side, about one-half mile above
the bridge. A party went out to rescue them. They proved to be Company D
boys from Sergeant Custard's command. They said that when they heard the
howitzers in the morning, Custard ordered a corporal to take five men and
go forward to see what the firing meant. They had proceeded but a short distance when they were cut off from Custard's escort. Pursued by the Indians
they struck for the river, but only three of them succeeded in crossing to the
south bank and one of these was killed before the friendly shelter of the
chaparral was reached. The nineteen men remaining with the train under
Custard were also surrounded, but made a brave fight from ten in the forenoon until three in the afternoon. From that time there was an ominous
silence . . ."[18]

The Army forts remained, so the Indians had merely scored a rhetorical
victory. But this is the Anglo point of view, accustomed to large tactics and
hospitals full of thousandfold pain and death. The Plains culture put the
highest value on individual daring. Thus it was more prestigious to touch an
enemy than to kill him, and the enemy body count was not as important as
how one killed them. It was only a little less meritorious to touch coup on a
dead body than a live one. There was also great prestige in raiding and seiz-
ing livestock, particularly horses. But the attitude of the white settler, living
in a culture as equine as that of the Indian, was that horse-stealing was a
crime only a little less reprehensible than killing your grandmother. And the
capture of women and children, regarded as meritorious and useful by the
Plains Indian, was viewed by the whites with a horror reserved for rape.
Every settler's diary recounts the stories (many of them true) of white cap-
tives abused (the details are left to the imagination), and this is a corollary of

the notion that native man, ungoverned by Christianity, is exceptionally potent.

The forts—Fort Phil Kearny and Fort C. F. Smith—presented a difficult target to nomadic warfare. Their stockades could not be forced by arrows, bullets, or ponies, and their guns "spoke twice"—once when they were fired and again when the explosive shell landed at the end of its long arc. So the Indian strategy was to lure soldiers outside these defenses, where they could be fought by traditional Indian methods. The practical side of Indian thought was demonstrated by the fact that they postponed their campaign until after the autumn hunts. A decoy attack was made on December 6, but it failed to catch any soldiers in the open. Another place was picked for the ambush. Was it chosen by Red Cloud of the Oglala? Or by one of the Miniconjous Sioux—in particular, High-Backbone? Was Red Cloud even present? Accounts vary, depending upon which tribe or band gave the information (a practice not entirely unknown among white historians).

On the afternoon of December 20, 1866, the Sioux and their allies reconnoitered this more promising spot and the Sioux sent out one of their shamans, a homosexual visionary. ". . . Half man and half woman— Hē ē măn ĕh"—with a black cloth over his head, riding a sorrel horse, pushed out from among the Sioux and passed over a hill, zigzagging one way and another as he went. He had a whistle, and as he rode off, he kept sounding it. While he was riding over the hill, some of the Cheyennes were told by the Sioux that he was looking for the enemy—soldiers. Presently he rode back, and came to where the chiefs were gathered and said: 'I have ten men, five in each hand; do you want them?' The Sioux chiefs said to him: 'No, we do not wish them. Look at all these people here. Do you think ten men are enough to go around?' The Hē ē măn ĕh" turned his horse and rode away again, riding in the same way as before. Soon he came back, riding a little faster than before and swaying from one side to the other on his horse. Now he said: 'I have ten men in each hand, twenty in all. Do you wish them?' The same man replied, saying, 'No, I do not wish them; there are too many people here and too few enemies.' Without a word the half-man-half-woman turned his horse and rode off. The third time he returned, he said: 'I have twenty in one hand and thirty in the other. The thirty are in the hand on the side toward which I am leaning.'

" 'No,' said the Sioux, there are too many people here. It is not worthwhile to go on for so small a number.' The Hē ē măn ĕh" rode away.

"On the fourth return he rode up fast aand as his horse stopped, he fell off and both hands struck the ground. 'Answer me quickly,' he said. 'I have a hundred or more,' and when the Sioux and Cheyennes heard this, they all yelled. This was what they wanted. While he was on the ground, some men struck the ground near his hands, counting the coup."[19]

Next day there was a small attack on a wagon party of woodchoppers, at work on a ridge above a creek. At the sound of firing, Col. Carrington sent one of his officers, Captain William Fetterman, out to rescue them. He had eighty-odd soldiers, both mounted and on foot, and orders not to go too far from the fort. Another small party of young warriors, including Crazy Horse, lured the captain far out onto the ridge. At that point, signalling with pieces of mirror, all the Indian forces, hidden down below in the brush on either flank of the ridge, attacked at the same time.

Though the Indian allies had few guns, and these were old flintlocks that had to be patiently reloaded with every shot, they had their traditional bows and arrows. It is a fact that an arrow is not a feeble weapon: it can pierce and kill a heavy buffalo, especially at close range. And it had the tremendous advantage that one could carry a whole quiver full of arrows and fire them in rapid succession, which gave the bow the power of concentrated and steady attack. Nor was the Indian lance a contemptible weapon. It had to be used, naturally, at close quarters, but such combat was traditional in Plains warfare, and white troops had not the experience of such intimate combat. The slopes on both sides of the ridge were slippery with snow and ice, and were not easy to climb. It was so cold that "blood running from wounds soon froze."[20]

By noon, the fight was over. The entire company of white soldiers, including their two captains, were dead. "After all were dead, a dog was seen running away, barking, and someone called out: 'All are dead but the dog; let him carry the news to the Fort,' but someone else cried out: 'No, do not let even a dog get away'; and a young man shot at it with his arrow and killed it . . ."[21]

The Indian allies lost about two hundred men, but both sides considered it an Indian victory. Col. Carrington was relieved of his command, and the newspapers, edited by and for whites, called it the "Fetterman Massacre". The Indians called it "The Battle of the Hundred Slain". Both names were rhetorical rather than true, as the dead, pale or dark might have testified.

5

This engagement was an intersection of luck and intelligence. Red Cloud had matched the technology of the invader with his own traditional weapons. It was not to happen that way ever again until the vain tragedy at Little Big Horn ten years later. In 1867, Red Cloud led his warriors against another wagon train of woodcutters and soldiers, but the enemy was armed with breech-loading, quick-firing, Springfield rifles. Captain Powell, who led the defense behind a barricade of logs and wagons, thought the Indian losses were about sixty; the Sioux admitted six dead and six wounded, but they stampeded and captured a herd of horses and mules, which by Plains standards, was the real prize of war. It's as if the Union claimed Gettysburg as a victory by the number of horses it had captured, instead of the number of Rebels it had slaughtered in the Pennsylvania woods.

The Cheyenne, too, assembling more than 1500 warriors, attacked thirty whites near Fort Smith; they were decimated by the same new rapid-fire weapons. Any sensible Indian should have concluded that the firepower of the white soldiers, the terrible product of a more and more industrialized society, would certainly overwhelm them, and they had far better quit. They didn't. Like any other general in the history of armed conflict, they were still fighting the last war, not the present one.

Yet it was certainly clear that in 1866 and 1867 the U.S. Army was temporarily overextended. Indian attacks, tiny, or simply small, were annoying enough to deny protection, not merely to the wagon trail that cut across Wyoming, but to the more southerly and still unfinished line of the Union Pacific Railroad. The railroad companies had the same power in the decades after the Civil War as oil corporations were to have a hundred years later. Supplying fuel or transportation, they dealt in a commodity absolutely essential to the expansion of business and were given much the same tenderness. The railroads, in 1867, were more sacrosanct than Army forts.

It was nicely symbolic that Washington appointed a Peace Commission, on which sat four generals, including the redoubtable Sherman. "We must act with vindictive earnestness against the Sioux, even to their extermination, men, women and children. Nothing else will reach the root of this case."[22]

The Commission came to the disputed territory in a specially fitted railway car. Typically, such cars had a plenitude of fringed chairs and horsehair sofas, and gleamed with spittoons and mirrors, neither of which were of much use to the Indian. But Red Cloud never came to the peace councils. He had heard from Man-Afraid-Of-His-Horses that the great Sherman wanted the Sioux moved back out of their present hunting grounds all the way east to the Missouri River. Instead of meeting Sherman, Red Cloud sent a proud and reasonable message:

"The Great Father sent his soldiers out here to spill blood. I did not first commence the spilling of blood. . . . If the Great Father kept white men out of my country, peace would last forever, but they disturb me, there will be no peace. . . . The Great Spirit raised me in this land, and has raised you in another land. What I have said I mean. I mean to keep this land. . . .[23]

". . . We are on the mountains looking down on the soldiers and the forts. When we see the soldiers moving away and the forts abandoned, then I will come down and talk."[24]

At the end of July, Fort Smith was abandoned, and Red Cloud and his followers came riding in to burn it down. Similarly, the Cheyenne burnt down "their" Fort Kearny. On November 6, Red Cloud came down to the Platte River in the south and entered Fort Laramie. Here he signed the famous and disputed peace treaty of 1868. He was, of course, illiterate, but only in the Anglo sense of the term, for the Plains Indians had for many generations kept written historical accounts of their particular bands by symbols

Red Cloud, center, and delegation in Washington, D.C., visit prior to 1876. Probably 1870.

National Archives, Washington, D.C.

painted on stretched elk skin. These symbols were well-known and readable
by Indians who spoke quite different languages. No such symbolic translation was prepared as a companion document to the little black markings of
the U.S. government. In fact, only the first clause of the treaty was ever read
and translated aloud: "From this day forward all war between the parties to
this agreement shall forever cease. The government of the United States
desires peace, and its honor is hereby pledged to keep it. The Indians desire
peace, and they now pledge their honor to maintain it."[25] The other sixteen
articles—which covered trading rights in the Platte River area, dollar annui-
ties, gifts of ammunition and blankets, areas of settlement, and other such
severely practical matters—were never read word by word, but merely
explained verbally. The understanding of the whites and the understanding
of the Indians on every one of these points were crucially different.

Who was lying? The generals, and their religious assistants (Father
Pierre Jean De Smet, Catholic, and Reverend Hinshaw, Protestant), and
their interpreter—who said they told Red Cloud exactly what was in those
last sixteen clauses? Or the Indians, like Spotted Tail, who said, "All these
words have proved to be false"? Both sides, possibly; not an unknown situation, even when adversaries read the same language. In addition, it must be
noted that there were mixed counsels in both parties. The whites of the
Wyoming Territory, on one hand, wanted to prospect the Powder River
country, while the pro-Indian "peace" policy of the U.S. government at this
time was to avoid a costly war with the Sioux. Yet Washington put the administration of this peaceful policy in the hands of Civil War generals.
Among the Indians, Spotted Tail's people got a substantial reward for moving to the Missouri, well out of the right-of-way of the Union Pacific railway.
But Red Cloud—temporarily famous among his own people, the only thing
that really counts, and judging himself victor over the entire white army—
held out for greater honors and greater rewards. He was not going to budge;
and he agreed to take the train to Washington in order to tell the Great
Chief, Ulysses S. Grant, exactly that. Such was the quadruple complication
that followed the 1868 treaty.

And what about the ordinary white or the ordinary Indian whose name
appears nowhere, even in the most intimate histories? What voice did he or
she have in this shuffle of treaties? Not much. There are no treaties, even in
the most advanced societies of the past or present, signed by the people
whose life or death they will subsequently determine.

6

In the back country of Peru, a white visitor was asked by an Indian if
World War II was really as violent as he had heard. "How many were
killed?" the Indian asked. "A hundred?" "No, far more." "A thousand?"
"More than that," the visitor told him. The Indian took a long time before he
asked if it could possibly be ten thousand. The white answered, rather sol-

**Indian boys at Indian boarding school, *ca.* 1895. Note absence of any sort of Indian clothing.
Tribe not known.**

National Archives, Washington, D.C.

emnly, that the number of dead was far greater, even, than that. In the next
few days, he became famous for miles around as a terrible liar.

Much the same incredulity must have been the feeling of the Plains
people about the American Civil War. One might think that the Indians
would stay ironically aloof, hoping the whites would destroy one another. Instead, the southern tribes—the Creek, Choctaw, Cherokee, Chickasaw, and

even the Seminoles of Florida—volunteered thousands of soldiers to the Confederate armies. Naturally, they did so as separate tribes, not as a nation nor even an alliance. There was, and still is, some sort of belief that Indians, though they practiced cultures as vastly different as the agricultural Hopi, the fish-and-berry-eating Kwakiutl, and the nomadic Blackfoot, had some sort of national consciousness. They did not. Tribe fought tribe and were driven from their lands and destroyed exactly that way, tribe by tribe. For instance, the Sioux drove the Crow out of the rich buffalo land at the begin-

Chief Red Cloud at the age of seventy-eight, photographed by Heyn, of Omaha, Nebraska.
Library of Congress

ning of the nineteenth century—the very land the Sioux declared was sacred to them by ancestral rights. Their lack of cohesiveness was certainly not a fault of Indian character. The distances between them were too vast for any sort of extended common action, and when the distance was short, there was bloody competition for the scarce resources of that hunting ground. When even that was no longer true, they were still prisoners of their own culture. For example, when the Brule Sioux bands under the leadership of Spotted Tail had obeyed Washington and settled in a reservation on the Missouri, two hundred of his young men raided a Pawnee camp in Nebraska, the old Brule hunting grounds.

That was in April, 1870. In early May, Spotted Tail, too, was persuaded to go to Washington to see President Grant and his officials. The Indians' ridiculous appearance was explained by that remarkable historian of the Sioux, George Hyde: "They were all wearing handsome buckskin costumes, but it was the deplorable taste of officialdom at that period to dress all visiting Indians in black suits, white shirts with starched fronts, uncomfortable shoes, and hats. Spotted Tail and the others refused to put on shoes, which hurt their feet and made it almost impossible to walk, and they covered their hated black suits by keeping wrapped in handsome blankets."[26]

Spotted Tail and his companions reached Washington on May 24, and the Brule chief was first taken to see Secretary of the Interior Jacob D. Cox, to whom he boldly complained that the 1868 treaty was being violated. He said his people didn't want to live on the Missouri; game was scant there, and whiskey abundant. Cox replied, through the interpreter, "Tell him that a man must expect some trouble in his life and should face it in a manly way, not by complaining."[27] It's odd how patient and forbearing an official can be—for the other fellow. Spotted Tail replied, "Tell him that if he had had as much trouble in his life as I have had in mine, he would have cut his throat long ago."[28] In frustration, he went to see President Grant, who praised, again, the virtues of farming. According to Hyde, the chief was not impressed. He had three wives and eleven children to support, and his sons were fighters, not flowers. The oldest son, sixteen, had already taken a Pawnee scalp.

On June 1, 1870, Red Cloud arrived with his own delegation and was housed in a suite in the same Washington hotel as Spotted Tail. There is still controversy about whether Red Cloud resented this rival chief. Possibly he did because Spotted Tail had killed one of Red Cloud's relatives the previous year. What is certain is that Washington had given Spotted Tail fine saddled horses for his group, but had furnished Red Cloud with carriages, which were considerably cheaper. It also cost the government $281.65 "for furnishing lemonade, cigars, tobacco, oranges, nuts, etc.," and there was a strangely large sum—$750—for medical expenses. Carriages, doctors, lemonade: there is no doubt that both delegations were meeting white civilization eyeball to eyeball.

They were taken next afternoon to visit the Capitol, where they sat in the balcony listening to a Senate debate on an Indian Appropriation Bill. They made no comments, but merely sat fanning themselves. June is hot in Washington. Next day, they were driven to the Arsenal, and it was pretty obvious why this sort of military show was staged. First, a fifteen-inch Rodman gun was fired; the sound was formidable, and the shell skipped like a stone down five miles of the Potomac River. Red Cloud measured the muzzle of the gun, and a little later was taken on an inspection of the workshops that turned such gun barrels on enormous lathes. The whole party was then escorted, somewhat reluctantly on their part, on board an ironclad ship.

"They doubted, though, that it was made of iron because anyone knew that iron would not float."[29]

7

On Monday evening, they attended a banquet at the White House. Red Cloud and his friends insisted upon taking off their white men's suits and shoes for this occasion and instead wore buckskin garments, moccasins, and blankets—clothing not as proud as it might seem, for blankets were standard trading-store items, made in New England. Red Cloud is said to have made the same touchy point about his own clothing when asked by the famous Matthew Brady to pose for him. But the photograph shows Red Cloud wearing a white shirt, a cravat, a dark vest, dark cloth trousers, and button shoes.

The Indian party was particularly astonished by the candles burning in the crystal chandeliers of the White House. They enjoyed the strawberries and ice cream, and one of the chiefs used the occasion to say that the whites certainly had plenty of food, but didn't send much of it to the Indians. One of the white guests remarked that the whites had plenty because they had settled down and farmed, upon which Spotted Tail remarked, rather sourly, that he'd be glad to do the same if they gave him a nice big white house like this one. So the Indian chiefs, it is apparent, retained a shocked, saddened and confused dignity.

An ironic twist, common enough in human affairs, was that the Indian Bureau of the Department of Interior was in sharp controversy with the Army. The latter claimed that the Indian Bureau was giving its wards—in order to hunt the diminishing quantities of game—better guns than the Army had to punish those very Indians. This curious argument disregarded the fact that most Indian attacks were made, for reasons already given, with traditional bows and arrows and lances. But this was only the initial irony. The Department of Interior was escorting their guests, led by Spotted Tail and Red Cloud, on a tour of U.S. military muscle, including a full dress parade of Marines, and the Commissioner of Indian Affairs who conducted the tour was himself a Seneca Indian from a reservation in upper New York State. His name was Hasanoanda when he was young, but he was renamed Donehogawa when he was made one of the eight Iroquois Confederacy chiefs from the Seneca tribe, and had gone to Albany and Washington, while still in his late teens, to oppose the sale of his people's reservation. To pursue this historical joke even further, he changed his name to Ely S. Parker and took a college degree in engineering at Rensselaer Polytechnic Institute, thus acquiring a profession that was at the hub of American industrial and social expansion—the very tide that swept repeatedly and murderously over the Indian.

Ely Samuel Parker owed his present position not to merit, though he certainly had that, but to his friendship with Ulysses S. Grant, whom he had met in Illinois when the great general was a clerk in a harness store. He

Bigfoot, Oglala Sioux Chief, dead at Wounded Knee Creek, during massacre of about 200 in his band, including women and children, by the Seventh U.S. Cavalry, December 29, 1890. This was the end of any Indian resistance.

National Archives, Washington, D.C.

subsequently, and not without great trouble because he was an Indian, became General Grant's aide, and wrote out in a fine hand the general's condition for Lee's surrender. Parker did a study of the whole Indian question for Grant in 1864:

"General: In compliance with your request, I have the honor to submit the following proposed plan for the establishment of a permanent and perpetual peace, and for settling all matters of differences between the United States and the various Indian tribes . . ." It is no surprise that he recommended that the Indian Bureau be transferred to the War Department. But his reasons were strong and unequivocal: "As the hardy pioneer and adventurous miner advanced into the inhospitable regions occupied by the Indians in search of the precious metals, they found no rights possessed by the Indians that they were bound to respect. The faith of treaties solemnly entered into were totally disregarded, and Indian territory wantonly violated. If any tribe remonstrated against the violation of their natural and treaty rights, members of the tribe were inhumanly shot down and the whole treated as mere dogs. Retaliation generally followed, and bloody Indian wars have been the consequence, costing many lives and much treasure."

He feared the possible extermination of this "portion of the human race." He therefore urged that a special Committee of Indians be appointed to visit all the tribes in the United States, and persuade them to take up farming, and "to convince the Indians of the great power and number of the whites; that they cover the whole land, to the north, south, east, and west of them."[30] So it is possible, though not certainly known, that Commissioner Parker, in conducting this military tour for Red Cloud and Spotted Tail, was simply trying to warn the Sioux that they were facing an enormous and brutal ratio—a million-headed industrial society against the puny weapons of a few thousand mounted warriors.

It was Commissioner Parker and Secretary of the Interior Cox who met Red Cloud and Spotted Tail (the latter for the second time) in the offices of the Department of the Interior. Cox sat at a table with the chairman of the new civilian Board of Indian Commissioners, and told Red Cloud that the tour of Washington was not arranged because President Grant was afraid of them. Red Cloud made no direct reply to this curious threat. Instead, he solemnly shook hands with all the whites at the table and said, "I came from where the sun sets. You were raised on a chair; I want to sit where the sun sets."[31] It should be remembered that the hired translators were not scholars but tradesmen and adventurers, and one wonders whether they did not occasionally alter and florify the Indian speech into the white man's conception of how a noble savage ought to speak. Also, the translation had then to be taken down in shorthand, and the Pittman method, first published in 1837, depended on devices like the same symbol rendered heavy or light; consequently it suffered errors in both directions. Still, Red Cloud's speech as he sat on the floor in this closed, panelled room, has all the accidental marks of authenticity:

"The Great Spirit has received me naked and my Great Father I have not fought against him. I have offered my prayers to the Great Spirit so I could come here safe. Look at me. I was a warrior on this land where the sun rises, now I come from where the sun sets. Whose voice was first sounded on this land—the red people with bows and arrows. The Great Father says he is good and kind to us. I can't see it. I am good to his white people. From the word sent me I have come all the way to this house. My face is red yours is white. The Great Spirit taught you to read and write but not me. I have not learned. I came here to tell my Great Father what I do not like in my country. You are close to my Great Father and are a great many chiefs. The men the President sends there have no sense no heart. What has been done in my country, I do not want, do not ask for it. White people going through my country. Father have you or any of your friends here got children. Do you want to raise them. Look at me I come here with all these young men. All are married have children and want to raise them. . . .

"The white children have surrounded me and have left me nothing but an island. When we first had this land we were strong, now we are melting like snow on the hillside while you are growing like spring grass. . . .

"When you send goods to me they would steal all along the road so when it reaches me it was only a handful. They hold a paper for me to sign and that is all I get for my goods.

"I know now the people you sent out there are all liars, and Mr. Bullock may now have some of the orders along with him. Look at me, I am poor and naked. I do not want war with my government. The railroad passing through my country now. I have received no pay for the land . . ."[32]

There were further conferences after that, including a vague and inconclusive one with President Grant. At last Secretary Cox faced the issue by quoting from the 1868 treaty, which Red Cloud had signed. Red Cloud said, "This is the first time I have heard of such a treaty. I never heard of it and do not mean to follow it."[33] Pressed on this point, Red Cloud said, "I do not say the Commissioners lied, but the interpreters were wrong. I never heard a word, only what was brought to my camp. When the forts were removed, I came to make peace. You had your war-houses, or forts. When you removed them I signed a treaty of peace. We want to straighten things up."[34] When offered a copy of the treaty, Red Cloud refused: "I will not take the paper with me. It is all lies."[35]

If this did not reflect the whole truth, it certainly expressed a raging despair, mixed with scorn and pride. Some reports even say: "That night one of them tried to kill himself, saying he could not go back to Powder River and tell the people how they had been swindled."[36] The same author, George E. Hyde, in another book on the Sioux, wrote: "After this council on June 10 some of Red Cloud's chiefs attempted to commit suicide in their rooms at the Washington House. They said that they were ashamed to go home alive to tell the people how they had been lied to and cheated into signing the treaty in 1868. From Red Cloud down, they now all demanded to be taken home at once, for they considered their mission a tragic failure."[37] Which chiefs and under what circumstances these suicides were attempted is still unknown. There is still the even more unlikely legend that one of the delegates hung himself in the closet of the hotel room, but was cut down before he died.

8

Maybe it really was a calculated white act of treachery not to have read all the clauses of the treaty of 1868 to the assembled chiefs. Even if they had, it would have taken several weeks to analyze and negotiate, because this treaty had eighteen clauses, each of numbing length, and a total of some three thousand words. Imagine translating that key provision, Article 2, into Sioux: "Article 2. The United States agrees that the following district of country, to wit, viz: commencing on the east bank of the Missouri River where the forty-sixth parallel of north latitude crosses the same, thence

along low-water mark down said east bank to a point opposite where the
northern line of the State of Nebraska strikes the river, thence west across
said river, and along the northern line of Nebraska to the one hundred and
fourth degree of longitude west from Greenwich, thence north on said meridian to a point where the forty-sixth parallel of . . . etc."

It's no wonder that the grandiloquent first paragraph of Article 1 was the
only one people bothered to remember: "Article 1. From this day forward all
war between the parties to this agreement shall forever cease. The government of the United States desires peace, and its honor is hereby pledged to
keep it. The Indians desire peace, and they now pledge their honor to maintain it." The rest of the article promised punishment for any crime committed by whites upon the Indians, and vice versa.

Article 3 promised to give any Indian who could find 160 acres of land fit
to farm, additional land outside the reservation. This was a form of pressure,
the one point of agreement by all white factions, to make Indians settle down
and cultivate the land like any decent Christian. Articles 6, 8, 9, and 14 were
more of the same futile inducement, allowing the prospective farmer 320
acres if he were head of the family or 80 if he were not, an allowance for
seeds and farm tools, a provision for educating him in their use, plus a bonus
for good crops. This solemn treaty also provided, for each Indian over four
years old, a pound of meat and a pound of flour every day, and when they
reached their teens "good, substantial woolen clothing"—of the modest
white man's fashion, naturally. Further, if any Indian should actually ". . .
commence farming, [he would get] one good American cow, and one good
well-broken pair of American oxen . . ."[38] Thus there was double pressure
on these hunting societies: either go to farming, or give up their land and be
fed and clothed on steadily shrinking and barren reservations.

In return for this, the U.S. government pledged to forbid white settlement in "the country north of the North Platte River and east of the summits
of the Big Horn Mountains." The treaty further provided that no more land
was to be ceded except by a three-fourths majority of all adult male Sioux.

The first real force to violate these crucial clauses would be Long-Hair
Custer, leading a whole train of wagons and guns into Indian land six years
after the treaty was signed and four years after it was explained and clarified
in Washington to Red Cloud and his people. The truth was that this treaty
represented a compromise between the military establishment, naturally
powerful after the Civil War, and the pressure of the new western settlements. The Indian Peace Commission was in the middle, as its half-civilian,
half-military makeup plainly showed. But deeper and more persistent than
all these divisions peculiar to the time, and implicit in the treaty itself—
where "blacksmith" is mentioned three times, surely unique among the
treaties of the historic world—is the clash of a mass industrial culture based
on the manipulation of iron and fed largely by cereals, with a sparse culture
based on individual hunting talent directed by a special and spiritual vision

and fed largely on raw or stewed meat. It was a contest so unequal, that except for local and temporary circumstance there could only be triumph for
the iron-tooled farmer and defeat for the mystic hunter.

Would a wiser, more anthropological approach have served the Sioux
any better? Could he, with his horse-herding culture, have been less radi-
cally persuaded, possibly to move toward a semi-nomadic role as a herdsman
in American society? Indians were quite open to new ideas and new tech-
niques; it is well-known that the horse and the bullet were adopted by them
from the whites. But they could not be changed too quickly or too utterly
without losing what every human being instinctively needs—connection
with his cultural group, however small.

9

On the eleventh of June, 1870, Red Cloud and his group were persuaded to go to a final conference in Washington. Someone, perhaps Commissioner Parker, had worked out a compromise, not to change the Treaty of
1868, but to reinterpret it. Red Cloud and the Sioux under his control did
not have to go all the way back east to the barren Missouri, but would be expected to stay in the vicinity of Fort Fetterman, a name which must have
given the Indians an odd and nasty turn. The Indians agreed to this interpre-
tation—but why? Perhaps they were overwhelmed by what they had seen of
the Anglo power and multitude, yet they were, unfortunately, dependent
upon this very culture to preserve their own. They had not traded since
1864, and they were in terrible need of everything from kettles to ammunition, because they were essentially a Stone Age culture, unable to smelt or
work the metal they had come to need.

Red Cloud sat on the floor of the conference room and declared: "What
I said to the Great Father, the President, is now in my mind. I have only a
few words to add this morning. I have become tired of speaking. Yesterday,
when I saw the treaty and all the false things in it, I was mad. I suppose it
made you the same. The Secretary explained it this morning, and now I am
pleased . . . We have 32 nations and have a council house, just the same as
you have. We held a council before we came here, and the demand I have
made upon you is from the chiefs I left behind. We are all alike . . ."[39]

He went on to discuss the history of his problems with the whites, and
came around to mentioning a white woman who had been captured by the
Sioux: "Look at that woman. She was captured by Silver Horn's party. I wish
you to pay her what her captors owe her. I am a man true to what I say, and
want to keep my promise. The Indians robbed that lady there, and through
your influence I want her to be paid."[40] This curious interjection still makes
little sense except as an assertion of badly wounded pride, which all of us
have felt, and with somewhat less politeness.

Secretary Cox was very happy with the compromise, and urged Red
Cloud to visit New York City so they could buy presents in the great metro-

politan stores. Red Cloud made a reply which revealed his underlying anger: "I do not want to go that way. I want a straight line. I have seen enough of towns. There are plenty of stores between here and my home. I have no business in New York. I want to go back the way I came. The whites are the same everywhere. I see them every day."[41]

There was still another conference on Sunday, June 12. Red Cloud wanted two particular men for traders, and they must, in any case, be civilians. He also wanted seventeen horses at his disposal when he came to the end of the railway line. Cox was equivocal on all these requests, and they parted on a curiously hostile note. Red Cloud said: "You have your land fenced in and do not want us to come on it. We have our land fenced in and do not want you to intrude on us. All nations are around us. I do not want to make war with the Great Father. I want to show I go away peaceably. I want to raise my children on my land, and therefore I want my Great Father to keep his children away from me. . . . I want good horses, the same as you gave to Spotted Tail. I am not mad with you. I have got a better heart. I am going home. If you will not give me horses, very well. God Almighty raised me naked. I am much pleased with your offer to give me presents, but I do not want any."[42] However, Red Cloud changed his mind and decided to go to New York City after all.

10

The voice of conscience has never been still in America, nor particularly genteel, nor polite. It rarely moved or even swerved the heavy locomotives of history. If it pushed in the same direction, it perhaps speeded, and more certainly, rode forward upon them, but when it opposed a train of irresistible events, it fell apart and was gone.

There was, of course, no formal Peace Party in America urging capitulation to the heathen Sioux, but there were many individuals who sympathized with the Indian. For example, Henry Ward Beecher, the divine who had preached abolition and in a manner, won, now undertook to see justice done to the Indian—a cause, which, by 1870, was substantially lost. Another such futile voice was that of the inventor and businessman (these occupations in later nineteenth-century America were often indistinguishable) Peter Cooper. His expertise was in iron, and iron was the skeleton on which America expanded, as copper was its nerve. He had built the first American steam locomotive, had rolled up huge investments in the iron industry and in transatlantic cables, and controlled the company that owned more than half the mileage in American telegraph lines. Like many self-educated and self-made men of the period, he had a strong belief in the education of the common man. In 1859, he built Cooper Union in New York City for just that purpose.

It had a large auditorium, and there the New York friends of the Indian proposed that Red Cloud speak. Cooper himself, a man of seventy-nine by then, went to visit him, but the chief was in a bitter mood and refused to see anyone. Again he changed his mind overnight. On the fifteenth of June, he met with the government commission in his rooms at the Nicholas Hotel and delivered a recital of grand and petty wrongs:

"My Friends, The Great Spirit placed me and my people on this land poor and naked. When the white men came we gave them our lands, and did not wish to hurt them. But the white men drove us back and took our lands. Then the Great Father made us many promises, but they are not kept. He promised to give us large presents, and when they came to us they were small; they seemed to be lost on the way. I came from my people to lay their affairs before the Great Father and I tell him just what I mean and what my people wish, and I gain nothing. I asked him for seventeen horses for my young men to ride from the border to our camps, and he does not give them. I wish no stock and no presents. The Great Spirit placed me here poor and naked. I appear so before you, and I do not feel sorry for that. I am not mad—I am in good humor—but I have received no satisfaction. I am disappointed. I cannot change my claims. I am not Spotted Tail. What I say I stick to. My people understand what I come here for, and I should lose my power if I did not stick to one course. You are my friends. You always talk straight to me and I am not blaming you."[43]

Peter Cooper, who was present, replied that if the government was too stingy to donate the horses, he would offer to do so. At this point, Red Cloud agreed to accept the presents and the horses. This was not mere greed, but an established ritual of Plains culture—that the exchange of gifts was a proof of friendship, a custom not wholly unknown to white culture, either. Further, he agreed to speak at noon the next day at Cooper Union Institute. Then there followed a strange entertainment indeed. The Indians were driven up Fifth Avenue so thousands of white faces could gawk at them, and in the evening, at the suggestion of the notorious Jim Fisk (who just nine months earlier had caused a financial crisis by cornering all the gold in the United States markets), they were guests at the Grand Opera House, where they saw half-naked girls posturing in an entertainment called "The Twelve Temptations."

By noon next day, the Cooper Union Hall was already packed, and there were so many hundreds outside that there was a relay speaker posted in the open air. Peter Cooper introduced Red Cloud, who wrapped his blanket around him and pointed to heaven as he spoke:

"My brethren and my friends who are here before me this day, God Almighty has made us all, and He is here to bless what I have to say to you today. The Good Spirit made us both. He gave you lands and He gave us lands; He gave us these lands; you came in here, and we respected you as brothers. God Almighty made you but made you all white and clothed you; when He made us He made us with red skins and poor; now you have come . . .

"The Great Father made us poor and ignorant—made you rich and wise and more skillful in these things that we know nothing about. The Great Father, the Good Father in heaven, made you all to eat tame food—made us to eat wild food—gives us the wild food . . .

"Colonel Fitzpatrick of the government said we must all go to farm, and some of the people went to Fort Laramie and were badly treated . . .

"In 1868 men came out and brought papers. We are ignorant and do not read papers, and they did not tell us right what was in these papers. When I went to Washington I saw the Great Father. The Great Father showed me what the treaties were; he showed me all these points and showed me that the interpreters had deceived me and did not let me know what the right side of the treaty was. All I want is right and justice . . . I represent the Sioux Nation; they will be governed by what I say and what I represent . . . I am no Spotted Tail, to say one thing one day and be bought for a pin the next . . .

"I was brought up among the traders and those who came out there in those early times. I had a good time for they treated us nicely and well. They taught me how to wear clothes and use tobacco, and to use firearms and ammunition, and all went on very well until the Great Father sent out another kind of men—men who drank whisky. He sent out whiskymen, men who drank and quarreled, men who were so bad that he could not keep them at home, and so he sent them out there . . . I don't want any more such men sent out there, who are so poor that when they come out there their first thoughts are how they can fill their own pockets.

"We want preserves in our reserves. We want honest men, and we want you to help to keep us in the lands that belong to us so that we may not be a prey to those who are viciously disposed. I am going back home. I am very glad that you have listened to me, and I wish you good-bye and give you an affectionate farewell."[44]

11

Red Cloud's speech was that of a condemned man. The process described so precisely by Parker in his formal letter to his friend Grant, the destruction of the original Americans in order to make room for the swarming increase of conquering strangers, had begun with the second expedition of Christopher Columbus and continued until the seaboard edges of both American continents were all bloodied and captured: Brazil, Argentina, Chile, Peru, Columbia, all of Mexico from sea to sea, California up to the Sierras, and the Northeast all the way to the Missouri. This proceeded over the course of three and a half centuries, tribe by tribe. It hardly slackened, much less ended, with the Civil War of white against white. In fact, when the war was settled, the ferocious energies that were no longer spent in hideous and ceremonious battles burst open and overwhelmed the remaining virgin territories of the continent.

Andrew Johnson, successor to Lincoln, was perhaps not the worst

American President, but he tried. His speech at the inauguration was almost incoherent, he was so drunk, yet he only spoke what many Americans, both north and south, felt to be perfectly obvious. He included in his 1867 message to Congress the following bit of honest jargon: "If the savage resists, civilization, with the ten commandments in one hand and the sword in the other, demands his immediate extermination."[45] The ordinary Indian, not constrained to make speeches, described the process with bitter simplicity: "I remember the big council fire when we signed away our first land. At that time the country was full of buffalo and when I was 20 summers I killed a cow and calf with one arrow. Then came swarms of grasshoppers and ate up all the grass for four seasons. Then bones of the buffalo became white on the hillsides and they were poor and of little meat, so that the hunter got not much but the blanket in the hunt. Then the grasshoppers turned into white men and killed off all the buffalo that did not starve. This made great changes to the Indian. He could eat the buffalo and the grasshoppers, but he could not eat the white man. So we had to sell off more of our land to the great father at Washington for meat and blankets."[46]

The inexorability of these historic crimes, the flat fact that the Indian could not win, that negotiations between former enemies and the consequent treaties that pledged eternal peace merely reflected the awful imbalance of weapons—these were the real reasons for Red Cloud's angry depression. Worse yet, he, who had been the hero-chief of two years of local victory, had to go back to his constituency and explain how they must bear a future of endless defeat.

He came back by train, of course, via Buffalo and Chicago, and arrived at Omaha again, where he had to wait two days for the horses that were promised. His rivalry with Spotted Tail, if it was ever serious, did not prevent Red Cloud from posing with him in Frank Currier's studio in Omaha. In 1868, he had been photographed, seated on the sort of fringed chair that was the odd style of that period, and shaking hands with a visiting Englishman. So Red Cloud was familiar enough with that other, more subtly sinister machine of the whites—the camera. Some tried to explain it as one of the marvels of the sun—plausible enough, because the summer dance to the sun was the principal ceremonial of the whole Plains culture. But that hardly made the camera less powerful, merely more invincible. It was said to suck out some part of one's soul; else how could it be gotten to look so much like oneself? The same was said by the Indians whom Catlin painted in the 1840's. And in a sense, they were right: Every image of oneself, even in a mirror, diminishes one's inflated fantasy. Here also, in the spiritual world, the whites had dangerous and irresistible tools. There are no smiling Indians in nineteenth-century photographs. Red Cloud, too, faces the glass eye with grave and dignified doubt.

He still had considerable power of character; his coups could, in his middle age, not be denied. But his tribal reputation by late 1870 was growing precarious. He had got in Washington only an agreement that his people need not go to the Missouri to trade, but precisely where would that agency be? Of course, Spotted Tail had got the same agreement and was only too glad to get his folk away from the Missouri agency, where whiskey was to be had so easily that his whole band of Brule Sioux was being debauched and poisoned; further, there would be less pressure on them to disgrace their manhood by farming. But neither Spotted Tail nor the other chiefs (and there were a half dozen of them) could agree on the new location.

They held council at Fort Laramie, where they learned that Washington wanted to put them forty miles north of the railway. Sitting Bull, chief of another band of the Sioux, refused to have anything whatsoever to do with the whites. He would sign no treaty, keep no peace, and hunt where he chose. And Red Cloud's description of his journey to Washington, of the multitude of white men with iron guns, had a strange and reverse effect. Some Indians said it was all an illusion; there were no such gigantic, unbelievable camps as Chicago, Washington, New York. The whites had probably thrown magic dust into Red Cloud's eyes. Sitting Bull said, "The white people have put bad medicine over Red Cloud's eyes to make him see everything and anything they please."[47] That statement was the beginning of Red Cloud's slow fall from power.

It was the unyielding, narrow patriots, ignorant of the immense forces against them, who became the new and desperate leaders of the Sioux. One was the sullen, sardonic Sitting Bull; another was the younger, mystic, and xenophobic Crazy Horse. The last was especially bitter about Red Cloud, for Crazy Horse was madly in love with a married woman who was a member of Red Cloud's band, and he even succeeded in eloping with her and her three children. He was pursued and shot in the jaw by her husband, and tribal opinion made him return the woman. But the enmity of the two factions remained. When Red Cloud accepted a new location for a government agency where he could trade, Crazy Horse's group remained intransigent. His story is unreservedly tragic, he would die at thirty-five after a white guard's bayonet had pierced him through the side. Sitting Bull himself, playing the pet Indian in Bill Cody's touring Wild West shows in the year of the Ghost Dance—the Sioux's last gesture of futile defiance—would be arrested by Red Cloud's warriors in 1877, dragged out of his own house, and killed by a rifle shot fired by a Sioux policeman.

Red Cloud lived on his reservation for many decades. He occupied a wooden shack whose interior was decorated with chromos of the Virgin Mary and American flags of differently numbered stars. He was blind by then (as, some say, Sitting Bull had foretold), and died December 10, 1909, in a world broken and changed and altered, visibly and invisibly, from the one in which he had been born.

In 1871, Congress passed a law that stated: "No Indian nation or tribe within the United States shall be acknowledged or recognized as an independent nation, tribe or power."[48]

3

A Long Track to China

Look over these prairies and observe everywhere the life and activity prevailing. See the railroads pressed beyond their capacity with the freights of our people; the metropolis of the state rearing its stately blocks with a rapidity almost fabulous, and whitening the Northern lakes with the sails of its commerce; every smaller city, town, village, and hamlet within our borders all astir with improvement; every factory, mill, and machine shop running with its full complement of hands; the hum of industry in every household; more acres of fertile land under culture, fuller granaries, and more prolific crops than ever before; in short, observe that this state and this people of Illinois are making more rapid progress in population, development, wealth, education, and in all the arts of peace, than in any former period, and then realize, if you can, that all this has occurred and is occurring in the midst of a war the most stupendous ever prosecuted among men. [1]

THIS effulgent optimism, in words suitable for a national anthem, was, like many an American boast, quite accurate. In particular, it was true of the railroads, for the wasteful prosperity of war had paid their debts and their dividends. New England now had a tight network of rails, but the geographic distribution in the South was loose and inefficient. Surprising is the extent and richness of the railway system in Ohio, Indiana, and Illinois. These agricultural states poured food into the freight cars that fed the Army, while New England forged the iron weapons.

The railroad was one of those strange and energetic symbols that alter the subconscious of a whole people, and indeed, make it possible to have such a commonality. It is at once perfectly real and iconically powerful. It is like the sun that became a symbol of power, the cross that became a symbol of suffering, and the mushroom cloud that became a symbol of both. The locomotive, though, is purely secular magic. Curiously, it's not the diesel nor the electric locomotive that has such mana; they are not animal enough. The steam locomotive audibly chuffs and breathes, roars down upon you like any proper dragon. It exhales white clouds by day, dark clouds by night against a moonlit country, and in the darkness we can see the fiery mouth of its furnace raging by. It eats coal or wood insatiably and drinks water for its iron veins. And its rails, pistons, and boiler have an ancient phallic drive.

But none of this would have haunted the nineteenth-century American imagination if it were not real and particular at the same time as it was legendary, as in this account:

"Last Wednesday I was invited to a picnic at Covington eighty miles distant it was the first time the cars had gone into the place . . . and several hundred people old and young, white and black, had gathered to see the show when we came off the people harrahed [*sic*] and cheered the women taking off their hats as well as the men but when they let off steam and whistled the crowd ran in every direction falling head over heels crying and screaming . . ."[2]

The steam engine itself was the product and the quickener of England's earliest industrial growth. It was invented in 1698 by Thomas Savery and simply improved seventy years later by James Watt. But this was a stationary engine, useful to pump water and service mines. Rails, too, had a slow evolution. At first these were simply wood; then they were plated with strips of iron, which sometimes tore loose and, bent by the pressure of wheels, curved upward and impaled the bottom of the following coach. The iron rails that replaced them were improved by Americans so they could stand by themselves and be fixed into place with simple spikes and plates. This was a more crucial change than it appears, for instead of using semi-skilled metalworkers, cheap and unskilled labor could be hired, and since the 1840s these were the Irish and they were considered expendable. The physics of wheeled vehicles remained much the same, for the principle had been known as long as the potter's wheel—the one was the derivative of the other, though it's not certain which came first. Nevertheless, it took a sudden intelligence to see it: a wheel rolls with less friction if the road is extremely smooth. And what is more smoothable and enduring than an iron surface? Best of all, with iron rolling on iron, the point of instant contact between the circle and the line is almost infinitesimal. Thus: "One horse could haul twelve tons of stone."[3]

The early railway system in America dates from the fourth decade of the Republic, but it was by no means uniform. "An obstacle to traffic in all parts of the country was the different gauges of the railroads. On the New York and New England roads the rails were laid 4 feet, 8½ inches apart; in Ohio, the West, and south of Philadelphia, 4 feet 8½ inches and 4 feet 10 inches; in Canada and some parts of Maine 5 feet 6 inches; in some special cases 6 feet. There were at least eight different gauges in the several states. In no direction could cars run long distances without changes and delays. The Hudson River and the New York Central cars passed directly from New York to Buffalo, but could not run to Chicago over the Lake Shore route without changes on the five lines between Buffalo and Chicago . . ."[4]

Yet the train had become a native of the American landscape, not without its price in American blood and sweat, as Thoreau, that visionary of the real, noted in *Walden:* "We do not ride on the railroad; it rides upon us. Did you ever think what those sleepers are that underlie the railroad? Each one is a man, an Irishman, or a Yankee man. The rails are laid on them, and they are covered with sand, and the cars run smoothly over them."[5]

Enthusiasm for its use was sometimes neutralized by government limitations on railroad profits, which reached as high as 25 per cent. But more often, the expense was reversed; state and city governments put up nearly a third of the construction capital. It has been shown, most clearly by the historian Elisha P. Douglass, that while in Europe the railroads and the canals built by private means eventually became public property, in America the whole thrust of individuals straining their way upward put a heavy value on private sweat and private gain. The government was to interfere only when profits were low, and even then simply to restore gain to a normal level, and then, as quickly as possible, to sell the utility back to private ownership. Such were the morals of our secular religion.

2

Salesmen, in the last third of the nineteenth century, did not have the sad name that our culture has now given them. They embodied the virtues of industrial America. They were tireless, aggressive, and they wrote regularly to their mothers:

My dear Mother . . .   Sunday, 3/29/1868, Brooklyn, N.Y.
    I start for Detroit tomorrow night . . . Charles Clement . . . has a good position in the Pennsylvania Railroad—headquarters of the road being at Altoona—that is the Superintendent and machine shops are there. They employ 1500 men in the shops, which I examined in company with Charley. They disburse about $100,000 a month there—own the hotel and have large fine offices and houses . . .
    . . . Eight miles on a branch road and we rode in the "cab" of the engine. Such a smokey country! As we came back in the dark we saw fires all around us on the ground where they were burning coal to make coke.
    . . . Charley explained the way they did their business and although it reminded me by its magnitude of government undertakings . . . *economy* is the great controlling idea . . .[6]

The expansion of these metal rails was extraordinary. In the two decades before the Civil War, their mileage tripled. Five years after the Civil War, it had doubled again. Where did the construction money come from? Ultimately, from the capital savings of the upper and older middle class. Income from property and mills was, of course, inherited, for death taxes were tiny or nil. But more and more often the inheritance was protected by a trust, and these trusts were held and administered by insurance companies, which were already powerful. Rich with these legacies, they invested in railroad bonds, secured by legislation that made United States bonds take second mortgage to the private bonds. The trusts made a commission on each transfer. They were thus the instrument by which America was being rapidly transformed from a nation of small holders and small craftsmen into a group of interlocking clusters of machinery.

The connection of the railroads and the trusts set up by insurance companies was logical and, given the nineteenth-century American premise of infinite profit and expansion, probably necessary. But there is another close connection that was one of the more curious nuptials of history: the love affair between the railroad and the Army. The earliest grants specified either free passage on the railway for troops and their supplies, or at worst, one-half the normal rate. Speed of assembly and intensity of force are the two classic aims of battle, and there was no speedier, more concentrated way of getting vulnerable men and iron weapons to the chess board of military campaign than a steam locomotive pulling a train of crowded cars. Then, quite naturally, the railway line itself became an objective of war. But this fact was only slowly realized. By 1864, the Northern strategists sent General Sherman around the flank and rear of the South expressly to tear up a latitudinal railway of the Confederacy, to warp its rails with special devices, and to burn its sidings, yards, and environs. At the same time, industry in the North felt the rude pressure of unlimited expansion. And this was true even in the most ordinary trades.

What was formerly a home craft, practiced for hundreds of years, an interlocked skill of brain and hand, became a simple mechanical procedure. And the small shop where the craftsmen lived as well as worked, became the long horizontal of the factory bench and assembly line. The demands, crucial to the course of the Civil War, were not only for food and rails, but also for shoes and uniforms. The sewing machine invented in 1846 by Elias Howe, was adapted for industry as early as the 1860s. And the cobblers, whose tiny shops were familiar in every crossroads community, were displaced by rapid and highly improved shoe-stitching machines by the second year of the Civil War. A Massachusetts newspaper reported that ". . . operatives are pouring in as fast as room can be made for them; buildings for shoe factories are going up in every direction; the hum of machinery is heard on every hand."[7]

And there was one particular necessity, true of every war from its invention as the bloody arbiter of human conflict—metal. For if man is killed by the sharp difference between the tensile strength of metal and that of human skin, flesh, and blood vessel, he can use the same metal to dig himself into the safety of the ground:

Dear Mother—
    . . . I've been very busy indeed. We are now filling a government order for the U.S. Quartermaster . . .   200 dozen shovels, long and short handles.[8]

Iron, of course, had been used for millennia. But this metal must be wrested from its ore, or, to use a nice chemical word, "reduced," generally by heating with carbon—coal or charcoal or coke. The resulting free metal is contaminated not only with carbon but with phosphorus and half a dozen other impurities. A method of burning away these impurities with a blast of air was invented by the British in 1856. The process produced steel, which is simply a finer, more durable alloy of iron. Thus England, and hence western

Europe, became the steelmaker and the industrializer and, so armed and so enriched, the rulers of the early–nineteenth-century world. But the United States rapidly overtook England. In steam engines, England had one-third of the horsepower of the known world, and Europe made it up to a half. But even at that date, in 1850, the United States already possessed the other half: 5.6 million horsepower.

For the most part, the United States was making not steel rails but iron rails, and those in huge quantities—over 200,000 tons in 1860 and 356,000 by 1865. Such iron rails often failed under the driving weight of the more and more massive locomotives. Therefore steel made by the English method began to replace iron after 1865. The heavy need for steel rails in turn stimulated a change in technology: coal and coke replaced wood and charcoal; forging, unchanged since 4000 B.C. as the work of a hammer, an anvil, and a man, became the teamwork of pouring molten iron out of buckets two stories high. This change did not alter the intimate experience of the man who worked in such a mill. The ladling and tending of molten metal was still the hottest, most glaring and exhausting work in industry—as it is today.

The twelve-hour day in steel mills was not abolished until 1923. It was based on the twenty-four-hour operation of the blast furnaces. Now twenty-four hours can be divided into sixes or eights as well as twelve-hour shifts, and before 1887 shorter hours were not the rule, certainly, but not the exception either. But by 1887, with the approval of the contemporary steelworkers union, the whole industry went back to the twelve-hour day—and the twelve-hour night. In 1910 the U.S. government surveyed the manufacture of steel and iron, and in particular, the current hours of labor. Not quite half the men worked a twelve-hour day—sometimes with Sundays off, sometimes not. On this platform of immense human labor, the American steel industry was built. The railroads that ran metal wheels on metal rails were both the result and the cause of this vast flood of metal across America.

There is no army in the world that has purely military aims. The force of weaponry confers both power and responsibility, and it was logical that the U.S. Army promote the expansion of the American railway system. Senior officers, and especially the realist General W. T. Sherman, felt that the great necessity of their age was a transcontinental line, to bind, with a double steel thread, the West to the East, and make one nation out of what would more naturally be two separate republics with the high wilderness of the Rockies and the dry prairies in between. Sherman, as early as 1849, pushed a survey by military engineers of a plausible route across the formidable wall of the Sierra Nevada. So the actual construction of a continental railroad took on a decidedly military color.

Granville Dodge was a young construction engineer before the war, doing railway work in the West. He was thirty when the Civil War began, led a volunteer brigade at the Battle of Pea Ridge, and was made a brigadier general after the victory. He repaired railways for Grant and later for Sher-

man, and led a corps during Sherman's invasion of the South, where he was
severely wounded during the siege of Atlanta. Like Sherman, he fought Indians in 1865 and 1866, and in May of the latter year, took on the job of chief
engineer for the newly formed Union Pacific Railroad Company. His old
friend and superior, General Sherman, wrote him on January 16, 1867:

My Dear Dodge: I have just read with intense interest your letter of the 14th, and
though you wanted it kept to myself, I believe you will sanction my sending it to
General Grant for his individual perusal, to be returned to me. It is almost a miracle
to grasp your purpose to finish to Fort Sanders (228 miles) this year, but you have
done so much that I mistrust my own judgment and accept yours. I regard this road
of yours as the solution of the Indian affairs and the Mormon question, and, therefore, give you all the aid I possibly can, but the demand for soldiers everywhere and
the slowness of enlistment, especially among the blacks, limit our ability to respond.
Each officer exaggerates his own troubles and appeals for men. I now have General
Terry on the upper Missouri, General Augur with you, and General Hancock just
below, all enterprising young men, fit for counsel or for the field. I will endeavor to
arrange so that hereafter all shall act on common principles and with a common purpose, and the first step, of course, is to arrange for the accumulation of the necessary
men and materials at the right points, for which your railroad is the very thing. So far
as interest in your section is concerned, you may rest easy that both Grant and I feel
deeply concerned in the safety of your great national enterprise. [9]

In his reports to the United States Senate, General Dodge's words have
a distinctly military ring—exact, colorless, and mined with profound implications:

"The organization for work on the plains away from civilization was as
follows: Each of our surveying parties consisted of a chief who was an experienced engineer, two assistants, also civil engineers, rodmen, flagmen, and
chainmen, generally graduated civil engineers but without personal experience in the field, besides ax men, teamsters, and herders. When the party
was expected to live upon the game of the country, a hunter was added.
Each party would thus consist of from eighteen to twenty-two men, all
armed. When operating in a hostile Indian country they were regularly
drilled, though after the Civil War this was unnecessary, as most of them had
been in the army . . . The location part in our work on the Union Pacific was
followed by the construction corps, grading generally a hundred miles at a
time . . . At one time we were using at least ten thousand animals, and most
of the time from eight to ten thousand laborers . . . the work was so system-
atically planned and executed that I do not remember an instance in all the
construction of the line of the work being delayed a single week for want of
material . . .

". . . The Union Pacific and Central Pacific were allowed to build, one
east and the other west, until they met . . . The reaching of the summit of
the first range of the Rocky Mountains, which I named Sherman, in honor of
my old commander, in 1867, placed us comparatively near good timber for

ties and bridges . . . Engineering forces were started to their positions before cold weather was over, that they might be ready to begin their work as soon as the temperature would permit. I remember that the parties going to Salt Lake crossed the Wasatch Mountains on sledges and that the snow covered the tops of the telegraph poles . . . Spring found us with the track at Ogden, and by May 1st we had reached Promontory, five hundred and thirty-four miles west of our starting point twelve months before."[10]

The organization of work was little different from that of an army engineer corps, and this is no artifact of an antiauthoritarian bias. A contemporary (1869) observer wrote:

"One can see all along the line of the now completed road the evidences of ingenious self-protection and defence which our men learned during the war. The same curious huts and underground dwellings which were a common sight along our army lines then, may now be seen burrowed into the sides of the hills, or built up with ready adaptability in sheltered spots. The whole organisation [*sic*] of the force engaged in the construction of the road is, in fact, semi-military . . .

"We, pundits of the far East, stood upon that embankment, only about a thousand miles this side of sunset, and backed westward before that hurrying corps of sturdy operators with a mingled feeling of amusement, curiosity, and profound respect. On they came. A light car, drawn by a single horse, gallops up to the front with its load of rails. Two men seize the end of a rail and start forward, the rest of the gang taking hold by twos, until it is clear of the car. They come forward at a run. At the word of command the rail is dropped in its place, right side up with care, while the same process goes on at the other side of the car. Less than thirty seconds to a rail for each gang, and so four rails go down to the minute. Quick work, you say, but the fellows on the Union Pacific are tremendously in earnest. The moment the car is empty it is tipped over on the side of the track to let the next loaded car pass it, and then it is tipped back again; and it is a sight to see it go flying back for another load, propelled by a horse at full gallop at the end of 60 or 80 feet of rope, ridden by a young Jehu, who drives furiously . . ."[11]

3

Certainly it was a long, inconvenient and dangerous distance from the goldfields of California to the bank vaults of New York, Boston and Washington. Much has been written about the overland passage. Travel across the mountains and plains was very great. In 1864, 150,000 people went through Kansas and Nebraska to the West, but it was harsh and tedious and often took up to six months. Almost as common was a maritime route. Between 1860 and 1866, about 200,000 people came and went via Panama. The sea voyage was 2,000 miles from New York harbor to Panama, and 3,300 more from Panama to San Francisco. In those years, of course, there was no Panama Canal, but there was a railroad across the isthmus. "It is well built, its bridges of iron—indeed, iron is used wherever possible, for the wood rots in a year or so. The length is forty-eight and one-half miles, the fare twenty-five dollars, and freight accordingly; so you can well believe that it pays well. Most of the hands are blacks, but all the conductors are Americans. It does an immense business and is a great enterprise, but it cost four thousand lives to build it amid the swamps and miasma of that climate."[12] Such a trip was amazingly fast. A typical schedule would take a traveler from New York City on October 22 and arrive at San Francisco on November 14—only twenty-three days. But it was expensive and scarcely had the patriotic thrill of a transcontinental railroad. Our commercial traveler wrote to his mother from Brooklyn in 1865: ". . . I heard addresses last Wednesday night from the Senators from Nevada, on the mineral wealth of that and all the Pacific states. They want the Pacific railroad completed. They say there is more mineral wealth in the one state of Nevada than in all the rest of the world. All they want is facility of transportation and capital to work with. Horace Greeley presided and made a few forcible remarks. I never saw him before and he is funny enough, both in manner and dress, but when he speaks he shows the force of his intellect . . ."[13]

To such considerations there was added a wild but curiously prophetic notion—that a transcontinental railroad would open China and Japan to the products of American factories. This idea was urged by Stephen Douglas, Lincoln's opponent from the booming state of Illinois. But a French company had already begun work on the Suez Canal, connecting Europe and the Mediterranean with the Red Sea, India, and the Far East, and this canal was completed by 1869. So future American trade with the Orient was little more, at that time, than a debater's argument whose deeper reasons were less Marxist than emotional: "RESOLVED, That this excursion party, here assembled in the center of this vast continent, now offer up our heartfelt gratitude and thanks to Almighty God for His manifold blessings, among which we enumerate that country subject to the jurisdiction of the United States of America, Republican institutions, civil and religious liberty, the freedom of speech and the press, a Union unbroken and indestructible, with all the material resources necessary for the comfort of mankind in a high and rapidly advancing state of development, and with a vast net-work of railroads and telegraphs, essential not only to our national prosperity and the interests of all our people, but also to the civilization and commerce of the world, including, among the most important of them all, that vast work—the Union Pacific Railroad."[14]

This popular rhetoric was shared by shrewd men on both sides of the slavery issue. The southern caucus wanted the transcontinental route through the South, where Texas, already a slave state, would grow rich on the easy transport of cotton. Sam Houston was a notable advocate of the southern route, for example. The northerners in Congress were just as stubborn about a northern route, for this would guarantee the solidarity, via economics, of the Northeast and the West. The controversy went on for more than a decade. It's generally forgotten that in 1853 Jefferson Davis was secretary of war in the Washington government. He authorized a number of military surveys for a transcontinental route, and it was he who decided in 1854 that the way through the South was the best and the cheapest. In Congress, each group blocked the other, so nothing was settled until 1862, in the second year of the Civil War. Then, with the enthusiastic help of Lincoln, the northern route was chosen. He was exceedingly generous with the Union Pacific. The law gave them, for example, a 400-foot right-of-way, plus a checkerboard of ten sections of land along with the timber and the minerals, for each mile of railroad. All this plus a subsidy in U.S. bonds of $16,000 a mile on the plain, and up to $48,000 a mile in mountainous regions. Perhaps this largesse was needed to get the project going, but it was certainly hasty, particularly because the railroad going west, the Union Pacific, did not exist before the act was passed.

Lincoln was in a great hurry. California, which only fourteen years earlier had been discovered to be awash with gold, was by no means firmly Union. It had traditions of benevolent peonage, if not outright slavery, in the *fincas* owned by the missions and worked by California Indians. And California bitterly opposed the military draft, perhaps for personal rather than political reasons, for California volunteers fought on both sides. Rowena Steele, contemporary author of *The Family Gem*, "received much publicity when she christened her baby Jefferson Davis Lee Stonewall Jackson." It would not help the boy very much, but a transcontinental railroad between the North and California would bind the state to the Union in spite of its doubts and divisions.

The newly created Union Pacific did nothing for two years. In 1864, by Act of Congress and at the earnest request of Lincoln, who called the railroad a military necessity, the 1862 gift of land was doubled. The future railroad was given twenty sections per mile (a section is 640 acres), and the status of the U.S. bonds was reduced to a second mortgage, so that the Union Pacific might issue thirty-year bonds of its own.

Does it make sense more than a hundred years later to question the motives for such generosity? One must recall that, at least since the beginning of the nineteenth century, the construction of canals was sweetened with the same sort of gift and in the identical pattern—a great mile-square checkerboard of land on either side of the watery passage. The railroads, for example the Illinois Central in a bill passed under the sponsorship of Stephen Douglas, had already received 375,000 acres of land absolutely free of charge. The consequence was that the railroad owners grew rich while the construction made Chicago the magnate of the Midwest and the most powerful city in the central plains of the United States.

Very few voices, editorial or religious or political, were raised against these gargantuan presents, which totaled an area bigger than Texas. Business and the nation were the legendary double-headed man of Mark Twain's invention, and in any case the West seemed illimitable. And if a man might grab all that he could and be admired and emulated, a railroad, and all the more a patriotic railroad, could certainly do the same. This was firmly believed, and well into the twentieth century. But is it true? Need a transcontinental railroad have been financed by such means? Was the gift of an estimated 180 million acres absolutely necessary? Could not the work have been done—Lincoln thought not—by the federal government? Or could the railroad have been built more slowly, as the earlier railroads were built? And at far less cost in human life—most of it Irish and Chinese? Further, if the transcontinental railroad was necessary to a booming American industrial economy, was such a development the happiest way to live on the North American continent? Certainly in 1869 it seemed inevitable.

4

One needs only a couple of months acquaintance with any large organization—civil, military, or academic—to realize that the innovators, the architects of novel solutions to novel problems, are not necessarily the brass of the enterprise. More usually they are a mixed and shifting team of the young and anonymous. Consequently, there is no way to fix credit or blame for the wild growth of the American railway system. Still, if General Dodge can be called the grand marshal of the transcontinental drive westward, the tutelary genius was a more furious and dedicated man, Theodore T. Judah, who initiated the concurrent move eastward. He was an engineer from Connecticut, brought west to build a small line from the California goldfields to Sacramento. There was little local workmanship, so steel rail was imported from England around the southern tip of South America, and locomotives had to be shipped from New England the same way. Freight charges were therefore tremendous. Morally outraged by these difficulties, Judah surveyed the arduous route over the Sierra Nevada Range and decided that the best way was over the Donner Pass, where only fourteen years earlier, five women, three men, and a boy had survived a December snowstorm by eating the emaciated thighs of the dead.

In 1860, a year before the Civil War, Judah assembled four California entrepreneurs: Collis P. Huntington, Leland Stanford, Mark Hopkins, and Charles Crocker. Hopkins and Huntington ran a hardware business, Crocker a drygoods store, and Stanford was a wholesale grocer. Judah met with them in an empty room upstairs from the hardware store at 54 K Street in Sacramento—four huge, heavy, bearded, prosperous, and aggressive men facing a thin, zealous, monomaniac engineer. He asked their support for a transcontinental railroad—a rather exaggerated request to make of four small-town businessmen. Nor was this the only evidence of madness in the scheme. Even in 1862, California had only twenty-three miles of railway in the entire state. The four men, all of them together, did not even have enough capital to build a line to Nevada, far less than halfway across the United States.

But the U.S. government did. So deep was the impression that Judah had already made in his repeated visits to Washington, that the line eastward was awarded to the minute Central Pacific Railroad of California. Possibly Judah was a bit eccentric; the proof was that he could not bring himself to steal from his own company. His four Sacramento backers enraged him by organizing a construction firm wholly owned by them, to which they naturally awarded the contract. Judah was cheated out of his financial interest in the Central Pacific and decided to go east to fight these respectable thieves—one of whom, Stanford, had just been elected governor of California. In October, 1863, Judah shipped via Panama, where he caught yellow fever and died within sight of New York harbor. The first rail of the transcontinental line had been hammered down a week before.

The scientific art of building railroads presents three kinds of choice, and the first defines the size of the power plant. Huge locomotives can be and were built, but while they were marvelous monsters on the straightaway, they could not bend with the deep curves that were necessary to get through the American mountain ranges. Secondly there was a choice of how to join and fix the rails. Again, to speed up the process, there had to be an American simplification so that semi-skilled labor could be used instead of highly-skilled metalworkers, of which there were very few. The third choice, and little recognized, was how to make the roadbed itself: how to grade, how to curve, and how to bridge. The American method was to blast, dig, and smooth it as quickly as possible, to use iron instead of steel, and timber instead of iron. Of course, wood for the crossties was not as easily found as one might expect. ". . . [W]est of the Missouri River the country is almost entirely destitute of trees, and excepting a limited supply of cottonwood, similar in fibre and strength to the old Lombardy poplar of the east, there was nothing from which railroad ties could be obtained. East of the Missouri the forest conditions were quite similar, so that in a short time it came to pass that the very ties on which the railroad has been constructed had to be cut in Michigan, Ohio, Pennsylvania and New York, and teamed over the country at an expense sometimes of two dollars and seventy-five cents per tie."[15]

In the West, all three of these technical choices were strained to their limit by the stubborn mass of the Sierras, which interposed a series of high, broken ridges and precipitous valleys. Such wild and picturesque country was hardly suited to straight lines in any direction. "At the top of the Sierra route was a 40-mile segment, much of which ran through a series of tunnels. But the granite was so hard that blasting powder would shoot out from the pitted walls, like cannon shot, without damaging the rock. Picks and chisels merely blunted against the granite . . . Despite 500 kegs of black powder daily, the tunnel progressed by only eight inches a day."[16]

It took a lot of money, perhaps a little more money than it should. The

Temporary and final railway trestle.

Photograph by Andrew J. Russell, 1868, Citadel Rock, Green River, Wyoming. Beinecke Rare Book and Manuscript Library, Yale University, Western Americana Collection

U.S. government loan to the Central Pacific specified a cost of $16,000 per mile. It provided, however, three times that rate when it met the mountains of the Sierra. But where, precisely, did the mountains begin? Judah had surveyed this point and determined it to be thirty-one miles east from Sacramento. But this honest fanatic was overruled. Collis Huntington went to see President Lincoln, and with General (then Senator) Sargent in tow, presented fake geological evidence that the place where the mountains began was only seven miles from Sacramento. "Lincoln was engaged with a map when the Senator substituted another, and demonstrated by it and the statement of some geologist that the black soil of the valley and the red soil of the hills united at Arcade. The President relied on the statements given him, and decided accordingly. 'Here, you see,' said the senator, 'how my pertinacity and Abraham's faith moved mountains.' "[17]

Such frauds were more magical than mere explosive, though that too was a product of human ingenuity. Discovered by the Italian scientist Sobrero and produced commercially by the Swede Alfred Nobel, nitroglycerin was an extremely powerful and dangerous compound. In its most potent form, it is freshly made of nitric acid and glycerin, and this oily yellow liquid goes off if it's heated, struck, or merely jarred. Premature explosions, even with gunpowder, were not uncommon, but no count was ever kept of casualties. (However it was recorded that Superintendent Strobridge lost an eye.) The Central Pacific Railroad employed a Scotch chemist named Howden to make nitroglycerin on the spot, and it blasted open a path through the conglomerate of the Sierra Nevada.

Seven hundred miles of track were laid at elevations above five thousand feet. The slopes were gradual on the western side, but precipitous on the eastern flank. Despite this, the Central Pacific Railroad—under the driving, ambitious, greedy, heavyweight Crocker, a self-proclaimed engineer, goldminer and mining-hardware storekeeper—drove its work force over this barrier and through the Rockies and down along the valley of the Humboldt River. "The higher they went the more stubborn the rock became, until they tackled an outcropping dubbed Cape Horn, which almost defeated even Charley Crocker. It was solid granite and its lower sides fell away in 1,000-

Tunnel construction, Union Pacific Railroad.

Photograph by company photographer Charles Russell, 1868 or 1869. Beinecke Rare Book and Manuscript Library, Yale University, Western Americana Collection

foot cliffs with no toeholds anywhere. Swathed in a great fur coat and hat like some mammoth bear Crocker conferred with his two assistants. Montague was for trying to locate another route even if it meant abandoning miles of track already down, but Crocker roared his veto. Didn't they know the Union was rushing west across the easy sand hills while they stalled here, freezing under the crest of the 'Hill'?"[18] Characteristic of that part of the American character which it shared with the Plains Indian, personal glory was as important to him as mere gain. Nor were the two really distinguishable.

The Central Pacific started work on January 8, 1863. Stanford, whose interest was something more than symbolic, lifted the first shovel to the blast of bugles and ceremonial gunfire. The Union Pacific line coming west from Omaha began must less enthusiastically. Their lack of working capital was at last remedied by the backing of a Boston firm that made shovels.

The Union Pacific hired what was already traditional in this country—Irish labor, which consequent to the great potato rot and famine at the end of the 1840's had come to the United States in great and increasing numbers. They were farm people and found work, as all immigrants do, only at the bottom of the economic pyramid. They were unskilled and semi-skilled workmen, earning their pay by muscle. They did the heaviest work—shoveling. And lifting and throwing a shovel full of broken rock, hour after hour, day after day, as long as there is light in the sky, is not the most agreeable labor in the world.

The Irish laborers, whether by company policy or not, raised traditional hell on the seven nights before Sunday morning:

"The first place we visited was a dance house, where a fresh importation of strumpets had been received. The hall was crowded with bad men and lewd women. Such profanity, vulgarity and indecency as was heard and seen there would disgust a more hardened person than I.

"The next place visited was a gambling hall where all games of chance were being played. Men excited with drink and play were recklessly staking their last dollar on the turn of a card or the throw of a dice. Women were cajoling and coaxing the tipsy men to stake their money on various games; and pockets were shrewdly picked by the fallen women of the more sober of the crowd. We soon tired of this place and started forth for new dens of vice and crime and visited several similar to those already described.

"At last about 10 P.M. we visited the theater and were asked behind the curtain to see the girls. From here I left the party and retired to my tent fully satisfied with my first visit to such places."[19] Cheap alcohol, risky games, and temporary women—these places were the very fantasy of the unattached male.

It is astonishing that no such scenes were provided on the more arduous route of the Central Pacific Railroad coming east from California. They had a severe shortage of iron, wood, water, and men. But the real reason was a little more involved and a little more crass. Crocker, in testimony before a Congressional Commission in 1876, put the matter rather frankly:

"Q. Did you commence the construction of the Central Pacific with white or Chinese labor?

"A. We commenced with white labor . . . [but] could not get sufficient labor to progress with the road as fast as was necessary, and felt driven to the experiment of trying Chinese labor . . . I had charge of the construction, and Mr. Strobridge was under me as superintendent. He thought that the Chinese would not answer, considering what they eat, and other things, and from what he had seen of them; he did not think they were fit laborers; he did not think they would build a railroad. . . . [W]e tried them on the light work, thinking they would not do for heavy work. Gradually we found that they worked well there, and as our forces spread out and we began to occupy more ground, and felt more in a hurry, we put them into the softer cuts, and finally into the rock cuts. Wherever we put them we found them good, and they worked themselves into our favor to such an extent that if we found we were in a hurry for a job of work, it was better to put on Chinese at once."[20]

But there was, of course, a working hierarchy, as James Strobridge testified: "We made foremen of the most intelligent of the white men, teamsters and hostlers. We increased, I suppose to 2,000 or 2,500 white men. At that time we were working fully 10,000 Chinamen. . . . Finally, before the work was half done, perhaps, I do not recollect at what stage, the Chinamen had possession of the whole work. At last the white men swore they would not work with Chinamen anyhow."[20]

A more specific estimate of the value of Chinese labor was given at the same hearing by Frederick F. Low, a former governor of California and minister to China, "I was one of the commissioners when the Pacific railroad was in the course of construction on this side of the Sierra. . . . They paid the Chinese $31 a month, and they boarded themselves. To the white laborers they professed to pay, and did pay, $45 a month and board, which amounted, they considered, to two dollars a day."[21]

It was not until 1866 that the Union Pacific began work, but it proceeded with methodical fury to make up lost time. The construction was supervised by the former Brigadier General Jack Casement and his brother Dan. The construction of this track became not merely an industrial enterprise, but the elongated sculpture of an American monument. Simultaneously, and characteristically, it was touted as a spectacular sporting event. A $10,000 prize was set, to be awarded to the railroad that laid the most rail between sunrise and sunset. The Central Pacific won. The last year of work was described by Strobridge, the superintendent of construction under Crocker:

"From April, 1868, until May, 1869, eleven hundred miles of iron was laid by the two companies. In crossing the desert, water for men and animals was hauled in places for forty miles, while grain, fuel and all supplies came

Railway curve on Moffat Road, Colorado.

Photograph by William H. Jackson, 1869. Colorado Historical Society

from California. There was not a tree big enough to make a board for five hundred miles.

"Supplies cost enormously. I found a stack of hay on the river near Mill City, for which the owner asked sixty dollars a ton. He said I must buy it as there was no other hay to be had. The stack was still standing in his field when we moved camp and it may be there now for all I know. Another settler had a stack of rough stuff, willows, wire-grass, tules and weeds, cut in a slough. I asked him what he expected to do with it. Not knowing that he had a prospective buyer, the man answered, 'Oh! I am going to take it up to the railroad camp. If hay is high I will sell it for hay. If wood is high I'll sell it for wood.'

"There were no Indian troubles, one reason being that General P. E. Connor was sent out with a thousand soldiers a few years before and he cleaned up the country, destroying men, women and children indiscriminately. The Union Pacific was guarded by troops for years and the authorities offered to put some with the Central Pacific forces as guards, but I said, 'No guards,' and there were none. Mr. Huntington suggested that a military man, accustomed to drilling troops, should be engaged to put down the rails, but I said, 'Damn the military' and it was damned."[22]

There was an odd proviso in the federal law: that the two railroads should meet. But the law didn't say where—presumably because it could not be known in advance how much rail each company would lay. They were now both in Utah, where Brigham Young, the head of the Mormon Church, had a considerable stake. His son and his friend Spencer Sharp, a Mormon bishop, formed a separate company to hire Mormon laborers. They were to build the missing section of the railroad, with Brigham Young himself the chief contractor. They were a tuneful and reverential lot:

> Hurray! Hurrah! For the railroad's begun!
> Three cheers for our contractor,
> His name's Brigham Young.[23]

He was anxious to have the railroad pass through Salt Lake City and denounced the alternate course, to the north of the lake, by a thundering sermon in his tabernacle. But the forces of evil prevailed, and both

Celebration of the final transcontinental link between west and east, at Promontory, Utah, on May 10, 1869.
Photograph by a Mormon, Charles R. Savage. Beinecke Rare Book and Manuscript Library, Yale University, Western Americana Collection

branches, east and west, pressed toward Promontory, Utah. Yet it was not as
simple as that. Both railroads were paid by the mile, so, by the crazy logic of
economics, the eastward and westward tracks actually passed one another by
a hundred miles without managing to join. This arrangement had all the
stubborn ideology of war. In the words of General Dodge: "The Central Pacific had made wonderful progress coming east, and we abandoned the work
from Promontory to Humboldt Wells, bending all our efforts to meet them
at Promontory. Between Ogden and Promontory each company graded a
line, running side by side, and in some places one line was right above the
other. The laborers upon the Central Pacific were Chinamen, while ours
were Irishmen, and there was much ill-feeling between them. Our Irishmen
were in the habit of firing their blasts in the cuts without giving warning to
the Chinamen on the Central Pacific working right above them. From this
cause several Chinamen were severely hurt. One day the Chinamen, appre-
ciating the situation, put in what is called a 'grave' on their work, and when
the Irishmen right under them were all at work let go their blast and buried
several of our men. This brought about a truce at once. From that time the
Irish laborers showed due respect for the Chinamen, and there was no further trouble."[24]

It's been a Machiavellian bromide of leftist politics for at least a hundred
years, that the governors of the world provoke divisions between the governed, sect against sect, skin against skin, the better to rule and profit. No
doubt such ugly schemes were proposed, plotted, and even financed, and
still are. But it is always a waste of money. Men need no encouragement to
hate their fellows; they will do it for nothing.

5

So the two railroads met, except for the final rail, at Promontory Summit, Utah, a point forty miles from Ogden, where "the two trains pulled up
facing each other, each crowded with workmen who sought advantageous
positions to witness the ceremonies, and literally covered the cars. The
officers and invited guests formed on each side of the track, leaving it open to
the south. The telegraph lines had been brought to that point, so that in the
final spiking as each blow was struck the telegraph recorded it at each connected office from the Atlantic to the Pacific."[25] The final spike, made of
gold, was inserted in a pre-drilled hole in the hardwood tie. It was reported,
perhaps apocryphally, that when the cameras were set up, someone yelled,
"Shoot!"—whereupon a Chinese laborer, sensitized by the experiences of
the past weeks, dived for his life. Governor Stanford, more acquainted with
American vernacular, struck down on the final spike with a silver hammer—
and missed. Durant, President of the Union Pacific, missed too, maybe "out
of courtesy." It was finally driven home by the chief engineer of the Union
Pacific Railroad.

An examination of the photographs taken that day by the cumbersome wet-glass plate technique, shows the two locomotives face to face. They are of somewhat different design but each has a certain black and glittering pattern—the aesthetic of copper, iron, and glass—where the useful and the massive are made elegant. In this they resemble the scientific instruments of the early nineteenth century, for each age and culture makes tools in the taste, not of its own time, but of the generation preceding it.

And each locomotive has a sort of barred iron apron in front of it—the cow-catcher. It is decorative and logical, an extension of the design. But its purpose was ludicrously useful, for encounters with animals were frequent in the rural American continent. "Once a hog got under a locomotive and was instantly decapitated, derailing the engine and shaking up the passengers, especially an unidentified man who turned a somersault out an open window . . . A resourceful mechanic, unforgettably named Isaac Dripps, found a solution to the problem of cattle on the tracks. He proposed to get rid of intrusive livestock by attaching a pair of outthrust, wrought iron bars to the front of the engine to impale a wandering beast before he could slip under the wheels. This cow-prong worked so well that a bull was carried along for several hundred yards, wedged between the tines, and had finally to be removed with block and tackle. This encounter induced the inventor to modify his basic design into a sort of downthrust metal comb, the predecessor of all the cow-catchers that later became standard equipment on American locomotives."[26]

There is also an interesting class distinction in the photographs: the officials in their best clothes are hatless, but the workmen all wear dark felts. A number of ladies are present, but whether they are wives or mere *nymphs du grade* one cannot say. In one photograph a telegraph operator stands at ease high upon the crossbar of a telegraph pole, where above him waves the flag of a newly-united United States.

6

A story, probably untrue in its present elaboration, relates the kindness of the Indians to the first colonists in Virginia. Maize was then unknown in Europe, but was a staple carbohydrate in Indian culture. The Indians told the new colonists precisely how to grow it, Dig a hole of a certain depth, plant a fish, cover it with earth, put in a dry kernel saved from the previous year, fill the hole, water it, and sing a particular song—in the Indian language of the region, of course. In the spring of 1609, the whites planted their first corn. They dug the hole, planted the fish, covered it, put in the seed, leveled the ground, watered it—but sang no song at all. The Indians laughed at this error. Without poetry, no corn could possibly grow. But it did grow, and this frightened them a great deal; obviously the whites had a secret, powerful, magic song.

This sinister magic of the whites would change—not quickly, for it took three centuries—the whole face of the continent. Eventually the country

Wreck at Batavia, New York, February 18, 1885. New York and Central and Hudson Railroad.

Photograph by P. B. Houseknecht. Library of Congress

would be pitted with mines, laced with wires, scarred with explosives, grimed and blurred with chemical fog, beglittered with the nocturnal rhinestones of multiple cities, tattooed with highways and bound with the double steel tracks of a mesh of railroads. And all of these peculiar and powerful alterations would be done without magic songs by the secret power of white engineering. The railroad was only one of the most stunning of these doubtful miracles. Its start and its efflorescence had a profound effect on American life, and particularly on the last third of the nineteenth century.

The great squares of land given outright to the railroads were the basis for the historic introduction of "bonanza farming," which was simply the mechanization of agriculture by the same power that drove the locomotive, steam pushing iron. The Northern Pacific Railroad, for example, ran farms of 100,000 acres apiece, and these were plowed, harrowed, and harvested by machine, with the assistance of a few hundred migratory workmen hired only for the late summer season. "Flying dust, cracking whips, glistening straw, a ceaseless ringing humming—that was horse-power threshing as described by Garland. The wheat came pulsing out the spout in such a stream that the carriers were forced to trot on their path to and from the granary in order to keep the grain from piling up around the measurer. There was a kind of splendid rivalry in this backbreaking toil—for each sack weighed ninety pounds.' "[27]

Similarly, the enormous empty public and railroad lands that were too dry for wheat grew excellent fodder for animals. Herds of cattle, as vast as the bison before them, could be driven north, feeding on the grassy plains and loaded live into freight cars. Thence they were hauled to the stockyards, where corn from the Midwest was shoveled into their mouths to fatten their poundage and therefore their profit. By 1880 the cattle drives to the railroads had been transformed into a romantic American event:

"Spring was the usual starting time, and during the seasons of the large drives, May, June, July, and August saw almost a solid procession passing over the great trails. So near were the herds that the drivers could hear one

Wreck on the Fort Worth and Denver Line, June 3, 1918. Arrow indicates body of engineer.

Photograph by W. D. Orr. Library of Congress

another urging along the stock, and frequently even the utmost care could not prevent two companies stampeding together, entailing a loss of much time and labor in separating them.

"Once started, it was remarkable the orderly manner in which a herd took its way across the plains. A herd of a thousand beeves would string out to a length of two miles, and a larger one still longer. It made a picturesque sight. The leaders were flanked by cow-boys on wiry Texas ponies, riding at ease in great saddles with high backs and pommels. At regular distances were other riders, and the progress of the cavalcade was not unlike that of an army on a march. There was an army-like regularity about the cattle's movements, too. The leaders seemed always to be especially fitted for the place, and the same ones would be found in the front rank throughout the trip; while others retained their relative positions in the herd day after day.

"When skies were clear and the air bracing, the task of cattle-driving was a pleasant and healthful one. But there came rainy days, when the cattle were restless, and when it was anything but enjoyable riding through the steady downpour. Then especially were the nights wearisome, and the cattle were ready at any time to stampede.

"No one could tell what caused a stampede, any more than one can tell the reason of the strange panics that attack human gatherings at times. A flash of lightning, a crackling stick, a wolf's howl, little things in themselves, but in a moment every horned head was lifted, and the mass of hair and horns, with fierce, frightened eyes gleaming like thousands of emeralds, was off. Recklessly, blindly, in whatever direction fancy led them, they went, over a bluff or into a morass, it mattered not, and fleet were the horses that could keep abreast of the leaders. But some could do it, and lashing their ponies to their best gait the cow-boys followed at breakneck speed. Getting on one side of the leaders the effort was to turn them, a little at first, then more and more, until the circumference of a great circle was being described. The cattle behind blindly followed, and soon the front and rear joined and 'milling' commenced. Like a mighty mill-stone, round and round the bewildered creatures raced until they were wearied out or recovered from their fright. . . .

"Reaching the outskirts of the shipping-station the herd was held on the plains until the drover effected a sale or secured cars for shipment. Then the animals were driven into the stockades, dragged or coaxed into the cars, and were sent off to meet their fate in the great packing-houses. The journey had been a strange one to them, often accompanied by savage cruelties at the hands of heartless drivers, and the end of the trip with close confinement of yard and car, the first they had ever known, was strangest of all."[28]

So these two necessities of the mammal, protein and cereal, were produced in such abundance that the great, growing, abnormally swollen and still-expanding cities of the East and the Midwest could easily be fed, and fed rather cheaply. This, in turn, made the vast growth of factories possible.

Thus the industrial pyramid of the United States, largely built in the last third of the nineteenth century, was bound together and made safe from collapse by these double threads of iron railway. The grandeur of this means of transportation was an amalgam of the useful and the romantic, a very American indistinction, but real enough in the poetry of the mind: "What a fierce weird pleasure to lie in my berth at night in the luxurious palace-car, drawn by the mighty Baldwin—embodying, and filling me, too, full of the swiftest motion, and most resistless strength! It is late, perhaps midnight or after—distances join'd like magic—as we speed through Harrisburg, Columbus, Indianapolis. The element of danger adds zest to it all. On we go, rumbling and flashing, with our loud whinnies thrown out from time to time, or trumpet-blasts, into the darkness. Passing the homes of men, the farms, barns, cattle—the silent villages. And the car itself, the sleeper, with curtains drawn and lights turn'd down—in the berths the slumberers, many of them women and children—as on, on, on, we fly like lightning through the night—how strangely sound and sweet they sleep!"[29] The train, with its life-like pulsations, was like something frightening and divine. It did not become part of folklore (except in the blues of black culture), but of the sad, corny poetry of common life:

> On a dark stormy night, as the train rattled on,
> All the passengers had gone to bed,
> Except one young man with a babe in his arms
> Who sat there with a bowed-down head,
> The innocent one began crying just then,
> As though its poor heart would break,
> One angry man said, "Make that child stop its noise,
> For it's keeping all of us awake,"
> "Put it out" said another, "Don't keep it in here,
> We've paid for our berths and want rest,"
> But never a word said the man with the child,
> As he fondled it close to his breast,
> "Where is its mother go take it to her,"
> This a lady then softly said,
> "I wish that I could" was the man's sad reply,
> "But she's dead, in the coach ahead."
> Ev'ry eye filled with tears, when his story he told,
> Of a wife who was faithful and true,
> He told how he'd saved all his earnings for years,
> Just to build up a home for two,
> How, when Heaven had sent them this sweet little babe,
> Their young happy lives were blessed,
> His heart seemed to break when he mentioned her name,
> And in tears tried to tell them the rest,
> Ev'ry woman arose to assist with the child,
> There were mothers and wives on that train,
> And soon was the little one sleeping in peace,

With no tho't of sorrow or pain,
Next morn at a station, he bade all good-bye,
"God bless you," he softly said,
Each one had a story to tell in their home,
Of the baggage coach ahead.[30]

4

The Fires at Pittsburgh

I N 1861, THE FIRST YEAR of the Civil War, there were
31,000 miles of railway track, a three-fold growth over
the previous decade. By 1869, the year of the transcontinental railroad, the length of track in the United States was almost
47,000 miles. In 1880 the mileage was 116,000, more than doubled again. By
1890, there was almost another doubling: 208,152 miles of track—200,000 if
one subtracted street railways. By 1900, another 50,000 miles were added,
and by 1917 the total railway mileage on the edge of another war was
400,000, enough to cross the continent a hundred times.[1]

But in this smooth world of statistics, there are ugly excrescences. Between 1890 and 1917, there were 72,000 railroad employees killed and
nearly 2,000,000 injured, and these only on the trains and the tracks themselves, not in the railway repair shops and roundhouses, which counted a
total of 237,000 injured and 158,000 killed.[2] These are catastrophic losses,
certainly far greater than all the battle casualties of all the Indian wars put
together. And passenger deaths and injuries over the same period were
roughly as great, with total casualties a good deal over 212,000. There is no
doubt that the American railroad system, built with such furious energy,
was, by any human standards, unsafe at any price particularly for the crew:

"It is very difficult to look back to 1875 and give a clear picture of the
conditions under which railroad men worked at that time. Link-and-pin
couplings, of course, for all cars . . . Perfect coordination of mind and muscle
were an absolute necessity. Oftentimes it was necessary to walk between the
two moving cars. Wary feet, an alert mind, and chilled nerve were needed
every instant. A man lived only long enough to make one mistake. The un-
coupling of the cars was always the most dangerous job . . . There was not a
great deal of room for a man's body on the coupling beam. The handholds
were seldom trustworthy. If there was any miscue, or if the pin could not be
pulled, the trainman stood a fine chance of being thrown under the car . . .
Pins and links that broke during couplings and uncouplings took their toll in
fingers. One of the most common marks of a railroad man in the seventies
and eighties was a crushed hand or a shortage of digits . . . None of the
switch frogs were blocked with wood as now. A careless foot that strayed into

one of these tracks was cut off before it could be jerked out. If the trainman was lucky, he lost one foot . . . Rail ends at all switches were open, presenting the same trap as the frogs. The cars themselves were unsafe. Regular inspection was unheard of. Some of the handholds were wired, some patched up with nails. All brakes were set by hand. When a brake chain broke (a common occurrence), the trainman had a fifty-fifty chance of being thrown under the wheels. I estimate that in 1875 there were from three to five men killed or badly crippled in the Hannibal & St. Joe yards each week."[3]

Passengers or crew, nobody counted the burned and the broken and the dead before 1890; the sum of these earlier years could hardly have been inconsiderable. For example, between 1870 and 1872, the Chesapeake and Ohio Railroad ordered a tunnel one and a half miles long to be cut through a mountain of rock in West Virginia. The job took about a thousand men. "Most of them were Negroes, only seven or eight years out of slavery. Nobody knows how many of them died, for there seemed to be a studied effort on the part of both the railroad and the press to play down the casualties. If the danger became too widely known, labor might become too difficult to recruit. But guesses might be based on casualties reported at other tunnels. The *Wheeling Intelligencer* said on December 30, 1870, that 1,000 lives had been lost at Mont Cenis Tunnel in the French Alps. The *Kanawhat Chronicle* revealed on December 17, 1873, that 136 had been killed in boring Hoosac Tunnel in Massachusetts. The three great killers were tunnel sickness (from heat and foul air), explosives (nitroglycerin, dualin, and gunpowder), and falls of rock. At Big Bend, one slide of 8,000 cubic feet of rock was reported by the *Greenbrier Independent* on June 1, 1872, but the paper said nothing about casualties. Many must have been dead by then, however, for as the tunnel penetrated the mountain, the likelihood of deaths from foul air mounted with each day."[4]

Once the ties were set and the rails hammered into place, a new team of workmen took on the hazards of guiding this steam projectile. Of these, the brakeman's job was the most dangerous and the worst paid, and brakemen made up the largest job category on the railroad. To stop the train, the brakeman had to climb on top of the moving cars, and then turn a wheel on each one of them, until the brakes were set and the wheels brought to a scraping, sparking halt. Automatic air brakes were not mandatory till 1893. Here is one railroad man's story:

" 'When will you be ready to go to work?'

" 'Right away,' I said.

"The yardmaster looked at his watch.

" 'Well, I don't know but that you had better get your dinner first. It's now eleven-thirty. There's no use of your getting killed on any empty stomach.'

"Away I went to my hotel, highly elated at my success. I was now a genuine railroad man, I thought. To be sure, I didn't like all those references to killing and maiming, but I thought they had been thrown out only to try my nerve. I congratulated myself that I had shown no sign of flinching.

"I was wrong in my conjecture, of course. Like all railroad yards, this was more or less a slaughterhouse, and one poor fellow's life was crushed out of him that afternoon, although I did not hear about it until the next day— which was just as well, I guess, for if I had known of it at the time, I dare say I should have lost some of the nerve I felt so proud of."[5]

Another even more dangerous part of his job was to couple and uncouple cars by hand:

"It was four or five months before I 'got it.' I was making a coupling one afternoon. I had balanced the pin in the drawhead of the stationary car and was running along ahead of the other car, holding up the link. Just before the two cars were to come together, the one behind me left the track, having jumped a frog. Hearing the racket, I sprang to one side, but my toe caught the top of the rail. I was pinned between the corners of the cars as they came together I heard my ribs cave in like an old box smashed with an ax.

"The car stopped and held me like a vise. I nearly fainted with pain, quite unable to breathe. Fortunately, Mr. Simmons was watching. With the presence of mind that comes of long service, he called at once for the switch rope, and he would not allow the engine to come back and couple the car again, as that would surely have crushed out my life.

"It seemed to me that I would surely suffocate before they got that switch rope hooked onto the side of the car, although I knew the boys were hustling for dear life. I tell you, when your breath is shut off, seconds are hours. My head was bursting. I became blind. There was a terrible roaring in my ears. And then, as the engine settled back on the switch rope, I felt a life-giving relief as I fell, fainting, into the arms of the boys . . ."[6]

The injured man was carried to the company doctor, fresh out of college, who remarked, "There's nothing much the matter with him. Few of his slats stove in, that's all."[7] It took him six weeks to recover, and meantime, "the boys cheered me up greatly by telling of their own various mishaps. Few of them had escaped broken bones and smashed fingers; and I was assured that broken ribs were nothing, absolutely nothing. Their talk restored my spirits wonderfully, for I had been disconsolately thinking that I was now a physical wreck, fit only for a job of flagging on some road crossing at twenty dollars a month. Even Simmons, who appeared to be a particularly fine specimen of manhood, told me he once had fallen while running ahead of a car, just as I had been doing, and twelve cars and the engine had passed over him, rolling him over and over, breaking both his legs, and, as he said, mixing up his insides so his victuals didn't do him much good for a year afterward."[8]

If a brakeman were hurt, he was immediately unemployed. The management of the Pennsylvania Railroad put its employees on notice: "The regular compensation of employees covers all risk or liability to accident. If an employee is disabled by sickness or any other cause, the right to claim compensation is not recognized."[9]

The fireman's job had somewhat more prestige, though it's hard to see why. The job was hot, laborious, and monotonous. Hour after hour, he had to pitch pine logs into the furnace or else shovel soft coal—most of it slate— into the burning, glaring mouth, and this, of course, in every sort of weather, broiling or freezing. The roundhouse worker was hardly better off. For example, in 1872, an apprentice in a Pennsylvania Railroad shop was paid only fifty cents a day for his first year of work. He worked iron with iron tools—chisel, bit, and file—which did permanent damage to his hands. By his fourth year, though, he earned a dollar a day. Why did men take such dangerous and ill-paid jobs in the first place? The truth was that these were the best jobs available and were the best way to be assured of bread, meat, and rent. Once on the job, they stayed as long as they were physically able to work, for there was no workmen's compensation until 1929, no national social welfare until 1935, no railroad unemployment insurance until 1939, and no disability insurance for railroad employees until 1947. In the nineteenth century, a man killed on the railroad had no further worries, but if he were merely injured, he had to depend on religious and local charity.

In these dangerous and difficult jobs, there was a hierarchy, with the locomotive engineers, those aristocrats of steam, at the very top, but they were not immune to exhaustion: "At times of heavy traffic it is not admitted that men need rest or sleep; and I have had a roundhouse foreman indignantly ask: 'What's the matter with you, that you register for rest? You've only been at work twenty-four hours! Some of you fellows ought to get a job clerkin' in a drug store.' "[10] In this reproach we hear the accent of the rude, brawny male—of the foot soldier, the iron puddler, and the ordinary seaman—a bravado that curses the work, but takes a sullen pride in its very danger and even in its monotony. This idea, this value, is not an invention of skippers, generals or railroad superintendents, but is the creation of the anonymous victim. If one is doing a hard, dangerous, uncomfortable, badly paid job, it is a requirement of one's human dignity to be proud of necessity.

But whatever the inner rhetoric, the external facts remain the same:

"I got down to oil while the fireman was taking water and discovered that the link-lifting spring was broken; and, while I was looking at it and wondering how that could have happened without my knowing it, the head brakeman came up with an order for me to weigh that coal.

"My back was almost broken; I was more than half dead with fatigue and worry; and now I had to weigh thirty carloads of coal without a lifting spring. The big cast-iron links and long eccentric rods must have weighed at least two hundreds pounds, and as it is necessary in putting cars on the scale to move the engine back and forth continually, I saw what a nice time I was going to have handling that old reverse lever.

"I telegraphed the dispatcher, telling him how I was fixed and asking permission to use another engine to weigh the coal with. The answer was short: 'Use the engine you have.'

"Back I went to the yard and weighed that coal. In order to back the engine, I had to brace both feet against the front of the cab and, pulling with all my might, raise the heavy links. If I had the misfortune to move the cars half an inch too far, I would get a signal to go ahead a bit. As I unhooked the lever, it would fly forward with such force as to nearly jerk me through the front windows. (Remember, I was nearly dead with fatigue and hunger when I started on this delectable trip.) Somehow I got the coal weighed and coupled on. The conductor, coming ahead, began to tell me how far we could go if we hurried up and got out ahead of Train 12. I cut him short by telling him to go into the office and tell Chicago I couldn't go another foot until I got five or six hours' sleep. Off he went, grumbling that we'd never get anywhere that way. Back he came in a few minutes.

" 'Chicago says, "All right. Go to sleep." '

"I pulled into a convenient siding, picked as smooth a lump of coal as I could find in the tender, upholstered it with waste, and, spreading my coat on the foot-board for a mattress, I dropped the curtain and curled myself into the short, hot, dirty cab for a few hours' rest . . .

"My back ached so, I was so tired, and my position was so cramped and uncomfortable, that it was some time before I could even doze . . .

". . . Having been fifty-two hours without rest (for the short spell of comparative quiet in the yard could not be so termed), I entered on the register this request: '9:30 A.M. Have been fifty-two hours on duty. Do not call me until I have had eight hours' sleep.' I then crawled slowly and painfully over to the hotel and went to bed.

"I was so completely fagged out that it was some time before my aching back would allow me to sleep. I had just dropped off when I was rudely shaken by the caller and saluted with, 'Hey, hey! Are ye awake now? I've been callin' ye fer ten minutes! You're wanted for a stock train.'

"When I got my wits collected enough to realize who I was, who he was, and what he was talking about, I asked him the time.

" 'Ten-fifteen.'

" 'What! Have I only been forty-five minutes off of that engine?'

" 'That's all.'

"Without another word I tumbled back on the pillow and pulled the bedclothes over my head . . .

". . . just as I was beginning to get my ideas into a pleasant state of haziness once more, the door was fired open with a bang. Rolling over, I beheld the exultant countenance, safely outside the door this time. He was holding up for my inspection a sheet of dirty yellow-colored paper, which I knew was a telegraph form.

" 'Read that now, an' see if ye'll get up or not!'

"I took the paper and read: 'Engineer M——, don't you delay this stock train. W.S.B.'

"A combined order and threat from the train dispatcher, signed with the division superintendent's initials, was a peremptory order, to be unquestioningly obeyed. I borrowed the caller's pencil and wrote underneath the order: 'W.S.B.—I have been fifty-two hours on duty, am unfit to take stock train or any other train. J.B.M.' I handed it to the caller, and, telling him that if he disturbed me again for any reason, even though the house should be afire, I would brain him, I once more retired. Although I had no doubt that I had signed my death warrant, I slept the sleep of the utterly weary.

"I got my medicine—thirty days suspension for refusing to obey an order . . ."[11]

2

The Homestead Act of 1862 was intended to provide an escape mechanism for a man badly employed or not employed at all. After all, it was free government land. But no one can plow without a plow and plows cost money, and so does a team of horses, and so do shovels, hoes, seed, wagons, sawn timber, and carpenters' tools, not to speak of the seed stock of piglets, chickens, and calves, and food all winter and spring for man, wife, and beast. All these might easily cost upward of $1,500—not an easy sum for a workman to save, steal, or borrow. So the great empty rich utterly free frontier never really existed. Many hundreds of thousands worked instead in the new factories and the new roundhouses and shops and locomotives of the sprouting, flimsily built and badly graded railroads, and were thus subject, as industrial labor, to that mysterious illness of industrial society—the panic.

There had been recurrent bad times since the founding of the Republic. There was one in 1873, and another panic in 1857. But by far the most severe and the most stubborn began in 1873, when over a hundred banks failed, forcing the air out of the boom in business and railways.

In New York City, "Christmas was not festive that year [1873]. The whole city stirred uneasily under the burden heaped up by conscienceless speculators. Many street meetings followed to burn into the hearts of all, tragic demonstrations of human need. . . . The unemployed filled the city's streets and squares and marched to conferences with aldermen and mayor at the City Hall. It was a folk movement born of primitive need—so compelling that even politicians dared not ignore. There is something about a marching folk group that rouses dread. Those in authority did not rest comfortably. The press began hinting at the 'Commune.'

"[One] morning people began assembling early in the Square. I reached the Square a little after ten. It had been a drill field and playground and though a bit out of repair, was commonly used by the working people for general gatherings and speeches. A high iron fence surrounded the park, with wide gate entrances. Soon the park was packed and all the avenues leading to it crowded. The people were quiet."[12]

Several journals were sold among the assembly. One of them, in the convention of leftist rhetoric, was called *The Volcano*. "It was printed on bright yellow paper and its articles set up in red ink. In accord with their distribution of family responsibility, it was [the editor's wife's] business to sell these papers, and her working dress (masculine garb) served to attract attention while the big stick she always carried was her rod and staff of defense and support. The couple had three children—Eruptor, Vesuvia, and Emancipator."[13]

At 10:30 A.M., a fresh crowd began to enter the Square. For no apparent reason, police were ordered to charge them with clubs. Simultaneously, mounted police galloped forward and attacked a large group of men, women, and children who were waiting in the side street. "It was an orgy of brutality. I was caught in the crowd on the street and barely saved my head from being cracked by jumping down a cellarway. The attacks of the police kept up all day long—wherever the police saw a group of poorly dressed persons standing or moving together."[14]

It is astonishing how often in a democracy, as in a tyranny, the police crack down on the majority. It appears that any action that breaks the constraints of normal society—mass picketing, marching mobs, obstructions to traffic, or the noise of screams and curses—makes an officer of the law at once fearful and righteously angry. He can do violence to strikers because he thinks them violent already. Nor is the policeman immune to the social anxiety of bad times.

By 1877, a good third of all the railways in the United States were in bankruptcy. Their customers were in trouble too, for 22,000 businesses had failed. The passenger dollars came to a total of $108 million in 1871, and rose to $132 million the following year. But in 1873, it had only risen to $137 million, and in 1877 it was only $125 million. The same was true of freight loadings, which were reckoned in ton-miles. These remained stagnant during the years of depression. They amounted to 7.48 billion in 1873 and only rose to 8.75 billion in 1877.

Since railroad management had acquired the habit of huge and easy profits, they found these figures painful. Four large eastern railroads met in committee in April, 1877, and agreed to a general wage cut of 10 per cent for all their employees. At the same time, they doubled the length of their freight trains, so they could fire 50 per cent of their crews. This stretch-out and this cut in wages was not local, but general throughout the principal railroads of the country. It set off an explosion never yet seen in this country—a social conflict, flaming and deadly, real and not rhetorical, between the paver of industry and the resistance of its workmen. It began, like any stage tragedy, with a small, ominous, local event.

On the large Baltimore & Ohio Railroad, the agreed 10 per cent reduction was put into effect on Monday, July 16, 1877, cutting the pay of firemen "from $1.75 and $1.50 per day, to $1.58 and $1.35 per day, according to the efficiency of the men. The pay of brakemen was fixed at a little less. One hundred miles was made to constitute a day's run. No allowance of time was permitted for delays at way stations."[15] Groups of employees formed committees that day and appealed to the management to restore the cuts; they were refused. At 5:00 P.M. at a railway junction near Baltimore, forty firemen left their engines and took the brakemen with them. "Reports came in rapid succession from the West, announcing that the railroad men at Cumberland, Martinsburg and other stations along the line were restless, discontented and insubordinate, and that the canal-boatmen had quit work and abandoned their boats."[16]

This sympathy strike of the canal men, themselves not employed by the railroad but working in the far older form of transportation, was the signal that the concept of *strike*—a forceful, symbolic word for simply quitting what has become intolerable—was a deep and moving concept to a great many more people than a few thousand firemen, brakemen, and repair mechanics. By evening, the semi-skilled craftsmen in the Baltimore factories—"boxmakers, sawyers, and can-makers"—had struck for higher wages. During the night of July 16–17, no freight train left the yards; "the control of the immense property of the Baltimore & Ohio Railway Company had passed out of the hands of the officers and was held by the strikers."[17] King, vice-president of the Baltimore & Ohio, who had refused to listen to the elected committee on the morning of the sixteenth, now asked the governor of West Virginia to call out the state militia, which Governor Matthews did at once, putting his own aide-de-camp in command.

Early on July 17, Captain Faulkner ". . . at once proceeded to the railway track and deployed his men as a guard for a West bound freight train, which the Railway Company determined to dispatch in spite of the orders of the strikers. The train started, and had proceeded nearly to the switch at the Company's yards, when suddenly one of the strikers, named Wm. Vandergriff, ran forward and seized the switch-ball for the purpose of opening it to 'side-track' the train. At this time the train was moving slowly. A guard of militia was on the engine. The movement of Vandergriff was observed by John Poisal, a member of Captain Faulkner's command, who immediately sprang from the pilot of the engine where he had been stationed, and attempted to replace the switch in order to allow the train to proceed. Vandergriff resented this action, drew a pistol and fired two shots at the militiaman, one of which took effect in the side of his head. Poisal returned the fire, shooting Vandergriff through the hip. This firing led to a regular fusillade. A number of shots were fired at Vandergriff and he was shot in the head and arm. The report of firearms, speedily attracted to the spot a great multitude of railroad men and citizens. The excitement was intense. The engineer and fireman who had engaged with the Company to run the train, fled when the firing commenced. Captain Faulkner ordered the mass of strikers to keep back, and commanded them to disperse. This order was received by them with jeers and threats. Finding that the engineer and fireman had deserted the train, Captain Faulkner declared that he had fully discharged his duty, marched his command to their armory, where they were disbanded, leaving the strikers in full possession of the field. The road was now completely blocked up with standing trains. The cars were all uncoupled, and the links and pins were either hidden or broken."[18]

Dispatching the militia was somewhat ineffectual, because two of the four companies of state militia openly fraternized with the strikers. Next day, Governor Matthews asked the President of the United States for military help.

Republican Rutherford B. Hayes had been elected President the year before in a rather interesting manner. A former brigadier general and governor of Ohio, he lost the popular vote to Samuel Tilden by more than 250,000. But the Republicans a hundred years ago were the more radical, anti-southern party, and they challenged the election returns as fraudulent in Oregon and in three southern states: South Carolina, Florida, and Louisiana. Two separate sets of delegates from these four states arrived in Washington to vote at the Electoral College. Thus there were two electoral returns sent to Congress, one electing Tilden, the other electing Hayes. To decide the matter, Congress set up a commission of fifteen members. Eight were Republicans and, to no one's surprise, this commission voted eight to seven to put Hayes into office. This result was made palatable to the South by Hayes' pledge to withdraw all remaining federal troops from the formerly Rebel states, an act which had grave consequences in the Reconstruction.

One of the innumerable ironies of human history is that Hayes was rather a decent person, and by no means a blind reactionary. He fought for civil service, was considered by his contemporaries to be pro-labor, and in later years became something of a socialist. But the railroad strike plainly frightened him, and he ordered all union pickets, peaceful or not, to quit the streets and the depots and go home on or before twelve noon on July 19. Why, even with the smug hindsight we now have toward these contradictions, was a strike of 4,000 workmen in Baltimore so awesome? In part, certainly, it was fear of a parallel to the events in France. There, six years before, a popular uprising in Paris had overthrown the government and had begun to put into practice the principles announced in the scarlet rhetoric of young Marx and the younger Engels' *Manifesto* of 1848. This municipal coup was put down by the execution of some 20,000 Parisians. American public opinion did not reckon whose was the slaughter; it simply scared them.

What President Hayes and Governor Matthews feared, in the confusion of 1781 with 1871, was some sort of Robespierrean Commune. What Vice-President King of the Baltimore and Ohio feared was a little more realistic: a marked reduction in the rate of profit. The Missouri journalist, previously quoted, agreed on both these points. First:

"The vast numbers engaged in the strikes against the railroads, their apparent determination, the general belief that they were well organized and prepared, produced a dangerous effect upon the idle and vicious classes in all the large cities. Labor unions were suddenly aroused into unwonted activity, and displayed alarming vigor. 'The Workingmen's Party of the United States,' which is but another name for the 'International Association of Workingmen,' which has caused so much anxiety to the governments of Europe, came forth from its shadowy coverts, and what had been regarded as a phantom party, assumed a realistic attitude that caused a thrill of astonishment and terror to fall upon the urban populations of the country . . .[19]

". . . It was a wide spread belief among a large class of people in the lower ranks of society, who were reduced almost to starvation, that they had been wronged and oppressed beyond all endurance, that made the scenes witnessed in so many of the great cities of the country possible. It was an outcropping of the dreadful doctrines of the Commune which subsequently played so important a part in the great popular commotion accompanying the labor strikes."[20]

And of the second point:

". . . the managers of the great corporations in this country . . . have persistently sought to reduce wages of the laborers, while at the same time there has been a gradual increase in salaries paid to the managers and their assistants. Thomas A. Scott while receiving one hundred and seventy-five thousand dollars in salaries per annum, for managing property interests which in part belongs to himself, cannot very consistently insist upon a sum less than four hundred dollars per annum, as the proper compensation for the services of a man whose peculiar employment requires that he must be vigilant, prompt, and constantly exposed to danger.

"Then again, the system of watering stocks of railroads and other corporations, debars the managers from the privilege of pleading a failure to earn interest as an excuse for cutting down the wages of labor. Perhaps Wm. H. Vanderbilt is not able to secure ten per cent interest on the stocks of the New York Central Railroad. But it must be remembered that the par value of the stocks of the New York Central Railroad, exceeds eighty-two thousand dollars per mile, or upwards of fifty-five thousand dollars per mile more than the cost of the road—more than the actual cash investment. It is quite possible that Mr. Vanderbilt would have no difficulty in earning a dividend of fifteen per cent on the actual amount of money invested, and have enough earnings left to make a handsome dividend to every employe of the road.

"And here we find the immediate, potent cause of the Great Strikes . . ."[21]

3

The strikers' reply to the President's vague proclamation was exact and detailed. "They declared that they had submitted to three reductions of wages in three years; that they would have acquiesced in a moderate reduction; that they were frequently sent out on a trip to Martinsburg, and there detained four days at the discretion of the company, for which detention they were allowed pay for but two days' time; that they were compelled to pay their board during the time they were detained, which was more than the wages they received; that they had nothing left with which to support their families; that it was a question of bread with them; that when times were dull on the road they could not get more than fifteen days' work in a month: that many sober, steady, economical men became involved in debt last winter; that honest men had their wages attached because they could not meet their expenses; that by a rule of the company any man who had his wages attached should be discharged; that this was a tyranny to which no rational being should submit, and that it was utterly impossible for a man with a family to support himself and family at the reduced rate of wages."[22]

They therefore asked a total of two dollars per day for firemen and brakemen and no reduction for engineers and conductors. The truth of these complaints was so well understood that even at a time of scarce employment when no welfare or insurance was provided—these began three panics later in the 1930s—there was nobody the Baltimore and Ohio could persuade to run their locomotives. "About ten o'clock an attempt was made to start a freight train from Martinsburg toward Baltimore. A locomotive was fired up, while guarded by the military; a large company of strikers had assembled; the Sheriff was present with a posse; an engineer named Bedford was found willing to go, and he mounted to the cab . . . Just as the train was about to move away Bedford's wife rushed from the crowd, mounted the engine, and with agonizing cries besought him to leave the position. The engineer heeded the entreaties, and departed from the engine, followed by the fireman, which conduct elicited prolonged cheers from the strikers and their sympathizers . . ."[23]

The first encounters with military and police authority were generally peaceable. "An attempt was made during the day to arrest ten of the ringleaders of the strikers, on a charge of inciting to riot. Warrants for their apprehension were issued and placed in the hands of Sheriff Naderbusch for service. That officer summoned a posse and procured the services of a person named Engelrecht to act as a guide, and point out the persons accused. Going into the throng of strikers, they were quickly surrounded, and Engelrecht, being menaced, refused to designate the men, and the attempt failed. No personal violence was offered the Sheriff or his men. Later in the day, the arrest of Richard Zepp, supposed to be the master spirit among the strikers, was effected by the Sheriff. Zepp was committed to jail and a strong guard placed about it. He is a native of Martinsburg, is about twenty-five years old, is regarded as a man of undoubted courage and determination, and has served as a brakeman on the Baltimore and Ohio Railroad for the last five years. In person, he is rather below the medium height; is decidedly prepossessing in appearance, and is a man of more than average intelligence.

He is not addicted to strong drink; is fond of amusement; generally quiet in demeanor, and is exceedingly popular among his acquaintances. He has a wife and one child, who reside at Martinsburg . . ."[24]

Against such men, the United States Army now began to exert a ruder force:

HEADQUARTERS UNITED STATES TROOPS,
MARTINSBURG. W. VA., JULY 20, 1877

Due notification having been given by the proclamation of the President of the United States to those concerned, the undersigned warns all persons engaged in the interception of travel on the Baltimore and Ohio Railroad that the trains must not be impeded, and whoever undertakes it, do so at their own peril.

(Signed) William H. French,
Brevet Major-General United States Army,
Colonel Fourth Artillery Commanding[25]

Here was a typical military report: " 'The train was stoned at Sir John's Run, but no one was injured. The rain doubtless prevented a large gathering. Reached Cumberland without molestation at 12:45 a.m. Torpedoes on the track notified the strikers at Keyser of our coming. The regular engineer and fireman were taken off by the strikers and the train run on a siding. About one hundred strikers are at the depot now. My detachment is too small for effective operations, and there are poor accommodations . . .' "[26]

On the afternoon of Friday, July 20, 1877, meetings were held by several tiny organizations, of which one, at least, was connected with the First International. These were largely attended by immigrants, Germans, and Poles. The fiery speeches were reported to be "for war, swift, terrible, relentless, in order that the wrongs of working men might be redressed."[27] The platform of one of these parties reveals its ambitious demands:

"The Workingmen's Party of the United States proposes to introduce the following measures, as a means to improve the condition of the working classes:

"1. Eight hours for the present as a normal working day, and legal punishment of all violators.

"2. Sanitary inspection of all conditions of labor, means of subsistence and dwellings included.

"3. Establishment of bureaus of labor statistics in all States as well as by the National Government; the officers of these bureaus to be taken from the ranks of the labor organizations and elected by them.

"4. Prohibition of the use of prison labor by private employers.

"5. Prohibitory laws against the employment of children under fourteen years of age in industrial establishments.

"6. Gratuitous instruction in all educational institutions.

"7. Strict laws making employers liable for all accidents to the injury of their employes.

"8. Gratuitous administration of justice in all courts of law.

"9. Abolition of all conspiracy laws.

"10. Railroads, telegraphs, and all means of transportation to be taken hold of and operated by the Government.

"11. All industrial enterprises to be placed under the control of the Government as fast as practicable and operated by free co-operative trades unions for the good of the whole people."[28]

By early evening, the presence of armed soldiers in Baltimore had brought out curious crowds in the neighborhood of the armories and along the streets between the assembly points and the main Baltimore depot, where the railroad was to attempt to dispatch a symbolic train. "Those crowds were composed of a few railroad men, workers in machine shops, factories, mills, foundries, and vast numbers of those who live by preying upon others—thieves, professional ruffians, the scum of the city, jail-birds, or those who were hurrying with rapid steps to enter prison doors, drunken loafers, tramps just returned from making a circuit in quest of food and the pickings of rogues, with a considerable intermixture of peaceable citizens who had come out to gratify an idle curiosity, and been drawn into the seething mass of grimy workingmen and odorous thieves."[29]

A military alarm was ordered by Brigadier General James R. Herbert. All the bells in the city were sounded at once. To this ominous tolling, small numbers of troops marched through crowded streets toward the Camden station in Baltimore.

"When the troops had reached the intersection of Frederick and Baltimore streets, the mob pressed so closely upon them that they were constrained to protect themselves. No command to halt was given; no orders to fire, but the men acted without orders. A sharp rattle of musketry rang out above the tumult of the mob. A whistling of bullets was heard, men were seen to drop, cries of agony were mingled with curses and howls of rage. Women screamed and fainted on the streets; children mingled their piercing cries with the general uproar. There was a shrinking back of the crowd for a moment, and the militia marched on. But the rioters quickly rallied and by the time the troops had proceeded two squares the throng was as great as before, and the mob threatened to rush upon and disarm and murder the soldiers in the streets.

"When opposite the office of the *American*, newspaper, another halt was called, and another volley of bullets were poured into the midst of the howling mass of men who pressed upon the marching column. Men sank in their tracks and expired. This second discharge was received by the rioters with mingled cries of agony, threats and jeers. Paving-stones were gathered from the streets and hurled by strong arms into the ranks of the soldiers. The determination of the mob was a fearful exhibition of aroused passions. The momentary check given the rioters was taken advantage of by the militia to continue their march. But again the mob rallied and assailed the troops as the head of the column turned into Charles street. Another halt, another fusilade, a few more dead on the streets, was the result. Then the soldiers proceeded, amid the hoots and jeers of a maddened populace, to the depot."[30]

There were ten dead and twenty-three wounded by bullets. It's interesting to read their surnames: Byrne, Gill, Sinovitch, Rheinhardt, Murphy, Hourand, Frank, McDowell, Manck, Doud, Roke, Kemp. Except for Italians, who were yet to arrive in this country, it reads almost like the fictional roster of a bomber crew in its mixture of national origins. Yet the soldiers hit by stones had much the same mixture of origin.

The bitterness of the ordinary Baltimore citizen was directed against the Sixth Regiment, many of whom stripped off their uniforms, abandoned their weapons, and thus escaped the city. In the morning, the ten civilian coffins, each carried by four policemen, were moved from a local police station to their homes, watched by "a vast multitude" in complete silence. By ten that evening, over 10,000 people assembled near the Camden Station of the

MARYLAND—THE BALTIMORE AND OHIO RAILROAD STRIKE. **The Sixth Regiment, N.G.S.M., firing upon the mob, on the corner of Frederick and Baltimore Streets, July 20.**

Contemporary print, 1877. Library of Congress

THE GREAT STRIKE—DESTRUCTION OF THE UNION DEPOT AND HOTEL AT PITTSBURGH.
Contemporary print, 1877. Drawing by Fred B. Schell. Library of Congress

B&O. Soldiers on duty there were ordered to load with ball cartridges. A police charge, flailing their clubs and firing blanks from their pistols, dispersed the crowd. "About fifty of them were captured, taken to the station, tied with ropes, and laid out in the gentlemen's waiting room."[31]

Baltimore was only a few hours from Washington, and Washington was frightened. The order to send Marines to Baltimore had been cancelled, but after the Navy had mobilized two warships, the Marines were ordered to proceed after all.

By the evening of the twenty-first, in spite, or perhaps because of, the deaths, funerals and arrests, the B&O announced that it would not try to man and run any more trains. But it had no plans to meet with the strikers either. The strike, thus, was at a critical stage. One one side was the overwhelming majority of the citizens of Maryland and West Virginia; on the other were the inadequate and untrustworthy forces of government at every level. Baltimore was divided, much as it had been during the early months of the Civil War.

Late on the twenty-first, the two companies of Marines started for Baltimore. They marched in full battle dress through Washington to the depot, and crowds gathered in the streets of the capital to hiss and boo them as they went.

4

The strike that paralyzed the B&O in that violent midsummer of 1877 was only the beginning. The chief railroad companies had made the same cuts as the B&O, and their concert, it is supposed, was not accidental. Their employees undertook the same drastic remedy. On Thursday morning, July 19, the crew of an early freight train on the Pennsylvania Railroad refused to take out a double string of cars, and before noon no train moved out of Pittsburgh.

It's unfair, but fascinating, to see the alteration in style of the public statements that accompanied this crisis in American life. Here is a union call to a convention in 1869:

"WORKINGMEN OF NEVADA: To you we appeal in the great crisis now being forced upon us by the sordid selfishness of the money kings, who, for the lust of lucre, are striving to check the progress of our young State, and bring ruin and poverty to ourselves and those dependent upon us for support and maintenance. Day by day, and little by little, they have advanced their nefarious scheme. By degrees, and insidiously, has the enemy drawn nearer; and to-day, from his ambuscade of honeyed seemings, he rises a monster, which will require our united and firmest action to defeat . . ." The remainder of this call was something less than noble in motive: ". . . There is danger brooding near; ruin floats on every breeze; poverty hovers over every rooftree; while desolation awaits anxiously the fruition of the dream of the sordid spoiler—the firm seating of Chinese labor in our midst . . . Already they have left the railroad lines, and are working in the mills and mines of Humboldt county; and if we defer action, how long will it be before every mill and mine in the State will be worked by Chinamen and *we* be left to starve or seek for employment elsewhere? . . ."[32]

Compare this, both for style and content, with the bald, exact language of the Pennsylvania strikers of 1877:

"1. The undersigned, a committee appointed by the employes of the Western Division of the Pennsylvania Railway, hereby demand from said Company, through its proper officers, the wages, as per departments, of engineers, firemen, conductors, and brakemen, received prior to June 1, 1877.

"2. That each and every employe that has been dismissed for taking part or parts in the present strike, or meetings held prior to or during said strike, be restored to their positions held prior to the strike.

"3. That the classification of each of said departments be abolished now and forever hereafter; that engineers and conductors receive the same wages received by engineers and conductors of the highest class prior to June 1, 1877.

"4. That the runing of double trains be abolished, excepting coal trains.

"5. That each and every engine, whether road or shifting, shall have its own fireman."[33]

The reply of the railroad management was just as precise: "The Sheriff of Allegheny County, at the request of the railroad officials, about twelve o'clock at night visited the headquarters of the strikers at Twenty-eighth street, and ordered them to disperse. This they refused to do. Sheriff Fife remained there until after three o'clock in the morning, but his authority was defied. He was frankly informed that trains should not go out if they could prevent it, and they did not care for any posse he could muster, or any troops that could be brought against them."[34]

The good sheriff appealed to the governor of Pennsylvania; unfortunately, the governor had gone West. Some unknown person undertook to post a bogus proclamation in his name, but the trick was too obvious. Nevertheless, the sheriff read it aloud from the tender of a locomotive carrying armed troops; he was followed by Gen. Pearson, who issued a verbal ultimatum, interrupted by: " 'Who are you?', 'Give us bread!' and similar cries . . ."[35]

Meantime, warrants were got to arrest "the ringleaders of the riotous crowds."[36] The sheriff tried to organize a posse of 100 men to serve these warrants and make these arrests. He could only get fifteen—the same number, by chance, as the number of arrests he had to make. With these deputies, reinforced by 250 militia, he marched out to do his duty by his state, his country, and his railroad. Between five and six on Saturday evening, the sheriff, openly accompanied by Cassatt, vice-president of the Pennsylvania Railroad, and backed by federal troops, faced a great crowd of strikers and their sympathizers at the Twenty-eighth Street crossing. An attempt was then made to serve the first warrant and make the first arrest. In reply to a single, anonymous man's shout of defiance, General Brinton ordered his men to fire. ". . . Platoon after platoon poured showers of bullets into the terror-stricken company assembled on the bank overlooking the railroad tracks."[37] The official military report was somewhat different. It stated that after a bayonet charge, ordered to enforce the writs of arrest, a striker was wounded. The crowd was said to have answered with stones and pistol shots, to which, without an official command, the soldiers replied with rifle fire for about ten minutes. "It was at this time that the Pittsburgh troops threw down their arms and fraternized with the strikers, Hutchinson's Battery and a cavalry company alone excepted."[38]

Whatever the details, there is no doubt that sixteen citizens were instantly killed by soldiers' bullets; it is still astonishing to note that among the dead were several Pittsburgh militiamen. As the news spread, almost the entire population of Pittsburgh rushed into the streets. At the Twenty-eighth Street crossing, there were now—at eight in the evening—over 20,000 people. At a little past 9:00 P.M., gun shops were broken open and looted. A vast crowd moved through the dark streets to the scene of the massacre that afternoon.

Troops were quartered in a Pennsylvania Railroad roundhouse, and volleys of gunfire from the crowd broke all the windows. The militia did not reply. At 1:00 A.M. that same night, boxcars by the hundreds were set afire with oil and shoved down the tracks against the roundhouse.

A curious fact, noted by several observers, was the strong participation of women, "boldly urging the men on to acts of outrage and bloodshed . . . The appearance of women among the rioters was something unusual in this country . . . and women were the boldest and most heartless creatures in the mob . . ."[39] The women, and there were thousands who took part in these street conflicts, were denounced as the moral equivalent of *les Petroleuses*, the women of the Paris Commune of 1871. But these Pittsburgh women were hardly ideologues; they had domestic, earthy grievances. Their neighborhoods were unpaved and filthy with animal and human excrement. There was no indoor plumbing. Water for drinking, cooking and washing had to be carried upstairs from courtyard pumps, or from the nearby Monongahela River, which "was the catch basin for the refuse and sewage of the more than 60,000 people living along its banks. It also carried the refuse from mills, glass houses and slaughterhouses which stood on both sides of the slow-moving river."[40]

During the first fires, an assault began against the troops fortified inside the railroad roundhouse. The strikers used two field cannon captured earlier in the evening. Lacking shells, the guns were loaded with iron bolts and pins. A hole was blown in the stone wall of the roundhouse, but the attack was driven back by rifle fire. They now pushed a freight car, loaded with coke and primed with barrels of oil, right up to the roundhouse and set it afire.

By this time, it was past 6:00 A.M. The amount of confusion in this battle may be gauged by the fact that the militia inside simply marched out, apparently without being observed. But they were attacked as they and the two Gatling guns they possessed were retreating along the Pittsburgh streets in the early morning; they lost eight killed and several wounded. Meantime, the fires set in the yard and at the roundhouse continued to spread.

"The most striking feature, perhaps, of the day's developments, was the complete apathy with which the tens of thousands that thronged the city, looked upon the riots, the bloodshed, and the burning of millions of [dollars worth of] property. They seemed to take the same kind of interest in these tremendous events as they would take in a sensational drama . . ."[41]

Looting began, with its typical mixture of the violent and the ludicrous. "Here a brawny woman could be seen hurrying away with pairs of white kid slippers under her arms; another, carrying an infant, would be rolling a barrel of flour along the sidewalk, using her feet as the propelling power; here a man pushing a wheelbarrow loaded with white lead. Boys hurried through the crowd with large-sized family Bibles as their share of the plunder, while scores of females utilized aprons and dresses to carry flour, eggs, dry goods, etc. Bundles of umbrellas, fancy parasols, hams, bacon, leaf lard, calico, blankets, laces, and flour were mixed together in the arms of robust men, or carried on hastily constructed hand barrows."[42]

The spectacle was intrinsically American of the late-nineteenth century—a view of disaster as theatre, of riot as a form of sport. But it had no permanent consequence. In this respect, it was like Red Cloud's victory over the same armed forces. On Monday, rather suddenly, all passions petered out. It was quiet—in Pittsburgh.

5

Although in all the strikes that followed, no more than 15,000 men were involved, it was the fierce, if brief, determination of the employees and the geographical spread and nearly universal support for this powerful idea— refusing to go to work at wages not big enough to eat and to live on—that frightened every organ of government. For the strikes were not confined to the B&O, the Pennsylvania, the New York Central and the Erie Railroad, but spread west to the Michigan Central Railroad, the Chicago and North-western at Chicago, the St. Louis and Southeastern, the Illinois Central, and many others. As it had happened in Baltimore, strikes occurred in many other trades. Miners, for example, "marched from one mine to another, with loaves of bread stuck on poles."[43]

President Hayes was harassed by telegrams from railway officials de-manding that Pennsylvania be declared in rebellion, under the assumption that the railways and the U.S. government had identical interests—and at that period and under that pusillanimous administration, perhaps they did. It was Hayes' Secretary of State, William Evarts, who held that "as a mea-sure of political reform in this State the restriction of suffrage [be made] on a basis of a moneyed qualification."[44]

The U.S. Marines were sent to guard the railroad depots and such trains as could be furnished with crews. Later they were reinforced with ordinary troops, many of them veterans of the Civil War. Their conduct was not tem-perate. The Second Division of the Pennsylvania National Guard, under Major-General William J. Benton, marched into the railway junction of Reading, Pennsylvania, at 8:00 P.M. in the evening, unseen in the dim light, and after filing into a cut near the depot, directed rifle fire into the crowds on both banks. They were answered by stones and pistol fire, and replied with repeated volleys. "The streets resembled a small battle field, and the pave-ments were stained with many pools of blood."[45] These shots reverberated round the United States. On July 26, 1877, two open-air mass meetings were held. One was in a square in a tenement district of New York City, and was sympathetic to the men striking all over the East and Midwest against a cut in wages. The other meeting, at Battery Park in the same city, was addressed by Reverend William H. Acres, who "made a very fervent prayer, during which he implored Heaven to protect the city of New York from the power of the ruthless men that were seeking to destroy its peace, that it would kindly extend Its all-powerful aid to the police and help them to maintain order and quiet, and that it would soon cause the present difficulties to melt away like snow before the beams of the sun."[46]

His prayer was granted. The strikes of 1877 failed, by and large, within the next two weeks. One reason is obvious: Men without work are men without money. The very reason for their strike is the reason that they have little in savings. A second reason is the use of strikebreakers, a consequence of the first reason, for most of them were the very men who were previously on strike. In one case, however, the mining company brought in wagonloads of black miners guarded by the guns of hired guards against the hatred of the local whites—though of course, there were blacks among the strikers, too.

A third reason for their failure was the arrest of the strike leaders by federal troops. In East St. Louis the troops were commanded by a General Jeff C. Davis, (not the former President of the Confederacy, who was writing his memoirs on a farm in Mississippi), and a U.S. marshall under his command, Col. James Roe. The latter "had hardly arrived on the ground when he put detectives, which he had brought with him from Springfield and Chicago, on the track of the leaders conducting the strikes. The detectives were not long in ascertaining the prime movers, and as fast as they were discovered, warrants were sworn out against them. These warrants embraced . . . all the members of the original Executive Committee, together with the added members of the new, nine in all. [Those arrested] were placed in the guardhouse, which consisted of an empty freight car, and were taken that night to Springfield, where they were subsequently tried, found guilty of contempt of court in disobeying the decree of the court in interfering with trains . . ."[47]

The final, and perhaps the main reason for the failure of these strikes, which had reached a national stage, was the fear the strikers had of the deadly force applied against them. Only someone who has been locked in a crowd facing a charge of police clubs can understand the instinctive fear and rage which such an assault conveys, all the more so if it is a show of bayonets, a volley directed upward and ricocheting from the cement faces of the buildings or bullets aimed straight at the nearest bodies. A killing or two, and certainly a score, will arouse the curious conscience of a whole city. But it will also bring in federal troops under the flag to arrest and imprison the obstinate leaders, enforce the riot proclamations, and kill again if necessary. Men without equal arms or leadership or symbolic flags as deeply rooted in childhood veneration, experience the fatigue of continuous courage. They are exhausted, by excitement if nothing else. Their lives have never been optimistic of victory. Accustomed to living from day to day, they accept failure as consistent with their own experience. This the peasant that endures in everyone: Only survive, that's all that matters.

Then where is the joking optimism that is still supposed to be the fire inside the American spirit? The truth is again complex. The feeling that everything will turn out fine somehow, is still one of our American illusions. It was certainly strong in 1861 on both sides of the Civil War, but by 1865 it became obvious that one might be torn apart by a shell burst and die in pursuit of happiness. In the following ten years, the growth of the iron pyramid of factory life, the weight of machines now grown far bigger than a man, and the tyranny of industrial time forced a reluctant submission to a society too powerful and too successful for the ordinary man to resist. In 1877, strikes were called out of the energy of despair. The workman quit work and took to the streets. He stoned and he burned; he ran cursing from the parallel guns; he buried his dead. If blacklisted (and hundreds were), he starved or moved West. If not, he went back to work at reduced pay.

Above all, the failure of the strikes reflected the lack of precisely what the government feared—a central leadership and unified philosophy, even of the most practical sort.

5

Dig Up and Bury Again

IN DENVER CITY, COLORADO TERRITORY, on May 1, 1863, a man named John W. Grannis went to a general store run by Woolworth & Moffat and bought a notebook. He would use it to continue his diary. He was married, thirty-three years old and had a young son. He had been raised in Indiana, and now worked as a hired hand for the ranch owners Clark and Griswold:

"*Saturday, February 7* Herded the cattle as usual had some words with Mrs. Grannis & spatted her on the mouth

"*Sunday [February] 8* This morning Mrs Grannis concluded to make her Bed By her Self & leave me for ever & take her chances in life with Mr Griswold on the free love Principal"[1]

Then there was silence for three weeks. The preceding events were not only painful, but no doubt confusing as well. He wrote again on March 1:

"*Sunday, March 1* Quit work for Clark & Griswold Went up Town to Canon City Tried to trade of my house

"*Monday, March 2* Went up to Canon to look at a mule Got on a Big Drunk for the first time in my life. Came Home was carried in and Put to Bed

"*Tuesday [March] 3* Staid at Home.

"*Wednesday [March] 4* Went up to Canon City and made a Bargain to sell my house

"*Thursday, March 5* Went up town & Sold my House for 25 dollars

"*Monday [March] 9* Hunted Cattle for Chas Nacktrieb But did not find them

"*Tuesday [March] 10* Started for California Gulch"[2]

He had begun one of those periodical pilgrimages of the American male—the search for gold. Caught in the recurrent tide of men full of hope and moving steadily toward fortune or despair, Grannis described it in much the same way in his own elaborate language in a "MEMORANDA" appended at the end of the notebook: ". . . this morning we Passed the graves of 4 Persons who have fallen By the way side on their Pilgrimage to some Distant land (I am the creature of fortune Cast abandoned on the world wide

Stage And doomed in Scanty Poverty to Roam at no Distant Day some
traveler may see my name written upon a lone Board By the way side where
I have wandered in Pursuit of happiness which alas has flown forever and for
why Simply because I even loved a woman yes, my wife and She Played
me false for another man) Happiness thou Boon of heaven thou hast flown
from me forever Never again can I lay my head Beside my wife and enjoy
happiness."[3]

In mid-March of that year, he went to Denver City to buy equipment.
He mentions packsaddles and rope, but he must have bought beans and salt
pork and flour, like the other gold seekers; possibly a gun and ammunition;
certainly a pan. But he didn't buy a pick and shovel. In the midst of this business, he made this entry for March 24:

"*Tuesday*[*March*] *24* My wifes Birth Day. She is (37) years of Age

Grannis went with a partner, designated in the diary as "X," but he was
delayed while the latter got back some stolen stock. They didn't get started
till May 2. The following Sunday:

"*Sunday* [*May*] *3* Found our Animals 1–½ m^s up the creek Packed
up and Started at 8 O– Crossed Rock creek Cool creek & Boulder
creek killed a Rattle Snake the first Snake of the Season camped on the
Uranus Creek. Made 23 miles no wood"[4]

They made better than twenty miles a day:

"*Saturday, May 16* Started at 7 O c. & came to Duck Lake to Dinner The country is a wide Barren waste no wood But Sage & no water that
is fit to Drink the ground here for some distance is covered with a kind of
Rock formed of Shells Made Barren Springs at night in a Rain Storm this
spring is strongly impregnated with sulphur. Made 21 ms."[5]

As he traveled, he noted the great events of the day in words as equable
as those he used for geography:

"*Saturday* [*May*] *30* The Donkeys Stampeded & Run off 2 or 3 miles
got them Back & Started on with the ox team Crossed a great many small
streams of good water Passed the grave of a man who Died July 5th 1850—

Camped on Bear river traveled 22 miles

"*Sunday, May 31* Came to Soda Springs this morning 8 miles Saw
Mrs Grannis & Clark & Griswold^s outfit — Went around to see the Springs.
Went Down to Mormon town & to a Dance in the Evening Made 8 miles

"*Monday, June 1* Started at 6–½ o clock. Saw the Celebrated Steam-
boat Spring Passed the graves of 4 Persons who have Died while journey-
ing to some Distant land."[6]

He showed no astonishment that his wife, too, had joined the crusade:

"*Tuesday* [*June*] *2* . . . Got a nice mess of strawberries at noon & had a
talk with Mrs Grannis Passed the graves of 2 small children & five men the
men were killed By Indians Aug. 9–1852.

"*Wednesday, June 3* Stood guard over night Started at 6–½ O

clock   met a party of Indians at 8 o clock correlled for a fight But they
Proved to be friendly   Passed the grave of a woman who Died 1850   Came
to Snake River & camped   traveled 18 miles."[7]

The gold seekers were often homesick, but never lonely. It was a community in movement:

"*Sunday* [*June*] *14*   Went up the Creek   Saw Mrs Grannis   She was
washing   Saw a great many men from Cal Gulch Saw Mrs Till   Chas Wetherbee got in"[8]

Not until the eighteenth did Grannis actually look for gold:

"*Thursday, June 18*   Went Prospecting in the forenoon & worked in
the afternoon for 2 dollars

"*Friday* [*June*] *19*   Went Prospecting Down the creek for 5
miles   Came back in the evening Did not make much

"*Saturday* [*June*] *30*   Went up some Dry Gulch above town for a wheel
barrow & went to Rocking with Chas Wetherbee made 85 cts"[9]

"Rocking" is simply the human labor of shoveling gravel into a "cradle,"
flushing it with water, and shaking it vigorously to persuade the heavier gold
dust to settle at the bottom; the results were not always spectacular. Three
days labor for $2.85 left Grannis despondent.

"*Sunday, June 21*   [I]t was a fine warm morning. got up Rather
late   got my Breakfast   went up the creek & washed. Read the Bible   My
thoughts are sad —   O happiness thou gift of Heaven thou hast forever
flown. Done nothing   there was a stampede for some Immagined new discovery in the evening"[10]

Five more prospecting days were no more lucky, so Grannis took off for
Virginia City, Nevada, where chances were little better:

"*Thursday* [*July*] *16*   Rained a good Deal during the night and some
during the forenoon   Worked all Day in the Ditch. Was sick with the Diar-
heo

"*Sunday* [*July*] *19*   Went to Discovery to a miners meeting   looked for
my Poney But Did not find him   Went Down town in the afternoon. it
Rained & the wind Blew quite hard. Mrs Grannis Bot a claim to Day for $200
in Dust

"*Saturday* [*July*] *25*   Went to hunt my Poney But found him not   got
on my hunt & went out to the new gulch   went to the head of the gulch &
camped for the night Heard Mrs Grannis was making 50 Dolls. per Day from
her claim"[11]

Boasting was common enough. Goldmining was like gambling in this
and most other respects, if one neglects to mention the exhausting, daily,
obsessive labor:

"*Monday* [*September*] *14*   Worked in the tail Ditch   was 34 yrs old to
Day

"*Thursday* [*September*] *17*   Was sick to Day   Went up to the Discovery & staid till noon   Came home & went to Bed   could not Sleep nor lay

comfortable   thought of the home I once had   But alas for a false Hearted woman I was betrayed"[12]

Now Grannis and his former boss Clark, working a claim together with three others, built a set of wooden sluices: essentially a series of water traps, where the stream could cascade from one level down to another, leaving the heavier gold as a residue at the bottom. The days became more profitable now:

"*Saturday, October 10*   Sluiced the Dirt from 3 Days Drifting   Done the hardest Days Shoveling that I Ever Done   Got 129.70"[13]

But the week's profit had to be split five ways:

"*Sunday [October] 11*   Settled up with the Co & Divided the money 85 Dollars each   went up to Discovery & Saw Mrs. Wetherbee then went Down town and Saw Mrs Culver from California & a lot of Boys from Colorado   Saw Mrs G and talked about a Settlement"[14]

The next week his share was $20.00., the week after, $38.00. Nor did Mrs. Grannis get much kinder:

"*Wednesday [November] 4*   Went to town to see Mrs Grannis   could not settle with her. She commenced suit for a Divorce in the territorial Legislature   Sluiced. got 56.70"[15]

The mountain weather got colder every hour, and his weekly gains remained small—$40.00 for the week ending Saturday, November 28, 1863, and $37.00 for the week following. Then there were the usual misfortunes:

"*Wednesday [December] 16*   Cold & clear. went up for my oxen   found them   old Buck had fallen Down the mountain & Broke one of his horns off & Broke 2 or 3 Ribs in & Bruised himself Badly   I took them Down town and sent them to a Ranch   Saw a Dead man that was found Dead on Stink water"[16]

Now, for the first time, Grannis began to be drawn into the live theater of the town itself:

"*Saturday [December] 19*   Warm & pleasant   I worked on the Drifting Cars Got the news of the arrest of Some prisoners for the murder of Nicholas Tevalt

"*Sunday [December] 20*   Warm & pleasant. I went Down town to see what was going on the Court was trying one Geo. Ives for murder   there was a very large crowd of miners present   I went on guard for the night

"*Monday, December 21*   After Pacing the heavy watches of the night away morning Dawned clear & Pleasant   the Court came at an early hour and was called to order by Judge Byham   the Lawyers was given until 3 o clock to get through & Submit the case to the Jury   at 3, O. the case was Submitted, the Jury came back in ½ hour with a verdict of guilty

"*Tuesday [December] 22*   After Some Preliminaries the Prisoner was taken out & hung By the Neck untill he was Dead (22nd)   Went Down town again to the trial of George Hilderman for the murder of N. Tevalt   He was Banished in ten Day   Came Home in the Evening

"*Saturday* [*December*] 26   Cold & Clear. Worked to Day   Got our Drift cleaned out

"*Thursday, January 14th* [1864]   Cloudy & clear By Spells   obeying a notice of the vigilance committee I went to Virginia [City] this morning. the whole gulch turned out By 10 oclock   the town was Surrounded By a guard and a Search was commenced for Some parties Implicated in the Road Agency Business. After a search of 4 or 5 hours we had six prisoners, Some having escaped. of these six 5 were found guilty and taken to the gallows & hung untill they were Dead. their names were—Jack Gallagher, Boon Helm, Frank Parrish, Hayes, Lyon, and Club footed George. I was on guard nearly all Day & saw them hung. the five was hung in a Row. all of them maintained their innocence to the Last & cursed the Vigilance Committee. the Bommers [Boomers] were very Quiet all Day. there were at least 500 men in town armed with Revolvers & Double Barrel Shot guns. the guard that was about the Prisoners was Released from Duty as soon as they were Dead & I came home after Dark a little while Being very well Satisfied with the Days work   Saw five men hung and not a very good Day for hanging neither."[17]

Even at this distance one still feels his numb fatigue:

"*Thursday 3d March*   Commenced to Start a Drift   had a Bad cave [cave-in]   I made a Sluce Box & some false Bottoms   was cold & Stormy

"*Friday 4th* [*March*]   Cold and windy this morning   Did not work to Day   was Getting my fortune told"[18]

And a month later:

"*Monday 4th April* . . . George told me of Mrs. Grannis' Marriage with Mr. Griswold which took place last night at Nevada (Joy to them)

"*April Monday 11th*   Pleasant But cool was sick all night & worse this morning   Did not go to work. Joe & Tom went to work cleaning out the Water Ditch till noon when the alarm was Given that 2 men was buried in a Drift on No. 29 Digget & Moon's Claim   Every Body immediately Ran to the Scene of the Disaster   when it was found that they would have to be Drifted out the best Drifters went to work   they could hear one of them alive and they worked with all speed to get him Before he would Die   in about 5 hours they got one man out Dead   his head was Broken and he was Badly mangled   the other one was not Rescued until 9 oclock although the Best Efforts were Put forth   the Best Drifters was on hand & took turns and Done their Best   he was taken out alive at last after 9 hours of intense suffering But had only to suffer till 12 O 20 minits when he Died, if he could have Been Rescued 3 or 4 hours he would probably have lived. he was not Badly Bruised & no Bones were Broken. Alas what Dangers will not men encounter for the Sake of Gold."[19]

About a week later:

"*Sunday June 19th*   Was Pleasant   I went to the Discovery this morning to Bid Mr & Mrs Wetherbee Good-Bye & wished that I was Ready to go with them to the States But have not made my Pile yet   I feel lonely without them   I could hardly check the Rising Tear as I kissed Mrs Wetherbee & Said that Dear old word Good Bye. came home and took a long Sleep   I feel the need of Rest   a years hard work in the mine has made me feel ten years older. But hard[work is what is needed here to make it Pay and I must not Dodge it

"*Monday June 20*   Arose this morning   felt well But thought how time had changed Since 13 years ago. 13 years ago this morning I was married, young & Buoyant with hope   I thought not of what awaited me in lifes journey. I have tasted of the Sweets & Sorrows of life to a great extent   Still life Does not look Dark   I am as hopeful of the future as ever although I am passing the Meridian of life, my health Somewhat impaired By a life of hard toil. Still I can look Back on my Past life & Point to it with Pride & hope for the future   it will Soon Be two years Since I left my wife   God grant that She has Spent those two years as happy as I have"[20]

His friends had given up gold mining to farm or to open a butcher shop. But Grannis persisted:

"*October, Thursday 12, 1865*   timbered up my Shaft & Set my Sluces

"*[October] Friday 13*   Started to Sluce   Did not get Pay

"*October, Saturday 14*   Sluced to Day But got no pay.

"*November, Friday 17*   Was cloudy all Day But Did not Storm much   Studied Dutch [German] part of the Day and Split wood part of the time   Staid at home all Day"[21]

He also went to Dancing School, and he gambled: "Won a watch Playing Poker." But the dancing was more useful:

"*Thursday, February 22, 1866*   Cold to Day   Went to Nevada and got a partner to go to a ball   Ball in Virginia[City]   Came Back to Virginia early the evening

"*Friday [February] 23*   Danced all night till near Daylight and went home with the girls in the morning   Came home afternoon   Was not So Cold to Day"[22]

Sex was implied, but never stated. Somehow we tend to think of our ancestors (like a child does its parents) as sexless. It's more probable that they were not; and where there is sex, there is, even in the crudest circumstance, emotion:

"*Friday, March 16*   We must part awhile; A few Short months — though Short they must Be long, without the Dear Society; But yet we must endure it and our love will be the fonder after parting

"*Wednesday [May] 16*   Went up town to Day with Mrs Mulvaney   it Rained nearly all Day   we both got wet   wrote to my true Love

"*Thursday [May] 24*   Went to town & Brought Mrs Reed home with me for a visit   was very warm"[23]

He despaired of his old claim, and moved on to "the New Mines on Elk Creek" in northern California, spending time along the way at that universal nineteenth-century American sport—looking for lost stock:

"*Thursday, May 3*   lost our animals this morning and Did not find but

2 of them to Day   Did nothing but hunt animals and write a letter to
Tom Everts

"*Friday* [*May*] 4   Packed the aparahoes on a poney and went to Mul-
keys hunted mules all the afternoon   Was Rainy & wet

"*Saturday, May 5*   Hunted Animals most of the Day   found them near
night   Was Rainy

"*Friday, July 6*   Was at home most of the Day   Went up to the Quartz
lode toward evening   looked for my poneys

"*Saturday*]*July*] 7   hunted my poneys to Day for a long time   failed
to find them"[24]

But California didn't "pan out" either. He returned to Virginia City.
Nothing had changed there except the names of the people:

"*Saturday, July 14*   Worked on the Shaft this forenoon   Went to town
after Dinner   Spent the afternoon in Virginia went to Nevada in the evening   Saw a man By the name George Rosenbaum Receive 50 lashes on the
bear Back for Stealing, By the Vigilantes"[25]

But his "true love" Ellen was living in Nevada, too.

"*Thursday, September 27*   My hand is not well yet   am laid for two
months & over   went to Nevada to Day   Saw Ellen   had not Seen her
Since April 13th   had various trials Since and considerable Bad Luck if
there is Such a thing as luck

"*Friday, September 28*   Ellen is well But is going to Salt Lake City
Before long and as I am not Situated to keep her here I must be without her
company again for a long time"[26]

The months after that were monotonous and unprofitable:

"*Friday, December 31*   this year has Been Bad luck to me from the first
to last. Been Sick and went to Elk Creek and lost one Thousand Dollars   Have Done nothing since July"[27]

The gold fantasy had been, as he put it, a "Bilk."

2

In all the astounding chronicle of human illusion, nothing exceeds the
passion for gold. Since it is corroded only by powerful acids, it is commonly
found in its free and elemental form—in flakes, dust, or sometimes remelted
and resolidified into nodular pebbles. For the same reason, it persists for
long periods without change, unlike iron or bronze which slowly decay into
rust and verdegris. Because of its second quality, softness, gold is easily
shaped, and can be beaten into sheets that are thin, delicate, and all but
eternal. So it became the very symbol of immortality, and funeral masks for
the courts were made of gold in cultures as far apart as dynastic Egypt and
imperialist but pre-Colombian Peru. It is a beautiful, rare, and almost entirely useless metal, and therefore is the very archetype of magical force.

It was magic that men sought when they dug and sweated and suffered
and fought for gold. But at the same time, it was real, because we as a species

Fred W. Loring with his mule "Evil Merodach."

Photograph by Timothy H. O'Sullivan, 1871. National Archives, Washington, D.C.

are profoundly and universally, if not uniquely, capable of making symbols
and then treating them as real. This psychological power is at once our virtue
and our weakness, the glory of all art and the staggering course of our stupid-
ities. For we confuse the realities of experience with the symbols of that experience. To someone alien to this assumption of our common culture, the
search for gold is uniquely insane and incomprehensible.

One does not have to invent a Venusian to see how this would be. The
Indians of North America had expressed this astonishment. As the Indian
lawyer Vine Deloria put it, why would any sane man labor (and kill if prevented) to take material out of the ground that he melts into bars and puts underground again in the locked cellars of Fort Knox?

We are forced to consider these general matters because the course of
gold has dug deep channels in American life, and it did so particularly in the
last half of the nineteenth century. Indeed the symbolic drama of gold has
been more potent in the Americas than in any other continent, with the possible exception of the tip of Africa. And in both cases gold was sought and
conquered by a brutal, invading, and domineering culture. There was, in
the first discovery of America 20,000 or more years ago, no interest in gold.
To the hunters who crossed the frozen or the dry and uplifted Bearing
Straits, food was fundamental. They pursued the hairy mammals of that earlier age to Cape Horn and very likely over-hunted and destroyed them. Gold
was ignored because it could not sustain a sharp edge. Fint was sharper and
better. The barbarian and cannibalist kingdoms of the Aztecs and the Incas
valued gold only as an ornament of the noble classes, a material for art and
decoration. They used it not for personal power, but for the glorification of
their mummies. In addition, they valued it because it was the symbol and
the presence of the almighty sun.

The America rediscovered by the Nordics was frigid and unpromising.
It was that part of the double continent that could be reached across the
short waters between Greenland and Nova Scotia; longer voyages would
probably have been impossible in Viking technology. But the Renaissance
mariners of southern Europe, in more seaworthy vessels and possessed of a
theory that the world was circular and therefore circumnavigable, found
what they were looking for—a tropical America. They went in search of
trade, and trade equals money, and money equals its mesmeric symbol
—gold. In 1493, Columbus wrote his friend Sanchez: "Finally, . . . I promise, that with a little assistance accorded me by our most invincible
sovereigns, I will procure them as much gold as they need . . ."[28] The Mexican King Atahualpa, while a prisoner, raised a gold ransom that filled a room
300 feet square as high as Pizarro could reach his arm. These were not the
Inca ruler's property, but the gold images and gold vessels that belonged to
the temples of his religion. In return for this largesse, he was allowed to
confess, with burning straw pressed to the soles of his feet, that he intended
to kill Christians. So he was condemned to death, but was spared the

punishment of being burned alive because he accepted baptism before his strangulation.

Great as were the gold treasures of the Americas, the Spaniards (in fact, most of the European governments) looked to find more and still more. For one thing, the one-fifth tithe of all gold that went to the Spanish crown hardly paid the cost of these transoceanic expeditions. But the visible gold gave out, and no more was discovered. This fact led to the acquisition of wealth and power by other and slower means. The Spaniards peonized the Indians, grew cattle and corn, and became lordly, prosperous criollo proprietors riding their huge *fincas* on horseback and fertilizing the country women of their villages. The Spanish system of rule which once extended over the vast lands of Mexico, Central America and South America (except for Brazil) also prevailed in Florida and California. Those Americans who came in modest numbers to these Spanish enclaves prospered in California, particularly if they could get a team of oxen. Or, if too poor even to afford that, they could always sell whiskey.

3

In 1847, the total United States gold production was only 43,000 ounces, much of it from the mines of north Georgia. A year later, gold production was more than ten times as great, and in 1849, gold production was almost 2,000,000 ounces. If we put the average value of an ounce at $16.00, the gold added $32 million to the wealth of the United States—and practically all of it came from California. It was found, not by search or design, but by accident.

Gold is not bound chemically into the rock where it is to be found. It is in fact an intrusion from the deeper part of the earth from a molten magma, forced up by superheated steam and water, the heat of the earth's interior, till it penetrates cracks and fissures of the cooler rock above it. These thin, torn, twisted sheets of gold are sheared by earthquakes, exposed to weather, worn down, and fragmented as the milennia pass, by water rough with gravel from the mountains. These fine gold pebbles settle to the bedrock, are covered with new stones, season upon season, and only sometimes are washed downstream into the valleys.

The goldminer must wash and sieve this gravel for its heavy gold, or dig to the bedrock to find it. This is how it was: ". . .[T]aking our pans, crowbars, and picks, we commenced operations. Our first attempt was to search around the base of a lofty boulder, which weighed probably some twenty tons, in hopes of finding a crevice in the rock on which it rested, in which a deposit of gold might have been made; nor were we unsuccessful. Around the base of the rock was a filling up of gravel and clay, which we removed with much labour, when our eyes were gladdened with the sight of gold strewn all over its surface, and intermixed with a blackish sand. This we gathered up and washed in our pans, and ere night four of us had dug and

Cradling for gold near Virginia City, Montana Territory.

Photo by William H. Jackson, 1871. National Archives, Washington, D.C.

washed twenty-six ounces of gold, being about four hundred and sixteen dollars. The process of pan-washing is the simplest mode of separating the golden particles from the earth with which it is amalgamated. A common-sized tin pan is filled with the soil containing the gold. This is taken to the nearest water and sunk until the water overspreads the surface of the pan. The earth is then thoroughly mixed with water and the stones taken out with the hand. A half rotary motion is given to the pan with both hands; and, as it is filled, it is lifted from the water, and the loose light dirt which rises to the surface washed out, until the bottom of the pan is nearly reached. The gold being heavier than the earth, sinks by its own weight to the bottom, and is there found at the close of the washing, mixed with a heavy black sand. This is placed in a cup or another pan till the day's labour is finished, when the whole is dried before the fire and the sand carefully blown away. The gold which we found the first day was principally procured by washing, although two pieces, one weighing thirteen and the other seventeen dollars, were taken from a little pocket on the rock. We returned to camp exceedingly elated with our first attempt; and gathering some green branches of trees built a fire, cooked some venison, crawled into our holes and went to sleep."[29]

In May and June of 1849 when grass was just high enough to feed horses and oxen, close to 50,000 immigrants came overland "to see the elephant," a phrase from the popular poem about the blind men who disagreed about the shape of this preposterous animal. Between 1848 and 1850, the California population increased from 20,000 to 100,000. A few made their fortune. Several, like Grannis, made a poor living, and many never even got there at all.

The motive was not simply greed, but a deeper force, less conscious and less socially approved: the restlessness of the individual cramped into a cell of circumstance—his occupation or the lack of it, his family responsibility or the lack of that, too, and the sting of reality that is wound up in the popular phrase, "This is it, wasn't it?"

Certainly the economic panic of 1857 did fire up the Pike's Peak gold rush of 1858 and 1859, and the even more severe depression of the years after 1873 drove men by the thousands to the Black Hills of South Dakota. But these crises in American life only exacerbated and made plausible the wish in all men to break open the strictures of their own lives:

"Not a few of them had started out with only such clothing as they wore on their backs, and small bags containing a few pounds of corn meal and meat. We met two individuals, one fifty and the other sixty-two years old, who had left with just 20 lbs. of corn and only 1.68 dollars in money. There were innumerable poor hand-cart and foot-men hungry, in rags, shoeless, with sore and swollen feet and without shelter from the rains and chilling winds. Not a few had to meet death in its most awful form, starvation; and, what is worse, were driven by the maddening pangs of hunger to acts of *cannibalism* [he probably had the Donner party in mind]. . . . The trails were lined with cooking-stoves, clothing and even mining tools, thrown away to lighten loads; and with the rotting carcasses of horses that had perished on the way. Also with many *fresh* graves. Upon a secluded island in the Platte were the bloody remains of a little girl with a broken skull . . .

"For the whole journey to this country was, a *race;* in which 30,000 men were using all their energies to outstrip each other, during the whole distance of 2000 miles—property, by hundreds of thousands of dollars, was destroyed & throw away, cattle & horses & mules hurried along on poor feed, till they dropped down, and the topic of interest to all, was onward, & onward—By following our track one would suppose, that a large army had been flying in hot haste, only careing to save their own lives—Wagons and ox-yokes were used for fuel—huge bonfires made of bacon and pork [so the Indians wouldn't get it]—Thousands of kegs of powder blowed up—broken guns & pistols strewed the road—sacks of flour & provisions throw in large heaps upon the ground—In one day I counted forty ox chains by the side of the road, & passed fifty head of stock, dead & dying—It is supposed that one half the stock that left the States last Spring, for California died & was lost — As I look back upon this great crusade, this rush for Gold, I am lost in wonder, that so few left their bones to be a monument of this great march . . ."[30]

In old, crowded, habit-crusted Europe, rebirth into another life was only possible by going to America. Once here, it was always tempting to change one's life again and replant it in the sparse, rocky wildness of the Far West; gold (or silver, or copper, or even lead) was as much an excuse as a motive.

But the realities of hunger, fatigue, and despair were inescapable, because we drag our bodies with us as we attempt, once more, the roads toward utopia. As Libeus Barney wrote to his hometown newspaper in Bennington, Vermont, death and worse was never too far away. He quotes the account of a goldseeker rescued by an Indian:

" 'Two brothers of mine, myself and five others left Whiteside County, Ill., the latter part of February last for Pike's Peak. Leaving Kansas City, Mo., the first of March with a pony for packing our provisions, we pushed on for the Eldorado. After being out for a few days the pony, for want of food and drink, became exhausted and died. We were then compelled to carry our own grub, which we continued to do until it was all consumed, then we had no resource left but the scanty game our guns could supply. Soon, however, this failed, for our ammunition became exhausted.

" 'Four of our company now started ahead to find, if possible, a settlement. A Mr. Roach and my brothers were left behind, being already too weak for pioneers. By and by the strength of Roach failed him and starvation looked us all full in the face. We killed our dog one day and devoured him; next day Roach died of starvation, and upon his corpse we subsisted till it was consumed to the very marrow in its bones. My eldest brother, conscious

Broadway Street, Round Pond, Oklahoma.

Photograph by Mr. and Mrs. Robert Kennett, January, 1894. National Archives, Washington, D.C.

he could last but a little longer implored us to feed upon him as soon as he should die, and travel as fast as possible while he lasted, and endeavor to find a settlement, and if fortunate enough to find our way out, then return to our once happy homes, and for the love you bear a brother, forget not my bereaved widow and fatherless children. He died and we devoured him. Next my younger brother died, and was eaten by me. After consuming the flesh, gnawing the bones, and breaking them for their marrow, horrible to relate, but oh! how desperate is hunger, I mangled the skull, and breakfasted upon my brother's brains!'

"When the Indian found him he lay upon his back, nearly blind and too weak to get a drink of water from the creek but a few yards distant. In the morning the conductor and I went with him and the Indian, and found the

Climbing Pike's Peak, *ca.* **1890, site of a false gold stampede.**
National Archives, Washington, D.C.

remains of the younger brother as he related. The bones, which were perfectly fleshless, lay in a little bough house, and the head about fifty yards
from them, the skull broken and brains absent; thereby corroborating the
story thus far. We buried the skeleton remains, the flesh which had preserved a brother from starvation, and left the wolf to howl his funeral dirge,
and the prairie winds to sigh his requiem."[31]

4

Gold was not the sole possession of the gilded state of California. It was
found in what is now the state of Washington as early as 1850, and again, in
1859, on the banks of the Similkameen, a rapid stream that runs along the
northern border. Three thousand men dug and washed the gravel in that
small river. When the placers gave out, more gold was discovered in the
mountains. A typical boom town "had a main street three blocks long, strung
with eight saloons, two dance halls, and three general stores."[32]

In Colorado, a year earlier, a hundred dollars worth of gold was panned
out of a small area on the South Platte River. "We were surprised this morning to meet Mons. Bordeau and Company, old mountain traders just in from
Pikes Peak. They came in for outfits, tools, etc., for working the newly discovered mines on Cherry Creek, a tributary of the South Platte. They bring
several ounces of gold dug up by the trappers of that region, which, in fine-

ness, equals the choicest of California specimens."[33] But T. H. Watkins notes: "The inaccuracies in the paper's story are magnificent: the gold region was a good sixty miles removed from Pikes Peak; the gold had not been discovered on Cherry Creek, but the South Platte; the discoverers were not trappers, but miners."[34] Still, the idea that gold was near a recognizable monument like Pike's Peak was too lengendary to disbelieve, whatever the labor. Early in 1859, a hundred thousand Americans left home and started west for Pike's Peak. Only one-fourth of them ever got close enough to discover the hoax.

Colorado paid off better in the discoveries at Cripple Creek, in the basin of Poverty Gulch. In 1890, the population there was fifteen; two years later it was over 2,500. By 1900, there were 50,000 in the districts around Cripple Creek, and by the year of World War I, it had produced nearly $350 million worth of gold.

Obviously, the streets of America were not paved with gold, but there were subterranean paths that shone with fortune, if one could only discover them. In Nevada, too, gold was seen as early as 1849, but the lovely dust was polluted with annoying amounts of an ubiquitous blue ore. Not till July, 1859, was it realized that the stuff was rich silver carbonate, worth about $3,000 a ton. Virginia City, mentioned by our diarist William Grannis, was the city consequent on this discovery. It contained three parallel streeets, each one a terrace on the side of Mount Davidson. The Comstock Lode, part gold and part silver, was in that mountain, which had to be dismembered to get to the treasure.

If one survived cholera, poisonous water, and accident by gunfire, there was always the gambling possibility that one could find a personal heaven.

"Among the first to . . . garner real wealth were Sandy Bowers and his wife, known as Eilly Orrum. Coming to Johnstown in 1851, Eilly had scrubbed, mended, and pressed for the miners; for her third husband, she took Sandy. Their claim yielded not more than $1,200,000 gross, and perhaps half of that was net profit . . .

"The $300,000 mansion of stone they built in the Washoe Valley was a showplace in its day, with doorknobs and hinges of silver bullion and a bronze piano adorned by mother-of-pearl keys . . . When Sandy died in 1868 at the age of thirty-five, his entire estate was appraised at only $88,998. Eilly opened the mansion as a resort, and when she lost this, she earned a meager living as a 'clairvoyant,' patronized by the wealthy who could afford it . . ."[35]

Montana, too, had its gold and silver and its lucky few and unlucky many. The first discoveries were in 1862 and 1863. Even richer areas, Confederate Gulch and Alder Gulch and Last Chance Gulch, together yielded over $100 million in the nineteenth century. South Dakota's Black Hills were long rumored to have gold, too, under the crags and the pines. But the Army, keeping the 1868 treaty with the Sioux, stopped at least three prospecting parties from invading this wilderness that the Sioux asserted was the haunt of their sacred spirits. Still, there were soon almost a thousand illegal miners in this area. Instead of expelling them, the War Department sent the flamboyant, long-yellow-haired General Custer to explore the region. He rode into the Black Hills with characteristic panache—a wagon train of a thousand soldiers, 110 wagons, and a brass band. He was there three pleasant summer months and reported that "the hills are filled with gold from the grass roots down."[36]

His words began another Western stampede of particular tenacity, because many of the prospectors were unemployed or bankrupt after the panic of 1873, which began a depression deeper and longer than any the Republic had yet endured. Spiritual rights had little weight against such realities, and I wonder if the Sioux were any exception to the old and effective human practice of hiding economic or cultural motives under the burning cloud of religious necessity. They offered to sell their sacred ground to the U. S. government, but their price was too high. In any event, on June 24, 1876, Custer lost his final battle—and the Sioux lost the war. Deadwood was the wry name of the chief town that rose up out of that stampede, and here was how it looked by April, 1877:

"Deadwood is a city of a single street, and a most singular street it is. The buildings which grace its sides are a curiosity in modern architecture, and their light construction is a standing insult to every wind that blows. Paint is a luxury only indulged in by the aristocracy. . . . Wells are dug in the middle of the street, all sorts of building material occupies them and every manner of filth is thrown into them. The city is honeycombed by shafts run down into the bowels of the earth from every yard. A keen-eyed, money-grabbing set of men makes up the population, but they are far from the bloodthirsty scoundrels the average newspaper correspondent would make them out to be. Shooting is not frequent; fighting is only occasional; and property is perfectly secure."[37]

By 1862, Idaho had its own gold stampede, and the next year, silver was found in the quartz too. In the area around Bannock, $20 million was taken out by 1900. But the biggest find was near Couer d' Alene in 1885—a vein of mixed ore which contained glittering cubic or octahedral crystals of lead, zinc, and silver sulphides. These metals were not free but chemically bound, and therefore had to be powdered and smelted. It was not a job for a man, or even a partnership, but for a corporation. Only these could afford the machinery. And their product was corporation size, too, for the yield was eventually on the order of a billion dollars.

Individual mining, which is simply a more laborious form of roulette, still offered one more chance, and it was the last grotesque historical gesture of the independent and anonymous man. In Rabbit Creek, an icy stream that fed into the Klondike River in Alaska, "color" was discovered in August of 1897. The claim was filed by George Washington Carmack and his two In-

United Verde Mines, Jerome, Arizona, *ca.* **1900. Typical of large-scale crushing and smelting.**

National Archives, Washington, D.C.

dian brothers-in-law, Skookum Jim and Tagish Charlie. The latter was a chief in the Siwash Tribe, and the former was famous for carrying a 156-pound pack of bacon over lofty Dyer Pass. It was in the United States, all right, but it was very cold territory. Lincoln's secretary of war, Seward, had finally bought it from the Russians in 1867. Thirty-one years later, a hundred thousand newborn prospectors left the States in search of Alaskan gold. The ships to Juneau charged a $1,000 a passenger. After that, the goldseekers had to climb Chilkoot Pass, thick with eternal snow, and slide down the other side to the gold fields, which were actually in western Canada. Of the 100,000 or so miners, only about 4,000 ever found any gold. They had invested about $50 million in transport and supplies just to get there, but the gold yield in the Klondike in a rich year, 1898, was hardly more than $10 million. But mere arithmetic does not determine the passions of real people—whether they think so or not. The fact is that for the last fifty years of the nineteenth century, this mania for gold was a recurrent mental illness peculiar to Americans and would have reached world epidemic proportions had it been easier for non-Americans to get to the mines.

The four and a half months it took to travel from Missouri—where most of the supplies were bought—to California, Nevada, Colorado, or Montana were an epic of despair, illness, and death. Once arrived at the place where fortune and happiness lay hidden like the prize in a child's treasure hunt, under broken rocks or glittering at the bottom of rapid water, the internal immigrant was forced into the special culture of the mining camp and the mining town. Having spent his savings on the long travel to his improvised Eden, he generally went to work at wages for someone who had already found and posted a claim, though it might be no more than twenty feet of a slanted rocky ledge. He was lucky to earn enough to pay his grocery bill. Here, recorded by a miner in California, was a storekeeper's bill for two persons:

One box of sardines,	$16	00
One pound of hard bread	2	00
One pound of butter,	6	00
A half-pound of cheese,	3	00
Two bottles of ale,	16	00
Total,	$43	00 [38]

Ties to children, parents, or lovers, which when torn open, leave spiritual wounds—these were endemic in these camps, for nothing is more temporary than gold. But other illnesses were much more tangible.

Scurvy, of course, is a nutritional disease. The human species cannot manufacture vitamin C, which is nevertheless essential to health. We have to get it in our food, and the miner's food was simple, dry, portable, and flatulent: salt pork, smoked beef, flour, and beans, augmented if one had the luck and the time, with fresh deer and fresh if redolent brown and grizzly bear. There were no vegetables, though dried apples or peaches could be had on rare occasions. There were no eggs and no milk. It is not surprising that there was little fish, either, because fishing notoriously takes time. The miners lived on this high calorie, low vitamin, low calcium diet, and they complained only because they had to stop grubbing in the ground and go make a fire and cook. In the wilderness about them were wild plants and herbs that would have given them the vitamins they needed. But this, they thought, was weak food, fit only for Indians and Chinese.

There were two universal beverages: one for daylight, one for darkness. The first was coffee, whose reputation as a comfort and a stimulant had been established in the bivouacs of the Civil War. The second was whiskey, or what passed for whiskey anyway, for it was sometimes a good deal more powerful, being made of an infusion of sage, cayenne pepper, and two plugs of tobacco to a gallon. Such commercial medicines served to narcotize the aching muscles and to alleviate that chronic disease of the young—homesickness.

One of these miners observed: "The camp was peopled with young men from 18 to 35 years old, and but few exceeded the latter age. Old men were scarce in California in those days, and as for women and children, except Indians there were none; and it was not till the immigrants with their families crossed the plains that our eyes were gladdened with the sight of either . . ."[39]

Sex has never been a great respecter of age. But it must be granted that among the young the urge to procreate, habitual in living organisms even before they separated into plants and animals, is more frequent and more persistent.

"There are but a few *ladies* here yet there are many female of questionable morality about town, some in bloomer costume and some in gentlemen's attire throughout, while squaws are more than plenty."[40]

The ratio of women to men was one to ten, and this included females "of the line." The phrase gets its name from the layout of a mining town, which generally had one short street where the main saloons, dance halls, gambling houses, groceries, assay offices, lawyers, and even an occasional doctor would be located. Then there was often a short straight parallel street, "the line," with wooden shacks big enough for a bed and a wash basin, each posted with a first name—"Jessie" or "Sadie" or other fond dimunitive—on a sign board over the door. Butte, Montana, once had almost 7,000 prostitutes in its red light district. This was merely an exaggeration of the average, for these commercial ladies were the solace of every mining camp for the last fifty years of the century.

It takes but little knowledge of human nature to realize that a town whore can receive, along with her money, a good deal of free manly affection. An English lady named Julia Bulette went into business in Virginia City in the late 1860s, when a considerable part of the rich Comstock strike passed through her hands. On Sunday, January 20, 1867, she was robbed and murdered. A contemporary newspaper account describes her as "thirty-five years of age, belonging to that clan denominated 'fair but frail,' yet, being of a very kind-hearted, liberal, benevolent and charitable disposition, few of her class had more true friends. Julia Bulette was some time since elected honorary member of Virginia Engine Company No. 1, of this city, in return for numerous favors and munificent gifts bestowed by her upon the company; she taking always the greatest imaginable interest in all matters connected with the Fire Department, even on many occasions at fires working at the brakes of the engines. She was still an honorary member of the company at the time of her death, therefore it was deemed eminently just and proper that she should be buried by the company."[41]

Curiously, the dance hall hostesses, the "hurdy-gurdies", were not necessarily prostitutes. Country Swedes or Germans, they earned a vigorous living by dancing for a fee with the booted, hatted, bearded young miners, bent on illuminating the town with a tiny bag of gold dust not unmixed with sand. There was an astonishing amount of traveling theatre too, from *Romeo and Juliet* to Lola Montez, former mistress to the mad King of Bavaria, who performed a tarantella about a woman pursued by spiders. But the true theater was the coarse, everyday spectacle of violence. Every man carried a gun or two, and a large knife for work at close quarters. Quarrels in the heat of whiskey were ordinary events and "any fight drew a modest audience."

Here we begin to see, though as yet dimly, the outlines of a change in American character. Typical tragedy up to the middle of the nineteenth century had been, for the most part, the drama of kings—English kings, at that. Also popular were sentimental comedies about the American country lout outsmarting the town sharpie. There was little question in the minds of the audience as to whether the stage, however crude, was real. It was not. Now in the adolescent isolation of the mining town, life itself became the substance of drama:

"The killing of the notorious Sam Brown was as follows: Brown was a heavy man about 200 lbs weight was noted as a lawless desperado whose name was terror to all who knew him or had heard of him. He made his brags on the day of his death which was his 30th birthday that he had killed eleven men & was going to have the 12th one for his supper. Brown had frequently stopped at my station in previous times always acting like any other civil traveller paing [*sic*] his bills and behaving himself and while he bore a bad reputation I had never had occasion to feel that he would in any manner interfere with me or my business, but on the day of his death he in company with a young man who subsequently state that Brown compelled him to come with him, rode up to the door of my then public house and while in the act dismounting as I supposed to stop for the night, I stepped out with the remark shall I put your horse up Mr. Brown, just as I would to any traveller who seemed to be desirous of staying with me. He in a very gruff manner said No you Son of a ———— I have come to kill you and at once drew his gun. Being entirely unarmed and knowing the character of the man I at once left the scene, for he following with a gun & cocked I passed in through the dining room where there were some 20 men seated eating supper, they of course were alarmed by the sudden appearance of my hasty entrance, followed by so formidable a character as Brown was known to be, Brown exclaimed in a loud tone where is the Son of a ————?

"Seeing so many men he dropped his gun from its position and put out and got on his horse and rode away in company with his young traveling companion. I secured my own gun, got on another horse and at once went in pursuit of him overhauling him in ¾ of a mile from the house, and when as I supposed within shooting distance I called to his companion to look out, and as he pulled away from Brown, I shot at him, but being at too long a range failed to hit him. Brown turned & returned my fire, I again shot, this time relieving him of his hat and burning his face with my fire, but again failing to bring what I was after, namely his head. He now pulls out and putting spurs to his horse drove away at a furious rate, I reloaded my gun and took after him again. In 3 miles I again got within what I supposed was gunshot range and turned loose again, he returning the compliment dark coming on and he losing his way I headed him off and thus reached the point where he intended to go, ahead of him, & awaited his arrival. I knowing he would surely come abided my time, well knowing that it was a matter of self protection with me, as if I failed to kill him he would without a doubt kill me the first time he got a chance. I therefore waited till he rode up within short range, when stepping out I said as he had previously said to me you son of a b——h I have got you now, and at once ended his career putting seven buckshots right through the center of his body, death being instantaneous, he falling from his horse without muttering a word that could be distinguished from a groan, thus ended the life of a man that had few if any redeeming traits to relieve a life of blackness and infamy."[42]

Thus there was born in the American spirit a morbid taste for the real, in which the audience is itself half spectator, half participant. In this way as in many others, the culture of the mining camp colors the American mind.

If the look and taste and filth and freedom of the mining camp were the crux of individualism, what happened next was the victory of the new industrial age. For when the gold dust filtering into the bankside gravel of mountain streams was all sieved through and exhausted, miners dug with pick and shovel and dynamite down through sedimentary rock to find the old beds of vanished rivers. And when that too was gone, there was still the penetration of gold into the original fissures of ancient and ubiquitous quartz.

But to really get at these riches which were far upstream and deep underground, slanting or vertical shafts had to be cut and timbered, and the metal pressed between walls of stone had to be got out by shattering and

grinding the rock. The ratio of metal to useless mineral was small, and no individual miner could really afford the time and the labor. Nor did the shifting personal partnerships ever have the money needed for the first investment.

However crude, two things were absolutely necessary—a stamping
mill, sometimes with as many as forty or fifty hammers, and secondly, the
power to move this heavy iron mechanism. Though there was generally
moving water available, it was often nowhere near the mill itself, which had
to be close to the ore. So money had to be invested in digging long ditches
and flumes and sometimes a massive diversion dam to bring the rush of
water down over the hills and into the main wheel of the mill. In the 1860s,
the stamping mill itself still cost up to $10,000 to build. The average man
never had that much money at one time, or if he did, it wasn't for long.

Thus after each major discovery of gold, the superficial flakes of metal,
got at by filtering the loose stones or by simply scraping the rock with a
knife, were quickly gone. Gold, sooner or later, had to be industrialized like
any other metal. This inevitable process, with all its benefits and its evils,
had begun as early as 1851. The noise of these huge, rounded iron hammers,
lifted and dropped forty times a minute, was like eternal thunder in these
mountain valleys. By 1879, the pans, sluices, and arrastras (primitive grinding contraptions) had become crude chemical factories.

As the shafts went deeper, getting fresh air was a nagging problem.
Miners died for lack of it, an ironic corollary to the utopian desire to go West
where the air was bracing and the mountains glistened against pure blue
skies and the limitless outdoors might be a paradise for free men. Nothing
much was done about ventilation until the invention and use of compressed
air drills. These had to be supplied with power, and this technical change
brought along ventilation as a secondary benefit. All of this cost money, and
was far beyond the resources of any small group of laboring men. For they
had spent whatever gold they had found; and by the 1870s, were looking for
work. They got it in the same locale, digging for gold or silver which they
would never own:

"We descend into the mine and get out by a cage, a small platform running between guides down a shaft. The sensation is peculiar. Three or four
men stand on this, the engine starts, and down we go rapidly in this shaft,
like a deep well. It grows dark, as down, down, down we go. We hear the
rope rattle over the pulley overhead and the rattle of the cage in its guides.
We know that a chasm hundreds of feet deep is beneath. We are hung on
this rope at a height twice as great as that of the tallest spire in the United
States.

"At last we strike the 'lower level' and step out into the mine, where we
find great timbers running in every direction. Here and there a candle sheds
a feeble light. Long, dark galleries or "drifts" run from the landing place,
with narrow railroad tracks in them, and little cars in which the ore is

moved. We hear the rumble of the cars on these tracks, and the distant clatter of picks and drills as the miners are loosening the ore and rock. Perhaps a heavy pump is groaning, worked by a powerful engine, to get the water out of the lowest parts . . .

"We ascend in the mine by ladders, stage beyond stage. Men are at work everywhere, digging the ore, getting it away, putting in the heavy timbers. Here galleries branch off; there great chambers have been opened. We walk along planks, through galleries, sometimes dry, sometimes dripping with muddy water. Look out! That little black hole by your feet may be deep! Only two days ago a miner slipped into such a hole and fell 115 feet; he was buried the day we were in mine."[43]

With the discovery of rich silver ore in Colorado, the process of industrialization reached a climax. The silver had not only to be pulverized, but roasted in smelters fed by wood furnaces. This process removed the sulphur; or else cyanide was added to the residue to form new gold or silver compounds which could be precipitated into metal by electrolysis. It was essentially a chemical plant, and such plants require buildings, machinery, expensive reagents, power, labor—and money to buy all of these. The miners who came by themselves or in small partnerships started from their original homes with something between zero and a couple of thousand dollars. If they came any distance (and quite a number came from China, Europe, and South America), very little was left by the time they got to the goldfields or the silver lodes—certainly not enough to build a mill or a smelter. What they might have, though, if they were lucky, were a few score feet of rock, a claim, which was soon bought up by a mining corporation, if it was worth anything at all. These speculative companies were, in fact, largely Eastern, and for good reason. The East was where the capital and the inherited property had had time to accumulate, but the way this money was got was more like blackjack than fiduciary investment.

The arithmetic was fascinating and thoroughly characteristic of the last quarter of the nineteenth century in America. Without any firmer collateral than a few running feet of mountain, they would issue a million shares of stock, generally at an arbitrary par value of a dollar each. Of these shares, most of a two-thirds portion was kept by the shrewd man who started the company. Whatever remained from this portion was assigned to the original owner of the claim—in lieu of cash, naturally. The remaining one-third of the stock issue was sold to investors at any price the market would accept. It might be $10.00 a share, or even more, depending upon what golden rumor was believed. The Eastern investor was blind:

Dear William Ward   April 8, 1876

It does me good to salute you. A sudden disability I suffered, on the 14th of last month, has caused me to be tardy in thanking you for the hundred shares of Colorado Mining stock you were kind enough to give me on such easy terms. I thank you now, however, with whatsoever of heartiness there is in my nature . . .

You will not doubt my sincerity when I say, I feel profound interest in the out-come of your 'Bonanza.' Mines . . . as a source of wealth . . . appear to me, to be in-dependent of Government and politicians, so soon as they become the property of private persons . . . Deposits of that kind can be 'removed' by labor but not by fraud. Mines cannot be burglarized—which is much in these times . . . Nothing in this country is now so enterprising as crime . . . But, shall no faith be put in man? . . . I still believe that the country abounds in trustworthy men . . .

We see, in New England, say, immense capital, directed by skill not to be sur-passed and administered with spotless integrity, failing of any remuneration what-ever—and why? Because the market value of the goods is less than the cost of them . . .[44]

This letter, from the elderly John Taylor Hall, indicates that the fall in the rate of profit in the older industries was forcing investment in the west-ern and speculative part of the United States. Rumors, of course, governed the daily price. The manipulation of stock, which is not entirely a modern device, guaranteed sudden wealth or sudden failure.

There are such restless, uncertain periods in the adolescence of every industrial nation. But in the United States it was prolonged and chronic, perhaps because from 1849 till well past 1900, there was in nearly every de-cade a recurrent and virulent gold fever that shook the nation loose of its habits and institutions. Before 1848, our immigrants to the West were me-chanics and farmers and their families; after that, the West was inundated by waves of young bachelors, many of them teenagers, and all of them gamblers at life. Gold, one naturally thinks, would make a nation rich, or are we still victim of this aureate illusion? But did gold really have an important effect on the nation's economy? On its ways of making a living?

5

It's true that in the fifty years or roughly two generations between 1850 and 1900, some $2 billion in gold was washed, scraped and pounded out of American rock. It seems an enormous sum, but it's not, for it only comes to an average of $40 million a year. We must compare that modest sum to the value of all things made or done in American society during the same years. For the decade 1869 to 1878, the first for which there are decently accurate records, this "gross national product," was about $23 billion a year, if ad-justed to 1958 prices. Therefore the ratio of gold to other trade was about one to six hundred. If we examine the same ratio for the following decades, we come to much the same conclusion, only more so. From 1879 to 1888, the ratio of gold to other products was one to a thousand. In 1890, it was one to thirteen hundred, and as the gross national product increased to $120 billion by 1910, and the production of gold had greatly diminished, the ratio was simply absurd.

So we are temporarily forced to admit, against all intuition, that if no gold was ever found in the United States, it would not have made much difference. But we would be wrong. Gold did make a very great difference, but by means that are little appreciated. First, the prospective miner had to be outfitted with food, transport, tools, and even a gun or two. The average cost was $200 a person, and in 1859, upward of a hundred thousand went to the mountains; that's $20 million right there. And they had to be fed and clothed and liquored when they were in camp, and therefore wheat and cattle had to be grown and transported. Even their most primitive diggings needed timber and iron, and therefore a timber industry that included logging and sawmills had to be established, not to speak of the forges and blast furnaces and factories to make their shovels and pick-axes.

Once there, the great majority spent whatever gold dust they found and preferred not to go home to the sympathy of their friends or else were simply drained of the will needed for another move. Consequently, enormous numbers of the goldseekers settled down to work on farms and ranches, in the tall forests and screeching lumber mills, or on the new railway lines that were built to carry grain and flesh, ore, fuel, and stone to the smelter, then the plow and the harrow back to the farmer. Thus an economy doubled and redoubled itself by the very presence of these workmen. Further, the money they made, either in the digging of gold or in the daily work for wages, did not disappear. It went to the storekeepers, the professional gamblers, the saloonkeepers, and the prostitutes. Round and round the money went: ". . . It is stated that five thousand teams are steadily employed in the Washoe trade and other commerce east of the Sierra—not little teams of two horses, but generally of six horses or mules, often as many as eight or ten, carrying loads of three to eight tons, on huge cumbrous wagons. Clouds of dust arose, filling the air, as we met long trains of ponderous wagons, loaded with merchandise, hay, grain—in fact everything that man or beast uses. We stopped at the Slippery Ford House. Twenty wagons stopped there, driving over a hundred horses or mules—heavy wagons, enormous loads, scarcely any less than three tons. The harness is heavy, often with a steel bow over the hames, in the form of an arch over each horse, and supporting four or five bells, whose chimes can be heard at all hours of the day."[45] Gold was the spark that set off the great engine of our present lives.

Because the repeated discovery of gold in the West added a metallic luster to the whole conception of the West as an Eden of the future, it became one of the great prizes of war waged between the Southern slave-holding aristocracy and the farmers and wage-earners of the North. This was a war fought at first in the neoclassic chambers of Congress, and then in the dust and mud, along the railroad lines, and in the bloody corridors of hospitals. Now because that war was won by the industrial North, it was the North that built the transcontinental railroads, and not the South. This line and the succeeding and spreading network of rails that followed hauled food to the miners and to the ex-miners who had settled in the long valleys which they had seen from the thin-aired heights of their gilded dreams. How curious, but how logical, that the Central Pacific Railroad, builder of half the transcontinental line, should have been financed by the little sacks of gold paid by California miners in exchange for the picks and shovels and miscellaneous hardware of men like Huntington Hartford!

Such dislocations: the massive Civil War that moved two million men from their homes and the successive gold rushes that moved a million more in the next half century were the stimuli that conditioned men to settle elsewhere from where their fathers had lived, moved them from their job and landscape, released their energy in fresh views and fresh applications, and became the force that broke, several times in every generation, the ossification which any society tends to form inside itself. So the last half of the nineteenth century was for America a symbolic rush with inadequate brakes down a glittering, seemingly infinite track with gold glimmering ahead like the sheen of lanterns against the valley mist.

6

The Bottom of the Pyramid

THE exemplary American, Benjamin Franklin Jones, kept a journal between 1875 and 1901. In all of his hundreds of entries, there are perhaps a dozen personal comments. The diary begins with this note, "George W. Jones died Monday February 8, 1875 at five o'clock A.M. — Funeral Thursday February 11, at two P.M."[1] There is not a word about how he felt. Not that he had no feelings about this personal loss, I suspect, but that he was chary of putting them down on paper. Jones' next entry is on May 24, 1875:

> Spring Chalfant & Co.
> prices paid on three single plate mill
> boiler Iron 3.87-1/2 per ton
> No. 8 to 14   5.44
> 15 " 17   6.46
> Heads   5.27
> Heater gets 1/4 of above
> Screen boy and Shearman paid by Company[2]

Jones makes an assumption here that the very act of putting pen to paper is a sort of contract and must therefore be precise and factual. In this sense, he presages a new type in American life—the aggressive accountant, bold because logical, and innovative because exact: "Arranged with Committee of Coal Miners, to pay them at the rate of 4 cts per bushell [sic] for the first two weeks of this pay. And 3 cts per bushell for the remainder of the pay . . ."[3] Note that there are approximately thirty bushels to a ton.

Benjamin Franklin Jones was a fourth generation American. His Welsh great-grandfather came from London to Philadelphia in 1682. The family had lived in Pennsylvania for 150 years, and Jones was born August 8, 1824, in the small village of Claysville. His family could hardly have been poor for he was sent to a private high school for four years. He left home at eighteen to go to Pittsburgh. This city at the confluence of the Ohio and the Monongahela River was, at the time, simply a river port like many others. Before the Civil War, paddlewheel steamers loaded with bales of cotton up from the South would stop for dinner, amusement, and supplies. All night long the roulette wheels would whir in their luxurious floating rooms, immune from local authority, and if a young owner had poor luck he would "place his young colored valet on the gaming table and say, 'I'll raise you three hundred, Gennulmen.' "[4]

Young Jones got a job as junior clerk for the Mechanic's Line of Packet Boats, which transported goods both by canal and railroad between Pittsburgh and points East. ". . . These boats were built in two sections so they could be separated for the trip over the mountains. Each section was a complete boat. At the foot of the mountain, a section was pulled into a basin of water. The water was then drawn out, allowing the boat to rest on a car. The car was drawn [on wooden rails] up the inclined plane by means of an engine at the top of the mountain. Passengers alighted at the base of the mountain and were carried around by carriages."[5]

In two years, Jones became manager of the firm, and at twenty-one he was made an equal partner. There was no direct rail line to Pittsburgh until the Pennsylvania Railroad finished its route. With this direct connection, the canal line rapidly lost its market. Jones got out. He was twenty-nine years old and was married, with family responsibilities. Iron was the dominant industry of that region of Pennsylvania, and Jones was naturally drawn to invest in this business.

He bought a small rolling mill at Brownsville, Pennsylvania, dismantled it, took it by flatboat to Pittsburgh, and set it up on the banks of the Monongahela. He next formed a partnership with two German immigrants, the brothers Bernard and John Lauth, plus the owner of the Mechanics Line, Samuel Kier. The brothers were skilled ironmasters and already owned a plant with six furnaces adjacent to Jones's new property. Together, they built a larger factory on the same site. ". . . An eight fluted stack, probably the finest in Western Pennsylvania was designed and built by a Jack Heakly, who was working in the mills at that time. However, he made one error. Being an Englishman, he conceived the idea of putting an artistic crown on top of the stack. Legend has it that Mr. Jones, who came to the mills every day, saw the crown from his buggy one morning, called Heakly into his office and gave him a thorough tongue lashing that amounted to, "This is the AMERICAN IRON WORKS and in America there are no crowns." The next day Heakly filled in with brick and mortar the crown of the decoration, and from a distance, the top of the stack looked like a man's hat."[6]

In 1853, a Pittsburgh banker, James Laughlin, bought into the expanding company. In a historical sense, this arrangement was a classic three-way partnership: money, technical expertise, and business management.

The Lauth brothers were each paid $1,500 a year for supervising the rolling mills, and B. F. Jones got the same salary for managing the warehouse, keeping the books, and overseeing the finances. John Lauth returned to Germany in 1856, and his brother quit the business in 1861. The history of this company now ceases to be idiosyncratic, and becomes, by its practices, a striking model of American industrial expansion. The newly constituted Jones & Laughlin Company now had puddling furnaces and rolling mills on the south side of the Monongahela. They bought property on the north side, directly opposite, and built a series of blast furnaces, called the Eliza Furnaces, named after B. F. Jones's mother.

For years, the firm had only twenty-five employees yet was able to boost production to seven tons per day. It specialized in bright, polished, cold-rolled iron, which had 75 per cent more strength than ingots turned on a lathe. By this time B. F. Jones had begun his diary, and his company, the creation of his drive and persistence, had survived the panics of 1857 and 1871. Here was a characteristic entry:

"*June 10, 1875* Agreed with Stephen Trautner to pay him at the rate of 27 cts per ton of 2240 pounds for all the Muck iron produced which is to cover all the repairs to the mill, i. e. he is not to be paid for any work except it be for entirely new erections or for work outside of mill. Reduced in December 1875 to 24 cts per ton."[7] The writing is extraordinarily hurried and uneven.

On November 17, 1875, he got one Jacob Shank to find out the pay of engineers in twelve other iron plants. He learned that, for example, one paid $2.417 per day, another $2.50 down to $1.60, a third plant $2.75 per day. Assuming a six-day week, the engineers, the highest class of employee at the mills, earned about $15.00 a week. Using the U.S. government consumer price indices, we find that the cost of living in 1875 was approximately one-third that of 1967—an average engineer's salary of $45.00 a week. Not exactly munificent. Jones noted, in his entry for November 29, 1875, the salaries paid workmen in the Altoona shops of the Pennsylvania Railroad:

"*Nov 29/75* Wages paid by PRR Co. at Altoona shops as per letter of W A Adams to I S Atkinson, dated Nov 28/75

Pattern Makers, 2.20 2.10 2.00 1.80 1.50 Labor 1.20
Machinists 2.30 2.20 2.00 1+¡30 1.80 1.60 1.50 1.40 Labor 1.20 & 1$
Black Smiths 3.00 2.80 2.60 2.40 2.20 2.00 1.80 1.60 1.50 labor
    1.20 that is helpers.
Moulders 2.10 2.00 1.90 1.80 1.60 1.50 labor 1.20
Boiler Maker 2.40 2.20 2.00 1.85 1.60 1.50 1.40 Labor 1.20 1.00
Outside labor 1$ per day"[8]

Note that ordinary labor, the most numerous, got $1.00 a day, which on the same 1967 scale would be $18.00 a week—not a great wage either.

Meantime, a revolution in the iron industry took place without any great notice from B. F. Jones. This was the adoption of the Bessemer process, which made iron with less carbon so it was therefore less brittle and more malleable. Andrew Carnegie, a Scots newcomer, had the immigrant's characteristic push in adopting the new process, which produced steel in continuous rolling mills—and at a cheaper rate, too. The demand for metal in America, for tools and tracks and nails and engines, was enormous and growing daily. Even during the stubborn depression after the panic of 1873, the Jones enterprise grew till it had seventy-five puddling furnaces, thirty heating furnaces, eighteen rolling mills, and seventy-three nail machines. In 1876 their combined capacity was 50,000 tons.

But on September 27th and 29th, 1876 Jones made two fateful entries:

"Sept. 27, 1876   Notice given Monday September 25th, 1876 to Laborers, and general day hands about mill—such as muck weighers, and shearmen, ash men and cinder wheelers and etc. that another reduction of 10 per cent would begin on that day."[9]

Two days later:

"Sept. 29, 1876   Arranged with Puddlers, Henry Ayers, James Pastonas and Edward Jones—being a committee, that for the first heat on each turn they shall be paid for not exceeding 500 lbs. on the remaining 4 heats the puddlers shall have a margin of 20 lbs. i. e. if he makes more than 500 lbs. he shall be paid for the excess up to 20 lbs. but no more and the whole turn shall not exceed 2500 lbs."[10]

It must be noted (as it is, repeatedly, by B. F. Jones) that the normal shift, whether day or night, was ten hours. In fact, certain employers tried to introduce an eight-hour shift, but they were bitterly opposed by their workmen, who could not accept a reduction in hours which meant a corresponding reduction in pay. As one can see from the price index given earlier, they lived at a level that could not easily bear a cut in wages.

Three months later, B. F. Jones makes note of a sudden and frightening storm:

"Tuesday, July 24, 1877   Since Saturday, July 21st the City has been you may say under the rule of a mob. The Penn reduced their hands' wages and the men struck, refusing to work or allow any freight trains to go out or in.

"The men becoming more excited would not permit even those who were not included in the strike to work and it slowly but surely gave evidence that it would all end in a riot. The military were called out and requisitions sent to the Governor to have troops sent here. A regiment came from Philadelphia, the men hooted at them and annoyed them so that they charged upon them killing and wounding quite a number of citizens.

"This started the riot and the working men throughout the country and city took it up and on Saturday night got beyond all 'law and order' marched through the streets declaring vengeance and robbing stores when guns or any arms were to be had.

"Matters grew from bad to worse and the crowd swelled into proportions beyond all control, made up of the worst element about the city, men out of work and who having nothing to lose were only too glad for this opportunity to become excited by drinks and heroic speeches. Whiskey flowed freely and what at first gave no one much thought became the all absorbing hopes, and fears for the safety of the city were shown on every face. The fires started about four miles out and burned everything belonging to the Pennsylvania Railroad from fence into the City—including the Union Depot and hotel, grain elevator—panhandle offices and etc. When we say about 200 locomotives each worth 18 or 20 thousand dollars were destroyed and that the Union Depot and hotel was alone worth half a million some small idea can be formed of the extent of the losses.

"Robberies were committed in the daylight cars broken open and contents carried off in a manner both terrible and ridiculous.

"All this has had a very bad effect on the laboring classes throughout the City and others, especially in this state. Today Tuesday the 24th nearly all the day hands about the mill have been in a state of excitement since coming to work this morning and now at 2 P.M. after holding an excitable meeting they have all (some 350 men) marched out of the mill saying they must have 25 cents per day added to their wages—that is for some a general advance of about 25 per cent."[11]

It's interesting and characteristic that Benjamin Franklin Jones repeatedly refers to himself in the third person. It is at once businesslike and strangely egotistical: "The committees met Mr. Jones about 3 P.M. and he told them he would think of their demands and let them know in a few days his decision."[12] He then listed in his diary the full names of the five men on the committee and precisely what wages they were paid. Four of them made $1.00 a day, and the fifth man earned $1.16. "The other committee from the forge hands was three of the cinder boys headed by Martin Meyers who we once put in workhouse for 30 days for calling for another man's money. They are getting 1.00 per day and asked for the 25 per cent advance."[13]

Meantime, measures were being taken by both employers and city authorities:

"*Wednesday 25th July 1877* The mill and store were guarded and watched last night—no signs of any riots or disturbance although had not everything about town become quiet through the aid of vigilance committees and military there is no telling what excitement might have caused them to do."[14]

Of course, B. F. Jones had no intention of negotiating. "The strikers still out and appear quiet—hardly likely they will get the wages asked and when they find out they are *not* to get it there *may* be trouble . . . [The strike] gives a good chance to take stock and more particularly because there is no shipping going on and of course orders cannot be gotten out."[15] Now we can see the inherent weakness of a strike by men without savings or union resources. They could not endure the daily loss, but B. F. Jones could. Indeed he was rather optimistic: "In the city today everything is quiet but the Railroads appear determined on the reduction . . .

"*Saturday 28 July '77* Nothing new developed about the strike—the city is well guarded by about from four to six thousand soldiers and it looks like the old war times. The mill is all stopped.

"*Monday July 30 '77*   Strikers weakening and frequent trains beginning to run again. Mill stopped but will be all right in few days—at least we hope so.

"*Monday August 6* [77] . . . Committee called the other day and say they still demand the 25 per cent advance in wages and ten hours work."[16] Note that although the basic work day was already ten hours, in practice the workmen often worked additional hours, for which there was normal pay depending upon the fraction of the day actually worked.

"Saturday night a large meeting of the 'unterrified' was held at 'Concordia beer garden.' Speeches were made advising the holding out of the men. Among the speakers Thos. Hawkins figured. It is reported today that if their demands are not agreed to by Wednesday they will then ask for a 50 per cent advance . . .

"*Wednesday August 15th* . . . Excitable meetings being held and in that way the men still continue in their demands and feel that they are injured heroes."[17]

Jones and Laughlin began to hire strikebreakers, with a somewhat mild consequence that a notice was circulated and posted:

"NOTICE TO WORKINGMEN The public are cautioned against working in American Iron Works as the employees are on strike for an advance of wages. Workingmen are earnestly requested not to interfere in this movement. By order of Committee."[18]

B. F. Jones' entry of August 27, 1877, lists eight men by name as speakers at the strikers' meetings. In addition, two other men were named as ". . . seen in skiff on river acting strangely supposed to have stopped men from going to work this morning."[19] There is no proof except by analogy, but the care which Jones took to write down the full names of committee members makes one suspect that, like the verified practice of the railroads, these men were subsequently blacklisted out of the trade. Their names— Robson, Hawkins, Stearns, Castle, Prescott, Bea, Miller, Assosky, Elmen, Boyle—are fascinating in another way. They are mostly English, with only two recognizably Irish, and one Pole—a situation that was to change extraordinarily in the next twenty years.

Jones' account in his journal now takes on a somewhat forced joviality. The strike had lasted almost six weeks:

"*Sept. 1, 1877*   The *muscular* clerks together with the bosses and Edward Gray with 3 of his clerks got to work and unloaded the 23 cars of ore.

"*Sept. 4, 1877*   Notices were put out by Wood saying New Mill would light up this A.M. and all hands wanting to go to work to put in an appearance. They didn't appear. I mean of course the laboring portion."[20]

The iron workers strike had begun on the afternoon of the twenty-fourth of July. The railroad strikes had been lost weeks before.

"*Sept. 18, 1877* The committee called this afternoon and said they would all go to work. The firm have made *no* concessions but will of their own accord raise some of the 804 men who are deserving of it to 1.00 per day and finding the time of going to work to be a little earlier here than at some other mills will change that also. Great rejoicing among all that the mill will start up tomorrow morning. So the strike is ended and we are *all* glad of it for it was becoming very monotonous . . ."[21]

Not valuing a workman as a human being—with a life span, a family, a character, and a set of instinctual needs encrusted with acquired habits—but simply as a digit of production to be kept as low as possible, is said by certain kinds of Marxists (including Marx) to be inseparable from the impersonality of large-scale production. This was never entirely true. But its obverse, the regard for human personality that is supposed to occur in small, personal enterprise, is fairly rare, too.

In any case, B. F. Jones' company did what other firms did, and probably for the same reason. In the first twenty years of its existence, and at extended periods after that, ready cash was chronically in short supply. Paper currency, issued by separate states, was not always worth the paper on which it was printed. So the industrial firms came to operate on credit, legalized by short or long term notes, which were often held by the local bankers. Since the management had to use credit, i.e., figures on paper, it was useful to have the workmen paid, at least in part, by the same manipulation. This was done by opening company stores where the workman could run up a bill for food and clothing, and that bill would be deducted from his nominal Saturday pay. His other chief need was shelter, and here the company intervened in exactly the same way. They bought land and erected inexpensive houses, which they rented to their puddlers and millmen and laborers, deducting the rent from their pay. Here is a typical entry, one of a hundred, by B. F. Jones:

"*May 17, 1877* L. Benz and Bros. have this day submitted a plan for building a row of 5 brick tenement houses of 4 rooms each on Sarah Street on lot we have next to Catholic Church, a portion of which lot the old Cole Road used to run on. They offered to build them for $4,000 or for $4,368—with finished attic. The project is now under consideration."[22]

Incidentally, the entry for the following day gave the approximate number of employees—1,590 at the mill and 30 at the store.

Production expanded with all the personal force and financial exactitude that was part of B. F. Jones' personality. His next entry after the strike gave a precise breakdown of the cost of expanding one of the mills by 5,600 square feet—exactly $2,867.57. Here was the core of his resistance to the ironmakers' strike—the inner need, the furious drive, not for profits as such, but for expansion. It's as though the mills were a great fire-eating, smoke-breathing animal, created and nurtured and loved by an owner who was also a manager. Money got for its bars, rails, plates, girders, and nails was immediately fed back to the growing beast. Eighty per cent of the Jones and Laughlin earnings from 1854 to 1908 were reinvested in expansion

Since this is a crucial division, it's interesting to see how it operated. From 1853 to 1869, no dividends were paid. Though the net earnings were over $1.5 million, it was all reinvested. In 1870, a fat and prosperous year, dividends were paid for the first time, but only half the year's earnings were distributed. The rest went into expansion. So in the first twenty years of Jones's company, dividends were less than 4 per cent of the net profit. From 1874 through 1893, the next twenty years, they rose to one-third of the profits. From 1894 through 1913, they sank to one-fifth of the net earnings. In every case, the rest of the money was crammed back into the business

Labor remained, if not exactly docile, at least cooperative:

"*Feb. 7, 1878* Pay day changed this time from Saturday night to Friday February 8 in order to give the men a chance to join in the grand tariff demonstration to take place on the 9th. A big turnout is expected. Music, badges, processions, and etc. and etc.[23]

There were, of course, some rare but annoying exceptions:

"*June 1, 1878* The year having expired today for which the agreement was signed between the Manufacturers and Boilers, a committee consisting of Edward Jones, John Broderick and William Probert called on B. F. Jones at 5 o'clock today wishing to renew the agreement for another year. Mr. Jones told them he would not sign it just at present but would await the action of the other manufacturers and would of course be guided by them. He thinks, owing to the great depression in business (particularly the iron) that the "sliding rate" should be a little lower—

"*June 3, 1878* All the depts. in the Mill have been on today except the "Forge' and as we have considerable muck bar on hand (enough to run a month) we could easily run for a short time without the Boilers. This muck being all of our own make we supposed that the Heaters and Rollers could not object to working it up but we were surprised by a Committee or rather all the Heaters coming to the office this afternoon and refusing to work longer than tomorrow unless the 'Boilers Agreement' was signed. This news was sent to Mr. Jones.

"*June 4th 1878* Mr. Jones over this morning but has not yet decided how he shall act in regard to the matters mentioned in the foregoing—"[24]

And the following year:

"*Saturday, June 7, 1879* At a meeting of all the manufacturers held this morning it was resolved that 'under existing circumstances it is inexpedient to further resist the unjust demands of the Boilers'— Mr. B. F. left for New York this afternoon with his family as his daughter sails for Europe with her instructresses next Wednesday (11th) on Steamer 'Scythia' about 4 P.M. Mr. T.M.J. sent for the Committee of Boilers and signed the scale for another year—so that on Monday the 'wheels will again go round.' "[25]

Having been away during this last piece of unpleasant business, Jones picked up the entries in his diary:

"*Wednesday June 18, 1879*   B.F.J. returned this A.M. looking quite brightened up by his little trip. He is offered a bargain in the "McTieman property" on Corner opposite the stores and is contemplating its purchase."[26]

The reader will have noted that the B. F. Jones mentioned in these entries is B. F. Jones himself. The capacity to remain at this distance in one's diary reveals both orderliness and precision of mind, but once again, it seems to me, an enormous egotism as well, for the "I" is separated from "Mr. B. F. Jones" as in the following entry:

"*Sept. 25, 1878 (Wednesday)*   President Rutherford B. Hayes arrived in the city Monday eve.

"Yesterday he visited our mill and appeared much pleased. We had made considerable preparation for his visit, the mill being thoroughly cleaned up and nicely decorated with flags. The machine shop looked very nice the machines all being handsomely polished up and trimmed with flags. In the Foundry Mr. Early had mouled [*sic*] in the sand the words, 'Welcome to President Hayes' which attracted much attention. At the small mill rolls, Edward Coates had a picture of Hayes above the rolls over which was the motto "Our Old Comrade"—(Coates I believe was in the army with Hayes.)

"Mr. B. F. Jones escorted Mr. Hayes through the mill in his best style and to the entire satisfaction of everyone especially I think to the President, taking care not to annoy or tire him by trying to show him *too* much. It was simply a glance at the most interesting parts of the works which was all there was time to do.

"The procession in the afternoon was a grand success ending by escorting the President to the exposition where speeches were made by Hayes and some of Pittsburgh's citizens. Thus ended an eventful day and whilst there was no *very* great enthusiasm the citizens and visitors from the surrounding cities all showed respect for our chief magistrate.

"The President's wife was also escorted about by a committee of ladies and gentlemen and appears to have charmed all by her quiet and elegant manners."[27]

And there is the same odd distance in the entry of July 15, 1879: "B.F.J. has been a little under the weather past two or three days but we are happy to say he put in his usual appearance this morning and 'the ball rolls again.' "[28] No imaginable secretary could have written in this jaunty fashion. It was Mr. B. F. Jones, preserving the history of Mr. B. F. Jones which was identical, or nearly so, with that of the company. His impartiality is even stranger in the entry of March 16, 1882: "B. F. Jones was taken sick with bad cold on December 10, 1881, was confined to home for some time—on getting better about February 1st '82, went to New York and Fortress Monroe or Point Comfort. Returned today March 16th, '82 and is now over to mill the first time since December 10th and "by a large majority" the longest time he has been away from the mill and from business in all his life. He will be around now until May 17th when he, accompanied by his family, sails for

Europe to be gone about 4 months. He is looking splendid and if he *feels* as well as he looks we shall all rejoice and wish him a long, happy, prosperous life—"[29]

His wish was granted; the enterprise flourished. In the early 1850s, the original capacity of Jones' mill was, at most, 15 tons a day, which is about 4,700 tons a year. By 1869, stimulated by the Civil War, it had risen to 30,000 tons. B. F. Jones recorded in his entry of January 2, 1879, the production at his plants for 1878:

Rolled iron	27,812 tons
Plate and sheet	2,560 tons
Rails	1,501 tons
Street rails	188 tons
Nails and railroad spikes	61,806 kegs [30]

Production in 1892 was quadrupled—126,667 tons. For 1901 the amount of steel ingots totaled 650,000 tons. By 1930, the Pittsburgh plant, and the new Alequippa plant built in 1905 and also owned by Jones and Laughlin, had the combined capacity to produce 3,250,000 tons.

We have looked at the Jones and Laughlin Company so closely because it is the very model of the tremendous rise in factory production for the last quarter of the nineteenth century. This is particularly true because the iron and steel made by B. F. Jones and his puddlers, millwrights, roughers, bar rollers, shearmen, nailers, feeders, heaters, and engineers—this white, molten fluid cast and rolled into grey and shining bars and strips—is the very bone of every other enterprise. For every machine now requires this hard, heavy, cheap, and durable stuff. And that is increasingly true for the farms, great or small, as well as the textile mills and the lumber yards and the railroad lines and the locomotives that carry the the grain and live flesh on the hoof, and clothes, and furniture. Each demand feeds the other, and production climbs hand over hand. But by what shall we measure this accomplishment? The problem is tricky, because the steel is interlaced with human nerve and muscle. For example, in 1907 and 1908, there was another in a series of spasmodic and painful American depressions, so Jones and Laughlin cut the wages of their rollers by 40 per cent.

". . . [T]he wages policy, which, while advancing the wages of common labor, has brought down the earnings of men of highest skill; which has anticipated increased output with cuts in the rates, and which has suffered the whole wage movement, unprodded by union demands, to lag behind the advances in prices of family necessities.

"With the employers no longer penalized by having to pay extra for overtime, the day's, the week's, and the year's work has been lengthened. Now the twelve-hour day is the working schedule for the majority; the seven-day week in 1907–08 claimed at least 20 per cent of all employes; and the twenty-four-hour shift comes once every two weeks for large numbers."[31]

Note that: ". . . Jones and Laughlin broke with the union in 1897. An employe of this company told me of an attempt in 1906 to hold a meeting to protest against Sunday work, but with no intention of organizing was a trade union. The men who were interested in the matter had engaged a hall. Word was carried to the company. The superintendent called the men together from the departments where the agitators were supposed to be and ordered them, with threats of discharge, to abandon the plan. When the time for the meeting came, a foreman, with several mill policemen, stationed themselves where they could see every man who went into the hall. As a result, no one attempted to go to the meeting . . . The Jones and Laughlin Company has some organization that keeps it sufficiently informed as to the likelihood of sedition breaking out, and the United States Steel Corporation has regular secret service departments. Its agents are thought by the men to be scattered through all of the mills of the Corporation, working shoulder to shoulder at the rolls or furnaces with honest workmen, ready to record any 'disloyal' utterances or to enter into any movement among their fellows. The workmen feel this espionage. They believe it exists, but they do not know who the traitors are. It may be that the friend of long standing who works at the next furnace is one of them, or, possibly, the next-door neighbor at home; they do not know. Is it any wonder, therefore, that they suspect each other and guard their tongues?"[32] And during all this time, the growth of the company may have slowed, but it never halted.

Suppose we try to reckon the final worth of this enterprise, first, in dollars. In 1879, the cost per long ton of unfinished muck iron—so B. F. Jones calculated—was $30.25. The finished bars cost "$42.04 per ton (of 2240 pounds) or $1.88 per hundred pounds." But what was the human cost? Naturally, it is hardly measurable in dollars, whether gold or paper. It must be judged by particulars:

"A puddling or boiling furnace is a brick structure, like an oven, about seven feet high and six or seven square, with two compartments, one a receptacle into which pig iron is thrown, the other a fuel chamber beside it where the melting heat is generated. The drafts are so arranged that the flame sweeps from the fuel chamber directly upon the surface of the iron. From five hundred to six hundred pounds of pig iron is put into the furnace at one time, after which the furnace is closed, and sufficient heat is applied to melt down the iron. Then the puddler begins to work it with an iron rod through a hole in the furnace door, so as to stir up the liquid and bring as much as possible in contact with the air. . . .

"Puddling is very hard, hot work. It is conceded by mill workers that few other positions in either an iron or a steel mill are so taxing, physically. There are always two men and sometimes three to a single furnace, and they take turn about at working the metal. No man could stand before the furnace and perform that back-breaking toil continually. Even when working by 'spells,' a man is often nearly exhausted at the end of his 'spell.' The puddler stands in the full heat of the furnace and works his rod through a hole in the door."[33]

A visitor to the mills, in 1910, noted how ". . . one of the highly paid vesselmen was struck by a tiny drop of molten steel—it was a very small drop, and his wages were good, he ought to have been satisfied—but he caught the drop in his eye and he came with his face distorted with pain to get aid from some one. The little piece of steel was embedded in the membrane of the eyeball, and my foreman friend removed it for him with the point of his pencil, and turned again to go on with his discussion of the high wage theory . . ."[34]

Nor was the expenditure of blood, bone, and life infrequent:

". . . In January, 1907, Number 2 furnace of the Eliza group, owned by the Jones and Laughlin Steel Company, exploded without warning, blowing out the whole side of the furnace and burning to death fourteen men. In February, March and May, accidents occurred in these same furnaces, resulting in injuries and loss of life. On November 15, 1907, nine men were badly burned by an outburst of flame and stock, while doing repair work at the top of one of the Lucy furnaces, owned by the Carnegie Steel Company. On February 12, 1908, at McKeesport, an explosion occurred at the Monongahela Furnaces of the National Tube Company, causing the death of two men and seriously burning three others . . .

"The open-hearth department is equally dangerous. I talked with a man who had been burned when the fluid steel broke out sooner than he had expected as he was knocking out the tapping hole. The steel came with a rush and his face and body were badly seared. This man had been a first helper, the man in charge of a furnace, but he gave up the job because, as he said, he lost his nerve over another accident in which a man under him was killed. A furnace had just been tapped. The crane lifted the huge ladle of molten steel out of the pit and was about to swing it around, when something gave way and the whole load dropped eight or ten feet, with an explosion as it struck the ground. Some of the metal flew completely over the furnace and striking the ground on the opposite side, rebounded and splashed over a workman standing some distance away. This man was horribly burned and died almost instantly. He had been standing where anyone would have thought him safe—on the far side of the furnace. Men standing near were severely burned, but recovered from their injuries.

"So long as steel is made there will be accidents . . ."[35]

The lack of compensation for injury was pretty much the same as that for the railroads. The commonly held view was that a man's accident or death was his own bad luck, and not the company's:

". . . The Jones and Laughlin Company has manifested considerable indifference to methods of reducing the danger of accidents . . . Their South

Side plant was badly overcrowded, and there were many dangerous machines which lacked proper guards . . . So far as compensation for accidents is concerned, the payments made by the constituent companies of the Steel Corporation in Allegheny County in the year studied, July 1, 1906–June 30, 1907, did not differ materially from those customary among other large companies of the district. In 33 out of 60 cases of married men killed in plants controlled by the Steel Corporation, it contributed nothing over funeral expenses, to take the place of the wages of the dead breadwinners; in 17 out of 28 cases, the same was true of their chief competitor, the Jones and Laughlin Steel Company. . . . No share whatever of the lost income was borne by the employer. The main economic loss in half of all the year's industrial accidents staid where it first fell—on the families of the men killed at work."[36]

By this time, Jones & Laughlin was no longer a group of iron mills and smelters in a single waterfront location. Iron ore was mined in Minnesota by a subsidiary company and carried to the smelter by a wholly-owned steamship firm. To insure another basic raw material essential for the reduction of the ore to metal, Jones and Laughlin acquired the Blair Limestone Company.

All these acquisitions not only made the Jones and Laughlin Company self-sustaining and self-contained, but allowed it to expand into other dominions: the Harbor Land Company, Adelaide Land Company, Woodlawn Land Company, Woodlawn Water Company, Woodlawn and Southern Motor Coach Company, Jones & Laughlin Steel Products Company, Louisiana Erecting Company, Inc., Roy L. Brower Corporation, Jones & Laughlin Steel Service, Inc., Frick-Reid Supply Corporation, and the Lucky Star Mining Company. As so often happens in the real, as distinct from the merely heroic, history of the world, certain exceptional men drive events forward, but these are events which were already in motion. They put their shoulder to a wheel already spinning. The primary impulse to buy the source and thus insure the supply of cheap raw materials and their transport is followed by an expansion outwards into related but not essential fields, and this was a process only beginning as the century changed from nineteenth to twentieth.

B. F. Jones, who pursued this inevitable course, died at seventy-nine, in 1903. However, the force of his personality remained in at least one Jones and Laughlin's executive's mind as late as 1929 when he was described as ". . . active and forceful unto the end, respected by his fellowmen, beloved and mourned by his friends and associates. To his children he has left a heritage of love and affection and an honored name. To his fellowmen he has bequeathed the record of a life of notable achievements, worthy of all honor and emulation. The impress of his personality will continue to live, and the work of his able hands and brain will carry on, in the beautiful language of one of the old poets: 'The torch of the great soul burns on long after his body has crumbled to dust.' "[37]

2

Benjamin Franklin Jones was not only an accountant, manager, and entrepreneur. He was also a salesman. This occupation became as necessary to the gigantism of the corporation as the puddler or the miner. Jones himself ". . . made two trips a year to Philadelphia to sell his products, make new contracts and generally advertise his business that was gradually growing up in the Monongahela valley. These trips were made on horseback, with all Mr. Jones' extra clothes, papers, and equipment packed in saddle bags. It took exactly one week from the time Mr. Jones left Pittsburgh until he reached Philadelphia, traveling about forty miles a day. This, however, was really a fast trip, because all other modes of transportation took from eleven to seventeen days to cover the same distance."[38] But at every link in the iron chain, from cold rolled bars to safety pins, there had to be salesmen to push the product into the enormous scatter of markets over the nation's ten million square miles. The lives and the labor of these salesmen focus into as sharp a picture of our country in that bloody and confused quiet between the Civil War and World War I, as the works and writings of Mr. Jones, albeit from another angle.

An interesting example of the rise and fall of a steel salesman may be found in the correspondence of William R. Russell. He was fourteen when he was sent away to a private high school, and he stayed with an aunt and an uncle. He wrote to his parents in Washington, D.C.:

My dear Father and Mother   Greenfield, Friday 21 May '58
     . . . My routine of the day is to get up at six in the morning and eat breakfast at 6–½, attend prayer meeting till I study my French until 8–½ then go over to Aunt's and recite until 9 then go to school. . . .
     . . . Both Uncle N. and Uncle John and Charley told me that the cultivation of my *memory* was of the greatest importance in *any* business, and so I am trying to remember every minute little thing . . .
     . . . The conversation here is about Religion just as it is in Washington about politics, and the different ministers are discussed as they come.
                              Your affectionate son[39]

Bill Russell drank from a farmer's cider press, found and killed a snake, described the comet of 1858, and recorded public opinion of the preacher: ". . . There are a great many people here who like him and a great many more that wish he was gone. Among the latter are, I guess, Uncle J. and Aunt Juliana for Uncle cannot bear his preaching and never goes to hear him and Aunt J. regularly tears his sermon all to pieces when she gets home. . . ."[40]

Russell graduated, went to New York, and got a job at another uncle's hardware store. His daily life in 1860 went something like this: ". . . I rise at 6–¾ and eat and breakfast at 7 and then rush out and down to Wall Street ferry and directly to the P.O. and then to the store and get there 10 minutes before eight o'clock. Then I hoist the curtains round the store and dust out. I was not allowed to dust till about one week ago and I consider it a kind of promotion."[41] He expressed great fascination with inventions, but perhaps in 1860's America, that was not too unusual. ". . . Sam [and his] Father . . . are engaged in the Steam Heating Business — Low Pressure Steam . . . It is an ingenious thing . . ."[42]

In March of 1861, William Russell was sent out on the road as a salesman. He wrote his sister from Oswego, New York: ". . . The towns were not handsome anyway: moreover I sold no goods up there, which was really worse than all. I then went to Pittston, stopping on the way at a town called Danville, where I saw tremendous rolling mills and furnaces, and went down, down, down into an iron mine . . . In Pittston I went into a coal mine so that I may be looked upon as having seen the whole Pennsylvania elephant . . . [Here in Oswego] I went right to see the customers and found that a desperately wicked and unprincipled man from a horrid bad company who make knives in Meriden Point, had the audacity to have been in town just before me . . ."[43]

Brooklyn Bridge under construction.

Museum of the City of New York

Miner in Comstock Mine, Virginia City, Nevada, *ca.* 1868.
Photograph by Timothy H. O'Sullivan. National Archives, Washington, D.C.

In the last year of the war, he expressed his dislike of salesmanship:

Dear Mother   Sunday evening January 22, 1865
    Someday I may want to get married—who knows—and I couldn't think of doing such a thing without money.
    I have been thinking that this kind of life does very well for a variety but after all as we have to die sometime it would be well to go for the best thing in the long run.
    And I can see no other solution of the problem as satisfying as the getting married and settling down.
    The more I think on the shortness of life and the many convenient luxuries a

man may have to himself as well as not before dissolution the more I am led to deplore a life spent in a garret during leisure and as hard matter of fact—Niggery--work, during the rest of the day—week, month, and year!

It may suit some people (that have no more brain than a kettle) to live thus but as for me—I can't see it . . .[44]

Yet three years later, he was once again on the road as a salesman for the same hardware store. ". . . I am not going to ruin my health in their service merely for their approbation as I only work there for the sake of learning the business and getting into business habits . . ."[45]

In 1871, he had relocated and set up his own shop in Fort Wayne, Indiana:

W. R. Russell
Importer, Manufacturer's Agent and Dealer in
CUTLERY, PISTOLS, GUNS, ETC.[46]

Thus, in the construction of the enormous iron pyramid of American industry, Russell was an inconspicuous and somewhat unhappy bolt. He, like so many millions of Americans before him and after him, was part of the historic deracination that was a necessity for industrial growth. In Fort Wayne, in 1872, long separated from his family, he was courting various young la-

Tunnel, Buckhorn Mine, near Prescott, Arizona, *ca.* 1900.

National Archives, Washington, D.C.

Vat of molten steel being poured into mold, at Jones and Laughlin Steel Company, Pittsburgh, Pennsylvania.

Below: Young German steel worker, Pittsburgh, 1908.
On the facing page: Maimed steel worker, 1910.

dies: ". . . I made the acquaintance of a new young lady lately—Miss Sweet-zer. My roommate took me to see her and we had a pleasant time at first until he and she got mad and finally he got mad with me and we went home separately, much to the disgust of Mss S. I guess. I don't think I shall make any more calls with him . . . I went to a splendid party on Berry Street lately—over 200 guests—and the journal says they were 'exclu-sively—selected from the elite'—! Ha! Big Injun!"[47]

Russell sent for his younger brother Johnny and put him to work in the hardware store. Johnny wrote home: "Tell Lou that all her alarms about Nellie Br—— are groundless for he does not care for any young ladie [sic] in particular at present as I can find out—You see we businessmen have no time for such follies time is money with us now, so we have to improve it . . ."[48] But the depression of 1873 had already shown its color in early '72: ". . . Three firms in town failed this month . . ." Russell took on a partner, Charles Washburn, to supply him with capital. ". . . Charly has orders every day for the machine [a bolt cutter at $75.00] and I believe he is making money but in such a business money is used in such quantities the first few years, that I suppose he don't really feel very rich . . . I have fixed my busi-ness very satisfactorily here and feel correspondingly elated . . ."[49] But the optimism is premature.

"Washburn is rather slow, but that is only what I expected, and if he improves with age, I think they will sell a good many of the machines . . .

"Business is dull—trade has not been good this spring. And the lookout for fall is not encouraging—I don't know what to do about Washburn unless I give him what I have and emigrate . . .

". . . Jack got mad last night and has been gone ever since—I suppose he is with some of his friends . . . Last week I only went out one day. Busi-ness is dully, but worse than that—money is very tight and collections are poor. The feeling is quite prevalent that the next six months will witness many failures. Under the circumstances I don't feel like forcing sales, and shall be content to make sales light for some time to come and collect up pretty sharp. Washburn has gone to Boston—he has gone to get money to buy me out. I don't really think he will succeed, but should be glad if he could raise the money. I have got tired of working so hard—Somehow or other since Washburn has got into the concern I have lost all interest in it."[50]

In spite of the continuing depression, Russell got married. He wrote his mother in 1875: ". . . Everything has been going on in the same old routine way here. Ella and I have joined the First Presbyterian Church, and have a pew. We are enjoying life very much. Business however is very bad. We are not making expenses now . . ."[51]

And in 1878, he wrote a long letter to his brother Jack, who had left Fort Wayne some time before:

". . . [I picked up] a thick lettered blank book bound in sheep which you used as a price book when you were in Fort Wayne, and which by some chance I made use of as a memorandum book for keeping track of the odds and ends of the stock which I still own. I took it up a few moments since and looked through its pages with an increasing interest, and something of a melancholy feeling too to think of those bygone days when you were with me. And a good boy you were and deserved better treatment than to lose so much of your money, but I hope someday to be able to pay that with interest. It has been close times with me lately. I have done nothing this spring, and do not now look forward to anything but will have to go into something as I cannot live on nothing very long—was brought up too well for that—appetite too good.

"We are very pleasantly situated now. [He had moved to Coldwater, Michigan.] Our house although small, is a nice one and we have everything arranged satisfactorily. I have my garden, and am very much interested in it. We have rhubarb pies made from our own plants—yesterday we had our first asparagus. My peas are up—so are the radishes, onions, potatoes, lettuce (and heading beautifully), beets. I have planted also, cauliflower, sweet corn, stringbeans (immense), tomatoes, parsnips and have a celery trench ready for the plants next month. We have the most ingenious chicken coop also, that ever was known—the chickens never venturing forth into the vegetable or flower garden (Ella attends to the flowers) and lay all the eggs we need. I am going to 'set' three hens as soon as they signify that their arrangements will admit of such a change in their methods of housekeeping. Mr. Bennett has promised me some eggs of the buff cochins—fine for spring killing—grow fast—very tender and juicy."[52]

These are pleasant triumphs, but the fact is Russell has lost the store and has no occupation: "I regret that I had not the moral courage to go to work to achieve something in a profession when at your age."[53] The steel ingots of Benjamin Franklin Jones had hardly made this middle-class salesman a fortune. It did no more for him than it had done for the laborer, the roller, the puddler, or the engineer.

3

Walt Whitman, in notes to his bitter, noble, 1871 prose poem, *Democratic Vistas*, quoted a speech by Vice-President Colfax on July 4 of the preceding year:

"From a territorial area of less than nine hundred thousand square miles, the Union has expanded into over four millions and a half—fifteen times larger than that of Great Britain and France combined—with a shoreline, including Alaska, equal to the entire circumference of the earth, and with a domain within these lines far wider than that of the Romans in their proudest days of conquest and renown. With a river, lake, and coastwise commerce estimated at over two thousand millions of dollars per year; with a railway traffic of four to six thousand millions per year, and the annual domestic exchanges of the country running up to nearly ten thousand millions per year; with over two thousand millions of dollars invested in manufacturing, mechanical, and mining industry; with over five hundred millions of acres of land in actual occupancy, valued, with their appurtenances, at over seven thousand millions of dollars, and producing annually crops valued at over three thousand millions of dollars; with a realm which, if the density of Belgium's population were possible, would be vast enough to include all the present inhabitants of the world; and with equal rights guaranteed to even the poorest and humblest of our forty millions of people—we can, with a manly pride akin to that which distinguish'd the palmiest days of Rome, claim, . . ."[54]

It was a claim shared by the great majority of Americans. The pride of mileage and tonnage and the patriotism of unrestrained growth were based on the daily realities of American production, even if the values with which they were saturated are not necessarily fixed and eternal.

Iron is the index of nineteenth-century industry, and putting aside the production of rails, we can follow the steep slope of its increase decade by decade. In 1860, 2,873 long tons of iron ore were cut and shovelled out of the earth; ten years later, it was 3,832; by 1880, this amount was nearly doubled to 7,120 long tons and more than doubled by 1890, to 16,036 tons. In 1900, iron ore shipped and smelted came to 27,300 tons; in 1910, it more than doubled again to 57,015; and in 1917, it was up to 75,289 long tons.[55]

The mining of soft coal, the principal fuel for most of the last half of the nineteenth century, had an even more astounding percentage of increase. In 1860, 9,057,000 tons were mined; in 1917, the amount of this botanical fuel was 551,791,000 tons.[56] But neither iron ore nor coal grows like a plant. It has to be dug, often from deep underground. And these tunnels, subject to flood, collapse, and the deadly odorless and colorless poison gas carbon dioxide, are not man's natural habitat. The man who goes into this underground night, day after day, though fully as patriotic as his company, does not view the upper world in quite the same way.

An anonymous anthracite miner was interviewed in 1902 by the weekly *Independent,* and though it was implied that the diction was his own, this is obviously not exact. The words were the reporter's, but the final account was checked by the miner, and it is thus, perhaps, more complete and more correct, and more painfully specific, then if he had had to write it himself:

". . . Day in and day out, from Monday morning to Saturday evening, between the rising and the setting of the sun, I am in the underground workings of the coal mines. From the seams, water trickles into the ditches along the gangways; if not water, it is the gas which hurls us to eternity and the props and timbers to a chaos. . . .

"Three of my brothers are miners; none of us had any opportunities to acquire an education. We were sent to school (such a school as there was in those days) until we were about twelve years of age, and then we were put into the screen room of a breaker to pick slate. From there we went inside the mines as driver boys. As we grew stronger we were taken on as laborers, where we served until able to call ourselves miners. We were given work in the breasts and gangways. There were five of us boys. One lies in the cemetery—fifty tons of top rock dropped on him. He was killed three weeks after he got his job as a miner—a month before he was to be married . . ."[57]

He was specific about the material rewards of a miner's life:

"My store bill for two weeks was $11. That makes $22 per month. The butcher gets $6 per month. Add them all, and it costs me, just to live, $42.50. That leaves me $17 per month to keep my family in clothes, to pay my church dues and to keep the industrial insurance going. My insurance alone costs me 55 cents a week, or $2.20 a month . . .

"Company stores are of the time that has been. Their existence ended two years ago. But we've got a system growing up that threatens to be just as bad. Let me explain. Over a year ago I was given a breast [an open seam of coal] to drive at one of our mines and was glad to get it. My wife took her cash and went around the different places to buy. When I went to the office for my first pay the 'super' met me and asked me if I didn't know his wife's brother George kept a store. I answered, 'Yes,' and wanted to know what that had to do with it.

" 'Nothing, only I thought I'd call your attention to it," he answered.

"No more was said then. But the next day I got a quiet tip that my breast was to be abandoned. This set me thinking. I went to the boss and, after a few words, told him my wife had found brother-in-law George's store and that she liked it much better than where she had bought before. I told him the other store didn't sell the right kind of silk waists, and their patent leather shoes were away back. Brother-in-law George had the right kind of stuff and, of course, we were willing to pay a few cents more to get just what we wanted.

"That was sarcastic, but it's the cash that has the influence . . ."[58]

This miner does not question the necessity for his labor. How can he? Yet there seems something odd about sending a two-legged primate, whose normal habitat for a million years has been the open savannah, to dig thousands of feet underground. The compelling reason for this labor was, and still is, to provide the raw material for the chemical factories called steel mills, and the function of the latter is to produce tools, rails, locomotives, and a variety of machines complex and ingenious to the point of madness.

The amount of machinery made between the Civil and World War I increased at much the same astonishing rate as coal and iron. In fact, one is puzzled sometimes to determine which is the cause and which the effect. In 1869, the first year in which an accurate count was made, $290 million worth of machinery was constructed. It had risen to only $313 million a decade later, but began to increase more rapidly as the century ended. The total was $562 million in 1890, and nearly $900 million in 1900. By 1917, the total value of newly manufactured machinery was almost $4 billion.[59] There are no quick and simple ways to determine what part of this increase was due to ordinary inflation. However, by looking at several kinds of indices, we can calculate for example, that if 1914 is considered as 100, the wholesale price of commodities in 1869 was 151—so obviously there was an actual drop in the cost of living. It fell to 100 in 1880 and again to 82 in 1890. The cost of commodities was about the same in 1900. Only in 1910 does the wholesale price index rise to 103 again. But by 1917, under pressure from the European War which had been in progress since 1914, the cost of living rose to 171. More crude yet still significant is the price of steel rail, which went from $102 in 1870 down to $28.00 a unit in 1910 and only rose to $40.00 by 1917. Similarly, coal—if we accept the relative cost as not too different from anthracite—was $4.46 a ton in 1871; it dropped to $3.35 by 1890 and even by 1917 was no more than $6.00 a ton.

The same was true of hard, durable consumer goods like wagons, carriages, tools, furniture, construction materials and—lest we forget—paper. The total sales of such manufactured goods was $291 million in 1870. Ten years later, the total had grown to $313 million, and in 1890, amounted to $542 million which by that time included bicycles; by 1900 the total of hard consumer goods was $900 million; by 1917, the figure included automobiles and came to nearly $4 billion. [60]

What conclusion can we see from these abstract but necessary figures? Simply that the vast increases in American production, even when counted in dollars, were real and not the result of inflation—at least until 1914. Our industrial expansion seemed infinite. And in the nineteenth century and the first decades of the twentieth, it was certainly limitless. We still have, in fact, great strata of coal, enough for another couple of centuries. Nor is there any close limit to the amount of iron we can dig out of the mountains. But there is, and was, one resource that our rapid society used up at a blind and reckless rate—our forest reserves, which once stretched in largely unbroken zones from the Atlantic Ocean to the Alleghenies, across the northern Midwest to the gigantic stands of Douglas fir and California redwood along the Pacific.

We slashed and cut and sawed our way from Plymouth Rock to Alcatraz Island. In the process, we altered our water and our climate and our soil forever. The amounts are incredible: 13 billion board feet cut in 1869; then an average of 18 billion every year until 1879; by 1889, 27 billion board feet a year; by 1909, 45 billion. [61] But again, this was at the cost of human lives—a difficult notion to accept, for it betrays our image of an axe clearing a new space for the pioneer plow. This was an idea shared even by the workmen. This group machismo is reported in one of the most remarkable studies of any American institution, done in 1973 by a priest of the Archdiocese of Seattle, Father Andrew M. Prouty:

"In their earlier years, *West Coast Lumberman* and *The Timberman* wrote column after column entitled 'Deaths' and 'Fatal Accidents' which list

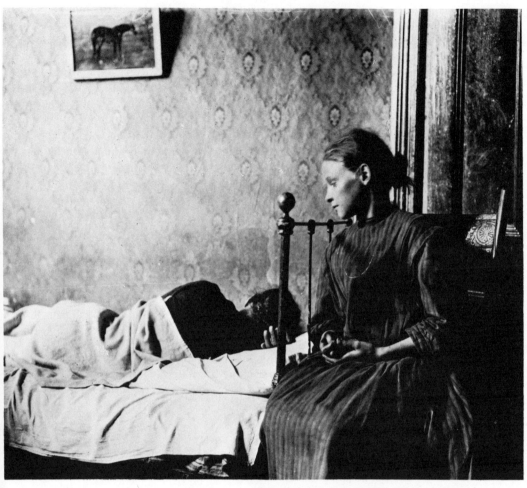

Girl with father dying of tuberculosis, *ca.* 1910.

Photograph by Lewis Hine. International Museum of Photography, George Eastman House, Rochester, New York

engineering and technological mishaps, incidents where men got cut in two by the rigging, squashed by falling snags, or dismembered by saws . . . In their cumulative effect, they have the horror of a battle report.

"Logging with animals, with its hazards of axe and saw, falling trees and rolling logs, breaking chains and cables parting under heavy strain, all this was dangerous enough; but the introduction of steam power—donkey engines and railroads, and that ultimate technological triumph, the rigged highlead tree—this new application of speed and power which sent logs flying through the air as often almost as it dragged them across the ground— began an era of injuries and death in which a domestic industrial occupation began to resemble a full scale war.

"[In one year] there were 31,000 industrial accidents [in the State of Washington]. There were 408 fatal accidents . . . 2239 permanently partially crippled men in 12 months—men who lost a leg or an arm or a hand, a foot, fingers or toes. In the woods alone [there were] 229 fatal accidents and 596 permanently disabled men."[62] Of course some of these deaths and injuries, grimly enough, were not in the logger camps, but in the sawmills.

There was no compensation for such acts of violence until 1911, when the Washington State Compensation Act was passe, a generous measure which ". . . provided burial benefits of $75.00 for a man killed on the job . . . it allowed a widow $20 a month for herself, and $5 a month for the first three children under the age of 16 years, the total not to exceed $35 a month. For 'permanent disability'—the loss of both legs or both arms, or a leg and an arm, paralysis, loss of sight and so on . . . single men received $20 each month, married men, with no minor dependents, $25."[63] This was perfectly fair by contemporary standards, for when a man worked in timber, he earned anywhere from $1.90 a day for a grease dauber up to $3.00 a day for a chopper—with, naturally, no charge for a bunk in a log cabin, but with a deduction of $5.00 a week for board. These immense meals contained upward of 8,000 calories a day—proof enough of the enormous physical labor that burned them up.

There is a natural lack of first-hand accounts by the men themselves. Like the gold rush camps, logging communities had few women, and families were rare. In any case, hard labor and long hours do not leave much will to write a daily account. But the muse of the semi-literate is poetry. I myself remember a fellow dishwasher who made up endless heartfelt lyrics in the darkness of the hotel barn where we slept. Father Prouty quotes similar lyrics by a slab-loader in a lumber mill:

> Down where the sun's gentle rays cannot beam,
> Beside the bright roll of Willamette's fair stream.
> A few faithful workmen each day can be seen,
> Whose hard, weary labor is dangerous and mean.
>
> The past dreary winter we toiled here below,
> Regardless a moment of frost, rain or snow;
> Determined to labor though meagre our pay,
> With huge rumbling slabs tumbling down as they may.
>
> Times without warning not even a sound
> Those slabs make us jump like wild bronchos around;
> The man throwing them down cares not for the slab,
> All he thinks is to quickly get next to his job.
>
> Last week unexpected glad tidings we found,
> In the cool gentle breeze it was wafted around,
> Claiming employes would get TWO-BITS raise,
> Rewarding the toil of their hard working days.

> The import was pleasing, though yet all a fake,
> It was only some flippant old babbler's mistake.
> Some may receive it, but one thing I know,
> Not by us toilers way down here below.
>
> Now, as a finale, I trust you will pay
> The humble slab-loaders $2.00 per day.
> The nerve of the writer I hope you'll excuse,
> With feeble shortcomings and talentless muse.[64]

In the specificity of this ballad, we feel the necessary paradox of our splendid statistical American pyramid at whose bottom, in his tens, his hundreds, and his thousands, there endures this humorous and bitter workman.

4

Then what was the daily quality of life for the ordinary nineteenth-century and early–twentieth-century man? For by any ethical standard, that's all that really counts.

". . . a steel worker has said . . . 'Home is just the place where I eat and sleep. I live in the mills.' Theoretically, the steel workers are in the mills twelve hours on each turn, from six to six; in practice, though, there is considerable latitude about the time of changing. It has come to be quite a general custom in certain departments for the men to work loner at night than on the day turn. The men prefer to work the longer shift at night because such leisure as they have when on the night shift comes at a time when it is hard to use it to advantage. They come home in the morning and go to bed, getting up at about four o'clock in the afternoon. There is little opportunity for pleasure or social intercourse before it is time to go to the mill again. By the time supper is eaten, most of the free interval is gone. The steel workers are united in saying that 'on the night shift you can't do anything but work, eat and sleep anyhow.' So home pleasures and social pleasures alike are entirely lacking during a full half of the time. Whatever opportunity for enjoyment of the home there may be, must come in the alternate weeks on day shift.

"The manner of dividing the twenty-four hours of the day into two turns varies. Judging merely from observation, I should say that the most general adjustment is an eleven-hour day and a man's work begins at seven in the morning. Most of the skilled workers live at least a half-hour's ride on the cars away from the mill, so if the man is to get to his work by seven, his breakfast must be ready at six o'clock, and he must be up and dressed before that. At six in the evening he is relieved by his "buddy," the man who holds the same position on the opposite shift. If he cares about his appearance, he will take fifteen minutes making himself presentable for the street, and if his car is not delayed he may reach home by a quarter before seven, having been absent twelve hours and fifteen minutes. But between six and seven the rush is at its height, and the man who can take the first car that comes along is fortunate. Sometimes one has to wait for half a dozen cars to go by before he can find one with any standing room left. With the best of luck it will be after seven before he can sit down to his evening meal. This is the program of a day that has been outlined to me again and again by the steel workers until I am sure it is neither overdrawn nor unusual in anyway. When I asked about the evening, the usual reply was: 'Well, I am mostly too tired to go out anywhere. I read the paper a little while, but I soon get sleepy and I go to bed so that I can get up early enough the next morning.' And this is the alternate week of comparative leisure!

Covered wagon and homesteaders, Loup Valley, Nebraska, 1886.
National Archives, Washington, D.C.

"The wife of the steel worker, too, has a hard day, and even a longer one than her husband's. To prepare a breakfast by six in the morning she must rise not later than half past five. The family cannot sit down at the supper table until seven or later, and after that the dishes must be washed. There is little time for husband and wife to have each other's company. It is only by an extra exertion that they can spend an evening out together, and the evening at home is robbed of much of its charm by the projection of the domestic duties beyond the time that would be required if the meal were served earlier. The father, too, has little time with his children. If they are quite small, he may go for weeks without seeing them except in their cribs. What the ultimate social effect will be of this stunting of family life may only be conjectured . . .

". . . There is not enough energy left at the end of a twelve-hour day to enable the average man to read anything of a very serious nature, and the reading done by even the most intelligent does not extend much beyond the limits of the daily paper. As for lectures and concerts,—to attend them would necessitate a change of clothing and a preparation for which a weary twelve-hour man has little heart. The difficulties that must be met before these cultural opportunities can be enjoyed are usually too great to be over-come . . .

". . . Working on the two-turn system, a man is obliged to get up at 5.45 in the morning in order to be at the mill at 6.50. He must stay there until 5.30 p.m., and then in order to make himself presentable he must bathe, as well as he can without proper facilities, and change his clothing, so it is after six when he gets home. He gets through supper some time after seven, and soon after that gets sleepy. If he sits down to read, he will fall asleep over a paper or a book. He has not read a book through in three or four years. Some years ago he read several of Shakespeare's plays, and while he was doing this he sat down to his reading each evening after supper and did nothing else. This is the only systematic reading he had done for years. He never uses the library, and the other mill men do not use it either. As a rule, they do not care for it, but they could not use it even if they wished to do so, for their hours are too long to permit the use of a library. They have a lecture course in the library, and every year have some of the best talent in the country, but this man seldom goes. The library and the lecture course are fine things for business men, women and children, but they are absolutely useless, so far as the mill men are concerned."[65]

By such means—the use of men's labor and time—coal was dug up and transported, and coal smelted iron, and raw iron was machined into huge tools, and these in turn built other machines, and by this process of mechani-zation, the productivity of the American workmen doubled between 1889 and 1929. But figures are only the foam at the crest of the wage. The change in America came in a rising flood toward the end of the nineteenth century. The marks of this flood can be gauged, for a start, by the value of manufac-tured goods. In 1849, $460 million was added by work and machinery; by 1914, the amount was $9.386 billion, an increase during sixty-five years of more than a 1,000 per cent.[66] If we reckon the amount added worker by worker, each man, woman, or laboring child created $680 a year in 1869, and by 1914, this amount had risen to $1,400 per workman.[67] But did wages rise in proportion to the greater value of the work?

Hardly. Factory wages in 1869 averaged only $300 a year. Decade by decade, the return to the worker crept up, but rather slowly. The average hand earned $350 a year in 1879; ten years later, $430. Wages remained at this level until at least 1899. Even by 1909, they had risen to only $510 per year. That would be the equivalent (again, in 1967 prices) to about $1,900 a year. Back in 1869, prices were actually higher, so that the annual wage of

$300 was only $750 by 1967 standards. For a median year halfway between 1869 and 1909—say 1889—the annual adjusted wage was about $1,600 a year, and this is reckoned not in dollars as of 1889, but in 1967 dollars. In short, if the millhand were working in 1967 at the same rate, he would have received, if he were paid 1889 wages, the equivalent of only $30.00 a week.[68]

How was it possible for a man to live on so low a wage? One can do without normal housing, without private plumbing, light, or toilets, but shoes and clothes, however soled and patched, are a necessity. Fortunately, they were not excessively expensive, because the people who made them came very cheap too.

It was natural for textile mills to locate in the South, close to the very fields where the white bolls of fiber were growing. But while raw cotton was tilled by blacks, the factories were manned by whites. To work in a mill in Augusta, Georgia, in, say, the early 1880s, was a privilege reserved for the white American poor—particularly for their children who were 25 per cent of the work force. Most adult workers made eight cents for an eleven-hour day, though a skilled carder or weaver might make as much as a dollar; the children earned forty cents a day. The president of the largest Augusta mill, Charles H. Phinizy, made child labor a moral issue, calling it "a matter of charity with us; some of them would starve if not given employment and others are forced upon us by their families."[69] The older textile mills in New England were more liberal. There mill hands were paid piecework rates, thus putting them in competition with men and women on the other machines. Even so, an average workman could hardly earn more than $1.50, and with frequent slack seasons, his pay—in 1882, for example—was $133 for the whole year. But then his family had time to scavenge wood in the countryside and coal in the railroad yards and to dig clams from the sandy spits of the Fall River. During a U.S. Senate inquiry, a mill hand was asked why he didn't move West, claim a homestead, and go to farming, all of which cost no more than $1,500. He said, "Well, I never saw over a 20 dollar bill, and that is when I have been getting a month's pay at once. If someone would give me $1,500, I would go."[70]

And here, painfully typical, was the account of a collar starcher in New York State, as late as 1905:

"The starchers work very quickly, of course. They have to, both for the sake of the collars and for the sake of their wages. It is possible to starch fifty dozen or more a day, depending on the style of collar. I have often done so. The straight band collar is easier than the wide turnover. If the work kept up at such a pace a starcher's wages would amount to ten or twelve dollars a week, but, unfortunately, the busy season lasts only three months in the year. A good starcher makes as high as fifteen or sixteen dollars a week during those three months. The rest of the year she is lucky if she makes seven dollars a week. The average, I think, is about six. The average wage the year round is between eight and nine dollars.

"In order to make good money during the busy season I get up at half-past five in the morning, prepare a hasty breakfast, leaving the dishes for my daughter to wash. By half-past six I am at work. In the middle of the morning I stop just long enough to take a cup of coffee and a piece of bread, which stay me until lunch time. Ten minutes' pause for lunch and I am hard at work again. Sometimes I work as late as eight o'clock . . .

"If a starcher drops one collar on the floor she is docked five dozen collars. In other words for every collar dropped on the floor the girl must starch five dozen collars for nothing. The starcher is even held responsible after the collars leave her hands. If the bars on which the collars are dried happen to be dirty the starcher is fined, although the bars are supposed to be cleaned by other workers. If a collar drops from the cleaning bars and is found on the floor, the four girls whose work is nearest are fined. Since it is not possible accurately to locate the carless one the four are punished in order to fine the right one.

"These are not all the excuses for docking, but they are the most flagrant and unjust ones. It has been said on good authority that our firm alone has recovered from its employees, in fines, $159,900 during the past ten years . . ."[71]

Still, these girls managed to survive. It becomes more comprehensible when we examine a sample food budget—this one for a downtown Brooklyn clothing worker in 1902:

"I made $4 a week by working six days in the week . . .

"I lived at this time with a girl named Ella, who worked in the same factory and made $5 a week. We had the room all to ourselves, paying $1.50 a week for it, and doing light housekeeping. It was in Allen street, and the window looked out of the back, which was good, because there was an elevated railroad in front, and in summer time a great deal of dust and dirt came in at the front windows. We were on the fourth story and could see all that was going on in the back rooms of the houses behind us, and early in the morning the sun used to come in our window.

"We did our cooking on an oil stove . . . the oil for the stove and the lamp cost us 10 cents a week . . . We lived well, as this list of our expenses for one week will show:

ELLA AND SADIE FOR FOOD (ONE WEEK)

Tea	$0.06
Cocoa	.10
Bread and rolls	.40
Canned vegetables	.20

(List continues)

Potatoes	.10
Milk	.21
Fruit	.20
Butter	.15
Meat	.60
Fish	.15
Laundry	$ .25
Total	$2.42
Add rent	1.50
Grand total	$3.92

"It cost me $2 a week to live, and I had a dollar a week to spend on clothing and pleasure, and saved the other dollar . . ."[72]

Food was 50 per cent of the budget, and this is roughly equivalent to what anybody on the poverty level spends, in any area. It was the first and prime necessity, because even on a reduced diet, the strongest young man or woman would slowly sicken and die. The cost of food was therefore an irreducible minimum, below which the weekly wage could not fall without serious personal and social consequences. The workman and his family could get along on his low wages because the cost of food was extraordinarily low, in fact between a quarter and a third of what it would cost in our comparison year, 1967.

And it was low because, precisely as the cost of expanding American industry—iron, coal, railroads, machinery, lumber—rested on the low pay of labor, so the low cost of labor rested on the even lower pay of the men and women and children laboring on the American farm. We must now abstain from any further arithmetic, distressing as it is, and look at the particular consequences. What was it like to work on the American farm in the latter part of the nineteenth century?

". . . [In Kansas] there were miles on miles of cornfields, yielding from forty to eighty bushels per acre, and for sale at twenty cents per bushel; tens of thousands of tons of hay, worth two dollars per ton in the stack; potatoes by millions, and more feed than the stock could eat. And there was the trouble. The people had not a sufficiently diversified industry. They had relied almost entirely on the sale of grain, and this year there was no sale, and they remained poor despite their immense crops . . .

. . . [N]obody ever makes a crop the first year in a prairie country— think themselves in luck to get fences built and sod broke . . . Raised a little corn and oats in 1873, and put thirty acres of the new land, sod broke in 1872, into wheat and went to work with a hurrah in 1874 to make a God-awful crop. Everything come a booming, and I thought I had the world in a sling. Corn, oats, potatoes and wheat just got up and laughed; they grew so fine.

Thought I never saw such a country for things to grow. Worked all the week, and used to set on the fence Sunday and calculate how rich I'd be. Went out one fine sunny morning about the first of June, and thought, by jiminy, the whole ground was a moving. Ten million hoppers to the square yard—all chawin' away as if the country belonged to 'em. Saturday morning they come into my farm from a ridge just south o' me—Sunday noon there wasn't a green thing where the corn, cane and potatoes had been. Job's luck wasn't a circumstance. My corn lot looked as if forty bands of wild Arabs had fell onto it. Not a smidgeon left—just bodaciously chawed up and spit out.

"Well, of course, I had the dumps. But I rallied. 'All right,' says I; 'got wheat and tobacco left anyhow.' Professor P—— said they wouldn't eat tobacco; but he's a fraud, sir—a barefaced fraud. The hoppers just went up on a ridge north of me and shed their second coats, and then come back on the tobacco. They eat every leaf clean to the ground, then dug up the roots and set on the fence and cussed every man that come along, for a chaw. About that time they got wings, and sudden as could be rose in the air and went off north a whirlin', like a shower o' white and yellow paper bits. 'All right,' says I; 'they've left my wheat anyhow.' Singular enough they didn't touch it; it was on t'other side the place, and out o' their track. Well, I rallied again, and counted on six hundred bushels o' wheat—and wheat's the money crop in this country. About June the middle, I noticed all at once that my wheat looked kind o' sick. Come to examine, sir, it was completely lined with a little, miserable, black and yellow, nasty-smelling bug. I took some to a man 'at had been here ten years. 'Neighbor,' says he, 'you're a goner; them's chintz-bugs, and every head o' that wheat that an't cut, 'll be et up in forty-eight hours.' Well, it was Sunday morning, and the wheat nothing like ripe; but it was a chance, and I got onto my reaper and banged down every hoot of it before Monday night. It cured in the sun and the bugs left it, and out o' the lot I got just a hunred and forty bushels o' shrunk-up stuff. It was a hundred and forty bushels more than any o' my neighbors got. You bet there was improved farms for sale in that neighborhood. My sheep had done well, and that was all I was ahead. Taking it by and large, the only sure crop is sheep."[73]

A young farmer near Newkirk, Oklahoma, kept a diary during the years 1889 and 1890. Here was a sampling of March:

"*Friday 8th* Built privy fixed stable helped Mr. Emmert haul in two loads of hay, etc.

"*Saturday 9th* Hauled out 3 loads of manure raised tool shed and put under a better foundation. Took out 2 pits of potatoes.

"*Monday 11th* Worked on the road hauling rock all day. Cool winds but pleasant.

"*Tuesday 12th* Went to town with Mr. Sager. Plowed the garden in the afternoon.

Round Pond, Oklahoma, January, 1894.

Photographs, by Mr. and Mrs. Robert Kennett. National Archives, Washington, D.C.

"*Wednesday 13th*   Sowed and plowed under oats on Watt place.

"*Thursday 14th*   Finished sowing and harrowing the 6 acre field on the Watt place.

"*Friday 15th*   Plowed patch by the house and sowed oats on it. Made garden and planted early potatoes.

"*Saturday 16*   Sowed a load of oats on the north of the wheat field by the house and the 3 acre sod field."[74]

Of course, sometimes the laborious cycle was interrupted by the vagaries of the weather or the pleasures of the hunt:

"*Tuesday January 7, 1890*   Rained in the night and froze to the weeds and bushes broke lots of trees down everything is covered with ice.

"*Wednesday 8 [January, 1890]*   Broke weeds on wheat stubble west of the stable and went Rabbit hunting Mr. Emmert and I shot 38 before dinner."

Or the excitements of music:

"*Thursday January 16, 1890*   Done odd jobs played for a party at Marshalls that night. Took second prize away."[75]

Often, like any soap opera, that simulacrum of ordinary life, the drama of illness, broke the monotony:

"*July 23*   Jenny taken sick in the morning spent the day taking care of her and the baby. At night she had 7 convulsions from 9 to 11:30 p.m. The doctor here after the 4th one she rested quite easy all the rest of the night.

"*Wednesday July 24*   Jenny is not in her right mind today but is resting easy about 7 p.m. she seems to commence to know people rested well all night.

Rural family, Tifton, Georgia, January, 1909.

Photograph by Lewis Hine. Library of Congress

"*Thursday* [*July*] 25   Jenny's mind is better today she knows every-thing and has good appetite sleeps well.

"*Friday* [*July*] 26   Plowed most of the day. Jenny gaining slowly.

"*Saturday* [*July*] 27   Plowed most of the day Jenny gaining.

"*Thursday August* 1   Plowed and done odd jobs made cellar door etc. Jenny sat up for the first time."[76]

But what were the wages of his labor? They varied a great deal, but it is difficult to find an account which proved the farmer rich. Len Carroll, for example, took a hog to market on December 4, 1889, which he sold to a packing plant at $3.10 per hundred. The hog weighed 380 pounds, so his sale gave him $11.78 in cash. It's very difficult to discover what percentage of this price was profit. For one thing, how does one reckon the cost of the farmer's labor? And here are some financial details from Iowa: "A farmer sold me good butter at four pounds for twenty-five cents; seed oats cost me twelve and one-half cents per bushel which was two and one-half cents above the market price; I purchased two two-year-old heifers nearly ready to freshen for $8 apiece."[77]

And this was wartime, 1862:

". . . The condition of the farmers was most unfortunate: although in the midst of plenty they were really very poor. Little hamlets were strung over those fertile prairies along the railway like tiny beads on a string. The village was usually on one side of the track and corn cribs without number on the other side. You might suppose that I would glory in those ample granaries filled to overflowing with the golden harvest, the result of making a thousand bushels of corn grow where only one buffalo grew before; but did you ever realize what it means to a farmer to sell a bushel—70 to 75 pounds—of corn in the ear for ten cents? Imagine him if you can, housed in a little, poorly-built pre-emption shanty, eight or more miles from a railway station on a treeless prairie and far from neighbors; and in a climate windy and cold for six months in the year; having always more corn in the field than he can husk and no money with which to purchase the most indispensable things or to employ help to gather in the fall harvest! Imagine, I say, such a farmer, out in the field by sunrise some frosty morning, with a span of horses and wagon, husking a load of corn, which means thirty bushels, and which would keep him at work all of the short autumn day. The next day he must take the corn to one of those long fence-board cribs at the station, ranged parallel with the railroad track—another day's work! And for all this labor of man and team—growing, harvesting and delivery—he received only three paper dollars!

"With these he crossed over to the store and traded the value of thirty bushels of corn for clothing for his wife and children and a few indispensable groceries. Is it any wonder that on his return home, after caring for the livestock and milking the cow before he seated himself at the family board—groaning with plenty—he spitefully threw a liberal supply of corn on the fire and said: 'Damn you, burn. You ain't worth anything at the station or anywhere else, so I'll keep warm until I enlist and then I suppose the Johnnies will make it warm enough for me without burning corn!' "[78]

Net income of farmers in the nineteenth century is difficult to disentangle, for the data are unreliable for any period before 1910. In that year, federal statistics show that the average farm family earned $652, a cash income which remained monotonously constant till the third year of World War I—1917—when it doubled to $1,282, which was scarcely a bonanza. And farm income was to drop to $340 per family per year in 1932.

Yet living on a farm had special advantages that are impossible to reduce to figures. The hours, of course, are dawn to sunset. But one can see the sun rise through the apple trees and set over the tight rows of corn in tassel. On a farm, autumn has flames in leaves and fire. Even in winter, there are horizons, however bare, that change subtly within any hour's walk. And earth under the leather of a farmer's shoes is a lot more complex than the uniform concrete of streets and factories. Unique to the farmer is the taste of new corn, hulled and boiled within the half hour; or the sharp, not quite ripe blackberries from the bramble that conceals and protects the rabbit's or the woodchuck's refuge in the heap of dislodged stones in the center of the plowed field. And then there is that most underground sense of all our images and kinesthesias, the sensation of odor: new, wet lilac or honeysuckle, cut hay or sileage, and distant fires of wood or straw; or even the animal pungence of manure steaming outside the barn door on a frosty day; and the scentless scent of winter, differing subtly according to weather. It is indeed the shift of the weather that dramatizes the laborious circle of the farmer's life, or of his children or his wife.

Yet beyond this unwritten beauty of change, there remains the real monotony of labor, recorded in farmers' diaries like marks on a prisoner's wall:

"*April 19, 1883* Worked down home all day at the stable.

"*20th* Sunday cold

"*21st* Worked on the stable.

"*22nd* Worked on the stable.

"*23rd* Went to Rushville and . . . worked on the stable.

"*24th* Stormed all day and worked on the stable

"*25th* Worked on the stable . . .

"*26th* Worked on the stable

"*May 13, 1884* Finished sowing barley today cleared manure in the forenoon lost one lamb today just one

"*14th* Cleared manure all day a nice day all day Cleared 42 loads today

"*15th* Cleared manure all day rained part of the day ground very wet and getting wetter some manure spred

"*16th* Cleared manure all day and finished clearing manure a better day today but very cold for the time of the year no corn planted yet

"*17* Plowed for corn today for the first [time] and finished the old barn yard and spred manure"[79]

Why do it? Many years ago, in the despondent 1930s, a half-grown boy

Three small-town women, Massilon, Ohio, _ca._ 1900.
Photograph by Belle Johnson. Massilon Museum, Massilon, Ohio

asked his father, somewhat irritably, why he kept his farm, loaded as it was with mortgages on the timber and the stone house and the cows and the very barn. The father did not answer that day, but took his son an hour before sunrise to the covered spring where last night's milk sat cooling in old-fashioned galvanized cans. The farmer wrested off the lid, and with a tin cup on a long handle, dipped and lifted up and drank a full pint of the top milk, heavy with cream. The farmer told his son that this nutriment is what kept him a man. The coming sunrise now was blood red in the sky, and so was the reflection in the cool of the spring, and on the inner, moist sides of the shed. So to the boy, anyway, it was pure, ethereal blood that his father lifted and drank every morning on his farm.

But the life of the outdoor male was made possible, in turn, by the labor of the women in his household:

". . . my husband has the stronger will; he is innocent of book learning, is a natural hustler who believes that the only way to make an honest living lies in digging it out of the ground, so to speak, and being a farmer, he finds plenty of digging to do; he has an inherited tendency to be miserly, loves money for its own sake rather than for its purchasing power, and when he has it in his possession he is loath to part with it, even for the most necessary articles, and prefers to eschew hired help in every possible instance that what he does make may be his very own.

"No man can run a farm without some one to help him, and in this case I have always been called upon and expected to help do anything that a man would be expected to do; I began this when we were first married, when there were few household duties and no reasonable excuse for refusing to help.

"I was reared on a farm, was healthy and strong, was ambitious, and the work was not disagreeable, and having no children for the first six years of married life, the habit of going whenever asked to became firmly fixed, and he had no thought of hiring a man to help him, since I could do anything for which he needed help . . .

"All the season, from the coming in of the first fruits until the making of mincemeat at Christmas time, I put up canned goods for future use; gather in many bushels of field beans and the other crops usually raised on the farm; make sour-kraut [*sic*], ketchup, pickles, etc . . .

"Any bright morning in the latter part of May I am out of bed at four o'clock; next, after I have dressed and combed my hair, I start a fire in the kitchen stove, and while the stove is getting hot I go to my flower garden and gather a choice, half-blown rose and a spray of bride's wreath, and arrange them in my hair, and sweep the floors and then cook breakfast.

"While the other members of the family are eating breakfast I strain away the morning's milk (for my husband milks the cows while I get breakfast), and fill my husband's dinner pail, for he will go to work on our other farm for the day.

"By this time it is half-past five o'clock, my husband is gone to his work, and the stock loudly pleading to be turned into the pastures. The younger cattle, a half-dozen steers, are left in the pasture at night, and I now drive the two cows a half-quarter mile and turn them in with the others, come back, and then there's a horse in the barn that belongs in a field where there is no water, which I take to a spring quite a distance from the barn; bring it back and turn it into a field with the sheep, a dozen in number, which are housed at night.

"The young calves are then turned out into the warm sunshine, and the stock hogs, which are kept in a pen, are clamoring for feed, and I carry a pailful of swill to them, and hasten to the house and turn out the chickens and put out feed and water for them, and it is, perhaps, 6.30 a.m.

"I have not eaten breakfast yet, but that can wait; I make the beds next and straighten things up in the living room, for I dislike to have the early morning caller find my house topsy-turvy. When this is done I go to the kitchen, which also serves as a dining-room, and uncover the table, and take a mouthful of food occasionally as I pass to and fro at my work until my appetite is appeased.

"By the time the work is done in the kitchen it is about 7.15 a.m., and the cool morning hours have flown, and no hoeing done in the garden yet, and the children's toilet has to be attended to and churning has to be done.

"Finally the children are washed and churning done, and it is eight o'clock, and the sun getting hot, but no matter, weeds die quickly when cut down in the heat of the day, and I use the hoe to a good advantage until the dinner hour, which is 11.30 a.m. We come in, and I comb my hair, and put fresh flowers in it, and eat a cold dinner, put out feed and water for the chickens; set a hen, perhaps, sweep the floors again; sit down and rest, and read a few moments, and it is nearly one o'clock, and I sweep the door yard while I am waiting for the clock to strike the hour.

"I make and sow a flower bed, dig around some shrubbery, and go back to the garden to hoe until time to do the chores at night, but ere long some hogs come up to the back gate, through the wheat field, and when I go to see what is wrong I find that the cows have torn the fence down, and they, too, are in the wheat field.

"With much difficulty I get them back into their own domain and repair the fence. I hoe in the garden till four o'clock; then I go into the house and get supper, and prepare something for the dinner pail to-morrow; when supper is all ready it is set aside, and I pull a few hundred plants of tomato, sweet potato or cabbage for transplanting, set them in a cool, moist place where they will not wilt, and I then go after the horse, water him, and put him in the barn; call the sheep and house them, and go after the cows and milk them, feed the hogs, put down hay for three horses, and put oats and corn in their troughs, and set those plants and come in and fasten up the chickens, and it is dark. By this time it is 8 o'clock p.m.; my husband has come home, and we are eating supper; when we are through eating I make the beds ready, and the children and their father go to bed, and I wash the dishes and get things in shape to get breakfast quickly next morning.

"It is now about 9 o'clock p.m., and after a short prayer I retire for the night."[80]

The duties on a farm, particularly for a woman, are multiple, and not so much monotonous as infinite; there is simply no end to these chores. From an economic point of view, the farm women were as unpaid as any slave, though of course they were given board, lodging, and, if they were young enough, the mixed pleasures of family and sex.

Thus we survey, from the bottom, the slope of the great steel pyramid of industrialized America. We glimpse at the top the great banking families, manipulators not so much of their own money, as of the accumulated dollars of several past generations: the profits of the old whaling companies and the early textile mills of New England; personal trusts and inherited real estate; and money that is even older—foreign capital from England and France. Below this powerful apex were the doers, the pushers, the obsessed managers, men like Benjamin Franklin Jones, less technocrats in the modern sense than inspired accountants who expanded a couple of smelters into an industrial complex.

Such men, powerful egotists, stood in turn on a numerous base of puddlers and millmen and plain laborers. And these subsisted on the textile workers and the shoemakers and, most especially, on the great majority of American farmers, growing their wheat and barley and oats and pigs and chickens at the cost of ill-paid and continuous labor. And in turn, these fathers, these husbands, these farmers were able to work and eat because at the very bottom of the pyramid was the great mass of country women—and their children. They labored all day and evening, not in social villages like their mothers or grandmothers in Europe, but in loneliness on newly broken farms, in the crude kitchen or the vegetable garden or the wash house:

"21st   Riley went to Mill   I washed

"22nd   I ironed   Darling gathere Apples   Riley James Sturt & Jenia Dug Potatoes   it is cold the wind blows & snowing

"23rd Saturday October 1869   Riley & James Sturt finished Diging Potatoes   cold all day   thawed in the sunshine

Apple pickers, Berkeley County, West Virginia.
Photograph by Smith Brothers, October, 1910. Library of Congress

"24th   cool wind   Sunday   Julias Baby was born   Darling & I went to see it   called to see Mr Wadley

"25th Monday   they finished sowing Wheat   I put up the onions   David took Dinner with us   Darling Covered the Apples   pleasant weather

"26th Tues   Riley Started to see his Father with James Sturt   Sallie Started home   Nancy went to see Julia   Darling gathered some Apples put up some Cabbage & several other Jobs   I swept & churned & knit a little   Jenia finished brushing in the wheat

"27th Wed   Hariet Calison & Sarah Dickerson come to get Nancy to help them sew on their Dresses   Nancy Bought one Table Cloth for 1 Dollar of a Pedler"[81]

Unpaid, overworked, they relied for the rewards of love on the kindness of the uneasy workworn caste next above them—their own men.

7

A Storm of Strangers

IN THE CENTURY between 1820 and 1920, the greatest movement of the human species in all of history took place, as 33.5 million people abandoned one continent for another. Of this unique migration, only 5 million came before 1860, so that in the three short generations upon which the present book discourses—that extended Sunday between wars from 1860 to 1920—the transplantation of men, women, and children totaled 28.5 million.[1]

Yet its effects were less than one might imagine. In 1830, only about 1 per cent of our population were immigrants. It rose to 4 per cent in 1840, and 5 per cent in 1850. Except for minor fluctuations, it stayed at that level until 1910. Even in that great tidal year, it was only 10 per cent, and by 1920, only half of that. So the percentage of foreign-born in the total population of the United States was never more than 10 percent, and rarely even that.

If we make another comparison, and match the numbers of all foreign-born—not only immigrants of that particular decade—as a percentage of America's total population, we see to our astonishment that, in 1850 the foreigners were only 5 per cent of the people, a figure which rose to 7 per cent in 1860, and the figure never rose above that by any more than a fraction. So it would appear that the immigration was only a small part of American life. That is true—except in the cities. For example, Boston in 1830 had 5.6 per cent foreign-born, but by 1855, only 61 per cent were native. In my own hometown, a small industrial city in New Jersey, one-quarter of the population in 1880 was foreign-born. By 1910, the proportion was 52 per cent.[2]

But if we consider mere numbers and remove the cities as exceptions, particularly the eastern ones, the transfusion of foreign life into American culture was never all that great. Still, the influx into the dense and influential urban centers was enough to be powerful and stimulating and even shocking, but in a psychological and economic sense, with the two intertwined as they always are. However, the domination, through their descendants, of the original, pre-1820 Americans is arithmetically incontrovertible. And here is the real reason, not very profound but still true, that America has preserved its uniformity. Of course there has been change, and seismic change, too, but on a scale of decades, it affected the first Americans and foreign-born Americans simultaneously, thus uniformly.

One of the pleasures of history is that it appears to preface probable effects with reasonable causes. For example, it's probably a fact that most Americans desired equality at the same time as they desired money, and that money was the very commodity which guaranteed the absence of equality. Could the source of this contradiction have been the leveling Protestantism of heretical northern Europe?

This much is true: Well before the nineteenth century, and certainly before the Civil War, the great majority of immigrants were from this European region—from England, Scotland, Wales, and from Scandinavian and northern and therefore Lutheran Germany. But unanimity they had not. Each, at first, despised the national origin of the other. Southerners during the Civil War, proud of their English grandfathers, thought everyone else was a nasty foreigner: "Mrs. Browne heard a man say, at the Congaree House: "We are breaking our heads against a stone wall. We are bound to be conquered. We cannot keep it up much longer against so powerful a nation as the United States of America. Crowds of Irish, Dutch and Scotch are pouring in to swell their armies. They are promised our possessions, and they believe that will get them.' "[3] She must not be considered mean and exceptional. For some maddening and unreasonable reason, the integrity of one's own group still seems to demand an uneasy contempt for all the others.

We now think of immigration as a great storm of untidy, if not downright dirty strangers, speaking Yiddish or Sicilian or Polish or some other gibberish that ought to be got rid of as soon as possible. And we still believe that the immigration from the British Isles was virtually over by the end of the eighteenth century. The figures, however, are less dogmatic and more confusing. British immigrants numbered 280,000 in the decade 1820–30. Then they tripled, and tripled again, in the next three decades. In 1860–70, the British immigration numbered 607,000. In the next decade, there were less—548,000—but from 1880–89, the number was only 200,000 short of a million. Even in 1910–20, 328,000 English came to America.[4] So of the 34 million immigrants to America in the century 1820–1920, almost 4 million spoke English and were, by a vast majority, Protestant.

The churches were not merely a periodic point of contact with one's particular God, but a social center that renewed every week one's communion with that equally intuitive force—the people of one's own language and background. The English and Scotch and Welsh of the nineteenth century, along with the Irish Presbyterians of Ulster, formed a continuity of taste and policy and value and custom with those of the previous century.

But one should not confuse a common culture with a common level of income. By the year of the Civil War, much of the English stock, particularly in the backward rural areas in New York and New Jersey as well as Appalachia, had little left but their pride. One must turn to the extraordinary diary of Mary Chestnut, herself of English stock, to get an accurate picture of these people in what easily might have been her third or fourth cousins:

"Today H. Lang told me that poor Sandhill Milly Trimlin was dead; that as a witch she had been denied Christian burial. Three times she was buried in consecrated ground at different church yards, and three times she was dug up by a superstitious horde and put out of their holy ground. Where her poor old ill-used bones are lying now I do not know. I hope her soul is faring better than her body. She was a good, kindly creature. Everybody gave Milly a helping hand. She was a perfect specimen of the Sandhill tackey race, sometimes called country crackers. Her skin was yellow and leathery, and even the whites of her eyes were bilious in color. She was stumpy and strong and lean, hard-featured, horny-fisted. Never were people so aided in every way as these people are! Why do they remain Sandhillers, from generation to generation. Why should Milly never have bettered her condition? My grandmother lent a helping hand to her grandmother, my mother did her best for her mother, and I am sure the so-called witch could never complain of me. As long as I can remember, gangs of these Sandhill women traipsed in with baskets to be filled by charity, ready to carry away anything they could get. They were treated as friends and neighbours, not as beggars. They were asked in, asked to take seats by the fire; and there they sat for hours, stony-eyed, silent, wearying out human endurance and politeness. Their husbands and sons, whom we never saw, were citizens and voters! When patience was at its last ebb, they would open their mouths and loudly demand whatever they had come to seek.

"One, called Judy Bradley, a one-eyed virago who also played the fiddle at all of the Sandhill dances and fandangoes, made a deep impression on my youthful mind. Her list of wants on one visit was rather long, and my grandmother grew restive and actually hesitated. Judy demanded: 'Woman, do you mean to let me starve?' My grandmother then attempted a meek lecture as to the duty of earning one's bread. Judy squared her arms akimbo and answered: 'And pray, who made you a Judge and the criterion of the world. Lord, Lord, if I had er knowed I had ter stand all this jaw, I wouldn't a took your old things.' But she did take them, and came again and again.

"There are Sandhillers born, and Sandhillers who have fallen to that estate. Old Mrs. Simons, now; Mr. Chesnut says she was a lady once. They are very good to her. She pays no rent for her house and the fields around it. She knits gloves, which are always bought for her sake. She has many children, all grown and gone, only one son left and he is a cripple. Once a year he has a drive in a carriage. Some uneasy candidate is sure to drive by there and haul the lame man to the polls. Everybody remembers that Mrs. Simons has seen better days. In coming from Society Hill once, Sally had Mrs. Simons's house pointed out to her. She stopped the carriage, got out and knocked at the door. All was silent as death. The old creature was locked in and barricaded, but after a parley she opened her door. When she saw it was Sally, she fell upon her neck and wept aloud. 'Why honey, to think you've come to see me.' I asked Sally: 'How did it all look there?' 'Sad and sorrowful, empty, clean, faded, worn out, just as poverty stricken and old as Mrs. Simons looks in that old shawl and bonnet of hers.'

"My mother had a protégée who had also fallen from a higher station. She was once a handsome young girl, of good family. A dashing young doctor in a gig fascinated her. He was to marry her and did not. She was ruined, and her severe parents turned her out of doors. Then began her Sandhill life. She lived alone with her child for awhile, and then she lived with a Sandhill man. She always spoke of him as 'He.' She came always with a half dozen daughters, all alike, gaunt, pale, freckled, white hair or sandy; and they sat in their oak-split bonnets all in a row. They all clutched bags and glared at us, but never a word spoke they. The eldest girl was named for my mother. The others we thought had no fixed names, but they were called Betsey, Sally, Charlotte, Amelia, according as the people happened to be present whose namesakes she claimed them to be.

"One day she drew my mother to the window. We saw her clutch my mother's arm and say something; then they shook hands, and tears were in the eyes of both of them. Afterwards my mother said to us: 'Did you hear her? She gripped me and said: "Woman! He has married me!" Neither of us said another word, but Fanny knew I felt for her.'

"At another time, these old friends met at church, a big meeting with more politics than religion in the wind. My mother proposed to take Fanny home in her carriage. 'No, no! Never mind me. I'm done in this world. Take your namesake. Let 'em all see my girl setting by you in your carriage.' "[5]

2

The accumulated capital of this country, which was to make possible the early foundation of the great industries built within the last two generations of the nineteenth century and the first of the twentieth, was money and property earned and accumulated by this Anglo-Saxon majority. It came from the whaling and maritime trade of the Eastern ports, from the textile mills of New England, and the slave farms of the South. But it is a corollary of the concentration of wealth that some are quite rich, while some larger number are merely prosperous, and the greatest number, the seamen and the sawyers and the weavers, remain poor. So in the first two-thirds of the nineteenth century the Anglos continued to have both the money and the power, industrial and political, in land and in railroads, power which was shaken but not moved by the storms of immigration. We must nevertheless reckon that most of the Anglos were, and remain, middling poor. Or they sank to that level in the whirlpools of economic change.

Here was a letter from one Anglo to another, a mill-girl to her friend Harriet Harrison Robinson:

Dear Harriet,

With a feeling which you can better imagine than I can describe do I announce to you the horrible tidings that I am once *more a factory girl!* Yes; once more a factory girl, seated in the short attic of a Lowell boarding house with a half dozen of girls seated around me talking and reading and myself in the midst, trying to write to you, with the thoughts of so many different persons flying around me that I can hardly tell which are my own . . . I am not so homesick as I was a fortnight ago and just begin to feel more resigned to my fate. I have been here four weeks but have not had to work very hard for there are six girls of us and we have fine times doing nothing. I should like to see you in Lowell once more but cannot wish you to exchange your pleasant home in the country for a factory life in the 'great city of spindles.' . . .

I almost envy your happy Sundays at home. A feeling of loneliness comes over me when I think of *my home*, now far away, you remember perhaps how I used to tell you I spent my hours in the mill in imagining myself sick and that the rattle of machinery was the rumbling of my charriot wheels but not alas that happy Act has fled from me and my mind no longer takes such airy and visionary flights for the wings of my imagination have folded themselves to rest; in vain do I try to soar in fancy and imagination above the dull reality around me but beyond the roof of the factory I cannot rise. . .[6]

In 1845, the Massachusetts State Legislature began an investigation of how these girls lived and worked, and in particular, whether a maximum ten-hour day should be enforced by law. The testimony of a weaver stated: "In the summer season, the work is commenced at five o'clock, A.M., and continued until seven o'clock P.M. The air in the room she considered not to be wholesome . . . about 130 females, 11 men and 12 children [between the ages of 11 and 14] work in the room with her . . . The children work but 9 months out of 12. The other three months they must attend school."[7]

The factory shoemaker was no better off:

" 'There is no class of mechanics in New York who average so great an amount of work for so little money as the journeymen shoemakers,' stated an article in the *New York Daily Tribune* in 1845. The number of journeymen out of employment is also large . . . There are hundreds of them in the city constantly wandering from shop to shop in search of work, while many of them have families in a state of absolute want . . . We have been in more than fifty cellars in different parts of the city, each inhabited by a shoemaker and his family.

"The floor is made of rough plank laid loosely down, the ceiling is not quite so high as a tall man. The walls are dark and damp, and a wide, desolate fireplace yawns in the center to the right of the entrance. There is no outlet back and of course no yard privileges of any kind. The miserable room is lighted only by a shallow sash, partly projecting above the surface of the ground and by the little light that struggles down the steep and rotting stairs.

"In this . . . often live the man with his work-bench, his wife and five or six children of all ages, and perhaps a palsied grandfather or grandmother and often both. In one corner is a squalid bed and the room elsewhere is occupied by the work-bench, a cradle made from a dry-goods box, two or three broken, seatless chairs, a stew-pan and a kettle."[8]

To complete the landscape of the Anglo laboring community, one must turn to the work of that extraordinary historian, Herbert Gutman, who has the rare gift for being as honest in his theory as in his particulars. We must be grateful for his apt discovery of a group of letters from Scots immigrants published in the weekly *Glasgow Sentinel*. They are painful in their specificity and give us a disturbing sense—rooted as most of us are—of what it was like to change countries, even among those of the same language and the same religion.

"We sailed from the Broomielaw on the 27th day of August, 1869, in the good ship Europa, commanded by Captain M'Donald, in company with 416 other passengers. . . . Scotland was disappearing from our view; again our thoughts are directed to scenes of our old haunts and pleasant associations, to the many true friends we have left behind us, to our dear wives and children who are mourning and sorrowful at our parting. Twelve o'clock on Saturday the Irish coast is coming in view, the weather is pretty stormy, the sea is running high, and sickness is beginning to get pretty general among the passengers. . . . My companion William. . . . in the very height of the storm. . . . was hard making love to a fine young girl. All at once she got frightened, and all William could do she would not be consoled. . . . One old woman, who was sure we were going down, kept shouting as loud as she could—'Holy J——s, is there not a man among you will go and tell the captain to make the ship stop pitching!' Another called out, 'Biddy, agra, light a candle, for God's sake, and let us see where we are going, any way.'

"Saturday, September 11.—Arrived in Boston. I am staying with my brother-in-law, and very kindly streeted indeed. . . . I have made up my mind to go to the mining districts; the wage there is better. It is money I want; if I can get it for the earning honestly I will have it . . .

"Taking all things into consideration, I must say that I like the country well. . . . The work has not begun to run steady yet. Some weeks you may get good work, and the next you may get hardly anything. . . . We have a dollar and 25 cents per ton for working it, and five cents per ton for every fifty yards you draw it after you leave your own platform. . . . On the days we were working we started at seven o'clock in the morning. We take breakfast before we leave home. I would like to see you sitting down before six in the morning to eat potatoes, beef, bread and butter, pies, and all kinds of fancy meats. . . .

"You will see from what I said that their is neither 8 hours nor 10 hours a-day here for the miner. All the day men, above and below, work 10 hours. The truth is, John, when the work is brisk every miner in the place works as long and as hard as he can—digging and drawing coals all day. . . . but this only when the work is running brisk 5 or 6 months in the winter; and if you be fortunate. . . . you can make over 100 dollars a-month; and 40 dollars, I am informed, can keep a very large family. Then, in the summer time they go half-time; they average about 60 dollars per month . . . In Maryland they work from 6 to 6, that is, when the work is running brisk (every place has a brisk and a slack time, as a rule). . . . In Pennsylvania it is all big coals; they work from 7 till 4; and in some places till 5, and in others till 6; and from what I have learned the wage is nearly the same, go where you like. . . .

"My dear sir, do not form a bad opinion of the country from what I have said about the work; wait till I let you know how they live and get rich. I assure you everybody lives well."[9]

The energy and optimism of the man shines through in every phrase. Whatever the statistics, it was this force, this attitude, that made one powerful strand of American character. For it was not special to M'Lachlan, who wrote the letter above. We can read it again here, in William Latta's letter to his friend Campbell in Glasgow:

"To own a house and lot is the ambition of the American workman, which may be done, if employed, with the savings of three or four years; but in the matter of constant employment, I think there is less of it than at home, and fully as difficult to get. That in spite of this, the working men are better is a fact, arising I imagine from the many business openings that present themselves. After a little capital has been scraped together, they take themselves off, but their places are as readily filled by "greenhorns," from the old country. Without it is some one that has made a break down of some independent move, or the loafer who won't work half his time, a man is scarcely to be met with who was wrought for wages more than nine or ten years . . . Forwardness is 'cheek'; 'cuteness' is a quality far more highly valued than independence. It will get more money—a thing that nobody despises. But I think fully as true of the people here as anywhere else. It is the idol they all seem willing to fall down and worship. I have heard the question put and answered at home—'What would the working man do with a vote if he had it? Of course, sell it!'. . . .

"I have now had some experience in housekeeping, and could safely vouch that, with the strictest economy, not less than 10 or 12 dollars will suffice to keep the household machine running per week—of course including rent and all other *et ceteras*. The average pay for tradesmen in the iron trades is 3 dollars per day, labourers about 1 dollar 75 cents. Can you imagine how much he can save out of this? They generally get hold of a lot and house of their own, and so save the rent—an expensive item; and the rise in value in a few years amounts to a considerable sum. Young men can board for about 5 dollars per week, and they, if anything well employed, can get along first rate. I have not made up my mind how long we may stay; perhaps we may stumble in upon you some day after we get rich, as we are likely to do soon . . ."[10]

And here was the same man commenting on the American system of values, or to be more precise, value: "To be successful, or rather to be rich, is the sure passport to influence, respect, and all the other things of that sort, to an extent you have no conception of. At home, amid the varied ways of getting dubbed right honourable, the value of each is relatively lessened. We have no other way here save the dollar . . ."[11]

These Scots workmen were sought and welcomed in America, because they already had skills that were a necessity to an economy in violent growth. Not only were they experienced miners, especially needed in the bituminous fields, but they were skilled in the mining and working of iron ores and the subsidiary metals like silver, copper, lead, and tin. They became the foremen and the skilled operatives of the steel-making furnaces and the rolling mills, the technicians of the complex processes and machines of the textile mills. They were easily cast in the American drama. And it was their special tragedy that as machines became more mechanical, so to speak, their skills were worth less and less. Brute semi-skilled labor became the primary need of the American machine as the century rolled to its tremendous close.

The Anglos—not the entrepreneurs like B. F. Jones or the professional doctors or preachers, but the skilled craftsmen—were shunted aside for the millions of non-English-speaking (with the grand exception of the Irish), cheap, young, unskilled, ex-peasant laborers—who were also, as it happened, non-Protestant. Did the American value system, based on money as the quantification of a man, therefore change? It did not. It has not.

3

In reading or listening to personal accounts by immigrants themselves, one is overwhelmed by a rush of envious admiration. These were very special people. Out of a European village only a few families would emigrate. And of these, only the youngest and strongest ever had the courage to leave. To abandon the landscape known to the eyes since childhood, never to see again the roads and paths and shortcuts that were programmed into one's muscles, to sever the invisible blood ties of parent and sibling; then to undertake a voyage of anywhere from three to five thousand miles pent up in the steerage of a rocking ship, imprisoned in a crowd of strangers; to feel, as the security of one's daily habits were altered or forgotten, the unacknowledged fright of the unconscious at all these changes; and then to arrive at last in another world which is crowded, indifferent, and for millions of immigrants, speaking another and unknown language, with alien names and signs incomprehensible—what fierce and contemptuous courage it took! The very process of emigration from one habitat and immigration to another was a kind of sieve that left behind the timid, the old, the marginally weary or ill, or those too dependent on daily touching and love. And it let through the young, the bold, the vigorous, those who had, like the United States, already declared their independence. By choice rather than inheritance, those who came across the sea were already a special breed.

This was just as true of the German immigrants as of any other. They had the same faculties of health, of furious survival, and of belief in oneself. To read their accounts is to find immodest proof of these qualities:

"I was born in Lindau . . . With my ninth year I acquired the art of swimming and diving, through the assistance of my uncle, who was an expert, and I was called one of the best swimmers and divers of my age in the country."[12]

At fourteen this young man was apprenticed to a coppersmith, and at seventeen set out to conquer the world. He was sold a fake diamond ring by a couple of sharpies, but "resolved . . . to find some other fool to sell it to . . ." He slept in a Hungarian peasant's hut, and in the copper region of the Carpathian Mountains got a graphic lesson on the reasons why Europeans emigrated. "As there was only one room in the house, and only one bed in the room under which the two pigs found a resting place, I was wondering

Immigrants on steerage deck of "S. S. Pennland," 1893.

Photograph by Percy Byron. The Byron Collection, Museum of the City of New York

where all of them would find sleeping room. The light was soon put out, and I saw that three of them were lying on the bed, while another made her bed on the table, and the other made her bed on the other bench. Thus, we all slept peaceably in one room . . . I found afterwards during my travels in Hungary, that their poor people are the most hospitable in the world. Money they have not to give you, but they will share with you what they have."[13]

He accepted a ride on a four-horse wagon, but when he could not pay, two men assaulted him. He fought them off with a cane and a knife, but they made off with his pipe; he was then about eighteen. He traveled in the company of two feather dealers, escaped an army recruiting officer, ate and drank and slept at a Gypsy wedding.

He noted that ". . . the working people, miners and farmer, were mostly serfs, they had to work for their masters three days of the week, just for their board, the other three days, they could hire out to do whatever they could find, and they would have to support themselves and families on these scanty wages.

"One day I was informed that three serfs, who had been caught stealing, were to be whipped at the nobleman's house. One of the men was to receive six lashes, one twelve, and the third, a young and stout man, was to receive twenty-five.

"The Hyduck, or private police, was on hand with a half dozen hazel sticks, and the nobleman stood behind the Hyduk [sic] with stick in his hand, for the purpose, I was told, if the Hyduck did not hit hard, he would himself be hit by the nobleman. So the first one, an old man of perhaps sixty years, was made to lie down on a bench, and two assistants, one at the head, and the other at the feet, held him down while the hyduk [sic] gave him the six lashes.

"After he had received them he got up on his feet and commenced shaking as with a chill, and the owner sent him to the kitchen to get a warm drink. Then the next man had to lie down on the bench, and he received his twelve lashes. When he was told to get up,—he could not stand on his legs, but fell over the bench, and was found dead. Fright seemed to have killed him, but this did not seem to disturb the nobleman in the least, and the rest of the programme was carried out by giving the last one twenty-five lashes. He was a young man and took his punishment very coolly. When he arose from the bench the blood was streaming from his wounds, and he calmly stepped up to the nobleman and asked him for a pipe of tobacco, which was given him, and he was told to go. That ended the tragedy, as they had no prisons in that country. Their only method of punishment was whipping.

"One day I saw a woman punished in this way, who had stolen some vegetables from a nobleman's garden. When caught she was stripped to the waist and driven through the streets by a Hyduk [sic], who carried a bundle of switches, and a drummer marched ahead of her, while the Hyduck applied the switches to the poor woman's back."[14]

The wonder is not why some peasants left for America, but why all of them did not go. It was partly because they simply had no money to pay the passage, and for others, to leave one's family, village, and employer took an effort of the will too great to be easily summoned.

Kuner's will was inexhaustible. Restless, impatient, he heard of a good coppersmith job in Smyrna, Turkey, and decided to go there. He refused to wait out the two weeks quarantine at the border, and so, within sight of Belgrade, he started back for Germany again. As the stagecoaches were being regularly robbed, he went on foot. At a crossroad in the thickness of the central European forest, he met a nobleman turned bandit, but he had nothing worth robbing. Kuner himself was wrongly accused of stealing copper, and beat up his accuser with a hazel stick. He served time in the army, took work as a sailor on a steamer that carried goods across Lake Constance, was given temporary command of a second vessel, and piloted it to a safe harbor in a storm. He got married in spite of his parents' disapproval, not a common decision in those times. And then, his bold and independent character got him into real trouble. In the violent days of the late 1840s, he got drunk in a wine shop and expressed his liberal opinions a bit too loudly. A warrant was issued for his arrest on the charge of "revolutionary proceedings, and insult to his majesty the King of Bavaria."

He parted from his wife, and accompanied by his three brothers, took ship from Paris to New Orleans. They intended to settle in Texas, where there was already a substantial German community. But hearing that Indians were attacking and killing settlers, they all went to Memphis, Tennessee. Here he got a job collecting dead animals for a soapmaker. When he quit this lovely job to invest in a farm that included a bakery, a smithy, and a general store, the soapmaker refused to pay him what he had earned. "This made me mad, and I grabbed him and commenced to choke him. He shouted for help, and his wife came in and begged me to let go, and he paid me. The next day we took possession of the farm, and I immediately wrote home for Mother, Father, Sister, my wife and my brother's betrothed, to come over as soon as they conveniently could."[15]

He learned how to bake bread, not always successfully. When frost killed the grapes on the farm they had hoped to keep, he moved on like any native-born American, and "after a long hunt I located in the town of La Grange, Tennessee."[16] Here he got into serious trouble by killing a dog that was raiding his kitchen. It happened to be a fine hunting dog owned by Bill Eggins, a rich and powerful local, who was a descendant of a previous wave of immigration. So our hero, Kuner ". . . resolved to remove the dog and bury him elsewhere. So that night about twelve o'clock my wife and I started out with lantern and shovel, the rain falling in torrents, but we did not mind that, and I proceeded to dig up the dog, and buried him again on the back of the river, and covered the place over with brush."[17] Since the evidence could not be found, the case was dismissed. Months later, he met the great Eggins himself, and invited him to have a drink. Kuner remembered, "I then apologized to him for killing his dog, saying that I had made inquiry before shooting him to find out who was the owner, but not hearing that anyone owned him, I had concluded that he was a stray dog. Mr. Eggins said he was sorry that he had caused me so much trouble, and that he was also sorry to lose him, as he was a valuable hunting dog. "But," said he, "what did you do to the dog?" I then explained the matter to him, and he laughed and said, "You are the d——est, smartest Dutchman I ever saw.' "[18]

He moved again in the autumn, and settled in Holly Springs, Mississippi, where he set up a bakery with a capital of exactly $5.00. He was a German with fairly liberal politics, and here he was in the pre-Civil War South, in the heart of the cotton belt at that. He was called an abolitionist, lost much of his business, and moved again, this time to Iowa City. Here too, his nationality got him into trouble. "When the Fourth of July came I was requested by my German friends to give a dance and have lunch served afterward. The only difficulty I experienced in getting up this party was the musicians. The only one in town was a violin player, and he could not play German music, but the boys all knew I could play the accordion, so I finally consented to give the party. They commenced dancing about eight o'clock in the evening, and everything went along smoothly until about ten o'clock when I had to stop playing and get the lunch ready. Then the violin player commenced playing the quadrille and the Germans commenced dancing the waltz. They started a row which soon became a free for all fight, and the Americans being in the minority ran outside and the Germans followed. They tore down a fence and used it for clubs and had a regular battle, and a little later several of them returned terribly cut up, with blood all over them, and asked for something to eat and drink. I never gave any more dancing parties in Iowa City."[19]

He ran a bakery and restaurant, played in a band, went hunting for deer and mallard, joined the Odd Fellows, begot five children, lost money in real estate speculations, was elected to the city council, had business problems so severe that he sold his bakery for $700, and moved again to Marshalltown, Iowa.

"In 1868 a temperance law was passed in the state of Iowa, which was so offensive to the Germans of that place that one day they made a public demonstration, riding about the city on sleds with music and song, and carrying an effigy of one of the principal temperance leaders, which was afterwards burned. We had to pay dearly for this piece of foolishness, as we were prosecuted and fined heavily."[20]

He sold out again and invested in a St. Louis vinegar factory, sold out there too and relocated the factory in Denver, Colorado, though he had so little capital that he made deliveries in a borrowed wheelbarrow. Finally, though, his mixture of mid–nineteenth-century German and urban American was more and more successful.

"In 1873 I joined the Denver lodge #14 I.O.O.F., and also the Denver

Turn Verein. In 1877 I was elected to the school board of district #2, and served ten years without pay. In 1878 I was elected county commissioner, and re-elected to that office in 1880, serving two terms. The latter year during the selection of the court house site, I was chosen chairman of the building committee, and after the completion of the building, I was presented with a diploma, of which I may well be proud. It was a token of ability, integrity, and honesty, shown during my term of office, and at the end of my last term I was presented with a fine gold headed cane."[21]

Hunting was part of both cultures but in the lower classes it had been for food—poaching. In America, it was, like the sport of a nobleman, hunting for fun: "I also accompanied a hunting party to the San Luis Valley, where twenty of us killed eleven hundred jack rabbits in two days . . ."[22]

He sold his interests in the Kuner Pickle Company and retired to travel to the 1893 World's Fair and Yellowstone Park. He had returned to his homeland twice in the preceding decades, a sufficient sign in itself of his advancing age and prosperity. And his memories, recorded in 1897, were transcribed by his great-great-granddaughter, Margaret McDowd Lieser, whose name alone is testimony to the limited intermarriage of tongue and country in the generations after him.

4

The European depression of the 1830s moved many Germans to America. One hundred fifty-two thousand emigrated between 1830 and 1840, and not all of them Lutherans, because they included the first wave of German Jews. There was a revolution in Europe in 1848 beginning in the narrow proletarian streets of Paris, spreading to a student revolt in Austria that toppled the monumental Metternich, and taking nationalism—that universal religion of the middle classes—to Berlin, Italy, Czechoslovakia, and the confederated petty kingdoms of Germany. The movement collapsed among the bloody uprooted paving stones of the barricades. The liberal governments ruled feebly, and in Germany, they fell under the onslaught of the Prussian army. The political exiles from this slaughter of democratic hopes came to America in October, 1848. They became the natural leaders of the German-American communities already in the United States. Other Germans followed, particularly after the blighted potato harvest of that year. The discovery of gold in California at the same time was a lucky coincidence and crystallized the image of America as the locus of gilded opportunity and personal energy.

There is a curious lag, nevertheless, between perception and consequent action. To leave one's home requires not only money and will and health and a particular character, but also a decent, brooding amount of time. The bad period must persist, experience must lie imbedded and ripen in the brain, and the desire for a new chance must burst forth, but often only in the following generation. And this because most ordinary people have more patience than energy. They endure—at least those who have not died early.

So in the decade following the European troubles in 1848, 435,000 Germans came to America. But in the next ten years, the number increased to almost a million. In the following two decades, the total immigration from Germany was 1.6 million, and in 1880–90, another million and a half.[23] The total contribution of Germany to our 34 million immigrants was 5.5 million—more by a million than any other. Now certainly not the main reason, but an interesting and important one, was the German vision of America as a heroic sort of Eden. The equal sign between wilderness and paradise is one of civilized man's oldest illusions, but in Germany there was something more—the figure of the woodsman with his mythic axe and rifle. James Fenimore Cooper's frontier romances, published from 1823 to 1841, had enchanted the English and the Scotch, but had also been translated into German and were extraordinarily popular in central Europe for a hundred years—so constant was the need for another, a free, distant, and adventurous land. In 1853, the German Heinrich Möllhausen joined a railroad survey that was sponsored by the United States Army, and drew sketches and maps from Arkansas to California. On the basis of these and other trips to the West, he wrote numerous travel accounts and eighty forgotten novels, which were once immensely popular in Germany.

It is impossible, without more personal evidence, to weigh the force of literature upon action. Like the Bible, its effect is probably additive, never primary. It tells us the ostensible reason we do or don't do something, especially when the basic drive is too deep or too shameful or too selfish. Maybe, though, the romantic conception of America as a flowery, feasting wilderness is what attracted most Germans past the Eastern cities and a thousand miles further into the Midwest. A more compelling reason would be simple economics—a rapidly growing agricultural economy based on the rich, deep soils of Ohio and Illinois. And the really vast, flat, treeless plains even further west had a great hunger for craftsmen who could build, repair, doctor, weave, butcher, and bank. The German immigrants, in turn, had come from a society governed by the possession of land. They may have hated the aristocrats (like Beethoven), but (like Beethoven, who put a "von" in front of his name) they wanted their privileges, too.

Many Germans, of course, went to the cities—or built them. In Boston in 1890, 5 per cent of German-born immigrants were professionals (if one includes musicians), 22 per cent were white-collar workers, and almost 50 per cent were skilled.[24] This, perhaps, does not seem extraordinary unless one compares the Germans with the Irish. Of the latter at the same time in the same city, 65 per cent were unskilled laborers. Ohio and Indiana had many towns where German was an equal and even a dominant language. John Roebling, a German immigrant, designed the Cincinnati bridge over the Ohio River, another over the Niagara Falls, and the great and beautiful

Brooklyn Bridge across New York Harbor. Chicago, too, had a great proportion of Germans and a correspondingly strong musical, architectural, and athletic culture.

They were a formidable political block. In the South they were so influential that, in 1843, Texas published its laws in both German and English. In the North, they were so completely antislavery that they were extremely helpful, if not decisive, in the curious election of 1860 that put Lincoln in the White House. Karl Marx not only commented on the Civil War for the *New York Herald Tribune*, but sent Lincoln a long letter of advice signed "T. Marx," whom Lincoln thought to be a clever woman. Among the first volunteer regiments for the North were German, formed around the nucleus of their athletic and social clubs. "The Ninth Wisconsin Regiment had a large band with special uniforms; it even published its own paper in the battlefield, *Der deutsche Kreiger*. The XI Corps of the Army of the Potomac consisted of twenty-six regiments, of which fifteen were entirely German. The

Bootblacks, New York City, 1896.

Photograph by E. Alice Austen. Library of Congress

5th and 11th New York Regiments were composed almost exclusively of German members of the Liederkranz and Teutonia Männerchor, 'whose musical directors,' said one, 'laid down their batons to become army buglers.' Of the total number of 2,018,000 Union soldiers, 289,080 were German—one tenth of the entire fighting force of the North. Of these, five hundred had officers who were born in Germany."[25]

5

For every engineer like Roebling, or lawyer and major general like Carl Schurz, or painter like August Bierstadt, there were thousands of German immigrants who labored at the bottom of the social scale. Many of these, quite naturally, were women. Jane Addams, the extraordinary social worker who ran Hull House in Chicago for forty years, described some of these in her autobiography:

"This piteous dependence of the poor upon the good will of public officials was made clear to us in an early experience with a peasant woman straight from the fields of Germany, whom we met during our first six months at Hull House. Her four years in America had been spent in patiently carrying water up and down two flights of stairs and in washing the heavy flannel suits of iron foundry workers. For this her pay had averaged thirty-five cents a day. Three of her daughters had fallen victims to the vice of the city. The mother was bewildered and distressed, but understood nothing. We were able to induce the betrayer of one daughter to marry her; the second, after a tedious lawsuit, supported his child; with the third we were able to do nothing. This woman is now living with her family in a little house seventeen miles from the city. She has made two payments on her land and is a lesson to all beholders as she pastures her cow up and down the railroad tracks and makes money from her ten acres. She did not need charity, for she had an immense capacity for hard work, but she sadly needed the service of the state's attorney's office, enforcing the laws designed for the protection of such girls as her daughters."[26]

In 1903, one of these women, a Miss Agnes M., told a reporter for the weekly *Independent* what her life was really like. There are no simple conclusions to be squeezed out of these rich, ordinary memories, any more than from the account of the coppersmith Kuner. It is either all quite true, or else, in her mastery of detail, Agnes M. was a great writer. She was born in western Germany, in the formerly French city of Treves.

"When I was eleven years of age I fell in love with a tall, slim, thoughtful, dark-haired boy named Fritz, whose parents lived in Frankfort. We used to talk to each other through the bars of the fence which divided our playground. He was a year and a half older than I, and I thought him a man. The only time I was ever beaten at that school was on his account. We had been talking together on the playground; I did not heed the bell and was late getting in, and when the Sister asked what kept me I did not answer. She insisted on knowing, and Fritz and I looked at each other. The Sister caught us laughing.

"Whipping on the hands with a rod was the punishment that they had there for very naughty children, and that is what I got. It did not hurt much, and that night at half past nine o'clock, when all the house was still, there came a tapping at our dormitory window, and when it was opened we found Fritz there crying about the way I had been whipped. He had climbed up one of the verandah posts and had an orange for me. The other girls never told. They said it was so fine and romantic."[27]

At fifteen, like Kuner, she was hired out to learn a trade, a properly feminine one, of course. "I went to work for a milliner. The hours were from eight o'clock in the morning till six in the evening, but when there was much business the milliner would keep us till nine o'clock at night. I got no money, and was to serve for two years for nothing as an apprentice . . .

"I heard about how easy it was to make money in America and became very anxious to go there, and very tired of making hats and dresses for nothing for a woman who was selling them at high prices. I was restless in my home also; mother seemed so stern and could not understand that I wanted amusement . . .

"I grew more and more tired of all work and no play, and more and more anxious to go to America; and at last mother, too, grew anxious to see me go. She met me one night walking in the street with a young man, and said to me afterward:

" 'It is better that you go.'

"There was nothing at all in my walking with that young man, but she thought there was and asked my eldest sister to lend me the money to go to America to my second eldest sister, and a month later I sailed from Antwerp, the fare costing \$55."[28]

Her older sister met her at Ellis Island and almost at once she got a job at a millinery, making four dollars a week. She paid her sister three dollars for board so she had one dollar a week left for herself. She found her married sister's house "dull," so she moved out in the only way she could afford; she became a children's nursemaid.

"The children were a boy of ten and a girl of eight years. They were restless and full of life but good natured, and as they liked me I would have stayed there till they grew too old to need me any more, but that something awful happened during the second summer that we were spending on Long Island.

"It was one night in June, when the moon was very large and some big stars were shining. I had been to the village with the housekeeper to get the mail, and at the post office we met the butler and a young man who sailed the boats for us. Our way home lay across the fields and the young man with me kept stopping to admire things, so that the others got away ahead of us.

"He admired the moon and the stars and the shine of the water on the waves and the way that the trees cast their shadows, and he didn't seem to be thinking about me at all, just talking to me as he might to any friend. But when we walked into a shadowy place he said:

" 'Aren't you afraid of catching cold?' and touched my wrap.

" 'Oh, no,' I said.

" 'You had better draw that together,' said he, and put his arm about it to make it tight. He made it very tight, and the first thing I knew he kissed me.

"It was done so quickly that I had no idea—I never saw a man kiss any one so quickly.

"I gave such a scream that one could hear it a mile and boxed his ears, and as soon as I could tear myself away I ran as fast as I could to the house, and he ran as fast as he could to the village.

"I was very angry and crying. He had given me no warning at all, and besides I did not like him enough. Such impudence! But I probably would not have said anything about the matter at the house but that the next day all the people in the village were talking about it, and some of them had the mistress in my place. She heard of it and called me in, and I told her the truth; but she seemed to think that I could help being kissed, and I grew stubborn then and said I would not stay any more."[29]

This was an aspect of immigrant life that one rarely realizes—the sexual fear and vulnerability of the stranger in a strange land. It is, indeed, both exciting and dangerous to be caught between deep, instinctual desire and the morality of one's church and childhood.

Agnes M. fled to another job. ". . . I secured another situation, this time to mind the baby of a very rich young couple. It was the first and only baby of the mistress, and so it had been spoiled till I came to take charge. It had red hair and green eyes, and a fearful temper—really vicious."[30] The baby wanted to be carried (another ancient instinct) but her own strict upbringing thought such behavior to be horribly indulgent:

"I read a good German book and let the baby rage. When it was crying it could not be sleeping, and it was far better to have it cry in the daytime than at night, when it disturbed the whole house.

"The baby threw everything out of its carriage, even its coverlets and pillows, and tried to fall out itself, but it was tied in. It cried till it exhausted itself inventing new ways of screaming. I sat at a distance from it, so that its screaming would not annoy me too much, and read my book till it had finished. Then I went and got some ice cream for myself, and gave the baby very little. I wanted to teach it to do without things. It had been in the habit of getting everything it cried for, and that had made it hard to live with. That night, again, the baby went to sleep without rocking, and the young mother was much pleased with my management and gave me a nice silk waist."[31]

She was astonished that she was fed the same food as her employers; in Germany that was never so. Her pleasures, meantime, became metropolitan: going to the beach by boat, and dancing "all the way there and all the way back." There's no doubt of her admiration for America, but it is specific, not general:

"I like Coney Island best of all. It is a wonderful and beautiful place. I took a German friend, a girl who had just come out, down there last week, and when we had been on the razzle-dazzle, the chute and the loop-the-loop, and down in the coal mine and all over the Bowery, and up in the tower and everywhere else, I asked her how she liked it. She said:

"'Ach, it is just like what I see when I dream of heaven.'"[32]

And then, exactly like a story in a "love and romance" magazine, Germany made up for its poor treatment:

"Two years ago, when I was with a friend at Rockaway Beach, I was introduced to a young man who has since asked me to marry him. He is a German from the Rhine country, and has been ten years in this country. Of course, he is a tall, dark man, because I am so small and fair. It is always that way . . .

"Herman is the assistant in a large grocery store. He has been there nine years, and knows all the customers. He has money saved, too, and soon will go into business for himself.

"And then, again, I like him, because I think he's the best dancer I ever saw."[33]

6

Americans are accustomed to moving, pushed on by unemployment, a change of jobs, a change of marriage, unfocused discontent, trouble with law or with love. Despite all that's been said about this enduring trait of American character, it was never easy and isn't now. We live in a web of friends rather than relatives, and cutting these intimate affectionate ties isn't simple or painless. Even the chords of dislike and irritation with a friend's character are, if snipped, a little bloody. So it takes an effort of the imagination to realize what it's like to go to quite another country and not even know how to speak and be understood.

"I was a man and stronger than most men. Yet my second childhood began the day I entered my new country [1906]. . . . My angers, fears, and joys were fleeting and childish and divided the new world into absolute categories—into good and evil. The new world cut into my clay and chronicled something which was not there before—another code of thoughts and feelings . . . I had to learn life over in a brand-new world. And I could not talk. My first desire was for chocolate drops, and I pointed my finger at them. My second was for fishing tackle, and I pointed my finger at a wrapping cord and heaved up an imaginary fish. I used baby talk. 'Price?' I asked. And later in the day, 'Vatsprice?' Saleswomen answered with motherly grimaces . . ."

This immigrant, Carl Christian Jensen, was a Dane. He was one of the half million Scandinavians who came to America in that final decade of the nineteenth century. New York City boiled over with immigrants:

"Frantic streams of sweatshop workers climbed the subway stairs,

leaped out of street cars, poured forth from ferries, rushed down from elevated stations. Children carried box wood home from wholesale stores and
market places. Bent old men carted bulky sacks of rags to their junk
shops . . .

"On West Street tangled teams and trucks and peddlers' carts blocked
the horse cars that clanged their bells with yowling petulance, while teamsters cursed, peddlers sang, ferries tooted. On one side of the street rows on
rows of immigrant liners lay moored. On the other side old tilting rooming
houses were crowded with dark-eyed children, and with women with Mona
Lisa faces, and with men lamenting in strange tongues.

"Labor bureaus shipped away immigrants to mines and mills and factories. The labor market was flooded. Weeping with gratitude they went.
Every day brought fresh hordes ashore. For every man who found work a
hundred others stepped ashore from the Ellis Island ferry . . .

"Along thirty miles of water front I wandered in search of work—around
Manhattan Island, on the Brooklyn, Jersey City, Hoboken, and Staten Island wharves—waiting through rain and sleet and snow with gangs of longshoremen to reach the boss before he finished picking the men he wanted. It
took strength, when a steamer arrived, to break the brawny barriers and
stem the tides of human muscles. Strong men crushed each other to the
ground in their passion for work.

"Thirty hours these longshoremen worked without a rest while thousands of envious idlers watched from ashore. Their eyes were wild with lust
for work. Tobacco juice mingled with sweat from their brows and froze into
icicles on their horned mustaches. Cargoes of wheat and fruit, coal and
brick, boxes, bales, and barrels, these tireless toilers carried, while their
gang boss, yelling like a demon, drove them in a continual trot.

"Accidents they ignored in their great urge for work. The paw of a hoist-
ing boom struck a toiler to instant death; a cable swept a row of men off the
deck, down on the drifting ice floes; a scaffold gave way under a dozen men,
who tumbled down with their barrels in a bleeding heap . . .

"The part of Manhattan that I learned to know best was the sweatshop
district. Between Canal Street and Greenwich Village I worked in several
hundred shops: glove shops with rows on rows of sewing machines, and
purring shuttles gliding out of and into thread loops, and the mad dance of
glinting needles around a thousand tiny leather fingers; lace shops with
looms growling appallingly, gears and pinions gnawing one another's teeth,
spindles and spools whirring, and shrieks from a jungle of belts; trouser
shops with forty layers of cloth cut by a pair of creeping scissors, and long,
clattering needle races along the inseams; handbag shops with dies,
punches, and curved knives, bronze, silver, and gold hinges, and a cargo of
warty alligator skins; feather shops with cellars of vats and blowers, airy dry-
ing lofts, and downy assortment rooms—all the shops crowded with bright-
eyed immigrant girls."[34]

New York City tenements.

Photograph by Jacob Riis. Museum of the City of New York

If we add all the Swedish, Danish, Norwegian, and Finnish who were immigrants between 1820 and 1920, there were a little over two million. At first, they were happy to survive. After that they became greatly interested in learning the American language:

"In Brooklyn I joined a public night school where immigrants gathered to learn the language of their new country. The teacher was a young American woman of wit and refinement. She handled her forty husky pupils well. There was in the class an old, half-blind Italian doctor who never learned to say 'I' instead of 'me.' There was also an English teamster, with black teeth and clothes that smelled of horses, who was learning a more limber handwriting. And there were many Swedes who after the day's work at the water front were tired and sleepy and always lost the page in their primers when they were called on to read. A German would leap up like a jack-in-the-box to show them the page and paragraph . . ."[35] that, this man could learn the terminology of a better trade. He became an electrician, and he realized he could rise no higher, unless he learned mathematics.

"One day I came upon a man bent over a sewing machine in a dingy sweatshop, a pale, thinly bearded Jew with the melancholy glow of his race burning in his eye. He had suffered his share in this life, having been driven from Moscow into the Siberian ice, during his student days, from whence he had made his escape to America. At noon we lunched together at a sidewalk counter, devouring—and relishing—a glass of synthetic lemonade and a nickle's worth of doughnuts. I treated to ice-cream cones, though this extravagance was more severe on my resources than if during my sailor days I had treated a crew. My apprentice wage of a dollar a day barely covered the four essentials of Manhattan—carfare, clothes, housing, food.

"My new friend was in a hurry to return. He was tutoring a youngster in mathematics, he told me. I held him back. Mathematics! The only language that made natural forces obey its command! The bridge between earth and the stars! The essence of voltage and amperage! He was preparing a youth for entrance examination to Cooper Union on the Bowery. 'If I took lessons, could I also enter Cooper Union?' I asked eagerly. 'One dollar I'll pay you every week.' He looked me over from head to foot—especially my head. 'Yes,' he said. 'I'll teach you.' "[36]

The largest number of Scandinavian immigrants didn't stay in the seaboard cities but went to the Midwest. This was perfectly natural, for their background was rural, and the trade they knew was farming. An exception were the 260,000 Finns "who came primarily from the lowest ranks of society." They were recruited to mine the copper in Michigan, the iron in Wisconsin, and the coal in Pennsylvania.

What they all had in common was poverty. A Swede, Axel Jarlson, put his reason for coming to America very precisely:

"Father had a little piece of land—about two acres—which he rented, and besides, he worked in the summer time for a farmer. Two of my sisters and three of my brothers also worked in the fields, but the pay was so very small that it was hard for us to get enough to eat. A good farm hand in our part of Sweden, which is 200 miles north of Stockholm and near the Baltic Sea, can earn about 100 kroner a season, and a kroner is 27 cents . . .

"A man who had been living in America once came to visit the little village that was near our cottage. He wore gold rings set with jewels and had a fine watch. He said that food was cheap in America and that a man could earn nearly ten times as much there as in Sweden. He treated all the men to brandvin, or brandy wine, as some call it, and there seemed to be no end to his money."[37]

Such stories, told literally by the millions in the nineteenth century, made America seem the one doorway to hope—and money. Not that the stories were always believed: ". . . My father and the other old men will not believe that there are any great cities in America. They say that it is a wild country, and that it is quite impossible that New York can be as large as Stockholm. When they hear about the tall buildings they laugh, and say that travelers always tell such wild tales."[38]

After a bad winter, his uncle paid for Jarlson's brother Gustaf to go to Minnesota, and the family got a letter from him the following August: "I have work with a farmer who pays me 64 kroner a month, and my board. I send you 20 kroner, and will try to send that every month. This is a good country. It is like Sweden in some ways. The winter is long, and there are some cold days, but everything grows that we can grow in our country, and there is plenty. All about me are Swedes, who have taken farms and are getting rich. They eat white bread and plenty of meat. The people here do not work such long hours as in Sweden, but they work much harder, and they have a great deal of machinery, so that the crop one farmer gathers will fill two big barns. One farmer, a Swede, made more than 25,000 kroner on his crop last year."[39]

Gustaf got a sixty-acre farm from the government and was eventually elected sheriff of his county. Axel joined him in America in 1899. In March, 1901, he bought himself a farm for $150, cheap because it was uncleared land except for two acres. He hired a half-breed French-Canadian Indian, rode toboggans over the snow, and cut timber for his house. The main beam was sliced from a trunk five feet in diameter. He noted that his tools and supplies cost $55.42. But the investment of labor was tremendous. They cleared the trees off an acre a day to make enough ground to plow and sow. They ate enormously—breakfast was corn meal mush, herrings, bacon, and coffee—and they slept on spruce boughs. They kept off scurvy by canning blackberries which they bought from the Indians. Azel Jarlson noted that in his second year, 1902, his cash income was $1,200 and his profit, $600.

"One thing I like about this country is that you do not have to be always taking off your hat to people. In Sweden you take off your hat to everybody you meet, and if you enter a store you take off your hat to the clerk. Another thing that makes me like this country is that I can share in the government. In Sweden my father never had a vote, and my brothers never could have voted because there is a property qualification that keeps out the poor people, and they had no chance to make money. Here any man of good character can have a vote after he has been a short time in the country, and people can elect him to any office. There are no aristocrats to push him down, and say that he is not worthy because his father was poor. Some Swedes have become Governors of States, and many who landed here poor boys are now very rich."[40]

7

If we compare three particular groups of immigrants—the English-Welsh-Scotch, the Germans, and the Scandinavians—we find astonishing uniformity: religion which is mostly Protestant; social group which is skilled

or semi-skilled and therefore lower middle-class; and geographical preference, which is for small town or rural life.

In the decade 1820–30, this triple group was a little less than a third of
all immigrants. In 1830–40, it approached a half of the total. It was well over
half in the decades 1840–50 and 1850–60. In the decade that included the
Civil War, this Anglo-Saxon group was close to three-fourths of all immigrants, a peak percentage from which it dropped only slowly in the decades
1870–80 and 1880–90, with one million out of two million and two million
out of five million—still more than half of all immigrants. Only in 1890–1900
did the percentage of Anglos drop to one million out of three million but this
is still a sizable third. Then in the period 1900–1910, the percentages were
remarkably altered: Germans, Scotch, English and Scandinavians sent only
one million of a vast total of eight million immigrants. By the final decade
under consideration in this study, 1910–20, they were only about 15 per
cent, a sixth of the total five million who came across the Atlantic to live
in America.[41]

Were the eleven million Anglo-Saxon immigrants all that different from
the other immigrants of that century? They were not. The European, the
source of 90 per cent of the immigration to this country, was such an historical hybrid of all the white varieties of man—Celts, Gauls, Greeks, and Bas-
ques, mixed with the Moors and the Huns, sometimes by choice and sometimes by rape—that there was no common marker of skin or eye color or
body build or even phrenological bumps. And in any case, the Anglo-
Protestants ate, sweated, smiled, loved, wept, worked, rationalized, defe-
cated, and died, like other human beings. But they certainly thought they
were different, especially from the four million Irish Catholics; and later,
from the millions of Slavs, Italians, and eastern and southern and central
Europeans. They felt they had a particular way of life. They thought themselves free, independent, hospitable, proud, humorous, frank, with a respect for hard work that was nearly religious, and with its corollary, a hypo-
critical and rigid morality. All others but themselves were immoral, idle,
dirty, saint-worshippers.

One sees clearly in accounts that are contemporary with the change in
the parts of Europe that exported toward America, how the Anglo's prejudice developed when he deduced a man's nature from his circumstance.
Here is one sincere, even sympathetic reporter, Jacob Riis: "[The Italian's]
ignorance and unconquerable suspicion of strangers dig the pit into which he
falls. He not only knows no word of English, but he does not know enough to
learn. Rarely only can he write his own language. Unlike the German, who
begins learning English the day he lands as a matter of duty, or the Polish
Jew, who takes it up as soon as he is able as an investment, the Italian learns
slowly, if at all . . . [The Jews] come here in droves from Eastern Europe to
escape persecution, from which freedom could be bought only with gold, it
has enslaved them in bondage worse than that from which they fled. Money

is their God. Life itself is of little value compared with even the leanest bank account. In no other spot does life wear so intensely bald and materialistic an aspect as in Ludlow Street. Over and over again I have met with instances of these Polish or Russian Jews deliberately starving themselves to the point of physical exhaustion, while working night and day at a tremendous pressure to save a little money . . ."42

Riis was an Anglo himself, a Dane, with a wry admiration for the strict way he had been educated, with its Calvinist emphasis on the moral value of hard labor.

Meanwhile, the skills of blacksmith, coppersmith, wheelwright, and dozens of other special trades were less and less useful as the century rolled to its close. The increase of iron and coal and thus of metal and the fire to put that metal into motion, not only to create goods but to fashion other machines that would make more goods—all this multiplication of energy by itself, this enormous engine of power and wheels, of warehouses and steamers, barges and freight cars, this pyramid of movement—had, in the end, one motive: to feed and increase itself by lowering the cost of labor.

It was no longer efficient to hire crowds of skilled labor. It was much cheaper to pay a few key workmen and support them with a great company of unskilled or semi-skilled. The McCormick Company, for example, increased its labor output by technical improvements from twelve reapers per worker per year, to forty per worker per year. Thus it increased its output from 1,500 to 55,000 per year, and its staff from 123 to over 1,400.

Where were all these eager, hungry, productive hands to come from? It was hard to coax a man from land he might himself own and work, in order to give him a monotonous job, which he would work twelve hours a day pushed to the limit of his energy, with restriction even on the time he would be allowed in what was then called "the water closet," imprisoned all day in a factory where the natural silence of nature was unknown. The new sort of immigrant, from 1870 onward—young, strong, illiterate, and hungry, but without land, resources or skills—was the ideal factory worker. Agents all over Europe lured masses of people to the United States with promises of cheap fare and instant employment. The character and origin of the immigrants changed because American growth required it. But the American promise did not create the European situation, namely, masses of unemployed and landless peasants from the west and the south of Europe—the Slavs and the Mediterraneans, particularly the Italians, and of these, especially the South Italians.

8

Was there no need for unskilled labor before the 1880s? Certainly there was. Bold enterprises were undertaken: the eastern canals, the railroads, the extension of roads and cities. These required hod carriers, pick and shovel men, and common laborers. And these were, in a large measure, Catholics from the southern provinces of Ireland. Only 54,000 came in in 1820–30, but by 1850–60, these immigrants were nearly a million. Even by 1880–90, the total of Catholic Irish immigration was 655,000. The grand sum of Irish who came in the century of 1820–1920 was well over four million, twice as many as the Scandinavians, a half million more than the total of the Scots, Welsh, and English, and only a million less than the Germans.[43]

But though they spoke English, and therefore were able to work, travel, and communicate from the moment they stepped ashore, they remained a depressed and separated enclave for a very long time. ". . . Although Irishmen were brought to the coal regions in great numbers by the operators, an . . . . antagonism existed there between them and the older races. The employers followed the policy of keeping the new group impoverished, thereby insuring their inability to bargain for better wages by refusal of work. Since the same policy has been adopted in dealing with later immigrant people, there is no reason for assuming that the Irish were obnoxious as a racial group to the employers. The growing numerical supremacy of the Irish. . . . aroused the fears of the prior inhabitants of the older groups, and intensified the racial problem."[44] A reckoning of the five main coal counties in Pennyslvania showed for example in 1870, that, there were 376,000 workmen, of whom nearly a fourth were foreign born. Of the latter, the Irish came to 44,000, about equal to the total of the Welsh, English, and German miners. It's not quite fashionable to say so, but every discrimination, even the most hateful, has two gainers, as well as two victims. The self-appointed bigot has the civilized satisfaction of being superior to someone, anyone. And the victim has the rather greater moral satisfaction of martyrdom, which ties all his problems into one great indecipherable knot. Each serves the other, one by creating a social ghetto, the other by enforcing it. In this separation, each can and does assume the role of the other.

The Irish, moreover, had the nasty aid of history. They were landless tenants, mostly, and Catholic; the landlord was usually English and Protestant. The sorrows of Ireland and the paternity of the Church were so intermingled that even to the Irish immigrant five thousand miles from home, there remained one single, glowing, touchy emotion. There was no way in which this very considerable minority could unite with the already powerful Anglo-Protestant majority which ruled American society politically, morally, and economically. One of the earliest divisions between the Irish and other Americans was the question of conscription to the Civil War army. It was a peculiar conscription, on both sides of the conflict, since a man could avoid it by paying $300 to buy a substitute. Very few Irish could raise a sum like this, which represented their earnings for half a year. The Irish earned the lowest income for the worst jobs, and therefore feared the competition of free blacks who would swarm north to take their work. This view was not entirely paranoid, for already in New York City a small number of fugitive slaves, all the more conspicuous for the rarity of their color, were working, as the Irish

Russian Jewess immigrant, 1905.

Photograph by Lewis Hine. New York Public Library

were, as common laborers. One of the few universals that is still true is that the consequence of fear is hate.

In the New York riots that began on July 13, 1863, and ended on Saturday, July 20, three policemen were killed and more than twelve blacks were lynched. Though no exact counts could be made, the number of dead rioters shot by police and troops was well in excess of 1,200.[45] There was a far milder New York Irish riot in 1871, when the Irish Catholics gathered to oppose a parallel march scheduled by Irish Protestants. Troops were mobilized, and when they were fired upon in the streets, they fired back in panic, killing thirty-one Irish and losing two soldiers. "A pile of dead men's hats stood on the corner of Eighth Avenue and Twenty-fifth Street untouched, and pale faces stooped over pools of blood on the pavement. The stores were all shut, and everything wore a gloomy aspect. The police stood near, revealed in the lamplight, but made no effort to clear the street . . ."[46] Is there any moral to these bloody tales, except the mysterious sadness of most truthful history?

9

The division between the Irish immigrants and the resident majority of the Anglo-Americans was largely self-perpetuating. Certainly it existed as late as 1905, though by then millions of Irish had come to America less out of young energy and natural restlessness than out of sodden despair. There were marked differences between them and other immigrants, quite apart from religio-patriotic emotions. Here was the account of an Irish cook, for example:

". . . We lived in a peat cabin, but it had a good thatched roof. Mother put on that roof. It isn't a woman's work, but she was able for it.

"There were sivin childher of us [sic]. John an' Matthew they went to Australia. Mother was layin' by for five year to get their passage money. They went into the bush. We heard twice from thim [sic] and then no more. Not another word and that is forty year gone now—on account of them not reading and writing. Learning isn't cheap in them old countries as it is here, you see . . . My father he never was a steddy [sic] worker. He took to the drink early in life. My mother an' me an' Tilly we worked in the field for Squire Varney. Yes, plowin' an' seedin' and diggin'—any farm work he'd give us. We did men's work, but we didn't get men's pay . . . What did we eat? Well, just potatoes. On Sundays, once a month, we'd maybe have a bit of flitch. When the potatoes rotted—that was the hard times! Oh, yes, I mind the famine years. An' the cornmeal that the 'Mericans sent. The folk said they'd rather starve nor eat it. We didn't know how to cook it . . ."[47]

Potatoes were a staple in Ireland as well as in Germany and for similar reasons. They are a vegetable easily and cheaply grown in cool, wet climates; secondly, they contain a good amount of protein, always the most expensive part of a poor man's diet; third, once planted and fairly grown, they did not require extensive care or weeding, so the men in the green Irish land could go to the towns to get work and a bit of money. But in 1846 and 1847, a root disease destroyed the potato tuber all over Euope:

"Maria—she was one of the twins—she died the famine year of the typhus and—well, she sickened of the herbs and roots we eat—we had no potatoes.

"Mother said when Maria died, 'There's a curse on ould green Ireland and we'll get out of it.' "[48]

When the rot was over, there were two million less Irish in Ireland. A million had emigrated, and almost a million had died. While only about a half million Irish emigrated to America before the horrible year of 1845, their numbers were 2.25 million in the next thirty years. Here again, as we've noted earlier, there was a lag, a reverberation; action follows necessity, but generally with a long lead time:

". . . The passage was $12. You brought your own eating, your tea an' meal, an' most had flitch. There was two big stoves that we cooked on. The steerage was a dirty place and we were eight weeks on the voyage—over time three weeks. The food ran scarce, I tell you, but the captain gave some to us, and them that had plenty was kind to the others . . ."

And many Americans were decent and kind: "When I got here Mrs. Bent let Tilly keep me for two months to teach me—me bein' such a greenhorn. Of course I worked for her. Mr. Bent was foreman then in Spangler's big mills. After two months I got a place. They were nice appearing people enough, but the second day I found out they were Jews. I never had seen a Jew before, so I packed my bag and said to the lady, 'I beg your pardon, ma'am, but I can't eat the bread of them as crucified the Saviour.' 'But,' she said, 'he was a Jew.' So at that I put out. I couldn't hear such talk."[49]

This feeling was not peculiar to this particular woman; it was part of the burden of parochialism carried by Irish-Catholic communities in America. Attacks on one's origin provoke an equal attack on one's enemies, so the psychological wall around the Irish Catholic was built not only by the native Protestant, but by the Irish Catholic himself and by his leaders, certain clergy in particular. One example among many others was the racist tract *The Celt Above the Saxon* written by Father Cornelius Herlihy. The powerful Archbishop O'Connell of Boston noted that the Irish masses "demanded . . . thoughts ready-made . . ." and he supported the myth of a submissive, jolly, dreaming traditionalist—subject to the affectionate vice of alcoholism. There's truth to all these prejudices. Whiskey, certainly, was traditional among the poor, and the Irish made a splendid unexception. As Jacob Riis notes in one of his worker's case reports: "In visiting a family referred to us by a church in the neighborhood, found a woman and two children living on the top floor with a neighbor. The woman stated that her husband was a confirmed drunkard, but for years she had borne with him, and tried in every way to reform him. She was in miserable health herself, but struggled doing odd day's work to support the family, until two months ago, when the man in a drunken stupor kicked her, fracturing her ribs so that she was unable to do any work."[50]

A good part of the resentment, hatred, and contempt that many Americans felt for the Irish was what they felt for alcohol itself. The temperance movement in the United States, especially in the prosperous and growing Midwest, replaced slavery with alcohol as the devil of the age. The movement was centered in, and motivated by, the Protestant churches. This was a new division between them and the Irish, who had a much more lenient view of this weakness. So the drunken, improvident Irishman became a stereotype embodied in popular culture:

This
fine ould Irish gintleman he was once
out upon a spree, and as
many a fine ould Irish gintleman has done and
        more betoken will do
        to the end of time he got about as
dhrunk as he could be,
His senses was completely mulvathered and
        the consequence was that he could
neither hear nor see, So they
thought he was stone dead and gone intirely,
        So the best thing they could do would
        be to have him waked and
buried dacintly,
Like a Fine Ould Irish Gintleman
All of the rale ould stock.[51]

In most other ways, of course, the Irish immigrant was like any other—hard working, frugal, determined: ". . . The McNabbs are no wasteful folk. I've worn one dress nine year and it looked decent then. Me and Tilly saved till we brought Joseph and Phil over, and they went into Mr. Bent's mills as weaver and spool boy and then they saved, and we all brought out my mother and father. We rented a little house in Kensington for them. There was a parlor in it and kitchen and two bedrooms and bathroom and marble door step, and a bell. That was in '66, and we paid nine dollars a month rent. You'd pay double that now. It took all our savings to furnish it, but Mrs. Bent and Mrs. Carr gave us lots of things to go in. To think of mother having a parlor and marble steps and a bell!"[52]

Their group feeling, cemented by outside hatred and ridicule, had its positive side: Irishmen tended to hire Irishmen. They took control of established political power in particular wards and localities—Tammany was only one instance—and this aroused the hatred of the frightened Anglo. ". . . The Roman Catholic element and the Copperhead, combined, just now, seemed to be imposing an unusually heavy strain upon our political institutions, to say nothing of certain fundamental moral interests which must share in the political peril. I hope it is the design of Providence . . . In public affairs we are accustomed to assign an overwhelming part to what is called Providence; a sentiment in harmony with the religious belief of so many of our people as look toward Heaven to find their God, and not toward Rome to propritiate by gifts and idolatrous sacrifices a sacrilegious counterfeit."[53] And so, before civil service and even after it, the Irish gave one another preference in the steady jobs of firemen and janitors and police.

The Irish who continued to come to this country long after the famine were those that obeyed the "sieving rule" of voluntary exile. In other words, only the young, strong, and healthy were capable of breaking out of their stone-and-thatch villages, and their ancient hierarchical social order. By that very choice, their energy propelled them upward in American society. In Boston, where better statistics were kept, the Irish middle class, which was only 10 per cent of the total in 1890, almost quadrupled their numbers by 1910. Their change in status, though, was slower than that of the Italians, for example, who came a generation later but also increased their middle-class status from 12 to 35 per cent, between 1910 and 1930, and halved the number of their unskilled and ill-paid workers.

Egalitarianism and prejudice were both American traits, and few people noticed that they were contradictory. This was particularly true in the extraordinarily mixed populations of the cities. It was the Irish who got the unskilled, low-paid, and insecure jobs, and one suspects that the common bigotry against these Catholic peasants was less an emotion than a rationalization.

10

These tiger passions, here to stretch their claws
In street and alley, what strange tongues are these,
Accents of menace alien to our air,
Voices that once the tower of Babel knew?
O, Liberty, white goddess, is it well
To leave the gate unguarded?[54]

This salvo of native eloquence, written early in the twentieth century, was typical of the new Anglo acceptance of the "imaginative Irish," who were now regarded as a people whose ". . . profound sense of personal dignity, gift of language, and fighting capacities go hand in hand . . . [and] . . . the Irish girl has the greatest refinement in her dress; she rarely chooses the extreme. Restraint and simplicity are the notes of her costume."[55]

The new objects of fear were those odd foreigners who were not only non-Protestant but also non-English-speaking, those who came to America from southern and eastern Europe. Those dark, distant, and corrupted kingdoms gave us over eleven million Slavs and Mediterraneans—Italy alone sent four million—in the years between 1880 and 1920 when the English, Germans and Scandinavians sent America a total of seven and a half million new people. We Americans gave them, in the fine old thoughtless tradition of Europe itself, a ready-made and plausible character according to their country of origin:

". . . Gifted, strong, with depth of character, grace and charm, the Northern Italian combines perhaps as many valuable elements in his composition as can be found in Europe. But the Northern Italian is only a very small part of our immigration.

"The Southern Italian comes to us with great capacity for work, and with a strong constitution. He is for the most part ignorant, where not positively illiterate. Of agreeable manners, he is passionate and uncontrolled in temper. He marries early and the ensuing large families finding it difficult to get along even with a simple and often insufficient diet, send their children early to work. The child labourer of the cities is par excellence the Italian child. The very early marriage of the Italian woman results in a lack of proper training of the children, for the Italian woman is uneducated and enters her mature responsibilities as an untrained child. Freedom from parental restraint and an early entrance without proper preparation of any sort into industrial life creates a second generation of Italians of inferior physique ready for physical or moral breakdown . . . and an increasing nervousness that tends towards heart troubles, insanity, and an excitement in general social intercourse, resulting in family friction and often in violence.

"The Southern Italian comes to us a strong labourer and an undisciplined personality . . . Gifted in the manual arts, with a taste for music and for simple social pleasures, the Italian, when freed from the most sordid conditions, has an aptitude for getting along with others that makes him most easy to assimilate . . . The Italian men also gather in cafes not only for gambling but also for news in regard to the home village, the prospects of work for the coming season, and all the gossip of the great Italian community, its loves, and murders, the opera and the respective merits of the latest Italian conductors. For the Ialian's love of music is an active form of recreation to him—no passive thing, as it is to so many American opera-goers who go to rest or pass the time away. The Italian goes to live within himself the great things of which the music tells. And nowhere are musical affairs so fought over, so vigorously debated, as in the humble cafes of the Italian workmen."[56]

How much easier is this not wholly truthful judgment, than a real grasp of the complexity and variety of actual, living human persons:

"When I was a very small boy I lived in Italy in a large house with many other small boys, who were all dressed alike and were taken care of by some nuns. It was a good place, situated on the side of the mountain, where grapes were growing and melons and oranges and plums.

"They taught us our letters and how to pray and say the catechism, and we worked in the fields during the middle of the day . . .

"Those were good times and they lasted till I was nearly eight years of age . . ."[57]

The narrator's name was simply "Rocco." He had no surname for many years. His background, like the very large majority of all Italians, was rural—a special kind of rural. They were either holders of small amounts of land that required intensive labor, or they were tenant farmers, or lower yet in the fixed hierarchy of the Italian social fabric, gang laborers hired by the great *latifundi* for the season. These country people were at least four-fifths of all Italian immigrants. We must not confuse the American rural style with the Italian. In America, a family of mother, father, their immediate children, and perhaps an elderly aunt or grandmother, lived in a separate farmhouse half a mile, if they were lucky, from the nearest neighbor. The Italian worked in the fields, but lived in clusters of stone houses, close and neighborly, returning at sunset every day to eat and gossip and love and hate the familiar faces of a greatly extended family of the same blood and often of the same surname.

Did a poor person like Rocco leave only because he was poor? Or were the economic reasons superficial? Did the drive to leave the place where he were born really come from deeper, less conscious motives? Or, to put it more succinctly, did the restless leave because they were poor, or did the poor leave because they were restless? Let's assume that persons of bold, energetic and impatient temperament can be found everywhere and are not, by the improvidence of nature, in one part of the world rather than in another. We can compare, for example, a province like Tuscany, halfway up the Italian boot, with a province like Calabria, at its rundown heel. The rate of emigration from rich Tuscany was fifty-two per thousand, one out of every twenty, while barren Calbria's rate of emigration had the astonishing ratio of more than one in every three persons. It's clear from this example what makes people move. It's pretty largely a matter of what is smeared on the daily bread. And this was just as true of Edinburgh as it was of Palermo.

Of course, for everyone who emigrates from anywhere, a great many more stay behind—the timid, the old, the weak, the unconvinced. This points to another little considered yet obvious reason for emigration: one had the example of a person in one's own social group, either family or village, who had already gone to America and had written back some sort of encouraging account. This process is particularly true of peasant societies. The first to do something unusual is considered mad. But if a madman succeeds, others cautiously follow. And then, by a sort of chain reaction, the whole community tumbles into line, no one wanting to be the last, which by that time would be considered an equally mad position. Common sense was, and remains, inherently conservative. The pattern is grounded in the truth of daily experience, and this pattern is rarely broken, but merely shifts or changes gradually. Thus whole families, one by one, brother by brother, cousin by cousin, and then score by score, took ship to America, carrying with them their invisible bundles—their psychological chains, their blood kinship, their mental landscape. For it is painful to break the ties with village and family, knowing the separation could very likely be permanent. Rocco (whom everyone called "Joe," because this was how one thought of Italians) recounted how it was with him:

"Now and then I had heard things about America—that it was a far off country where everybody was rich and that Italians went there and made plenty of money, so that they could return to Italy and live in pleasure ever after. One day I met a young man who pulled out a handful of gold and told me he had made that in America in a few days.

"I said I should like to go there, and he told me that if I went he would take care of me and see that I was safe. I told Francisco and he wanted to go, too. So we said good-by to our good friends. Teresa cried and kissed us both and the priest came and shook our hands and told us to be good men, and that no matter where we went God and his saints were always near us and that if we lived well we should all meet again in heaven. We cried, too, for it was our home, that place. Ciguciano gave us money and slapped us on the back and said that we should be great. But he felt bad, too, at seeing us go away after all that time."[58]

The young man with the gold in his pocket was probably a contractor, for he got these poor boys to pay for their passage by shoveling coal for the ship's furnaces. When they got to America, they were denied entrance because they had no money (the then substantial sum of $25.00 was required). However, they were rescued by three strangers, who swore that one of their number was the uncle of both boys. Quite naturally, this man, Bartolo, was their next employer; he used them to pick up old rags and bottles and bones from trash barrels.

"We came to Brooklyn to a wooden house in Adams Street that was full of Italians from Naples. Bartolo had a room on the third floor and there were fifteen men in the room, all boarding with Bartolo. He did the cooking on a stove in the middle of the room and there were beds all around the sides, one bed above another . . .

"Most of the men in our room worked at digging the sewer. Bartolo got them the work and they paid him about one quarter of their wages. Then he charged them for board and he bought the clothes for them, too. So they got little money after all."[59]

This was the common *padrone* system, which among other things, guaranteed a supply of fresh workmen to employers at lower wages than the Americans already here would demand. After 1900, the great railroad construction gangs were more and more Italian. The padrone would bring them West under contract. Once there, the local contractor, generally of the same region as the crew, took on the task of cheating them. What he could not cadge by raising hours and lowering wages, he got by "operating a saloon at each end of the tunnel."

The mines of America—grinding out copper, iron, and carbon for the steel furnaces, railroads, and metal tools of a voracious and expanding industrial complex—used all the illiterates they could find, at a conveniently low rate of pay, which actually was a lot higher than what they earned in rural Italy.

Why didn't Italians become farmers, as so many Scandinavians and Germans did? Some in fact did become agricultural laborers—cotton pickers in Louisiana, vineyard workers in California, even truck farmers on the marginal land near the growing cities. But they did not usually become individual middle-class farmers in the American sense. Part of it was the dragging weight of dependence, after generations of working for somebody else. Partly it was ignorance of how to get government or railroad allotments. But mostly it was simple poverty. Where would they get the money to buy seed, a plow and harrow, a team and harness and a wagon, not to speak of food until a crop matured? So they stayed with the padrone and the padrone gave them plenty of work but very little cash.

Yet, as the young Italian, Rocco, pointed out, American space and mobility broke apart the social tyranny of language and origin. "We were with Bartolo nearly a year, but some of our countrymen who had been in the place a long time said that Bartolo had no right to us and we could get work for a dollar and a half a day, which, when you make it *lire* (reckoned in the Italian currency) is very much. So we went away one day to Newark and got work on the street. Bartolo came after us and made a great noise, but the boss said that if he did not go away soon the police would have him. Then he went, saying that there was no justice in this country."[60]

Rocco and Francisco had advanced their careers in the land of opportunity. No longer rag-and-bone-pickers, they had become street laborers.

"We paid a man five dollars each for getting us the work and we were with that boss for six months. He was Irish, but a good man and he gave us our money every Saturday night. We lived much better than with Bartolo, and when the work was done we each had nearly $200 saved. Plenty of the men spoke English and they taught us, and we taught them to read and write. That was at night, for we had a lamp in our room, and there were only five other men who lived in that room with us.

"We got up half-past five o'clock every morning and made coffee on the stove and had a breakfast of bread and cheese, onions, garlic and red herrings. We went to work at seven o'clock and in the middle of the day we had soup and bread in a place where we got it for two cents a plate. In the evenings we had a good dinner with meat of some kind and potatoes. We got from the butcher the meat that other people would not buy because they said it was old, but they don't know what is good. We paid four or five cents a pound for it and it was the best, tho I have heard of people paying sixteen cents a pound."[61]

It was temporary work, though, and when it ended, they took the next step up the flimsy social ladder. They rented a basement and bought shoeshine equipment and became independent businessmen. They were so successful that they, in turn, had to hire cheap help. "We had said that when we saved $1,000 each we would go back to Italy and buy a farm, but now that the time is coming we are so busy and making so much money that we think we will stay. We have opened another parlor near South Ferry, in New York. We have to pay $30 a month rent, but the business is very good. The boys in this place charge sixty cents a day because there is so much work."[62]

They were tempted to become American citizens, but the law required a residency of five years, and though they were promised two dollars apiece for their votes, they refused to lie. Their view of American politics was rather odd. "There are two kinds of people that vote here, Republicans and Democrats. I went to a Republican meeting and the man said that the Republicans want a Republic and the Democrats are against it. He said that Democrats are for a king whose name is Bryan and who is an Irishman. There are some good Irishmen, but many of them insult Italians. They call us Dagoes. So I will be a Republican. I like this country now and I don't see why we should have a king. Garibaldi didn't want a king and he was the greatest man that ever lived."[63]

The Italian man, unlike the Irish, had a skeptical view of his Church. ". . . [A]s soon as we came to the country we began to go to the Italian church. The priest we found here was a good man, but he asked the people for money for the church. The Italians did not like to give because they said it looked like buying religion. The priest says it is different here from Italy because all the churches there are what they call endowed, while here all they have is what the people give. Of course I and Francisco understand that, but the Italians who cannot read and write shake their hands and say that it is wrong for a priest to want money."[64]

Their Sundays were spent like the Italian gentry back home:

"On Sundays we get a horse and carriage from the grocer and go down to Coney Island. We go to the theatres often and other evenings we go to the houses of our friends and play cards.

"I am nineteen years of age now and have $700 saved. Francisco is twenty-one and has about $900. We shall open some more parlors soon. I know an Italian who was a bootblack ten years ago and now bosses bootblacks all over the city, who has so much money that if it was turned into gold it would weight more than himself.

"Francisco and I have a room to ourselves now and some people call us 'swells.' Ciguciano said that we should be great men. Francisco bought a gold watch with a gold chain as thick as his thumb. He is a very handsome fellow and I think he likes a young lady that he met at a picnic out at Ridgewood."[65]

11

These Italians, Russians, Spanish, Portuguese, Greeks, and Austro-Czech-Hungarians, who came in their ten millions between 1900 and 1920, were—it was true—persuaded to come to America because there was work and pay here, particularly on the railroads and in the factories. But one must not have the misconception that industry is entirely or even mostly the man-ufacture and transport of steel objects over steel rail. It also requires millions of even more humble laborers—people to dig gravel, build roads, carry bricks, mix cement, dig sewers, take garbage away to the dump, grow onions in vacant lots and dismal suburbs, spin cloth and stitch garments and launder them when soiled, and cut hair and sharpen knives and shine shoes. This swarm of secondary jobs were worse paid than even the semi-skilled coal miners and steel-molders. They were allowed to come here because their labor, and what was crucial—their labor at low rates—was a necessity of industrial growth. Americans of the second and third generation, whether English, Irish, Finnish, or German, would no longer do such work.

First the Chinese, then the Irish, and finally the southern and eastern Europeans, which included the Jews, were a threat by their very numbers to the fragile structure of wage agreements in the last third of the century. Prejudice of one immigrant group against another was the disguise for economic fear, and though the prejudice was vile the fear was real:

"I want to congratulate to your noble lawful stand you are taken in regards to undesirable immigration. I am a Union workman, have been organizer of workmen's Unions for years and well able to know the opinion of organized labor regarding immigration and the fulfillments of the laws on this point . . . especially in keeping out they dirty low bread [*sic*] jewish and slavic element, those that live on hogs food and therefore work for a pittance. You wish you would be more stricter yet, as we have too much of this undesirable trash already. Let the nations that created them, take care of them . . ."[66] This was a letter written by a German immigrant to William Williams, Commissioner of Immigration at Ellis Island, in response to Williams' strict (indeed over-strict) application of rules against the immigrants at the end of the century.

Though we deplore the division of humanity into arbitrary and hostile groups, we must recognize how natural it is to the species. And yet how unnatural. Human beings from every group resemble one another right down to their hostility. The emigrations to America, whether by the English, or Welsh, Bohemian, Finnish, Sicilian, Pole, Montenegrin, Russian, or Jew unfolded in extraordinarily similar ways. "The village where I was born. . . ." Thus began the life account of what might have been any of the above nationalities, but was in this case the story of Lee Chew, a man from "the province of Canton on one of the banks of the Sikiang River." He describes his house and his early life:

"My father's house is built of fine blue brick, better than the brick in the houses here in the United States. It is only one story high, roofed with red tiles and surrounded by a stone wall which also incloses the yard. There are four rooms in the house, one large living room which serves for a parlor and three private rooms, one occupied by my grandfather, who is very old and very honorable; another by my father and mother, and the third by my oldest brother and his wife and two little children. There are no windows, but the door is left open all day.

"All the men of the village have farms, but they don't live on them as the farmers do here; they live in the village, but go out during the day time and work their farms, coming home before dark. My father has a farm of about ten acres, on which he grows a great abundance of things—sweet potatoes, rice, beans, peas, yams, sugar cane, pineapples, bananas, lychee nuts and palms. . ."[67]

Compare the feeling, not the detail (marvelous though it is), and the emphasis on family life apparent in this story, recorded in 1903, with the 1904 account of the Slavic immigrant Antanas Kaztauskis:

". . . It was a cold December. We were in a big room in our log house in Lithuania. My good, kind, thin old mother sat near the wide fireplace, working her brown spinning wheel, with which she made cloth for our shirts and coats and pants. I sat on the floor in front of her with my knee-boots off and my feet stretched out to the fire. My feet were cold, for I had been out with my young brother in the freezing sheds milking the cows and feeding the sheep and geese. I leaned my head on her dress and kept yawning and thinking about my big goose feather bed. My father sat and smoked his pipe across the fireplace. Between was a kerosene lamp on a table, and under it say the ugly shoemaker on a stool finishing a big yellow boot. His sleeves were rolled up; his arms were thin and bony, but you could see how strong the fingers and wrist were, for when he grabbed the needle he jerked it through and the whole arm's length up. This arm kept going up and down. Every time it went up he jerked back his long mixed-up red hair and grunted. And you could just see his face—bony and shut together tight, and his narrow sharp eyes looking down. Then his head would go down again, and his hair would get all mixed up. I kept watching him. My fat, older brother, who sat behind with his fat wife, grinned and said: 'Look out or your eyes will make holes in the leather.' My brother's eyes were always dull and sleepy. Men like him stay in Lithuania."[68]

The reasons for going to America were different, but equally thoughtful. The Slav was certain to be drafted into the Russian army, and like any sensible man, he saw no reason to fight for a cause not his own.

The Cantonese, also the son of a farmer, simply thought to better his life:

"When I was ten years of age I worked on my father's farm, digging, hoeing, manuring, gathering and carrying the crop. We had no horses, as nobody under the rank of an official is allowed to have a horse in China, and horses do not work on farms there, which is the reason why the roads there are so bad. The people cannot use roads as they are used here, and so they do not make them.

"I worked on my father's farm till I was about sixteen years of age, when a man of our tribe came back from America and took ground as large as four city blocks and made a paradise of it. He put a large stone wall around and led some streams through and built a palace and summer house and about twenty other structures, with beautiful bridges over the streams and walks and roads. Trees and flowers, singing birds, water fowl and curious animals were within the walls.

"The man had gone away from our village a poor boy. Now he returned with unlimited wealth. . ."[69]

The Chinese boy, like the Lithuanian, had to cut the arteries of family life, and the operation was painful, but more so to those who stayed than to those who left:

"The wealth of this man filled my mind with the idea that I, too, would like to go to the country of the wizards and gain some of their wealth, and after a long time my father consented, and gave me his blessing, and my mother took leave of me with tears, while my grandfather laid his hand upon my head and told me to remember and live up to the admonitions of the Sages, to avoid gambling, bad women and men of evil minds, and so to govern my conduct that when I died my ancestors might rejoice to welcome me as a guest on high."[70]

The Lithuanian boy also suffered the tears of uprooted love:

"My mother began to cry. 'He cannot go if his father commands him to stay,' she kept saying. I knew this was true, for in Lithuania a father can command his son till he dies.

"'No, he must not go,' said the shoemaker, 'if his father commands him to stay.' He turned and looked hard at my father. My father was looking into the fire. 'If he goes,' said my father, 'those Russians will never let him come back.' My mother cried harder. We all waited for him to say something else. In about five minutes the shoemaker got up and asked, 'Well, what do you say—the army or America?' But my father shook his head and would not say anything . . . My mother stopped crying and went out. Our house was in two parts of two rooms each. Between the parts was an open shed and in this shed was a big oven, where she was baking bread that night. I could hear her pull it out to look at it and then push it back. Then she came in and sat down beside me and began spinning again. I leaned against her dress and watched the fire and thought about America. . ."[71]

His mother died, and this event persuaded his father to let him go. He was twenty years old, and would have to do service in the Czarist army within a year. He went to see his girlfriend to say goodbye:

". . . It was ten miles and the road was dusty, so I carried my boots over my shoulder, as we always did, and I put them on when I came near her house. When I saw her I felt very bad, and so did she. I had the strongest wish I ever had to take hold of her and keep her all my life. We stayed together till it was dark and the night fogs came up out of the field grass, and we could hardly see the house. Then she said good-by. For many nights I kept remembering the way she looked up at me."[72]

The Chinese boy was too young for such attachments, but, like the Lithuanian on the other side of the world, he was astonished at the miracles of travel:

"My father gave me $100, and I went to Hong Kong with five other boys from our place and we got steerage passage on a steamer, paying $50 each. Everything was new to me. All my life I had been used to sleeping on a board bed with a wooden pillow, and I found the steamer's bunk very uncomfortable, because it was so soft. The food was different from that which I had been used to, and I did not like it at all. I was afraid of the stews, for the thought of what they might be made of by the wicked wizards of the ship made me ill. Of the great power of these people I saw many signs. The engines that moved the ship were wonderful monsters, strong enough to lift mountains. When I got to San Francisco, which was before the passage of the Exclusion act, I was half starved, because I was afraid to eat the provisions of the barbarians, but a few days' living in the Chinese quarter made me happy again . . ."[73]

The Lithuanian had many of the same emotions, for he too was a country boy unused to the rapid, mysterious, and brutal rhythms of industrial life in America: ". . . The boat was the biggest boat I had ever seen— the machine that made it go was very big, and so was the horn that blew in a fog. I felt everything get bigger and go quicker every day . . .

"That first night we sat around in the house and they asked me, "Well, why did you come?" I told them about that first night and what the ugly shoemaker said about 'life, liberty and the getting of happiness.' They all leaned back and laughed. 'What you need is money,' they said. 'It was all right at home. You wanted nothing. You ate your own meat and your own things on the farm. You made your own clothes and had your own leather. The other things you got at the Jew man's store and paid him with sacks of rye. But here you want a hundred things. Whenever you walk out you see new things you want, and you must have money to buy everything.'

"Then one man asked me, 'How much have you?' and I told him $30. 'You must buy clothes to look rich, even if you are not rich,' he said. 'With good clothes you will have friends.' "[74]

Why did the American unitary system of values, based on an oblong of printed green paper, astonish the Lithuanian and yet remain comprehensible to the Chinese? Because the essentially and firmly Anglo culture of this country was middle-class, above but not too far above the cruel boundaries of poverty. And it was a group that historically did not have great possession of land, which was the value currency of the European gentry, and did not base its whole vitality on such possession or tillage, as the European peasant did. By their very nature, middle-class values were upwardly mobile. And status and success could most easily be measured in the abstracts of currency. If the most valued and intoxicating power for the landed gentry of Europe was their control of masses of peasantry, the middle classes, the artisans, and the merchants risen by the power of money out of mere labor, put their trust and made their metric in pounds, rubles—dollars:

". . . We were tired out when we reached the stockyards, so we stopped on the bridge and looked into the river out there. It was so full of grease and dirt and sticks and boxes that it looked like a big, wide, dirty street, except in some places, where it boiled up. It made me sick to look at it. When I looked away I could see on one side some big fields full of holes, and these were the city dumps. On the other side were the stockyards, with twenty tall slaughter house chimneys. The wind blew a big smell from them to us. Then we walked on between the yards and the dumps and all the houses looked bad and poor. In our house my room was in the basement. I lay down on the floor with three other men and the air was rotten. I did not go to sleep for a long time. I knew then that money was everything I needed. My money was almost gone and I thought that I would soon die unless I got a job, for this was not like home. Here money was everything and a man without money must die."[75]

Lee Chew, whose father was a prosperous peasant and a member of a very highly evolved if pre-industrial society, was close to the lower edge of the middle-class. Money, and money as measure of the world and of oneself, was not a barbaric language. But to Antanas Kaztauskis, son and grandson and great-grandson of poor peasants, the acquisition and possession of land was entirely sane and natural, while there was something about money and especially naked money, that was hostile and mysterious. So that crucial difference existed between these two immigrants, along with their human similarities. Both had to eat, and both, therefore, had to get a job, and that as quickly as possible because they were both poor:

". . . A man got me work as a house servant in an American family, and my start was the same as that of almost all the Chinese in this country . . .

"I did not know how to do anything, and I did not understand what the lady said to me, but she showed me how to cook, wash, iron, sweep, dust, make beds, wash dishes, clean windows, paint and brass, polish the knives and forks, etc., by doing the things herself and then overseeing my efforts to imitate her. She would take my hands and show them how to do things. She and her husband and children laughed at me a great deal, but it was all good natured . . . I worked for two years as a servant, getting at the last $35 a month. I sent money home to comfort my parents, but tho I dressed well and lived well and had pleasure, going quite often to the Chinese theater and to dinner parties in Chinatown, I saved $50 in the first six months, $90 in the second, $120 in the third and $150 in the fourth. So I had $410 at the end of two years, and I was now ready to start in business.

"When I first opened a laundry it was in company with a partner, who had been in the business for some years. We went to a town about 500 miles inland, where a railroad was building. We got a board shanty and worked for the men employed by the railroads. Our rent cost us $10 a month and food nearly $5 a week each, for all food was dear and we wanted the best of everything—we lived principally on rice, chickens, ducks and pork, and did our own cooking. The Chinese take naturally to cooking. It cost us about $50 for our furniture and apparatus, and we made close upon $60 a week, which we divided between us . . ."[76]

The Slav went to the Chicago stockyards to look for work. Why didn't the Chinese do the same thing? Or, obversely, why didn't the Slav open a laundry? Here we have come to a central fact. Immigrants, for want of deeper ties, tended to follow the road already cleared by their own group. They may have hated such employment, but they felt it was safe. Their contacts were there. The experience of those who spoke or acted as they did, Cantonese or Lithuanian, had already made the strange job familiar:

". . . [W]e went to the yards. Men and women were walking in by thousands as far as we could see. We went to the doors of one big slaughter house. There was a crowd of about 200 men waiting there for a job. They looked hungry and kept watching the door. At last a special policeman came out and began pointing to men, one by one. Each one jumped forward. Twenty-three were taken. Then they all went inside, and all the others turned their faces away and looked tired. I remember one boy sat down and cried, just next to me, on a pile of boards. Some policemen waved their clubs and we all walked on. I found some Lithuanians to talk with, who told me they had come every morning for three weeks. Soon we met other crowds coming away from other slaughter houses, and we all walked around and felt bad and tired and hungry.

"That night I told my friends that I would not do this many days, but would go some place else. 'Where?' they asked me, and I began to see then that I was in bad trouble, because I spoke no English. Then one man told me to give him $5 to give the special policeman. I did this and the next morning the policeman pointed me out, so I had a job . . ."[77]

Both men felt the poisonous and explosive air of prejudice with every breath, though the Chinese suffered its distortions more deeply: ". . . We had to put up with many insults and some frauds, as men would come in and claim parcels that did not belong to them, saying they had lost their tickets, and would fight if they did not get what they asked for. Sometimes we were taken before Magistrates and fined for losing shirts that we had never seen. On the other hand, we were making money, and even after sending home $3 a week I was able to save about $15.[78]

The Lithuanian felt he was continually harrassed by urban dishonesty. His was the typical attitude, anywhere in the world, of the cautious, close-mouthed, anti-authoritarian peasant: ". . . At that time I believed that all men in Chicago were grafters when they had to be. They only wanted to push themselves. Now, when I was idle I began to look about, and everywhere I saw sharp men beating out slow men like me. Even if we worked hard it did us no good. I had saved $13—$5 a week for six weeks makes $30, and take off $15 for six weeks' board and lodging and $2 for other things. I showed this to a Lithuanian, who had been here two years, and he laughed. 'It will be taken from you,' he said."[79]

Just as the Chinese resented exclusion and yet wanted more of their own sort to come to America, so did the Lithuanian. ". . . All of us were telling our friends to come soon. Soon they came—even thousands. The employers in the yard liked this, because those sharp foremen are inventing new machines and the work is easier to learn, and so these slow Lithuanians and even green girls can learn to do it, and then the Americans and Germans and Irish are put out and the employer saves money, because the Lithuanians work cheaper . . ."[80]

Finally both men had that universal and curious illusion of all migrants: they remained homesick for a childhood landscape. Lee Chew went home in 1897, but returned the next year. The Slav never went back.

". . . We bought this song, which was written in Brooklyn by P. Brandukas. He, too, was homesick. It is sung all over Chicago now and you can hear it in the summer evenings through the open windows. In English it is something like this:

> "Oh, Lithuania, so dear to me,
> Good-by to you, my Fatherland.
> Sorrowful in my heart I leave you,
> I know not who will stay to guard you.' "[81]

12

The difference between these two young men was not only class, nationality, and color, but the fact that they came to different Americas. Chew came to San Francisco in 1883, and thus to the West and an economy bursting with disorderly growth. The Lithuanian came in 1900, when the American economy, while still vigorously growing, did not need the imported shiploads of labor to fill vacant jobs but to displace a work force from an earlier migration which was now becoming humanized, and therefore threatened to raise the cost of production. The Chinese became a businessman. The Slav raised his status, too, from cattle killer to cattle butcher. He joined a union led at first by the Irish, then by a Lithuanian who deliberately set them out on strike so that his countrymen would spend time and money in his saloon. The next union was a lot better:

"It has raised my wages. The man who worked at my job before the union came was getting through the year an average of $9 a week. I am getting $11. In my first job I got $5 a week. The man who works there now gets $5.75.

"It has given me more time to learn to read and speak and enjoy life like an American. . . ."[82]

The differences between these men are distinct enough and may obscure their similarities. They were both young men, torn up and moving away through the processes of their own will. They were both survivors of a rite of passage: a sea crossing, poverty, strangeness, each event as crucial as any circumcision. This violent and dislocating change was just as true of the young women, of which there were an astonishing number—at least a third of all immigrants. Their sexual status gave them a more specific coloring than the men had, so that it's harder, sometimes, to draw the general from the singular. Yet, for this purpose, let's look at the experience of two women, both immigrants, born tens of thousands of miles apart, and as different as the men were in skin color, in religion, and in language. They were of the same period—the generation before World War I. One was Japanese, the other Jewish.

The first element common to both was a certain sly courage, stamina, and a kind of testy wit. The Japanese women often came here to marry men almost unknown to them. The typical young Japanese laborer, at work in a railway camp or a lumber mill, could not afford to go all the way back to Japan to look for a bride. So the woman was married to his photograph. Both parties had a touching faith in the truth of the photographic image, which was generally altered by the American portraitist to remove bumps and defects.

"When I was aboard the 'Kashima Maru' bound for Seattle in 1918, I met many picture brides. Having plenty of free time, we talked about our personal affairs, and they spoke about their husbands whom they had never seen. Some of them proudly said such things as: 'My husband is the president of a company.' Or, 'Mine is the manager of a large store.'

"But when the boat finally landed, the 'president' and the 'manager' turned out to be unbearably disgusting, about 40 or 50 years old, and their humble job was working on the railroads. The brides were between 18 and 23. Some of them upon meeting their disappointing 'president' and 'manager' promptly said No! and pled to return on the same boat. Such refusals invariably put their husbands at a complete loss.

"This sort of case most frequently occurred when the man had sent a picture of himself which was taken when he was young. Some brides therefore, seeing their husbands darkened with sunburn, and with gnarled hands, found the image in their minds so different that they claimed to the immigration officials, 'This one is not my husband'—which got the husbands into trouble with the law. But even under such discouraging circumstances some of them gave up and went on into the marriage. There were others, however, who insisted 'No, no!' and stayed in Seattle hotels for over a month, crying and begging to go back to Japan. Still others in the interim of waiting for the next boat, got pregnant and then gave up. And of course there were some who, while refusing their husbands, found a better man and changed over to him."[83]

As the strongest hatred of the Chinese was in California, the prejudice simply spread to any Oriental because all of them, to the *keto* (the Japanese word for "hairy foreigner"), obviously looked alike. Yet there were strong and quite rational reasons for this dislike of one group by another:

"In Pike Place Market in Seattle my chickens and eggs sold well. Therefore, the people in the same business tried to exclude me, but our attorney, Mr. Custer, took care of it. However, for one reason or another they did violent things and mean tricks. When they came to ask me to sign a petition against the rules of the market, and I refused, they immediately picked up my eggs and started throwing them at me. Another time they came to claim that more than half the eggs I had sold were rotten. One day I was selling next to a lady who was trying to exclude me. I bought ice-cream and offered her some, but she spit on me and said, 'I don't want it!' and knocked my ice-cream out of my hands. Then at around 4 p.m., suddenly she started suffering from stomach ache. So I called her son for her and, getting the key for the storage locker, put away her possessions. After that she changed her attitude toward me."[84]

Sometimes as so often since its unhappy invention, dynamite, took the place of reason and decency:

"I'll never forget it. It was almost 40 years ago, on the 13th of April. With 5 or 6 other people I had been weeding the peas and had returned home awfully tired. I cooked dinner and finished the dishes, and as usual took a bath and went to bed at around 10 o'clock.

"I wonder how many hours later . . . with loud cracking sounds the house was shaking. I suddenly woke up. My husband jumped out of bed, threw on his robe and ran out. Beside myself with shock, I followed him. Just as I took a couple of steps out of the house, the second explosion took place. As I watched, pieces of flying wood were landing within two feet of my husband, and I was scared to death! It was dynamite that caused the explosion—some in the garage and some in the Dodge three-quarter-ton truck. Our house was wooden, about 20 feet from the hands' house. Their place was about 14' by 36', and half of the space was a garage.

"I was most afraid for Mr. and Mrs. Kurihara who were sleeping in the hands' house. I was terrified that they might be hurt, and so we went to them at once. They were standing outside with vacant, shocked expressions. Fortunately they were uninjured, and it was a tremendous relief. Immediately we took them into our house and spent the rest of the night in anxiety and fear.

"I was much more scared when I looked at the ruins early the next morning. The second explosion was from a bomb set under the truck. The fender had been blown 20 feet, and glass was scattered all over the area. The wall board separating the garage and the hands' house had all fallen over the Kurihara's bed."[85]

Not that the Japanese were entirely free of anti-white feelings. Indeed they were unexpectedly specific: "Along with the differences in the American style of living, I couldn't get used to American foods. The smell of celery got to my nose. It smelled like medicine and I couldn't eat it however hard I tried. Since in Japan eating raw vegetables was rare, we felt as if the whites were horses, watching them chomp away on raw celery, parsley and lettuce. Butter and cheese were also too smelly, and I could not put them in my mouth."[86] The Japanese believed that the food one ate gave each nationality its characteristic smell; the underarm odor of whites was reported to be really sickening.

These trials and prejudices were the lot of every Oriental immigrant.

More typical of women's experience is this description of a sorrowful departure:

"I left Japan dressed in pure Japanese style—kimono with light blue background designed with white waves and a plover flying. I had on a *Hakata* sash—white striped with black, blue and orange—and Japanese sandals with white and orange straps.

"On the way from Kobe to Yokohama I looked at Mt. Fuji standing loftily against the cloudless blue sky and in that moment I resolved: A woman going to America, depending on a husband she has never seen, should have the noble spirit of this majestic mountain. Such high-mindedness and eternally firm strength, indifferent to any weather, should be the spirit of Japanese women like me."[87]

Even more universal was the incredible labor of all women immigrants, and that was certainly as true of the women on the *Mayflower* as of those on the S.S. *Maru:*

". . . I arrived at night on July 31 at my husband's house in Spokane. But I had to get up at six the next morning to work! My husband was running the Rainier Laundry, with two other people, on Third Avenue West, doing washing, ironing and pick-up-and-delivery service. Each man had charge of one of the three jobs. At noon I had to prepare a meal for twelve. The employees worked from 8 a.m. to 5 p.m., but I began to fix the dinner at 5 p.m., cooking for five or six persons, and then after that I started my night work. The difficult ironing and pressing was left for me. At that time ladies' blouses were high-necked and long-sleeved, with much silk lace and other decoration. I could barely iron two blouses an hour, taking great pains to press out each scallop with the point of the iron. Frequently I had to work till twelve or one o'clock. Not only I, but all the ladies engaging in the laundry business had the same duties."[88]

There is very little to distinguish the Japanese wife from any other rural woman of the same period, since the universals of labor were much the same. However, the particulars were certainly different:

"Before we could afford a machine to cut wood, my husband and I cut the trees with an eight-foot saw, split the wood with a wedgehammer and brought it to the house on a sled. At the time we had two children, aged three and one, and with them to take care of I couldn't do so much work, so when a friend of ours went back to Japan, I asked him to take them with him. Sending them away when they were so adorable and young made my milk run so! I thought of them on the boat, calling for their mother, and I couldn't sleep for sorrow and loneliness. We cultivated new land and planted berries, but that year we didn't get any crop, so again we kept cows. We also raised fifty chickens.

"We had six children, and five of them my husband and I delivered without help. We bought rice and soy sauce from Furuya Company or Tsutagawa, and butchered two 300-pound hogs per year, making bacon and lard and canning the pork. Since we had our own milk, eggs and vegetables, we had no food problems. However, our life was very hard because of insurance payments on my husband's policy, complicated by poor crops and the rent payments. So for three years my husband went to Kent for work.

"While taking care of six children, I also took care of the cows and made cream and butter. Along with the vegetables and eggs, I loaded the cream and butter on the wagon and sold them to a store attached to a sawmill in Port Gamble. As I had language difficulties, I worried about it, but when I was leaving the store, a man said: 'Don't you want these empty boxes, too?' and he loaded crates and boxes on the wagon for me. Thus we finally paid off all our debts and heaved a sigh of relief . . ."[89]

Japanese women were rare, and Japanese men were not always conventionally polite about how they got them:

"Soon after I landed, when I was helping in a hardware store on Maynard Avenue which was run by my sister Suzue's husband, Komakichi Horikawa, I received a love letter from a young man who said he was the nephew of the manager of Matsuba-tei, a Japanese restaurant. If that were the only thing, it would have been a commonplace incident among young people. But when I didn't answer it, the man telephoned me and complained, 'You embarrassed me!' He threatened me, saying, 'I'll get even with you!' I was scared. Almost on the instant, I left Horikawa's house and moved to Miss Rumsey's Women's Home. However, since the man came to the Home carrying a gun, Miss Rumsey found me shelter in some white person's home.

"Like a madman, the man shot into the Horikawa's store and injured my sister on the forehead. Of course he was arrested, but at the request of his uncle we allowed the situation to pass. The man was released after six months and went to Alaska, but I heard later that he shot and killed an Indian woman and her daughter."[90]

For those women who didn't like, for example, weeding on their knees for hours every day, or carrying water "in two five-gallon cans on a pole," there was always another choice. They could become prostitutes in San Francisco or Seattle. A somewhat higher rank dealt only with white customers, and were called "white men's birds," and lived in brothels bearing the sign: "Whites Only." Or a Japanese woman could work in just such a brothel and still remain pure—a *nembutsuko*, a little Buddha:

"It was 1916 when I came to America from Hikone City, Shiga Prefecture. As my husband, Yosajiro, asked me to take over his job while he was working at Interbay Railroad, I began to do house-cleaning in a 'pink hotel' in the red-light district. It was on the corner of 6th Avenue and Lane Street, and it had no name. I went there at ten o'clock in the morning. My job was to clean the women's rooms, five rooms upstairs, two downstairs, the halls and staircases. When I finished I went to the downstairs shop selling cigarettes and soda water. I stayed there until twelve midnight or later.

"There were five or six women, white and black. Their customers came one after another and kept them busy. Since I didn't understand a word of English, I couldn't answer the women. To whatever they said, I had to answer 'Um-hum.' My salary was $30. According to my husband, who came here in 1902, there was one brothel where Japanese prostitutes lived. On the way back to the hotel at midnight they used to stop at my husband's grocery story on 6th Avenue and Lane Street, a block from their hotel, to buy penny candies. Anyway, hurrying back home from work, past eleven at night, I felt miserable to think why I had to live on like this, having come so far to America. But I had no choice; I had to survive."[91]

That universal longing of every immigrant for the early and the familiar, that profound craving for the milk of childhood, took a characteristic form for the traditionally literary Japanese in the homemade poem, the haiku:

> In spite of aging,
> Still the homesick child in me
> Who sailed so far out
> From Yokohama harbor . . .
> I still long for my hometown.[92]

And again:

> America . . . once
> A dream of hope and longing.
> Now a life of tears.[93]

A fierce passion, an incredible will to survive was also a general characteristic of every immigrant. In a new, strange, hostile, and laborious world, the ego is naked and must learn not to be vulnerable. And this will to stubbornly endure was especially true of women. So it is less as contrast than as proof that we listen to the voice of a woman who came to America in the same decade as these Japanese girls and from as great a distance, but from the opposite direction.

Mrs. G. was born in a Russian town now in Poland, destroyed in every generation by the fires and wounds of war. It had about a thousand people, of which, remarkably, four-fifths were Jews. "There was a couple rich people but the most were poor. Scholars. More rabbis there than anything."[94]

There were no pogroms there, within her memory, possibly because, as Mrs. G. said, "We organized how to protect ourself—defense league—the children they were going in the cellar—where they kept cabbage and everything so we went there—and my father went to shul [synagogue] he couldn't go out to fight but it was young people like revolutionists that time in 1904 in 1903 they organized a brigade . . . They had sticks, they had iron bars and there where you take out from the oven the food they had a [long wooden shovel] . . . They organized in case of fire, in case a pogrom."[95] In spite of the lopsided ration in the population, there was rampant prejudice: "The Jews, when a policeman came, I had to get off the sidewalk . . . I remember like now there was a big dairy farm but belonged to not to the Jews, so some girls went to buy on the gallons milk to carry milk I went too my momma didn't know I run away to go to the dairy and when I went back youngs boys 17 or 16 they come and take the jug and they threw it away the milk and they tear out half of my hair and I was afraid even to tell what happened . . . I was about 12."[96]

The town also had a certain local renown for its elaborate, powerful, and poetic superstitions. Many of these centered around illness, for it was common for half one's children to die before they were five. To cure diphtheria, for example, it was first necessary to determine who had spoken well of the child, and then one wrapped the child's throat in a cloth soaked in the benevolent person's urine. In the case of imminent death, a religious ceremony was conducted to change the victim's name, thus confusing—whom?

Life in this village was not the paradise of poverty and piety that later and more sentimental writers have imagined. The house in which Mrs. G. lived, with her parents, a brother, and two sisters, was a single room with an earthen floor. "Kitchen? What kind of kitchen? It was one room. In that one room was a big closet that made a bedroom like, and the clothes, and the other side was a big . . . screen. There we sold . . . candles—in the house. [My mother] didn't make in the house the candles, but she sold it, she made it in a far away out, because it was the candles a bad smell, so she used to go far away, it was outside gardens, far away, it was a couple of miles empty, you know, and a little shack in the middle."[97] The making of candles required boiling the tallow over an outdoor fire. Ordinary candles were made by dipping the linen wick over and over again; holy candles were made by measuring the wick around all four sides of the grave of a *tzadik*, a secret holy man, of which there are only thirty in the world at any one time; the work often took all night, and on such occasions, Mrs. G.'s mother was assisted by a house guest, a man who had once knocked at the door and asked for bread, and had stayed for the next twenty years.

Girls were rarely given much education, but Mrs. G. got hers mostly by proxy, for her father, a man "so tall my mother was ashamed to walk with him," taught only male pupils. She sat under the table and listened as the lessons droned on for hours all day. On Saturday afternoon, the pupils' fathers would come to hear the progress of their sons and wallop them if they hadn't done well. Mrs. G. would coach them from a special hiding place. "We had a big sofa so I used to crawl in there in the corner that nobody sees me but the chickens. We had a big like a bakery oven and on the bottom was a big hole, but when the chickens see me under the table they liked me, they recognized me, they came my father used to feel very bad about it."[98] In this peculiar manner, Mrs. G. learned to read and write.

When she was thirteen, Mrs. G. went to work far away, in the city of Vilna. Aside from steadfastly refusing to sleep with her boss, she had a rather good time in what was then a charming city, alive with political movements of all sorts. When she could save enough money, she visited her family. "I used to go up on the train under the bench and go home to see the family."[99]

On one of these visits, at the age of seventeen, she heard that there was a chance to go to America. Her older sister had gone two years before and had sent "a ship ticket." Her mother was so grieved by her first daughter's departure, that "she went to bed for a year, but she didn't go for me . . ." Mrs. G. went with a false passport, the identification of the daughter of a neighbor, because such papers cost money. The boat would depart from Bremen, Germany, and after crossing the border, she took the train. "The train was packed up just like sardines you couldn't even breathe. We were all standing all the time and no food . . . The boat was first class, second class, and I was third class. Downstairs, in the basement like . . . the mothers was killing the children because they give them the cushions, the pillows to bring to America, but nobody helped the girls to carry, but I had a net, was very light my mother put in where I should have food I should have where to sleep and she killed me with that. Heavy . . . The Germans they put you in line like they have soldiers in line and they was marching with us to the place where the boat. They gave you food but was worms in it, real worms, it was hard like rocks, I had to eat it. The pig that you hate, they would treat him better than they treated us. Then I was real sick. There was a lot of young people dancing, drinking, crying. The boat was going 19 days, it landed in Baltimore . . . I had to show $25 in American money . . . They put on me a tag that I'm not so good with the eyes."[100]

The truth was that she had had an eye infection when she was about eight, and when it persisted, her parents had taken her to a neighboring village where another secret *tzadik* had just died, and to cure her, they put his dead hand on her eyes. Years later, on her arrival in America, "they took me in a room . . . they put out a 5 about that big to see if I could read I told them I'm not coming to go to the houses to beg. I'm coming to work here what do you mean you put in that, it's a five, I see everything. The man laughed so hard he couldn't stop laughing . . . Even if you had bugs they're not going to let you in but they're not going to send you back . . . On the ship you don't wash, what kind of wash . . ."[101]

Tagged like a parcel, she was sent by train to Chicago. "They put us in a wagon like a bundle they have to bring you to the house and sign that you're [delivered]. It was a wagon with horses. It was no cars then so we were on the wagon and they didn't leave me out . . . They had to bring me home so [her older sister and her husband] were running after all the way through they were running after us [till] they brought us to that address my sister was only two years in America."[102]

Though Mrs. G. had been raised in a one room hut with no floor, the tenement in Chicago shocked her as deeply as the rural shacks of Oregon and Washington upset the Japanese women. Both had expected houses that would fit the splendid dream of America, and the reality of poverty is repeatedly and monotonously traumatic. "They lived in a shack in Chicago. It was a wooden house four flats . . . Was four rooms, one room was a front room, one room was a kitchen, and two little bedrooms and the bedrooms was with wire they shouldn't spill anything in the windows a little bit off there was a shul in the alley so the men when they came they put on my windows—they made like they ain't doing something . . . I thought I'll die I got so scared they didn't have no toilets so they went—on my window. And my sister I told her I said why don't you move nobody believed it. One woman downstairs [in the basement] from us had a husband a tubercular. Next door from us was a family with three boys upstairs was a little woman with children. And our family. And one toilet. The whole house was the toilet to stay in line. Outside? No! There was a little hole, inside, and it filled up a hole and we stayed in line for going in the morning. Bathtub? What kind of bathtub? Was a public place—a shower, a bath . . . I said, look, can't get in the toilet, the men stay and go and the rats in the walls I says [to my sister] if you'll stay another month I'll die here, I can't take it . . ."[103] It's fascinating, this interest that both the Japanese and the Jewish women had in toilet arrangements. Mrs. G. was particularly upset that America was so crude and vulgar as to provide a toilet "inside the house!" and she "used to run to the Pennsylvania Railroad station a mile to go to the toilet."

By sheer chance, one of her father's ex-pupils in that remote Polish village was now the assistant manager in a garment factory in Chicago. He got her a job for which she was scarcely suited, for she had never worked on any sort of machine before. "[It was] sewing, a big factory. Blouses and petticoats silk petticoats but I was working on a machine, I couldn't even see. Nothing. How did I learn, I learned the hard way because he took me in, I had a lot of nerve then now I haven't got the nerve so—the first week I made 60 cents that was piece work, I couldn't thread the needle in the machine."[104] Her friend Ida, whom she had met on the boat ("a shipsister"), threaded the needle. "I'm not handy you know the kup [head] thinks but the hand don't work, that was very bad, was very bad . . . When I worked piece work they didn't care . . . I was very fresh in the factory, it was a cutter and he was a very good man, and he cut very good work so then they sent away that cutter, then a young man came, and the forelady came, a big Polish girl, and she . . . wanted to throw out the Jewish girls, we didn't have too many, only about five."[105]

Mrs. G. protested because the new cutter, in order to save cloth, often gave them several pieces instead of a single piece to stitch. "They paid 12¢ a bunch, so you had to sew three times, and then they gave us all kind of colors and I with my eye, was a yuntiff ['a holiday'—ironically of course]."[106] She protested in her bad English, and the forelady—"a Jew-hater, she could eat me up every day for breakfast they don't care . . ."[107]—fired her. But she was restored to her job by the assistant manager.

These factory girls often sang as they worked. "One machine sing, and another machine sing, but they didn't sing all together like an opera . . . We used to sing sentimental—but this is a revolutionary song: [translated] Howl, howl angry wind, now is your time, drive the little birds from the branches, do whatever you will."[108] They also sang the "International": "Union, union, what kind of union? I'll tell you about the union, I was in the beginning of the union . . . The union started about 1914, they started to organize about a block or two away where you take the bus, and you talk with them outside, we should try and we should go down and we shouldn't be scabs . . . First it was New York organized and then it was Chicago, and Chicago was very hard to organize . . . so it took about half a year . . . They organized, asked for a five day week, eight and a half hours work, one half hour for lunch—I wore a sign, and picketing I did but I didn't holler, I can't fight, so I just walked . . . One man, he came to my house, he was blue, beaten up . . . He was scabbing, I didn't hit nobody, I didn't holler . . . but it was hard, was very hard [till] that factory signed. It was nine weeks . . . Union songs? A full book! . . . But it was the I.W.W. songs mixed in, it was no good, was too strict."[109]

A factory job requires a peculiar mixture of close attention and mental dullness. Most workers daydream all day, and although their hands are busy, a wide path in their minds wanders off into fantasy. For the immigrants this meant thoughts of home and childhood, however difficult these were in fact. The Japanese women from the islands of the Pacific were homesick, and so was Mrs. G. from the center of Europe. One of the former wrote:

> Every day I watch,
> Looking westward to Japan.
> What attracts me there?
> Fuji stands against that sky
> In eternal gown of snow. [110]

Meanwhile, Mrs. G. thought not of that muddy, dark down with the immense winters and the constant hunger and the stifling deaths of children, but of her first metropolis, Vilna: "Vilna was a beautiful city beautiful, good, the toilets was in the yard, but no flushing toilets but that time, it was harder, but here was hell. So then I insisted again to look for an apartment, the apartment we paid $12 a month and there was $14. Terrible, Chicago, I was very, very disappointed, but Vilna was very literary, people had libraries, Jewish, everything . . ."[111]

Mrs. G. was getting older—nineteen, twenty, twenty-one—and she was still unmarried. "The boss [in the factory] when he wants to unbutton my blouse—all the girls wore buttons on their blouse in the back—but I didn't come any more with [a blouse with buttons in the back]. And I didn't say anything. I had [a blouse] over the head, no buttons . . . so he smiled a little but he didn't say anything . . . He didn't go to the Jewish girls anymore, I didn't tell him yes or no, I turned around I picked up I went to the washroom . . . Was a good looking man but I wasn't for sale . . ."[112] Mrs. G.

was small and dark, and never thought herself attractive enough for marriage; her older sister was considered the beauty in the family. She was constantly kidded by the other factory girls. "They said my neck is dirty, so they took me to the washroom, they powdered, they said I don't wash myself so they rubbed they made me sick, I was so dark they didn't believe me, what could I do."[113]

She joined an amateur theatrical group and played character parts in plays like *God, Man, and Devil*—"I think he stole it from Faust"—and a very popular play called *The Yiddish King Lear*. It's astonishing how many immigrant groups kept a circle of warmth and kinship by staging amateur theater. The Japanese in Seattle performed kabuki plays: ". . . It was amateur performing in a basement theater, so naturally the properties and stage settings were insufficient. Wigs were made of paper, and the costumes were cheap and crude. It is said that the majority of the audience were prostitutes."[114] There were, of course, many Jewish prostitutes in American cities; sex has a way of eluding national boundaries.

One day the assistant manager of Mrs. G's factory took her aside and said, " 'Look, I kept you so long why don't you paint yourself up and go nice and look like everybody,' but I was ashamed to say that I was [already] married because married girls didn't go to work."[115] The truth was that she had had a boyfriend almost from the very first. "It was a parade from the first of May, so we went in the line . . . so my brother went to work and he introduced his friend to me, so he came and began to talk about marrying . . . He worked for Hart Sheffield, and Marx, he was going with me, I was going with him, my sister thought I should marry him, but here he was sitting there and sleeping so once he took me to a show, I look around, he's sleeping! So I went away home."[116]

Meantime, she had met another man. "T. came to my sister's house, he didn't go away no more, how could you not notice him, he used to sit till 2 o'clock at night . . . He was good looking, poor feller, he didn't sell anything, he wanted to be a moving picture operator, so he knew everything but he didn't have the language yet right, he came 1913–1914. . . . My sister made him potato pancakes and I used to scream at her, stop making them I don't want to see him. . . . I finally threw him out at 2 o'clock at night, and he talked and talked, he had so much life . . . I don't know, I thought I'd better put a ring on and tell my sister I'm married, she wouldn't bother me. T. didn't ask to marry, he didn't want to go out . . . He never said let's get married . . . I was supposed to sleep together without marriage but my aunty said she's going to call my mother and father from America write them a letter so I figured that's the end of me . . . I don't think I had a rabbi . . . He was worried a lot about a job, and he didn't have a job . . . I know one thing, that I didn't want to get married, not because I didn't like him, because what did the judge have to tell me go to sleep, I can go myself to sleep . . ."[117]

She lived, in the evenings, in vaguely anarchist and bohemian circles, and heard Emma Goldman speak fairly often. Here was a typical passage from one of Goldman's famous speeches: "Monogamy is a much later sex form which came into being as a result of the domestication and ownership of woman, and which created sex monopoly and the inevitable feeling of jealousy . . . The grotesque phase about the whole matter is, that men and women often grow violently jealous of those they really do not care much about . . . Take any couple dependent upon each other for every thought and feeling; without an outside interest or desire and ask yourself whether such a relation must not become hateful and unbearable in time . . . Compared with such horrors, open adultery seems an act of courage and liberation . . . [Each individual] is a small cosmos in himself, engrossed in his own thoughts and ideas. It is glorious and poetic if these two worlds meet in freedom and equality . . . All lovers do well to leave the doors of their love wide open . . ."[118]

But Mrs. G. despised such talk and such promiscuity. Marriage, then as now, was taken to be the natural objective of every woman. But a Japanese marriage meant working knee by knee with your husband in the strawberry fields. And for a Jewish immigrant woman, especially one raised in the medieval tradition that held it shameful for the husband to work when he should be reading and murmuring and nodding in the religious Study House if he had any intellect at all, marriage meant earning the daily bread for the family, as Mrs. G.'s mother the candlemaker had done. Mrs. G., with her personal force, her peasant intelligence, and her impatient endurance, carried the burden with precious few of the pleasures of ordinary life. "And T. didn't make a living, he didn't work, I worked . . ."[119] T. had been a vegetarian and a follower of Tolstoy ever since he was a child. "He didn't eat yet eggs no cheese so I used to make all kinds of dishes, for 10¢ you made a dish of supper . . ."[120]

When she was three months pregnant, "it start to show, so then I had a hundred dollars, he opened a paper stand in the neighborhood from the Polish people, and he always was liked by people, I'm telling you, and the people was crazy about him, then the war was just over, my brother had money so I took money from my brother, and I bought in Chicago in a fancy section and T. worked half days, and he made $5, and the customers used to like him and love him . . . I used to go and help him out to work in the stand . . . He used to deliver and I stayed by the stand . . .

"The rest is not interesting . . ."[121]

8

If You Don't Come in Sunday Don't Come in Monday

WE AMERICANS are not fond of the tragic view that great human dilemmas resist any remedy, especially the simple ones. We are all for quick, magic medicine, whether for the body mortal or the body politic. We are therefore easy marks for the trickster and the confidence man, especially if he promises heaven on earth, not in a thousand years but right now, or next summer at latest.

The great dilemma of the last third of the nineteenth century and the first decade and a half of the twentieth, this smoky Sunday between two giant wars, was to determine how to build the pyramid of industrial production at a rate that was almost irrational. For the desired rate of production had more to do with the ego of the entrepreneurs, the B. F. Joneses of American business, than it did with the arithmetic of profit. To reinvest and expand at this frightening speed, it was not only necessary to have strong young labor capable of working long hours, but it was essential to pay for this time, half of a worker's daily life, with the very least that the pressure of immigration and unemployment could impose. In this reckless, careening, and marvelously successful mania for expansion, it was also necessary to disregard how many men lost hand or foot or fingers or lives in the pursuit, not of happiness as Jefferson would have had it, but of industrial power—and this power not for themselves, but for others.

Developing in the shadow of that great growing power of owners and managers and presidents and superintendents of industry, and opposing them on issues of poor pay and dangerous labor and recurrent panic, was the bitter and difficult organization of union men. But the unions were just as subject as the rest of us to the lure of quick, easy, magical plans. Just as Lydia Pinkham's Elixir for all female disorders was 40 per cent alcohol, and therefore cured nothing, but made the housewife feel a lot better, so too the laboring man was prey to the illusion of instant relief. And labor organizations like the IWW, with its guarantee of a future utopia when all men would be part of one big Union, were as rhetorical as the evangelical religions they professed to despise. For utopia is that country never discovered, nor yet, luckily, quite discoverable. But maybe it is an illusion as necessary as Heaven. America, itself a stubborn utopia, has always had a rich crop of junior utopias guaranteeing to cure the sickness of its parent. One of the most curious of these movements, and yet characteristic of them, was the Commonweal of Christ of 1894. It was at once feeble, and crackpot, and immensely significant.

2

On Easter Sunday, March 25, 1894, which by no coincidence was his fortieth birthday, a man in Massillon, Ohio, proposed to lead an army of unemployed to Washington, D.C., where he would force the Congress to pass two laws he had himself invented. The first would issue a half billion dollars in bonds that would bear no interest, and the second would use the money so printed to hire the unemployed and build a network of good roads everywhere in America. The proposed laws were not entirely altruistic.

James S. Coxey was born in Pennsylvania and quit school when he was thirteen. He worked in a rolling mill and advanced from the ranks of common labor till he was the engineer of a stationary steam engine. When he was twenty-five, he sold scrap iron and with the profits went to Massillon two years later, where he bought several silica quarries. (The sand was sold for use in the open-hearth steelmaking process.) When he was thirty-five, he mortgaged his properties to buy a horse farm in Kentucky, and his financial problems began in that year, 1889. He also had a wife and six children to support.

"Coxey is a small man with round shoulders. His face is brown and oily. His mouth, which is of the order known to physiognomists as weak, is almost hidden by a scraggly straw-colored moustache. The chin is receding almost to a deformity and a pair of shrewd grey eyes look out through gold-bowed spectacles. Coxey talks little and smiles a great deal . . .[1]

"A visit was made yesterday at Coxey's home. It lies at the end of four miles of hills, slippery with mud and amply provoking to stir the anger of a less zealous soul than Coxey's."[2]

The magnificent solution to his problems did not occur to him till the summer of 1893, although he had formed a Good Roads Association two years before. He went to a convention in Chicago in 1893 called to promote the coinage of silver and the issue of paper money without reliance on gold. Gold! That strange symbol of all men's terrestrial desires was widely held to be the instrument of the devil, and in particular of his bloated and usurious demons, the eastern bankers. It was a native mythology that is not wholly disbelieved even today. And it is not entirely untrue. Fisk, Gould, the Rockefellers Junior and Senior, Carnegie, and Frick did exist. Of the delegates to the Greenback convention some were bitterly sincere, others merely bitter, but one of the most curious was a self-created character from Calistoga, California, named Carl Browne.

". . . Browne has a fleshy face. He has grown a beard in two spirals as an imitation of the old pictures of Christ. He is partly bald and when he smiles his nose wrinkles a trifle. Habitually he wears a Texas sombrero, a greasy bear-skin coat and top-boots. His hands are always grimy with dirt. He speaks in a hoarse voice which has a wheedling tone."[3]

Browne was born on July 4, 1849, in Springfield, Illinois. He was trained as a printer, and in the course of his occupation he taught himself how to draw and paint. He went to California in 1869 and painted several "panoramas," broad scenes of ranch life in Sonoma, California, and traveled with these rolled up canvases, lecturing upon them for a living. He worked in San Francisco as a newspaper cartoonist, and himself edited and published a small newspaper for working men, *The Open Letter,* whose main tenets were support for the Pennsylvania mine strikers and bitter opposition to Chinese immigration. Through this newspaper, he met an Irish immigrant, Denis Kearney, who took to the empty lots of San Francisco during the depression of 1877 to attack the monopolistic railroads and the evil, slant-eyed Chinese. The street rioting, arson, looting, and murder of Chinese in San Francisco caused no revulsion among the citizens of California. Instead, they revised the California state constitution to forbid civil liberties to the Chinese, and denied them the right to own property.

Kearney and Browne went together to Washington, D.C., where Kearney delivered another of his famous speeches—they always ended, "The Chinese must go!"—from the Capitol steps. Meanwhile Browne, mistaken by the Washington police for Kearney, got tossed into jail. He went back to California and bought himself a farm in Napa County, where he joined the Farmers Alliance and started a Greenback newspaper in San Francisco. At the Chicago convention he was singled out by the mayor as an agitator who ought to be expelled. He thus became locally famous and came to the notice of James Coxey.

Coxey invited Browne to visit him in Massillon and to join him in leading a grand army of the unemployed to Washington. In addition to his other talents, Browne was a theosophist. He believed that a part of Christ was bodily reincarnated in himself, and, generously enough, in Coxey as well. One of the banners for their army was a painted portrait of Coxey with the words, "Cerebrum of the Commonweal of Christ," and another of Browne with the words, "Cerebellum of the Commonweal of Christ."

So, with impeccable logic, their army was christened the Commonweal of Christ. Browne was a self-admiring artist of extraordinarily small ability, and he drew a Browne-ish Christ on a throwaway sheet for distribution during the march. "He Hath Arisen" was inscribed about the level of his beard, and above his head were inscribed the words, "Peace On Earth Good Will Toward Men," but below the drawing was the more sinister motto: "BUT

DEATH TO INTEREST ON BONDS." Another such sheet had the following plan for an American utopia, under the heading "The Prayer Answered": "Organized society as it should be, and would be if nationalization of money, land, transportation and general industry were once established. The Coxey Good Roads and Non-interest bond plan would inaugurate or bring this about—a 'New Heaven and a New Earth' or the 'Kingdom of Heaven at Hand,' as taught by Him on Calvary's Cross, Who died for this very idea—the destruction of Usury. Designed, drawn and copyrighted by Carl Browne, Calistoga, California, 1894."[4] The same throwaway had a caricature of a banker with a high hat, excessively Semitic nose, and both hands full of bonds. This drawing was accompanied by the slogan: "Rothschild's Gold Bond Basis For Money." Another slogan, whose relevance must have been clear at the time, declared, "Women's sphere solely that of wife and mother."

On March 14: "A crisis is thought to be approaching in the circles of the unemployed in Stark county, due to the concentrating here of scores of disreputable-looking strangers, who announce that their visit is for the express purpose of joining the march to Washington of J. S. Coxey's army of peace. There are at least 4,000 unemployed in the county, and it is difficult to determine how they will act under the fiery and inflammatory harangues of Carl Brown, who acts as organizer for Coxey."[5] Money and food were solicited from sympathetic Massillon merchants, themselves embittered by the national depression and the numerous bank failures that began in 1893.

The outside world looked at this movement as frightening and ludicrous. The latter it certainly was, but it had, somehow, an endearing quality. Perhaps all martyrs, moralists, and reformers are a bit mad. But how much of the Commonweal madness was showmanship?

"Even the boys and girls of Massillon are beginning to discuss Coxey and his "common-weal army" with all-absorbing interest. This morning a crowd of them trooped down the street at a discreet distance behind a thin, fidgety man with hair so long it swept his shoulders. He was clad in a buckskin jacket of ancient pattern, trimmed along its edges with fur, and held in place by buttons made of polished silver dollars. It was Carl Browne, self-avowed reformer, who is Coxey's chief adviser and lieutenant. He comes into town every day from the general's stock-farm, wearing each time a different costume, the least picturesque of which is enough to keep him constantly followed by enthusiastic children . . . ."[6]

And then there were the twenty-one young drummers, all noisily equipped. How, wondered General Coxey, was he to fit twenty-one bass drums into his marching band of fifteen pieces. Other logistics were in better order: Coxey ordered a coffee pot the size of a beer barrel, which Browne offered to decorate "with allegorical paintings." The men of the Commonweal were, of course, expected to march to Washington on foot, in order to fulfill the prophesy of "a petition in boots." But Browne would ride a percheron (a large heavy breed of brewery horse); Coxey's nineteen-year-old son Jesse would ride a bay horse named Chevalier and would carry a banner and wear a uniform the right half of which was blue and the left half grey, to symbolize the reconciliation of North and South; General Coxey himself would modestly ride a two-horse phaeton.

Labor encouragement was very real, if at times pathetic:

My dear Mr. Coxey: Pittsburgh, Pa. March 19, 1894
    The 'Bell Boys Union' about 50 strong, have determined to join you on your march to Washington . . . Since the move was first contemplated I have circulated about among the working classes and find them enthusiastic for the Commonweal. The B. B. Union is only one of several orders that will send delegations. The movement is a *glorious* one. Long live *Coxey*. All recruits from here will be provided with rations for two days. One mammoth chicken pie. Each man will have donated one chicken . . . I am satisfied that this is the turning point in the history of the United States. Indeed I may say the world. The results will be far reaching, and the name of *Coxey* will go thundering down the ages relugating to oblivion that of Washington and Lincoln . . .
    Press onward the people of the nation say amen The eye of God and the nation are on you. Don't thro this away but peruse it it is the sentiment of the people too amen Give it to the press if you have no time to read it.[7]

The reporter for the *Chicago Daily Record* also noted other signs of encouragement: "Yesterday the general was in receipt of letters from several dime-museum managers who want the two leaders of the commonweal to expose themselves to the curious public as soon as the march is over. Harry Davis of Pittsburgh offers $250 a week for several months to Mr. Coxey alone."[8]

Two more fine auguries would send the army eastward from Massillon. The first was a reading by the astrologer Dr. J. M. "Cyclone" Kirkland of Pittsburgh, who averred that April, 1894, would be "a hummer in a cyclonic way." The second fortunate sign was the birth of a new son to General Coxey and his second wife. The baby was immediately christened, "Legal Tender." On the Saturday before the march was to start, Coxey got a letter from a man named Platten, "who lives in the wilds of Wisconsin." The note was written in words of alternate red and black and suggested that the Commonweal get a beautiful girl to ride at the head of the army as the Goddess of Peace. Coxey tried to cast his eighteen-year-old daughter Mamie in the role, but her mother (the first Mrs. Coxey) said, "If Coxey and Browne induce my daughter to place herself in such a questionable position, I will have them arrested for kidnapping." So the general got a Massillon, Ohio, girl to wear the red, white, and blue gown.

Although there were rich promises of support—including an offer of a case of hard-boiled eggs, and another of 140 baseball players to conduct a traveling season for the Commonweal—not everyone was enthusiastic. Carl Browne tried to quiet the general fear of communities on the proposed line of march through Ohio and Pennsylvania: "If there be any timid persons

along the line of march who have become frightened by the press or addle-
pated mayors in ill-advised interviews charging that we are bums and van-
dals, let them dispel these fears. We have sufficient food promised us, so we
should as not to be as much feared as a state militia regiment of bankers'
clerks and other scions of dudedom marching through the country. Your
daughters are in no danger from us and your silver and gold are as dross to
men who believe in legal tender money of paper."[9]

He also composed a song to the tune of "After the Ball":

> After the march is over,
>   After the first of May,
> After the bills are passed, child,
>   Then we will have fair play.
>
> Many a heart will be happy,
>   As to their homes they'll away,
> For we will have no interest on bonds
>   After the first of May.[10]

Two more men joined the army on March 23. One was described thus:
"Abraham Lincoln Jenkins, a five-foot-three Irishman with a black eye, is
another recruit. He recently won a wager by eating four pounds of cheese at
a sitting. . . ."[11] The other was Louis Smith, who billed himself as "The
Great Unknown."

"The Great Unknown is a most provoking conundrum. He grows more
mysterious every day. He is evidently widely read and a man of considerable
wealth. That he has had a military education, probably in Germany, cannot
be doubted. He has a bluff, brisk way of ordering the men around that has
made him exceedingly popular with them."[12]

On Sunday, March 24, Mrs. Coxey and little Legal Tender went home.
At eleven in the morning, the Commonweal band played a march, and the
bugler, "Windy" Oliver, blew the military call for attention. The command,
"Everybody march!" was shouted by the Great Unknown, and the procession of a little over three hundred men marched out of town, headed by a
black man carrying the American flag. The march carried thirty banners,
painted by Browne in his best cartoon style.

"The motley procession left Massillon this morning nearly 200 strong
. . . The spectacle was indescribably grotesque. Nowhere outside of Bedlam
or the Midway plaisance has such a conglomeration of nondescript and out-
landish humanity ever been seen. There were beggars in rags and tags, agitators, patent-medicine men, negroes, tramps, cranks, Carl Browne, cow-
boys, cattle-punchers and last but not least, Honore J. Jaxon, professional
half-breed Indian."[13] These words, written in a mixture of contempt and
fear, were filed by a twenty-four-year-old newspaper reporter for the *Chicago Daily Record*. But as the march went east across Ohio, he began to
change his mind: "I am beginning to feel that the movement has some mean-

ing, that it is a manifestation of the prevailing unrest and dissatisfaction among the laboring classes. When such an ugly and grotesque fungus can grow out so prominently on the body politic there must be something wrong . . . I don't like to think of the army with a sober face, but it seems to me that such a movement must be looked at as something more than a huge joke."[14]

General Coxey was quoted as saying, "Not one percent of the people think I will ever get back to Massillon alive, but I have no fear. I shall go forward and do my duty regardless of consequences." At Canton, Ohio, where all the women had promised to make the army a hot breakfast of beans, ham, and potatoes, the men arrived and camped their tents in a snowstorm. Browne and Coxey, though, lodged and ate at the Hotel Hurford.

Their stop at Alliance, Ohio, also gave them a generous welcome: "Coxey came into Camp Bunker Hill to-day, waving two iron skillets over his head and shouting: 'A miracle; a miracle.' Some one had given him the skillets. . . .

"It was a busy day at the camp. Almost as soon as the tents were pitched recruits began to arrive in groups of two and three. Dr. 'Cyclone' Kirkland, astrologer and official weather-maker for the expedition, stood at one end of the big tent and mustered them in. Here is a sample of his examination of a new recruit:

" 'What is your name?'

" 'Peter Miesner.'

" 'Peter, Peter—that's a good name: you've heard of Peter the Great and Peter the apostle. You may some time be Peter the Great. Try. "Some men are born great, some achieve greatness, while others have greatness thrust upon them." Unborn children may yet rise up to call you blessed. What is your occupation?'

" 'Miner.'

" 'I see. You labor in the bowels of the earth. Be faithful and you shall receive your reward. Credit where credit is due. *Sic semper tyrannis.* Never call a man by a nickname. Now step inside and be good. You belong to the greatest army on earth. I have been moved to tears by scenes less pathetic than this.' "[15]

On March 28 they marched through the continuing snow into the Quaker town of Salem, Ohio. ". . . The windows were alive with people and the streets crowded. For a week or more Charles Bonsall, chairman of a committee appointed by the populists, had been preparing to receive the army in fine style. A considerable amount of provisions, ten yards of sausages, eight gallons of milk, a half-cord of bread and other things in like proportions had been collected in the office of Mayor Northrup, and the citizens generally cordially welcomed the army . . ."[16]

Next day, in Columbiana, Ohio, an old farmer died of a heart attack while cheering the Commonweal's arrival. Browne, meanwhile, ". . . had announced that he would deliver an address and explain his panorama in the evening and a crowd numbering many thousand persons gathered in spite of the icy air to hear him. The panorama consists of paintings on canvas so arranged that they will drop down one after another. Long use has worn them so that they strongly resembled mummy cases. Browne mounted the platform and began with an oratorical flourish to riddle the national banking system. A wind-whipped gasoline flare lit up the specimens of Browne's ghastly art."[17]

New recruits came from Medina and Akron. At Lectonia, where 2,800 people lived in the smoke of the iron mills, the army was received with great enthusiasm. Yet the Commonweal had shrunk, and now consisted of eighty-eight men on foot, eighteen on wagons, fourteen on horseback, and another fifty who were traveling more or less parallel to the route on freight trains. Yet to the common American, this insubstantial army was a symbol as fearful and powerful as a flag. They named their camps after contemporary and controversial heroes like Debs and Gompers. Indeed the army had the strong approval of most labor unions. One reason was the provision in Coxey's bill for the construction of new roads, on which men were to be employed at a wage of $1.50 per eight-hour day. Local sheriffs were therefore quite properly frightened. ". . . [T]he sheriff of Lawrence county which lies directly in the line of march, will be on hand to-morrow with a large posse of deputies and prevent the army of peace from passing out of Ohio."[18]

But on March 25, General Coxey got a long and important letter: "There have been no Washingtons, Jeffersons, Jacksons or Lincolns elected president of the United States in the last two decades. A soulless despot of alien origin is monarch of the commercial world. His name is money. His instruments of oppression are banks and bonds. His servants are administrative and legislative bodies."[19] The letter reflected accurately the current populist belief in the tyranny of abstract money. "The suferings of the people are the result of electing men to office who do the bidding of the money powers, which by legislation and administration have destroyed more than one-half of the metallic money of the world and cornered the other half. Twenty years of uninterrupted rule of banks and bondholders has concentrated the wealth of the world in the hands of the few and enabled them to seize the telegraph, the press and nearly every other avenue through which the people can obtain information of the cunning devices by which the parasites absorb what the masses produce."[20] The letter was not written by Emma Goldman or Big Bill Haywood or Mother Jones, but by Senator William M. Stewart of Nevada.

Then in Pittsburgh, on April 3, 1894: "The newsboys on the street corners have been calling 'Coxey, Coxey, Coxey' all day long. The crowds, packed forty deep on the dusty pavements, stood for hours and shouted 'Coxey, Coxey' until they were hoarse. Shop girls whispered 'Coxey' to one another in the half-deserted store. The children in the public schools were dismissed because Coxey was coming to town . . . The spectacled face of

Coxey glared from the newspapers and his name besprinkled every page. The band played 'Coxey's March' and a local theatrical company sung Coxey's songs. The bakers worked 'Coxey' into the frosting of their cookies and Coxey consommé was served at many a lunch stand . . .

" 'Gen.' Coxey rode in a carriage by the side of Snowball, his negro driver . . .

"During the march Coxey was presented with two little mince pies, a paper knife adorned with ribbons and an embroidered pin cushion with the general's name worked in pins on the top. As the army crossed North avenue a wagon drove past with this placard on its side:

> 1,000 LOAVES OF HOME-MADE BREAD
> FOR COXEY'S ARMY."[21]

Three members of the Commonweal, including Dr. Cyclone, left to join a dime museum and were refused permission to rejoin the army. They threatened to organize a "Counterweal." For by April 8, the daily march over the muddy hills of western Pennsylvania had begun to exhaust the army, and minor mutinies broke out like measles. A group of malcontents were expelled by the Great Unknown, and Carl Browne, not to be outdone as a disciplinarian, kicked out another forty men on the grounds that they could not speak English. He also read an official order discharging all dogs from the Commonweal, reasoning, "I have noticed that some of our number here evinced an unwarranted liking for dogs. The army should receive your deepening and purest affection. With this in view I order that all but the human dogs now accompanying us be dismissed."[22]

After long days of marching through spring snowstorms on roads alternately frozen or muddy, a new and more dangerous dissension arose in the army between the theosophist Carl Browne and the Great Unknown. Early on the morning of April 15: ". . . [A] carriage, furiously driven, was seen tearing down a distant mountain road. As it drew nearer the commonwealers recognized Commander-in-Chief Coxey, and greeted him with a cheer. His face was pale and his clothing bore evidence of the muddy road from Cumberland, over which he had driven between midnight and dawn.

"Without stopping to greet his lieutenants he began at once to question them closely as to the cause of the mutiny. He talked with Browne privately, and then he gave audience to the 'Unknown.' 'Now,' he said, 'we will have a talk with the army.'

"Mounting a soap box near the center of a big room over the Frostburg opera house, where the men had spent the night, he made a brief statement of the case. Then he asked all those who favored the Unknown as chief marshal to rise in their places. One hundred and fifty-eight men, all but four of the commonwealers stood up. It was plainly a case of mutiny. The Unknown was visibly exultant. Browne changed from white to brick-red and back to white again. He bit his lips in anger.

" 'I cast 154 votes for Brother Browne,' said Gen. Coxey calmly, 'and I further order that Mr. Smith, the unknown, be forever expelled from the army.' "[23]

The Great Unknown, wrote the reporter Ray Stannard Baker, had the "true" name of Dr. Pizzaro: "Dr. Pizzaro, [had] spent nearly all of last September selling a blood purifier in Chicago. He delivered addresses every day at 81 Peoria street on the subject of 'physiology,' and incidentally spoke glowingly of so and so's sarsaparilla."[24]

At Cumberland, Maryland, the army and its horses and wagons were loaded onto a boat to go down the Potomac part of the way to Washington. Carl Browne issued a nice description of the voyage: "When Capt. Wilson of our ship gave the order to cast anchor we sailed away in bright sunlight, buoyant of hope in our ultimate purpose, and our voyage has been like the languorous languor of the lingering day when Cleopatra floated down on her barge of perfumed sails to meet her Antony. In lieu of her silken sails is our starry banner of freedom and glorious banner of peace. For perfumery we have been regaled with the buds of spring-time. In lieu of her decks of beaten gold we have substantial boards of oak. Instead of caparisoned slaves our crew is a band of brothers, however ill-clad, the nucleus of a cooperative commonweal."[25] Meantime, General Coxey left for New York City to attend a horse sale.

On April 29, the men camped in a park just outside Washington, and after a heavy rainstorm that blew down the tents during the night and overturned the big "panorama wagon," they rose at 5 A.M. to march toward Washington. They were met near Rockville by hundreds of bicyclers whom Browne called "the army of the common wheel," a group certain to press for better roads. Mrs. Coxey and Legal Tender Coxey rejoined General Coxey as he rode into Washington and entered their final camp, Camp George Washington. Here Carl Browne astonished his General: ". . . He took him up into the parlor of the National hotel, where they are staying, and presented him to his daughter, Miss Mamie Coxey. At first the general could not believe his eyes. He thought that Mamie was far away in Massillon. Browne explained that he had sent Jesse Coxey to bring his sister to Washington and that she had consented to act as goddess of peace . . ."[26]

Coxey then proposed that the Commonweal, enlarged now by the addition of other citizen armies from the West, meet on the steps of the Capitol. This idea terrified the Washington police, who immediately consulted with Police Chief O'Mara of Pittsburgh and "scores of out of town detectives." They were especially worried by the fact that the Washington march was to take place on May 1, a date associated with foreigners and communards. On that morning, the men assembled in line of march, and while standing, swallowed a breakfast of bread, hardtack, and coffee. They were then each issued the four-foot oak "war club of peace." Browne told the men, "The greatest ordeal of the march is at hand. The eyes of the world are on you and you must conduct yourselves accordingly."[27] The men were then drilled in the war club for an hour, waving it three times in the air and shouting in unison, "Gloria, peace!"

The first Mrs. Coxey had relented and eighteen-year-old Mamie Coxey rode on a white horse, with her long yellow hair flowing down over her shoulders. She was flanked by two veterans of the Civil War, one from the Union, one from the Confederacy, since she represented the Goddess of Peace. Another pretty girl, Virginia LaValle of Philadelphia, wore a red, white, and blue gown and represented the Goddess of Liberty. The procession through the streets of Washington attracted a curious but scanty crowd.

". . . [I]t was a warm, bright morning. The road was heavy with dust, but the over-hanging trees shaded it somewhat from the fierce sunshine. When the column reached the asphalt pavement the crowds grew larger. The army passed the magnificent building in which the Chinese legation is quartered. It was greeted with the waving of gaily-colored handkerchiefs from the celestials in the windows. They appeared much interested in the strange procession. Near Florida avenue Citizen Redstone appeared with a bunch of flags in his hand and saluted Browne.

" 'I have 225 loyal men ready to join the army,' he said.

" 'Line up and fall in behind,' commanded Browne. At Thomas circle the great bronze statue of Martin Luther frowned sternly down at the procession, and a negro in a white apron tried to sell one of the band members half a dozen clams."[28]

They marched down Pennsylvania Avenue, through crowds that had become so thick that General Coxey's buggy was nearly crushed. At the B Street entrance to the Capitol grounds, Coxey kissed his wife (to thunderous applause) and joined Carl Browne on foot. But both men were literally lifted off the ground and carried across the street by "a wild, surging mob of men." Here they met the stone wall that surrounded the Capitol grounds. Permission to rally there had been forbidden the previous afternoon. But Carl Browne vaulted the wall; Coxey, following, didn't quite make it, fell down, and was, for the moment, swallowed up by the crowd going over the same obstacle.

Browne and the multitude who had followed him were immediately pursued by a hundred mounted Washington police, who forced their horses over the wall and onto the grounds. "A wild rush through the shrubbery took place, men and women rolling and tumbling over one another in the wild scramble."[29] After that, the mounted police simply acted out of a common hysteria.

". . . Women and children were ruthlessly ridden down. A commonwealer who had in some way escaped from the ranks, stood behind a tree and struck a policeman a terrible blow in the back with his war club of peace. The next officer that came up saw the attack and clubbed the commonwealer into insensibility and let him lie where he had fallen. . . .

"Just as Browne reached the corner of the steps he was seized by an of-

ficer. Without a moment's indecision the man from Calistoga swung his arm
quickly around and sent the policeman spinning far out into the crowd. The
next moment he was seized from behind and a clenched fist struck him several blows in the face. In the struggle that followed his clothing was badly
torn, and a string of his dead wife's beads, which he always wore around his
throat, was scattered. An inoffensive negro named Johnson crowded up to
watch the struggle and one of the policemen, blind with anger, struck him a
blow with his club . . .

"The fury seemed to spread and two mounted policemen closed down
upon the negro and hit him repeatedly until he sank to the ground with his
head terribly lacerated. Browne, together with Christopher Columbus
Jones, who had been arrested for trying to assist his friend in the fight, was
taken to the police station."[30]

Carl Browne was interviewed while in his jail cell; he was rather bitter:
"I've been talking for six weeks, and the people have not heard. I will leave
all to the public now." He was bailed out late that evening by "a wealthy
lady." Coxey, meantime, having tried to give a speech from the Capitol
steps, was seized by the police and forcibly put back into his phaeton. The
whole morning's affair caused a great deal of editorial sadness across the
country. A certain Mrs. W. P. Black contributed the following poem,
printed in the *Chicago Daily Record:*

> The Army of Peace
> March! march! men of the peace army,
> Never grow weary of tramping the moor.
> Every step counts for the worn, starving millions.
> Down with selfishness!
> Down with the cruelty!
> Go plead the cause of the suffering poor![31]

At the trial of Carl Browne and C. C. Jones, the judge charged them
with "lawlessly entering the Capitol grounds, breaking shrubbery, walking
on the grass, and displaying a banner which had for its purpose the bringing
into public notice of a certain organization known as the 'J. S. Coxey Good
Roads Association.'" Coxey himself was in court and upon being recognized
was promptly arrested for disregarding the signs, "Keep Off the Grass."
These peculiar charges gave the Commonweal a lot of extra publicity.
Money and food poured into their camp on the sluggish James Canal. "For
the first time in history, the Commonwealers ate spring chicken." Samuel
Gompers, head of the AF of L, went to visit Coxey to give him the symbolic
support of organized labor. The same day a new flag was presented to the
Commonweal, stitched by the women of Little Rock, Arkansas, depicting a
great yellow sun surrounded by smaller suns, in tribute to a line in Carl
Browne's poem about reincarnation. Coxey said, ". . . We will be joined, I
have no doubt, by thousands upon thousands of other unemployed people.

For myself I propose to lay aside every other occupation and remain in Washington until some action is taken by congress. If that body should adjourn without affording any relief to the unemployed we will simply demand that the president call an extra session. The presence here of 300,000 or 400,000 men—and by that time there will be that many here—will simply force the president to this step . . ."[32]

No such multitude ever assembled. This utopia simply obeyed the inner law of all institutions, which condemns them to sink sooner or later into the marshes of history. An effort was made to revive it by marching on July 4 to the steps of the Capitol again, to depict in pantomime the sad death of Liberty. The Goddess, dressed in a white gown and with long yellow hair, rode on a horse to the Peace Monument, followed by 246 Commonwealers, 10 mounted police, 26 foot patrolmen, and 2 paddy wagons. The Goddess was said to be an Egyptian damsel named Sarah Elkharf, but her speech was uncommonly coarse and guttural. She was, in fact, Carl Browne, who had cut off his beard and shaved his head for the occasion, and put on a gown and a wig. At the end of his speech, he slumped down from his horse, pretended to expire, and was put on a hearse which was drawn slowly, drums beating, to Mulligan Hill, where the corpse rose and the parade disbanded. It was the corny and symbolic end of a corny and symbolic movement.

And its every detail—marching, quarreling, demonstrating—is a narrow but historic window through which we can comprehend the special qualities of life, good or bad, in the late American nineteenth century.

Because the real and unresolved issues of that last decade—men without work, farmers without decent return, small businessmen perpetually walking the knife between debt and failure, workmen who labored killing hours for small pay even in times of prosperity—all these issues remained as potent and dangerous for the republic as ever. For in the same year as the march of Coxey's army, 1894, a war was renewed and fought for months with implacable ferocity—a war symbolic, but also utterly real, in a district of Colorado by the sinister name of Cripple Creek.

3

The 1877 railroad strike was the first giant spasm of collective discontent. The Commonweal of Christ was one of the last demonstrations of the American independent man; in this it resembled the expedition of Red Cloud to Washington. What happens first and last, though, has little real influence on history. What counts is always the repeated pattern of overlapping forces.

Let's look, for example, at the Cripple Creek drama of 1903. It was doubly ironic since the town is only a few miles from Pike's Peak where the manic gold rush of 1879 turned up nothing but empty rock, but where veins of gold were found in great quantities in 1889. By 1900, the old, individual claims had all been bought and merged by businessmen who invested money (a surprising amount of it British) to sink mines and build crushers and smelters. Shafts were gouged out of hills and mountains at elevations up to 11,000 feet, and a web of railroads was flung over the rich holes.

Miners' wages, even in the important gold mines, were only $1.75 per day, which is particularly stingy since food had to be transported from a considerable distance and was therefore much more expensive than it was elsewhere. The money left after food was rarely sufficient to pay rent, so a large proportion of the miners and their families lived in tents, a special hardship in the cold mountain nights at these altitudes. The Western Federation of Miners had begun to organize in this area of Colorado, but the U. S. Reduction and Refining Company hired informers to get the names of aggressive union members. Between August, 1902, and February, 1903, forty-two men had been fired. The union suggested arbitration, a move supported by the community and by the editorials of the *Denver Post*. C. A. MacNeil, general manager of the company, replied, "There is no trouble between our com-

On the facing page: **Leaders of Coxey's Army.** *Left to right:* **James S. Coxey, C. C. Jones, and Carl Browne, in jail after their arrest in Washington, D.C., on May 1, 1894.**

Below: **Departure of Coxey's Army of unemployed workers from Massilon, Ohio, on March 25, 1894, headed for Washington, D.C.**

Library of Congress

pany and mill workers employed by us. Our employes are now and have been perfectly satisfied with wages and treatment."[33]

The union, either patient or sluggish, took no action for six months. Then on August 10, 1903, a strike was declared at all the mines in the Cripple Creek district, except for two smaller ones which had already settled. Governor Peabody of Colorado said, "If an emergency arises I shall be prompt to order out the troops."[34] This was a sinister understatement, because he left it ambiguous as to whether the troops would be used against the strikers or the management.

At the other end of the state, at Telluride, the ostensible cause of the miners' and smeltermens' strike, which had begun in September, 1903, was complex—and typical. Miners hated the system of individual contract that obliged them to eat their meals at the company's boarding house and to buy their tools and blasting powder from the company stores. And the accident rate, high everywhere, on railroads and in the forest, was exceptionally high in the shifting tunnels of the mines. One must remind oneself that these figures are more than a row of digits grown cold in files. They were human pain and death. And this was true, not only in the nineteenth century, generally callous to industrial murder, but into the early twentieth, as well. In 1901, 1,087 miners lost their lives; in 1903, 528 were killed underground. Yet the main issue in both regions of Colorado was not money, or death by accident, but the eight-hour day. It had a curious history in Colorado, because the election of 1898 had returned a great many liberal legislators. They passed a mandatory eight-hour law the next year, which was promptly declared unconstitutional. In 1900, an amendment to the state constitution to correct this curious judgment was put to a referendum, and it passed by a majority of 46,000. But by that time there was a new legislature, and there was no majority large enough to get the enabling law out of committee. Consequently the eight-hour movement had to be fought out in the mines and the mining camps, not in the splendid new courthouses and resounding marble corridors of state government. The eight-hour demand was extraordinary in that it was meant to improve, not the wage, but the quality of life itself. No longer, it was hoped, would a man have to leave and come home in the darkness, exhausted, unable to be the father to his family.

The eight-hour issue was, I believe, even deeper. It touched the fundamental change in American character—if by character one means not merely the inner feelings of an American, but the complicated summation of all the ways one deals with the realities of life. Because certainly before 1861, the ordinary American male wanted to hammer out his own destiny. Even if he failed, he tried. And tried again and again, in different climates and different occupations. And even if he didn't try, he believed he ought to. He set his own pace, and he might work long hours or he might not, as he chose. Herbert Gutman quotes from *A History of American Cooperage* (the making of barrels): "Early on Saturday morning, the big brewery wagon would drive up to the shop. Several of the coopers would club together, each paying his proper share, and one of them would call out the window to the driver, 'Bring me a Goose Egg,' meaning a half-barrel of beer. Then others would buy 'Goose Eggs,' and there would be a merry time all around. . . . Little groups of jolly fellows would often sit around upturned barrels playing poker, using rivets for chips, until they had received their pay and the 'Goose Egg' was dry.

"Saturday night was a big night for the old-time cooper. It meant going out, strolling around the town, meeting friends, usually at a favorite saloon, and having a good time generally, after a week of hard work. Usually the good time continued over into Sunday, so that on the following day he usually was not in the best of condition to settle down to the regular day's work.

"Many coopers used to spend this day [Monday] sharpening up their tools, carrying in stock, discussing current events, and in getting things in shape for the big day of work on the morrow. Thus, 'Blue Monday' was something of a tradition with the coopers, and the day was also more or less lost as far as production was concerned.

" 'Can't do much today, but I'll give her hell tomorrow,' seemed to be the Monday slogan. But bright and early Tuesday morning, 'Give her hell' they would, banging away lustily for the rest of the week until Saturday which was pay day again, and its thoughts of the 'Goose Eggs.' "[35]

Now such an attitude became more and more antiquated as the decades ground forward with multiplied mechanical power. Driving belts, conveyers, and blast furnaces never stopped for a mug of beer, and the completely sane and logical studies of mine and factory work by people like Frederick W. Taylor were the final perfect artificial flower of the industrial jungle. His work was done in the last two decades, more especially the final decade, of the nineteenth century. A wonderful illustration of the resistance to his science was given in his own testimony:

"Now, the machine shop of the Midvale Steel Works was a piecework shop. All the work practically was done on piecework, and it ran night and day—five nights in the week and six days. Two sets of men came on, one to run the machines at night and the other to run them in the daytime. . . .

"As soon as I became gang boss the men who were working under me and who, of course, knew that I was onto the whole game of soldiering or deliberately restricting output, came to me at once and said, 'Now, Fred, you are not going to be a damn piecework hog, are you?'

"I said, 'If you fellows mean you are afraid I am going to try to get a larger output from these lathes,' I said, 'Yes; I do propose to get more work out.' I said, 'You must remember I have been square with you fellows up to now and worked with you. I have not broken a single rate. I have been on your side of the fence. But now I have accepted a job under the management of this company and I am on the other side of the fence, and I will tell you perfectly frankly that I am going to try to get a bigger output from those lathes.' They answered, 'Then, you are going to be a damned hog.'

"I said, 'Well, if you fellows put it that way, all right.' They said, 'We warn you, Fred, if you try to bust any of these rates, we will have you over the fence in six weeks.' I said, 'That is all right; I will tell you fellows again frankly that I propose to try to get a bigger output off these machines.'

"Now, that was the beginning of a piecework fight that lasted for nearly three years, as I remember it—two or three years—in which I was doing everything in my power to increase the output of the shop, while the men were absolutely determined that the output should not be increased. Anyone who has been through such a fight knows and dreads the meanness of it and the bitterness of it . . ."[36]

One has, despite sympathy for the badgered and underpaid worker, a sneaky admiration for Taylor's science. It was all so reasonable. It not only increased profits, but it also reasserted the identity of the factory and its growth with the ego of its owners and managers—and, as I've tried to show earlier with B. F. Jones, this was no small matter. What hurt one, hurt the other—not merely in the wallet, but in the entrepreneur's perception of himself as a man in charge of his own fate. Taylorism was the most confident assertion that the industrial plant, with all its work and workmen, was private property. Taylorism, the study and rationalization of work technique, simply omitted all question of why, for what purpose, how, and by what standard, the ordinary American was to live his limited hours on earth.

So there was bound to be a fight, open or hidden, over the very possession of time. I myself worked in a small New York factory that began work at 8:00 A.M., but whose owner did not get there till nine. Every morning before he arrived, we would hoist one of our number up on our shoulders, so he could turn the wall clock ahead twenty minutes. The owner, when he came in, would be overcome with fury and demand we lift him up, and he would turn the clock back forty minutes, correcting the crime and giving himself an extra punitive bonus. If he went to the toilet, he had no sooner closed the door than the same little drama was re-enacted.

It was for this privilege—to limit the authority of the owner, the manager, and the foreman to eight hours out of the twenty-four without reduction in wage—that Cripple Creek was fought. And lost.

4

It would appear obvious that to keep digging gold during a strike, men had to be gotten from communities far from Telluride or Cripple Creek, because group pressure alone would prevent any local man from working at a struck mine or smelter. Here the obvious, for once, was half true:

"During a St. Louis strike, company representatives visited Troy, Cohoes and Elmira, New York, as well as Scranton, Pennsylvania, in their search for skilled hands. Many mill owners desiring strikebreakers went so far as to specify 'skilled' workers in their advertisements, indicating clearly that recent arrivals from eastern Europe need not apply. Quite often agents or advertisements proclaiming the existence of large numbers of jobs in particular communities did so without mentioning the fact that a strike was in progress."[37]

From Cripple Creek, they went as far as Michigan, where they recruited mostly recent Scandinavian immigrants, very few of whom understood English. One who did, changed to the union side. It was a frightening experience:

Strikers in street battle in Bayonne, New Jersey, July 26, 1915.

Photograph by Greeley Photo Service. Library of Congress

"County of Teller, State of Colorado, Emil Peterson, being duly sworn, upon his oath, says: 'I am twenty-four years of age. I reside in Denmark; that is my native land. I came to America February 23, 1903. I then went to Fairchilds, Wis. I am not an American citizen. At Fairchilds the Lester Lumber Company paid only $26 per month. On the 8th of September I went to Duluth to get work. At Duluth B. B. Gilbert & Co., labor agents, 5 South avenue, west, employed me to go to work in the Colorado gold mines. I was to get from $3 to $5 per day to fire boilers in the mine. I was shipped here from Duluth. Mine owners of Cripple Creek advanced me $18 for car fare. The company would pay this if we contracted to work a month. About se-

venty-five men were shipped from Duluth. I don't know how many quit on
the way. Others joined at St. Paul, making near 150 altogether. I think that
about eighty of these, of whom only five had ever worked in a mine arrived
last night, Friday, September 18. B. B. Gilbert & Co. told us there was no
strike in Cripple Creek. They had a newspaper in the office, saying: "No
strike in gold camp; all men go to work." At Colorado Springs we discovered
there was a strike. Men with spectacles on who said they were mine lessees
met us in Colorado Springs and came on with us. I stayed last night at the
Rhodes house with a party of ten. We took breakfast and then went to a
building near where the shooting occurred. Here there were many others.
The men were lined up and an officer said: "Come on, boys, go to work." I
said out loud in Spanish, "Don't go to work," I started to run and he fired at
me with a pistol. I ran zigzag to avoid the bullet. He fired once. I got
away.' "[38]

But one must be careful not to generalize. It was certainly union dogma
that the only strikebreakers were foreigners, who should consequently be
banned from American shores. The uncomfortable fact was that to bring
hundreds of new immigrants across the country to break the strike was often
not worth the effort, because they were, by the 1880's, mostly peasants and
therefore unskilled in mine or factory. In addition, the pool of unemployed
laborers, skilled and partly skilled, now included both American-born workers and immigrants who had been here for years. The pressure to get a job—
any job—was enormous, because the alternative was literally starvation.
There was no unemployment insurance throughout all of this period—1865–
1917—and in fact there was none until 1934.

But the use of strikebreakers was a local declaration of war. Both sides
were armed. This was hardly unusual, since every American who lived anywhere near a mountain, forest, or open country of any sort, possessed a gun.
First of all, his own self-image as a man simply required it. Second, his gun
got his family a good and necessary source of protein: rabbit, squirrel, duck,
pheasant, and a surprising amount of deer. In every mining district, dynamite was a tool as common as a shovel. So there was certainly violence used
against the "scabs, finks, blacklegs." But it was sporadic, disorganized, infrequent, and ineffectual.

The companies, on the other hand, had formidable, trained, and brutal
armies. At first, these were private guards. "Among the distinguished
members that were employed on the El Paso [mine] were to be found such
celebrities in the criminal history of the state as the Gibson brothers, who
had just returned from a sojourn in the state's institution at Canon City, for
wholesale robbery and holdups. They had been residents of Canon City
(against their will) for five years and returned on parole to help break the
strike. Another gentleman with a criminal record that was of invaluable service to the association was Frank Vannick, who had also served the state with
distinguished dishonor to himself at Canon City, and was also at large on

parole . . . Dumps Benton, Esq., the man who killed George Potts, is still another . . ."[39] Such gunmen were not exceptional. They were, and still are, a characteristic pathology of labor problems, particularly in isolated areas of the United States where a single industry dominates the landscape.

The famous woman organizer, "Mother" Jones, wrote a very plain account of a strike in West Virginia:

"I took the short trail up the hillside to Stanford Mountain. It seemed to me as I came toward the camp as if those wretched shacks were huddling closer in terror. Everything was deathly still. As I came nearer the miners' homes, I could hear sobbing. Then I saw between the stilts that propped up a miner's shack the clay red with blood. I pushed open the door. On a mattress, wet with blood, lay a miner. His brains had been blown out while he slept. His shack was riddled with bullets.

"In five other shacks men lay dead. In one of them a baby boy and his mother sobbed over the father's corpse. When the little fellow saw me, he said, 'Mother Jones, bring back my papa to me. I want to kiss him.'

"The coroner came. He found that these six men had been murdered in their beds while they peacefully slept; shot by gunmen in the employ of the coal company.

"The coroner went. The men were buried on the mountain side. And nothing was ever done to punish the men who had taken their lives."[40]

Local police forces were sometimes immobilized by their own dilemma. The mining companies were the source of power and authority, and were generally obeyed. But at the same time, these police were related by common habits and family connections to the workmen they were asked to intimidate. Sometimes, not always, they simply did nothing, neither for the strike nor against it. As the sheriff of Teller County, where Cripple Creek is located, said publicly, ". . . There is no occasion for the militia here. I can handle the situation."[41] As a logical consequence, the state militia, always from another county, were sent in by the governor. As Governor Peabody of Colorado put it, "I will not withdraw the troops until the trouble is settled. They are at Colorado City to protect the rights of the miners as well as of the smeltermen. There are no agitators running this administration. This administration is to be run for the benefit of the people. If a man wants to work he has a perfect right to do so and the troops are there to see that everybody's rights are protected."[42]

The state militia were generally commanded by officers unsuited, by character and training, to civil problems of any sort, far less one in which basic issues of time, labor, money, and food were being fought and decided. They did what they were trained to do and simply waged a one-sided war: "September 13 found the military in complete control of the entire district. The troops dominated everything. A 'bull pen' was established. Men were taken from home and families at dead of night, made to get out of bed and go with the militia and placed in the 'bull pen' without explanation. They were

not allowed defense and there were no charges preferred against them.
Union meetings were, from the date given, broken into and obstructed
without apparent cause."[43] People arrested without warrant by the state
militia, included five boys aged from nine to fourteen, who were later released. The adults were kept for indefinite periods in a military enclosure,
awaiting future trial by a military court. Major McClelland, who was acting
judge advocate for this court, said, "To hell with the Constitution. We are

Stockyards strike, Chicago, 1904.

Chicago Historical Society

going by the governor's orders." A sinister circumstance of this militia was
that many of the hired gunmen were sworn into government service. These
were the men who enforced local vagrancy laws—originally meant to dis-
courage "tramps"—against men who were simply out on strike. For example, on March 1, 1904, thirty-four striking miners were arrested and
given the choice of reporting for work or leaving the county. The local press,
too, was raided by the military:

"Tuesday night, September 29, at 11:05, the busiest hour on a morning
paper, the *Victor Daily Record*, which had espoused the cause of the striking

Above: **National Guard, Ludlow, Colorado, 1913.**
Below: **Armed Strikers after Ludlow Massacre, 1913.**

United Mine Workers of America photographs

miners, was raided by the militia, and the entire force at work was 'captured'
. . . 'You're all prisoners of war!' bellowed Major Thomas McClelland.

"With that the *Record* force was marched to the 'bull pen' under an honorary guard of two companies of infantry, two troops of cavalry . . ."

That night after the raid, an extraordinarily handsome woman named Emma F. Langdon, the wife of one of the editors, went to the newspaper office and, locking the doors against the posted guard of militia men, set up the rest of the type. With the help of two men who had not been in the offices and had thus escaped arrest, she worked the linotype machines and got out the morning edition.

The battle for community support was fought in characteristically nineteenth-century American forms: rhetorical prose and limping doggerel. Union rhetoric was sonorous, windy, and generally true: "The straining muscles of the worker pushed back the frontier, subjugated the desert, gave a continent to civilization; his bloody sweat reared and cemented free institutions, but no law is written in legislative halls to protect his bread, and in the temple of justice his cry is unheard . . ."[44]

The style of the Mine Owners Association was somewhat less lofty: "During all these years an alleged labor organization, known as the Western Federation of Miners, has been endeavoring, with considerable success, to obtain a hold on this particular industry through the unionization of these mines, and the history of this campaign, with its record of murder, arson, dynamiting and riot, to say nothing of the more petty crimes, such as assaults, intimidation, threats and personal abuse, all committed for the purpose of intimidating and coercing men engaged in earning a livelihood, is enough to shock humanity . . ."[45]

Government rhetoric was much more restrained; it was also untrue:

State of Colorado, Adjutant General's Office, Denver, Colorado, March 23, 1904.
General Order No. 15:
The following proclamation is issued from these headquarters for the information and guidance of all concerned, and it will be obeyed and respected accordingly.
. . . I, James H. Peabody, governor and commander-in-chief of the military forces, by virtue of the power and authority in me vested, do hereby proclaim and declare the said County of San Miguel, in the State of Colorado, to be in a state of insurrection and rebellion.

JAMES H. PEABODY, Governor and Commander-in-Chief.
SHERMAN BELL, Adjustant General[46]

Poetry was quoted by the Union:

God give us men; a time like this demands
Strong minds, great hearts, true faith and ready hands;
Men whom lust of lucre does not kill;
Men whom the spoils of office can not buy.[47]

But anti-union doggerel, printed in red ink on the front page of the *Cripple Creek Times* and set to music, was more specific:

Cripple Creek's Liberty Anthem
One, Two, Three—Now altogether,
    You can never come back—No, Never.
You can never come back, no never,
    We will follow your track forever.
Though you promise and plead
    We will give you no heed,
For to this we're all agreed forever.
Chorus
You can never come back, boys, never,
    The game's all up with you forever,
We treated you square,
And the pay was fair,
And all would be yours yet,
    But now you'll beware
The W.F.M. is fated,
    And you'll stay there, you bet.[48]

But now a more effective method of breaking the strike was used at Telluride. Local businessmen, ranchers, and foremen organized an armed vigilante citizens alliance who patrolled alongside the official deputies. On June 7, 1904:

"Engineer's hall No. 80, W.F.M., was visited and the entire furnishings destroyed, including charters of many organizations that met in the hall. A beautiful new piano that was the pride of the Maccabees, was totally destroyed, being turned over and the sides smashed in. Many magnificent portieres were stripped from the windows, and after being torn in rags were piled in a heap on the floor.

"The library in this elegant hall was estimated at $1,000. The entire contents of the bookcases were hurled from the windows to the sidewalk below . . .

"On the blackboard in the reception hall of the building, after the horde had left the hall, was found the following threat, written in the blood of one of their victims:

" 'For being a union man, deportation or death will be your fate.' 'Citizens' Alliance.'

"By the evening of June 7, 150 men were prisoners and 100 others had been arrested and released and twenty-seven shipped out of the district."[49]

At Telluride, on Monday, the night of March 15, 1904, a union man named A. H. Floaten was at home with his wife:

"On Monday night I was at home with my wife. She had retired, and I was partially disrobed. I had taken off my shoes and was just getting ready for bed when I heard the knock on the door. I knew what was coming, for I had heard a number of men in the alley at the rear of the house. The man did not knock at the door with his hand, but with the butt of a gun. They broke in the glass panel of the door, and then my wife, who was upstairs, demanded to know who was there. The people outside said they wanted the man who was in the house. When my wife demanded to know who they were and what they wanted of me, they gave her no reply, but broke the lock open and came in, searching the house. I stepped into the bedroom downstairs, and then into the clothes closet, in hopes that they would not find me. I was discovered by Walter Kenley, who shoved a revolver into my face. I said: 'For God's sake, have you come to kill me!' Kenley, who is the same man who assaulted Attorney E. F. Richardson a few weeks ago, answered: 'You get up and come with us.' I asked him if he had a warrant for me, and he answered that he had. I told him to read it, and then he said that he did not need any warrant for me; that I would have to come anyway.

"He and his companion pushed me out of the bedroom into the hall. I asked him to let me put my shoes on. Then without warning he struck me over the head with a revolver, cutting a gash about an inch deep in the left side of my head, at the same time telling me that I did not need any shoes. They then pushed me out onto the sidewalk, and my wife came out after them, begging to let me put on my shoes and hat. She had my shoes and hat in her hand, but they would not allow me to put them on. Just as my wife was trying to give me my shoes someone in the crowd, which had gathered, struck me on the head again with a gun. Kenley then took me by the arm and marched me up the alley from my house to a vacant lot near the city hall. The ground was frozen with mud and ice, and my feet were bleeding before I had taken a dozen steps. I was being pushed by one man and then another.

"Before we had gone a block we came to a large pool of water in the alley, and someone in the crowd yelled: 'Shove the ——— through the water!' which Kenley did. When we got to the first street I asked them to let me walk on the sidewalk, but they continued down the alley. At this time Kenley was walking directly behind me.

"Again without warning he struck me on the head with a revolver, and at the same time someone yelled: 'Shoot him!' with an oath. When we got to the vacant lot near the city hall I found that there were a number of others there in almost my predicament. We were surrounded by armed men, some having guns, some revolvers and some both. We were forced to remain there until midnight. Then we were taken to an empty store room, where we were kept until 1:30 a.m. By this time over sixty men had been gathered there, and we were all marched to the depot, where a special train was waiting for us. As I entered the car, bleeding profusely, with my head tied up in handkerchiefs, someone shouted: 'If that fellow tied up in white ever comes back to this town he will be hung.'

"When the train started a fusilade of about 200 shots was fired by the mob as a parting salute. Fifteen members of the mob accompanied us to Ridgeway, forty-five miles out, where we were ordered to get off the train. Fifty-three of us then walked from Ridgeway to Ouray, a distance of eleven miles, where we arrived at 6 o'clock in the morning. The other men remained at Ridgeway, being unable to continue on the journey.

"There is but one reason why I did not defend my family and my home, and that is because of the union rule which was laid down at the beginning of the strike, to the effect that we must submit and not resist, so as to give them no excuse to do violence. There has not been one cent's worth of property destroyed during this strike."[50]

Deportation of Telluride miners beyond the county line was not a rash, exceptional action. It was a particularly cruel, violent, and wholly illegal measure taken against 227 union strikers—men who were not wild-eyed European socialists or anarchists with unpronounceable names. The overwhelming majority of them were of English, Scotch, and Irish extraction, with a few Germans and one Slav. In short, they were men of an earlier immigration. Kidnapping and deporting them was a blow aimed, not at anarchism or communism, but at the historic Anglo-Saxon rights embodied in the U.S. Constitution. The Adjutant General of the Colorado State Militia was frank about his reasoning: "I deported these men from the Cripple Creek district because in my judgment it was a military necessity.

"I sent them to the Kansas line because I believed it to be the most effective method of ridding Teller county and the state of Colorado of an organized gang of assassins, dynamiters, anarchists and lawbreakers.

"More than that, I sent them out of the district for their own safety. Martial law and the presence of the military is all that has prevented these men from being lynched by the indignant citizens of Teller and El Paso counties. My men have even taken ropes from their necks and saved them.

"The deportation was the quickest way of restoring peace. I don't want these men in Colorado. They are the leaders and participants in the insurrection now existing in the Cripple Creek district and it is my business to break that up. That is exactly what I propose to do.

"What steps I take as military commander concerns nobody but myself and my commander-in-chief, the governor of the state . . .

"I took charge of the district last week and I proceeded to clean it up.

"I had more than 300 men thrown into the bullpen, and I had every one of them put through the 'sweatbox.' The confessions they made were appalling.

"Today I have absolute proof that will send a dozen local federation leaders to the scaffold, and twice as many to the penitentiary.

"The men I deported were indirectly concerned in these crimes. Those I am keeping are directly concerned."[51]

At Cripple Creek, the owner of the Portland Mine had settled with the union, but on June 9, 1904, he was ordered by Adjutant General Bell to shut the mine down. The curious reason behind this order was the tragedy of June 6, three days before, when, at 3:00 A.M., a heavy dynamite charge had exploded under the wooden station platform while a crowd of non-union miners were waiting for a train to arrive. Thirteen were killed, and many more were crippled for life. Who triggered this explosion?

The Western Federation of Miners denied the obvious implication that this was a union act of revenge against the strikebreakers at the Findley Mine. The Citizens Alliance took immediate advantage of the horror, and called a mass meeting in the town of Victor:

". . . Clarence C. Hamlin mounted a wagon, which was used as a platform. He was accompanied by S. D. Crump, attorney for mine owners, and ex-convict Frank Vannick.

"Mr. Hamlin opened the meeting and his opening statement was:

" 'United States citizens must arm themselves and drive these Western Federation men to the hills.'

"In the course of Mr. Hamlin's remarks, he further said:

" 'For the blowing up of those brave boys fifty union men should be shot down like dogs and as many more swung to telegraph poles. Every Federation man is a criminal, and it is up to you men to drive them over the hills with your guns.' "[52] A union heckler in the crowd was seized, and in the mass frenzy that followed, five men were shot, two of them striking miners, and two of them strikebreakers. The fifth man was the chief of the local fire department. The same afternoon, the union hall was invaded: "We heard a noise at the foot of the stairs leading up to the hall, and, looking out, we saw a crowd trying to force an entrance. We warned them they were not wanted, but not once did we fire a shot. After awhile we decided to lock up the place and go to our homes. We left the windows and all of us were crowded at the head of the stairs preparing to descend when we were shot at from the outside. Then for the next few minutes a perfect hail storm of bullets were fired at us from the front, sides and through the skylight of the building. All we could do was to run alongside the walls or fall to the floor in order to protect ourselves from the terrible shower of lead.

"After awhile the firing ceased and one of our men ran out a white handkerchief as a sign of surrender. When that was done the mob and militia, who were at the foot of the stairs, ran up the steps and called upon us to throw up our hands. Such of us as were able, did so. The wounded were treated shamefully. They shoved a pistol down Ed McKelvey's throat, cursing and saying, 'Say its good, you ——— or we will blow your brains out!' One of the non-union men abused Peter Calderwood and started to finish him with his six-shooter but was prevented by the militia, who, by this time, were swarming into the hall. I verily believe we would have been murdered had it not been for the timely intervention of the militia. There was not a single shot fired from our side and had we started five minutes earlier we would have been out of the hall on the way to our homes."[53]

Every one of the men arrested for the crime at the Independence Railroad station was tried, and acquitted. No one else was ever arrested. Of course, there is no way, at this distance, to identify the murderers. Was the explosion the work of a paid provocateur? That would hardly be unusual. One such case was that of a certain Mr. McKinney, who was arrested for a bungled attempt to derail a passenger train, and who admitted at his trial that he was hired by the detective agency employed by the Mine Owners Association. His fee was $500, but he incurred further expenses because he was defended by a Mine Owners Association lawyer, who got him set free.

In the midst of this bloody civil war between miners and mine owners, a most extraordinary election was being held for governor of Colorado. Allegations of fraud were made by both sides. It was indisputable that the mine corporations, particularly in Huerfano and Las Animas Counties, voted their employees as a bloc, and very likely there was a fraudulent count in Denver County, which went heavily Democratic. The State Supreme Court, staunchly Republican, declared enough Democrats falsely elected to swing the lower House back into a Republican majority. In violation of the state constitution, this majority declared that the election of the new Democratic Governor, Adams, was invalid, and the seat should go to the former Republican Governor, Peabody. It was an awkward situation, for Adams had already been inaugurated. His inaugural address supported a new eight-hour law, and the creation of a board of arbitration for labor disputes. Of course, both these moderate ideas were violently opposed by the largest mine owners—and this was the real issue.

At first some twelve Republicans refused to go along with this astonishing fraud, but they compromised at last, after getting an agreement from former Governor Peabody to write out his future resignation, to take effect twenty-four hours after he was given the oath of office. To induce Peabody to shorten his new term to exactly one day, he was guaranteed a governor's salary for the next two years, by a fund to be made up by the mining corporations. So on March 16, Governor Adams was evicted, and Peabody was inaugurated. On March 17, Peabody resigned, and the Republican lieutenant governor was inaugurated governor of Colorado: "Jesse McDonald, of Lake County, made the third governor Colorado had had within 24 hours."[54]

Returning to his home in Pueblo, Colorado, Adams had his carriage drawn from the station by crowds of citizens. But he issued a bitter statement to the press: "To the People of Colorado: Force has triumphed. A brutal majority placed in the governor's chair a man the people repudiated. Ninety-five per cent of Colorado citizens know that Peabody was not elected. All of those connected with the crime know it . . .

"The greatest anarchists, and the most dangerous, are often the no-party, no-conscience heads of great corporations, who use the money and influence coming from the franchises and privileges that are the gifts of the people to control legislation, to dictate the personnel of courts and officials, to corrupt the ballot.

"They stand high in church and society; they drone their prayers with regularity; they are the 'holy Willies'—the 'holier than thou' politicians—no publican of old more pious and self-satisfied. They are full of homilies on political virtue; they preach morality and practice reason; their purse is open to the church and to the political corruptionist and lobbyist with equal liberality. For their disregard of the law there seems to be no relief, as they would have the laws so made, interpreted and executed as to exempt them from penalty."[55]

He ran again in 1906, and defeated the fraudulent governor, four to one.

5

At Telluride and Cripple Creek, not unexpectedly, the strikes were lost. The most active union men were blacklisted everywhere in the state by the Mine Owners Association, which issued cards to those miners identified as non-union men. Those without cards were turned away from the mines. It was quite open and official. Employers were asked to sign the following agreement circulated by the Citizens Alliance: "We, the undersigned merchants of the Cripple Creek district and employers of help, hereby agree not to employ help of any kind that is in any way connected with the trades assembly or the American Federation of Labor or the Western Federation of Miners or kindred organizations."[56] The ban on the AF of L was later withdrawn, because newspapers could not print without the typographers union. But the mine unions, like the steel unions, lacked the economic power to back their own leaders. In fact, so great was the solidarity of the mill owners that union leaders had to leave the industry, or starve.

Was there no alternative in democratic America, free of the old feudal laws, customs, and classes? Couldn't a blacklisted miner go to work on a western farm, for example? Very few of them did. What public land was left by 1904 was dry and only marginally fertile, and, as has already been noted, the homesteader had to have around $1,500 worth of tools, stock, seed, feed, and food for a year to get started. But if that was impractical, couldn't the blacklisted worker learn another trade? Probably. But we must look at this question from the workman's point of view, which raises subtler and less arithmetic problems. These were described by an acute and sensitive observer in a steel town of the same period: ". . . Young, unmarried men may shift about quite freely without incurring great danger, and many of them do. But married men cannot jeopardize the interests of their families by leaving the known for the unknown . . . He will not lightly tear himself loose from the city or the locality where all his closest friends reside and go so far away that they perhaps may never follow, and he may never return. Is it a small thing that the working people also love their homes and the associations of years? The home community often means more to a workman of slender means than it does to those more fortunate, for he knows just who are the trusted friends there who can be counted on in disaster . . ."[57] It was precisely this social, economic and psychological exile that the great coal, steel, gold, and railroad companies imposed on the brightest, most aggressive—indeed, most characteristically American—union men.

With all these weapons on one side of the labor wars, it is not surprising that the unions were for many years, from 1877 to World War I, a stark, bloody, and repeated failure. The great railroad strikes of 1877 were broken by troops, blacklist, murder, and simple lack of food. The motive for this repetitious drama of strike and strikebreaking was not simply profit, but power. For example, in the Augusta, Georgia, textile strike of 1886, where the workers were as young as five years of age, the Southern Manufacturers Association broke off negotiations because "to yield now is to yield the whole management of the mills, manufacturing, commercial and financial to them . . ."[58] Four months after this strike began and with awful irony, after whole-sale embezzlement of strike relief funds by union officers, the mill resumed operation. No wage increase was given and the mills worked the usual sixty-eight hours per week, instead of the sixty the strikers had, in their insolence, demanded. It was a pattern repeated in America for a hundred years from the earliest craft strikes in the nineteenth century to the wide industrial battles of post-World War I.

In steel, the crucial battle was fought at Andrew Carnegie's steel works at Homestead, Pennsylvania, in 1892. It's interesting that whereas Benjamin Franklin Jones, of Jones & Laughlin, faced the strikers of 1877 personally, a decade later the union had to deal with the much more brutal and rigid managers. In 1889, the representative of the Carnegie Brothers & Company was H. C. Frick, whose reputation was already excellent. He had crushed a coal strike several years before by the use of Pinkerton detectives. The steel strike began, on June 30, 1892, over the terms of a contract that would lower wages below the earlier minimum, but the real issue was recognition of the Union as the bargainer for its men.

On July 6, a force of Pinkertons was conveying three hundred strike-breakers by boat toward the mill pier on the river. The strikers piled up barricades, and behind them both men and women waited with the hunting weapons that everyone had. As usual, no one knows who fired the first shot, but in the battle that followed seven persons were killed, plus three more on subsequent days.

Finally, the two barge-loads of Pinkerton strikebreakers were forced ashore, and the passengers made to run up the slopes of the river shore and through a bloody gauntlet of strikers and their families. ". . . The first few passed through the lines without molestation beyond hoots, jeers and imprecations. Suddenly the fury of the mob broke out. A man struck a detective with his open hand. The example was contagious. Clubs and stones were used with demoniacal ferocity. Women, converted for the nonce into veritable furies, belabored Mr. Frick's janizaries with bludgeons, stoned them, kicked them and spat upon them. The hated Pinkerton uniforms were torn off and cast into the river . . ."[59]

The National Guard was sent by the governor of Pennsylvania, and under the protection of these guns, the company sent in two thousand more strikebreakers. They were men who, in the growing mechanization of the industry in the last decades of the nineteenth century, had no need for the old highly technical skills. The strike failed by October, and the union with it.

But this was a small disaster in comparison with the Pullman strike of 1894. The company town rented its neat houses to its own workmen, and even provided such rare amenities as a church and a hospital. But the panic of 1893 had caused an almost universal reduction in wage rates, sometimes justified, sometimes not. In the case of the Pullman Company, it was not. "During the fiscal year ending July 31, 1893, dividends of $2,520,000 had been distributed and wages of $7,233,719.51 paid; but for the year ending July 31, 1894, dividends rose to $2,880,000 while wages dropped to $4,471,701.39. The company enjoyed a paid-up capital of $36,000,000 and a lump surplus of $25,000,000 in undivided profits. The average daily wage, earned on a piece-work basis, in most departments was about ninety cents, [which came to about $25 a month] while the rent approximated eleven to twelve dollars per month."[60] Rent consumed about 50 per cent of the workers' income. George Pullman would neither restore the wage cut nor lower the rents. On May 10, 1894, two thousand Pullman workers went on strike. The powerful American Railway Union, organized on the basis of the whole industry, not just one or two elite crafts, voted not to handle Pullman cars on its tracks.

The General Managers Association, comprising twenty-four Midwest railroads, ordered its member companies to fire all employees who boycotted Pullman cars. The first such switchmen were discharged on June 26. The union called a strike to get them back their jobs. Up to this point there was no violence whatever, merely a silent test of strength and resources. But Grover Cleveland, the current President of the United States, instructed Attorney General Richard Olney to handle the emergency. The latter made an extraordinary appointment, naming as special U. S. attorney, Edwin Walker, who was a lawyer for the General Managers Association, and sending him the following telegram: "It has seemed to me that if the rights of the United States were vigorously asserted in Chicago, the origin and center of the demonstration, the result would be to make it a failure everywhere else and to prevent its spread over the entire country. . . . But I feel that the true way of dealing with the matter is by a force which is overwhelming and prevents any attempt at resistance."[61]

Walker got a federal injunction against the officers of the American Railway Union, prohibiting them from ". . . directing, inciting, encouraging, or instructing any persons whatsoever to interfere with the business or affairs, directly or indirectly of the railway companies."[62] To enforce this injunction, Walker asked for, and got, federal troops into Chicago. In response, thousands of people, obviously not all of them strikers, began to physically obstruct traffic on the struck railroads. Only six railroads out of twenty-three were able to operate at all.

Eugene Debs, president of the union, wired the local leaders: "Calling out the troops is an old method of intimidation. Commit no violence. Have every man stand pat. Troops cannot move trains. Not enough scabs in the world to fill places and more occurring hourly . . . Strong men and broad minds only can resist the plutocracy and arrogant monopoly. Do not be frightened at troops, injunctions, or a subsidized press. Quit and remain firm. Commit no violence. American Railway Union will protect all, whether member or not when strike is off."[63]

Particularly interesting was the populist resentment of all railroads: "In California, particularly, public sentiment was against the Southern Pacific Railroad for monopolistic practices before the strike, and the introduction of federal troops stirred up a fresh antagonism to the railroads. When the militia of Stockton and Sacramento were called out to fire upon the crowds, the soldiers removed cartridges from their guns and refused to use bayonets . . ."[64]

In Illinois, popular pro-labor feelings were crystallized in the actions of Governor Altgeld, who had pardoned two of the Haymarket prisoners, and who now asked President Cleveland to pull back the federal troops. There was violence by now. Two men, one a train engineer, had been killed by strike sympathizers, and the World's Fair buildings left from the grand Columbian Exposition of 1892 were set afire. The Chicago chief of police reported: "In some cases there were strong suspicions that the fires were set by Deputy United States Marshals who hoped to retain their positions by keeping up a semblance of disorder. . . . While there were some honest men among them a large number were toughs, thieves, and ex-convicts. . . . Several of these officials were arrested during the strike for stealing property from railroad cars. In one instance two of them were found under suspicious circumstances near a freight car which had just been set on fire. . . . They [the deputies] fired into a crowd of bystanders when there was no disturbance and no reason for shooting. . . . One of them shot and killed a companion by carelessly handling his gun and another shot himself."[65] A confrontation between state militia and crowds of Chicagoans ended with four dead and twenty wounded.

On July 10, 1894, U.S. Attorney General Olney ordered the arrest of Debs and three other officials. Next day, there was a call for a general strike across the whole country. The strike was successful in Chicago. The grievances of the sleeping-car-makers at Pullman were subsumed in vaster and more dangerous issues. After the arrest of Debs, the head of the AF of L, an ex-cigar worker named Samuel Gompers, forbade any of his member unions to join the general strike. Debs, defended by Clarence Darrow, lost his case before the Supreme Court and served six months in federal jail. Without leaders, and more dangerously, because of its very ambition, the general strike fell apart, and the railroads refused to deal with any labor leaders at all. Every active union member was discharged and blacklisted, and there were thousands.

On September 30, 1911, railroad shop mechanics—organized in the AF of L, but outside the four elite craft unions of locomotive engineers, firemen, trainmen, and conductors—struck two major rail networks owned by E. H. Harriman. They wanted a minimum wage plus pay for overtime, and they voiced the old native populist complaint that blacks and foreigners were undercutting their wages. This was a true grievance, if a selfish one. They instinctively hated the notion of bringing blacks and foreigners, by which they meant foreigners from southern Europe, into their unions. The energy behind the drive to abolish child labor had a similar economic, and not simply humanitarian, reason. This is no surprise, and is not meant as an indictment of human nature. Individual men and women can be moved by unselfish emotion. Organized into groups and blocks of any kind, their vision is narrowed down to what is good for them today, right now, and nothing else really matters. This was all the more true in this case, because their adversaries, the vast Illinois Central and the empire of Harriman railroads, were hardly more benevolent. It was force against force:

"On one occasion 800 furious strikers surrounded the Illinois Central depot. Newspapers carried stories of brutal physical assaults of both sides. In Carbondale workers subjected company roundhouses to gunfire, while in Mounds men sent volleys of bullets into passing trains. Under cover of darkness Illinois Central smuggled 200 strikebreakers into stockades at the railroad center of Burnside. A furious crowd rushed these buildings, stoned the occupants, and then advanced on them with clubs. Police issued a riot call in order to quell the battle. In Illinois, as in New Orleans, the company furnished shotguns to state and federal officials."[66]

It was 1877 all over again, for the mechanics were starved out, and the strike was reluctantly called off in December, 1914.

6

The cost of these battles—for that is exactly what they were—must not be softened by generalization, that easy sin of all historians. Truth has its root in specificity, and no strike has had more detailed reporting than the 1913 events in Ludlow, against the Colorado Fuel and Iron (C.F.I) Company, 40 per cent of which was owned by John D. Rockefeller, Jr. The company owned 300,000 acres, and no miner, even if he could afford it, was allowed to build or buy a house or a lot inside these invisible walls. Workmen had to rent a company house or live in a tent or a dugout on company soil. The water supply was bad, sewage worse, and often the two were identical. For many years, the C.F.I. paid its miners only in company paper, valid only in company stores. Their profits were therefore as large as 20 per cent. Schools, libraries, and churches were dominated by company managers. "J. F. Welborn, president of the company, considered it management's prerogative to fire ministers who opposed the firm or who exhibited 'socialistic tendencies.' A Commission inspector discovered that the firm censored movies, books, and magazines. It proscribed not only anti-capitalist literature but such works as Darwin's *Origin of the Species* and *The Rubaiyat of Omar Khayyam.* 'We wish to protect our people from erroneous ideas,' a company spokesman declared."[67] Of course, political offices were filled with company men. Sheriffs, judges, coroners, and juries were picked to assure that the C.F.I. would rarely lose a death or an accident case.

The old union had been broken. A new one, the United Mine Workers, organized the men in the C.F.I. by August, 1913, after a decade of failures. They then asked management for an eight-hour day, a 10 per cent raise, payment of wages in U. S. currency, and the right to choose the men who weighed the coal for which they were paid. The chairman of the executive board of the company, L. M. Bowers, refused even to meet with the union committee. He didn't want the company run, he said, by socialists and anarchists. The strike began late in September, 1913.

In October, John Chase, commanding general of the Colorado National Guard, deployed three troops of cavalry and one of field artillery. He then tried to disarm both sides: "I consulted the strike leaders, including John R. Lawson, and obtained from them, and especially from him, an assurance that if I first disarmed the mine guards employed through the Baldwin-Felts Detective Agency to guard the operators' properties, the strikers would then cheerfully surrender the arms in their possession . . ."[68]

He collected the high-powered rifles of the mine guards, and then paraded his troops through the miners' tent colony at Ludlow:

"The road for a half-mile or more between the point of detraining and the entrance to the colony was lined on either side by men, women, and children. Many of the men were in the strange costume of the Greek, Montenegrin, Servian, and Bulgarian armies; for the colony numbered among its inhabitants many returned veterans of the Balkan wars. The little children were dressed in white, as for a Sunday-school picnic. All carried small American flags and sang continually the Union songs. Through this line of men, women, and children the troops paraded—infantry, cavalry, and field artillery. Flags were waved in welcome, and an improvised band of the strikers heralded our approach.

"We passed by Ludlow, occupied the Berwind and Hastings canons, and then returned to the colony to receive the surrender of the hundreds of high-power rifles I knew the strikers to be possessed of. At this point occurred the first instance of bad faith on the part of the striking people. Expecting to receive hundreds, if not thousands, of arms, there were delivered into my possession some twenty or thirty weapons, many of them of obsolete pattern, the strikers topping off the humor of the situation by including in the delivery of arms a child's toy pop-gun . . ."[69]

The logic of the strikers in this mocking deception was no different from the logic of the 1877 strikers: (1) Lacking a base in government, either state or national, the workmen had no other force but to quit work. (2) Quitting work meant, of course, no wages. (3) The workmen had therefore to depend on union relief payments, on the credit of local merchants, or the charity of the sympathetic public. (4) All three of these were rather limited, so the strike had to be won in a few weeks or at most a few months, or their families would be faced, literally, with starvation. (5) If the company could get strikebreakers, it would have the resources to outlast even an extended strike. (6) In order to get strikebreakers through the strikers' lines, the company had to hire armed guards, or get armed deputy sheriffs, not always distinguishable from one another. (7) This use of armed guards exacerbated the situation, so the company was happy to request, and it generally got, the state militia, which "was largely made up of small property owners, clerks, professional men, and farmers"—and not miners, of course. (8) To oppose the transport of strikebreakers under armed guard the strikers had either to admit defeat, or use armed force themselves; poorly armed, they would generally rely on their greatly superior numbers and the courage of their desperation.

On November 8, a non-union miner was shot. On the same day, a mine guard, going to a dentist in the nearby town of La Veta, was stopped and taken to the union hall. He was rescued by other mine guards in a company automobile which was ambushed by armed miners outside of town. Both sides had weapons, which immediately contradicts the general's account of the disarmament. Three of the mine guards were killed, the fourth wounded. On November 20, George Belicher, one of the leaders of the detachment of mine guards hired by the Baldwin-Felts Detective Agency, was shot and killed on a street corner in Trinidad, Colorado, "by a Tyrolean Italian named Luis Zancanelli," who confessed to General Chase that he'd been hired by the union. The general also reported on the case of the famous, roving organizer, Mother Jones:

"On the 11th of January Mary Jones, or Mary Harris, alias 'Mother Jones,' appeared in Trinidad in defiance of Your Excellency, with the avowed and proclaimed purpose of stirring up trouble. I have discussed this woman elsewhere in this report. By Your Excellency's directions I arrested Mother Jones, placed her in San Rafael Hospital, a church institution, giving her every comfort, but depriving her of being at large to carry out her incendiary purposes . . .

"In view of her history in other places and the evident effects of her incendiary utterances in Colorado, Your Excellency deemed it wise and even necessary, as a military measure, to restrain Mother Jones of her liberty so long as she persisted in remaining in the strike region. Accordingly, upon the day of her arrival in Trinidad I arrested her and placed her in San Rafael Hospital, upon the outskirts of the city, where she was given every attention conducive to her comfort. She was advised that she was always at entire liberty to leave the disturbed parts of the state, but she pertinaciously and with great contumacy insisted on remaining in imprisonment . . ."[70]

A parade of women, the wives and daughters of strikers from Trinidad, marched on the hospital to free her. The soldiers were attacked with sticks and stones, and several of the crowd were arrested, women included. There was a hearing on this affair before a committee of the U.S. House of Representatives. One witness, said the general in his report, ". . . testified that she was shoved, pushed, jabbed in the back with a bayonet, arrested, and held in jail eleven days. The arrest and imprisonment are facts, but the rest of her testimony is largely fiction. She was a vociferous, belligerent, and abusive leader of the mob. She forcibly resisted orders to move on, responding only with highly abusive and to say the least, unwomanly language."[71]

The general further reported: "The examination of the prisoners revealed over and over again English-speaking men who had been in this country between twenty and thirty years, yet had never attempted to become American citizens, but remained still subjects of the British crown. These are the class of men who clamor most loudly about their constitutional rights."[72] General Chase himself was no doctrinaire believer in constitutional rights. He tried the arrested miners, not before judge and jury, but before a military commission appointed on November 20 for this purpose. They were all captains, majors, colonels, or generals in the state militia. One hundred seventy-two trials were held. "Of the prisoners, 141 were foreigners, 14 were Greeks, 46 Italians, 43 Mexicans, 24 Slavs, 14 other foreign nations. There were 31 Americans. The moral effect of the Military Commission was tremendous . . ."[73]

With arms on both sides, the strike was careening toward community disaster. On the morning of April 20, 1914, the National Guard, armed with machine guns, took up battle positions on a hill overlooking one of the larger of the miners' tent colonies. Major Edward J. Boughton then set off two bombs, as a signal, he said, to warn troops at other points. It's more probable that it was a military signal for simultaneous assault. In any case, someone—as usual his identity was never established—fired a single shot. Immediately, firing began from both sides. The National Guard, from its high ground, assaulted the tent colony below four times and was driven back four times. But they made a number of arrests, including that of a union leader, Louis Tikas, a graduate of Athens University and therefore indubitably a foreigner. A National Guard lieutenant, Karl E. Linderfelt, was involved in what happened next:

"Tikas was taken before Lieutenant Linderfelt. About Linderfelt at the time stood fifty or seventy-five militiamen, most of them members of Troop 'A' and acting in their double capacity as militiamen and mine guards. Hot words ensued, and although Tikas was absolutely defenseless, Linderfelt grasped his Springfield rifle by the barrel and broke the stock over Tikas' head. Linderfelt then strode away, and a few moments later there was a fusillade of shots. R. J. McDonald, stenographer for the militia officers, testified at the inquest that Linderfelt did not look around when he heard the shots. Tikas was shot three times in the back. The doctors who testified at the inquest said that he had been literally 'shot to pieces inside.' "[74]

Toward the end of the day, the militia launched a fifth and frontal attack under cover of machine gun fire. Three tents in the hollow burst into flames, and militiamen set fire to those that did not. Testimony before a U.S. Commission established that " '. . . men and soldiers seized and took from the tents whatever appealed to their fancy . . . clothes, bedding, articles of jewelry, bicycles, tools, and utensils.' 'So deliberately [sic] was this burning and looting,' the military commission stated, 'that cans of oil found in the tents were poured upon them and the tents lit with matches.' "[75] There were twenty-one dead, among them two women and eleven children burned to death in the union tents.

Surely one of the oddest confrontations in American history took place on January 27, 1915, before the House committee investigating this Ludlow massacre. ". . . Rockefeller maintained complete self-composure and calmly took his seat. Then he spotted Mother Jones. In a move which startled everyone, the millionaire stood up, reached across the table, and shook her hand. 'I wish that you would come down to my office at your convenience,' he said. 'There are so many things on which you can enlighten me.' Flustered, the elderly lady mumbled her acceptance. When she had regained her composure, Mother Jones also extended an invitation. 'I want you to come out to Colorado with me and see the things I have seen,' she told him. 'I am sure what you see will make you do things which will make you one of the country's greatest men . . . I don't hold the boy responsible,' she said. 'When I have a good motherly talk with him I believe I can help him take another view of the situation among his miners out west.' After their chat, Rockefeller announced, 'I find we are in full accord upon most of the subjects in which we are mutually interested.' He then invited other UMW officials to his office and praised them all as 'clean cut fellows.' Finally the young scion proclaimed that he had determined to visit Colorado in the near future. 'We have been misrepresenting him terribly,' lamented Mother Jones, 'and I as much as anybody else.' "[76]

The odd truth, it seems to me, was that Mother Jones and John D. Rockefeller, Jr. were modestly competing for a good media image. The admittedly pious Rockefeller, for all his testimonial concern for the miners, was lying. The C.F.I. refused Wilson's plan for industrial peace, and under Rockefeller's benevolent guidance, did not recognize the United Mine Workers until the social earthquakes of 1933. Fifteen months after it began, the Ludlow strike was broken.

7

If from this little distance we look more coldly at the long record of union failure, we are forced to ask ourselves whether its limited victories and its spectacular defeats have made any real difference in the course of American life. What was the average hourly pay, and at what rate did it increase under the union pressures of 1881–1917? In the soft coal mines, pay was eighteen cents per hour in 1890, and ten years later, still only twenty-one cents. By 1910, it had risen to twenty-nine cents, a weekly pay of $11.70. The pay in 1914 was almost the same at $12.11 per week. Iron and steelworkers earned an average of seventeen cents an hour in 1892, which by 1910 had risen to twenty-three cents an hour. Foundry workers' wages rose in the same double decade from eighteen to twenty-three cents per hour.

The rates in consumer industries were a good deal lower at both ends. A shoe worker earned sixteen cents in 1892, nineteen cents in 1910; a paper worker twelve cents an hour in 1892, seventeen cents by 1910. So there was a slow rise, no doubt about that. But this rise should be measured against the cost of living. If that index in 1913 is taken as 100, then the cost of living was, in 1892, only 77. But by 1910, the cost of living index had risen to 196, an increase of about 20 per cent. The coal miner during that same period got an hourly pay increase of nearly 50 per cent. Yet his actual pay raise measured against the cost of living was only 30 per cent, or about 1.5 per cent per year between 1892 and 1910.

But the partly or wholly unorganized workers in the consumer industries did far worse, because they started at a lower rate. The wages of paper workers rose 40 per cent, but the cost of living meantime rose 20 per cent, so their net gain was only about 1 per cent per year. The shoe workers' raise amounted to about three per cent during that whole period, against a rise of 20 per cent in the cost of living, so this large group actually lost ground between 1892 and 1910.[77]

How strong a part, in fact, have unions played in American life? We can get some rough notion by comparing union membership with the total of all industrial workers. The earliest decently accurate figures for union membership were in 1897. But let's start in 1900. In that year, the unions had organized 4.6 per cent of the factory, mine, and railroad workers. In 1910, union membership was 8.3 per cent. Even after a war that sent millions of young men into the armed services and therefore created a labor shortage, the unions in 1920 had only organized 13 per cent of the eligible workers.[78]

Maybe that is true of all our institutions—a reluctance in the American character to assume collective obligations? No, that is only part of the complex truth. For the churches, also a voluntary institution, had the allegiance of 34 per cent of the American people in 1890, 42 per cent in 1906, and 41 per cent in 1916. But none of them had their growth stunted by eviction, blacklist, kidnapping, deportation, arson, or murder.

But just as religious values motivate people who don't get around to going to church on Sunday, so union pressure affects not only the factory or the mine or the company or even the branch of industry toward which it is exerted by strike or the threat of strike. It also affects other mines and other mills by the very threat of future union. Therefore, it is important to see its justification; to calculate the real economic place of the worker during the splendid and feverish erection of the American pyramid.

In 1890, the yearly wage of an industrial worker was $486; though a miner only got $406, a railroad employee got an average of $560. How did these figures compare to less laborious, cleaner, and more prestigious occupations? In 1890, the average minister made $794 a year, a postman got $878, and a clerk $848—scarcely a fortune, either. An acid irony is petrified in the figures for farm laborer and schoolteacher in 1890: the first only got $233 a year, but that probably included board and room; a schoolteacher got $256 a year without these amenities. One must resist the easy temptation to regard these as mere figures, for they are also the spare and difficult means by which one survives day by day, and year by year.

How did these people do in 1910 two decades later? Industrial workers then got an average of $558 per year, coal miners about the same, clerical workers $1,156, a postman $1,049, while a minister made $802, a schoolteacher $492, and a farm laborer, on the bottom as ever, earned $336 a year. Meantime the cost of living went steadily up. Between 1890 and 1910, it rose from an index of 67.8 to 96.0, a climb of 41 per cent. So, by direct and indirect union pressure in all industries, how much did the average workman gain? His hourly rate seems to have risen, not markedly but decently. But his annual wage rose only 15 per cent, from $486 in 1890 to $558 in 1910. Put against the rise in the cost of living, 41 per cent, the average workman was actually making 26 per cent less in 1910 than he was in 1890. Even if we extend this comparison to 1914 (because after that, the European war complicates all statistics), the industrial workmen got $682 a year, but the cost of living index had risen to 102.5; so it cost 51 per cent more to live while the average increase in a workman's average annual wage over the same twenty-five years was barely 40 per cent—a net loss, in fact, of 11 per cent in the way he lived, ate, and clothed himself.[79]

And how did the industrial worker do in respect to that essentially spiritual, non-material issue of the eight-hour day? In 1895, foundry hands worked ten hours a day, iron and steel employees the same, while paper employees worked nearly eleven. In 1910, the latter had gained somewhat, for their average working day was now 9.7 hours; for foundry men, it was 9.3 hours, but in steel and iron, the average working day was still, in 1910, 10.6 hours. Only in August, 1923, years after the end of World War I, pushed by the moral pressure of the Interchurch World Movement, and under the surprising but cautious leadership of the then Secretary of Commerce, Herbert Hoover, the eight-hour day became general in the steel industry.[80]

Therefore, by the arithmetic of material and moral issues, the unions must be considered a relative failure. The reasons are not mysterious; the forces of management were simply too great to overcome. Early in the Bethlehem Steel strike of 1910, for example, a thousand workers left to seek work elsewhere. They didn't get it. They were named on a careful industry-wide blacklist. Furthermore, the strikebreakers came, not from the outside from the pool of unemployed, but from apprentices within the mills who earned nine cents an hour and stood to lose a hundred dollar bonus and a raise all the way up to eighteen cents an hour—after four years. Third, a new and potent weapon used against the strikers was the anger of the small town middle class—businessmen who were persuaded that it was in their interest to keep the plant open. But the final, most compelling, and most general reason was that no worker had money enough to survive a long strike. Nor did his union. The Bethlehem Steel strikers had endured 108 days without pay. No family man could make further sacrifice. Survival, which is natural, and, to this observer, moral, took precedence over naked principle.

8

The psychological consequence of all these bitter experiences was two-sided. The ordinary worker became cynical, depressed, and passive. At the same time he acquired a private belief in the essentially religious dogma that a time would come, and must be made to come, when the industrial barons and bankers, the devils of the industrial age, would be cast down from their luxurious heaven, and the worker would then live forever after in a just and equitable society. It was the old legend of a golden age, which is always put at either far past or far future, or sometimes, curiously, both.

An exceptionally intelligent and relatively prosperous steelworker, Ed Jones, expressed this view in 1910: " 'It is no use for them to try to regulate wages, anyhow,' he says, 'for labor is a commodity and its price is regulated by supply and demand. The only way out for the laboring men is to get together in a labor party,'—and this to him means the socialist party."[81]

Another Pittsburgh workman said, "Ninety-nine percent of the men are socialists, if by that you mean one who hates a capitalist."[82]

A steel union organizer, Mrs. Gertrude Hunt, told the Bethlehem strikers: "If they cannot run their steel business at a profit to clothe, feed and shelter their employees decently, if they cannot run it decently, then it is time the Government take possession and see that it runs the business for the whole body of the people."[83]

In 1908, the defeated strikers at Homestead held a similar belief: ". . . [T]he concerted action of trade unionism would be helpless to affect the conditions of work. A small but apparently growing group, recognizing that the industry is too large for them to cope with, look toward socialism for a solution. State interference seems to them the only means of changing the situation. Those who think thus are not extremists; they are workingmen who simply can see no other way out. These men held few meetings and attempted no propagandist work; they accepted the socialist program as an individual hope."[84]

This view can be found very early among American laboring men—for example in the preamble (later censored) to the hard rock miners union constitution adopted in Comstock, Nevada, late in 1866: "Whereas, in view of the existing evils which the Miners have to endure from the tyrannical oppressive power of Capital, it has become necessary to protest, and to elevate our social condition and maintain a position in society, and that we should cultivate an acquaintance with our fellows in order that we may be the better enabled to form an undivided opposition to acts of 'tyranny'— Therefore, We the Miners of Gold Hill have resolved to form an association for the promotion and protection of our common interests, and to adopt a constitution for its guidance, for without Union we are powerless, with it we are powerful;—and there is no power that can be wielded by Capital or position but which we may boldly defy,—For united we possess strength; let us then act justly and fear not."[85]

The Knights of Labor, that began as a secret organization with ceremonies like the Masons of Europe and the United States, became an open union by 1881: "The Order had a broad aim: the replacement of a competitive society by a cooperative one which would give workers the opportunity to enjoy fully the wealth they created. This was to be achieved primarily through reducing the 'money power' of banks, not through battles with individual employers. More concretely, the Knights' program called for the 8-hour day, equal pay for equal work by women, abolition of convict and child labor, public ownership of utilities, and the establishment of cooperatives."[86] Out of the real, repetitive, hopeless privation of which they had personal and daily experience, the workmen longed for a catastrophic change.

Even in the AF of L, which competed with the Knights and won, and where the possible and the practical—and too often, therefore, the cowardly and corrupt—began to dominate the craft unions, there still remained a strong flavor of utopian socialism. From 1886, its policies were framed by an extraordinary immigrant from London, a Jewish cigar maker, Samuel Gompers. Praised as a conservative and vilified as a reactionary, he was not quite either. The narrow craft divisions of the AF of L were integral to its Federation, and when Gompers tried to broaden them, for example by opening membership to blacks, he was faced with the refusal of certain of the railroad brotherhoods, and he retreated. Gompers' actual power was limited by craft autonomy, and he might be more accurately described as an arbitrator. Certainly he was not a socialist, but he was surprisingly respectful of the ideological power they had within the unions, particularly unions in the big cities of industrial America. In fact, Gompers lost the presidency of the AF of L, if only for the stormy year of 1895, simply because the socialists didn't want him. In self-defense, he wrote a famous letter to the communist Friedrich Engels, apologizing for the fact that he had exlcuded the Socialist Labor Party, the oldest American representative of Marx and Engels' First International, from membership in the AF of L:

Mr. Fred Engels
#122 Regents Park Road
London (N.W.) Eng.   Jan. 9th. 1891

Dear Sir:—I make so free as to write to you upon a question which I know you take a deep interest in, and from the further fact of having been a life-long devoted friend, thinker and writer to and for the labor movement . . . I have respect for your judgment, and as a student of your writings and those of Marx and others in the same line, I would not have your judgment formed upon the basis of erroneous information . . .

There has never yet arisen a question in our Councils whether a man was a socialist or not, whether he was an anarchist or not, in fact the greatest freedom and latitude of thought have been not only permitted but encouraged. Some of our best men and staunchest in holding as I do are well-known and avowed socialists . . .

Our movement is anxiously endeavoring to keep in touch with the wage-workers, to help organize them, to make them self-reliant, to coalesce them into one grand whole struggling against the unjust conditions that exist, and to supplant them with such that the noblest aspirations of mankind has conceived or can conceive.[87]

Engels never replied directly, but wrote to the editor of a New York German-language newspaper, that he agreed with Gompers. The latter had no real alternative. The very word "socialism" was to the American public—to that ambiguous part of it that formed public opinion—a grim and leveling monster risen from the grave of the Paris Commune. Never mind that the massacres there were done by the French army. Socialism was, in the press, indistinguishable from anarchism or communism or from the opinionated factions like the Socialist Labor Party of Daniel de Leon. Whatever the niceties of doctrine, it had simply come to mean unruly mobs led by frowsy wives carrying torches soaked in kerosene.

Of course, like many another false conception in our history, it became, at times, horribly real.

9

In Chicago, on February 16, 1886, twelve hundred men were locked out of the McCormick Harvester plant, simply because they had submitted a list of common grievances. A large number of these men held a mass meeting on March 2 and were attacked, searched, and clubbed by a force of 400 uniformed policemen plus 300 plainclothes Pinkerton detectives. In response, on the Sunday before May 1, 125,000 persons attended a meeting that called for a general walkout in Chicago. It met a very strong response. By May 3, 50,000 workmen were on strike under the general slogan of the eight-hour day. On the afternoon of that same day, wagonloads of police, firing their revolvers, broke up an attempt by the McCormick strikers to prevent replacements from entering the plant. There were shots fired on both sides, and six men were killed—all strikers.

On May 4, a mass meeting to protest these deaths was held in Haymarket Square at 7:30 in the evening. The *Chicago Tribune* of May 5 reported: "There was no warning given. The crowd was rapidly dispersing. The police, marching slowly, were in a line with the east and west alley when something like a miniature rocket suddenly rose out of the crowd on the east sidewalk, in a line with the police. It rose about twenty feet in the air, describing a curve, and fell right in the middle of the street and among the marching police. It gave a red glare while in the air. The bomb lay on the ground for a few seconds, then a loud explosion occurred, and the crowd took to their heels, scattering in all directions. Immediately after the explosion the police pulled their revolvers and fired on the crowd. An incessant fire was kept up for nearly two minutes, and at least 250 shots were fired. The air was filled with bullets. The crowd ran up the streets and alleys and were fired on by the now thoroughly enraged police. Then a lull followed. Many of the crowd had taken refuge in the halls or entrances of halls and saloons. As the firing ceased they ventured forth, *and a few officers opened fire on them.*"[88]

Seven police officers were killed, seventy wounded, and four Chicago citizens were killed in the police counterattack that followed. Eight socialists and anarchists were arrested that night, but no proof was ever offered that they had had anything whatever to do with the fatal bomb. The bomb thrower was never found or identified. Nevertheless, in the subsequent trial, seven of these eight leaders—six of whom were not at the Haymarket meeting at all—were convicted of murder and sentenced to die. There is no doubt that anti-foreign prejudice was one of the irrational facts of their trial. Samuel Fielden, one of the accused, testified, ". . . I was taken into the corridor of the court house. Lieutenant Shea was sitting on the table with about twenty-five detectives around him. Mr. Slayton said, 'This is Fielden.' Lieutenant Shea said, 'You ——— Dutchman, before you came to this country people were getting good wages.' I said, 'Mr. Shea, I am not a Dutchman.' He said, 'You are ——— ——— worse, you ——— ——— ———.' That is the language of the officers of the law . . ."[89]

Even the briefest account of the trial shows that the men were certainly proved guilty, not of murder, but of rhetoric. It is characteristic of America in the nineteenth century that two of the men, Fielden and Albert Parsons, each began their speeches to the court by reading a long poem; of which I quote only one peroration:

> Man of labor, up arise!
> Know the might that in thee lies,
> Wheel and shaft are set at rest
> At thy powerful arm's behest . . .
>
> Break this two-fold yoke in twain:
> Break thy want's enslaving chain:
> Break thy slavery's want and dread:
> Bread is freedom, freedom bread . . .[90]

Michael Schwab, another of the defendants, proposed a definition of anarchy, which turned out to be a marvelous restatement of the New Jerusalem, that ancient and heavenly country: "Anarchy is a state of society, IN WHICH THE ONLY GOVERNMENT IS REASON. A state of society in which all human beings do right for the simple reason that it is right, and hate wrong because it is wrong. In such a society, no laws, no compulsion will be necessary."[91]

The same utopian ideas were declaimed by Parsons, as well: "THE NATURAL MAN IS A HAPPY MAN. He is virtuous and right; truly so. Whoever violates the right of another, sooner or later publishes himself. Nature is inexorable. From her penalty there is no escape . . ."[92] But the rhetoric of violence was too intoxicating to resist, even in open court: ". . . here are the Knights of Labor and the trades unions, and all of the organizations without arms. They have no treasury, and a Winchester rifle costs $18. They cannot purchase those things. We can not organize an army. It takes capital to organize an army. It takes as much money TO ORGANIZE AN ARMY AS TO ORGANIZE INDUSTRY, or as to build railroads; therefore, it is impossible for the working classes to organize and buy Winchester rifles. What can they do? What must they do? Your honor, the dynamite bomb, I am told, costs six cents. It can be made by anybody. The Winchester rifle costs eighteen dollars. That is the difference . . . So today DYNAMITE COMES AS THE EMANCIPATION OF MAN from the domination and enslavement of his fellow-man. [The Judge showed symptoms of impatience.] Bear with me now. Dynamite is the diffusion of power. It is democratic, it makes everybody equal."[93] The men could have been convicted from the logic of that one passage alone, for it confirmed in the public mind and in that part of the public which was the judge and jury, that anarchism equals dynamite.

Two of these men had their sentences commuted, one killed himself, and four were hanged. The eight-hour movement was thus colored, in the general view, by the scarlet of the anarchist and socialist movements, and this fear was the unreasonable consequence of the French communards of 1871 and the nihilists of nineteenth-century Russia.

There is a disturbing parallel, in this curious and unsolved Haymarket bombing, to the dynamite blast at the Independence Station during the decisive phase of the Cripple Creek strike when the mine owners were in serious trouble, unable to get enough strikebreakers except by paying unacceptably high wages. In Chicago and the Midwest, the bomb blast came at the height of the eight-hour drive, and after almost a decade of union success, particularly in the iron mills (though not in the steel mills). Were both these murderous and theatrical explosions meant to be provocations? To shock public opinion into irrational anger? Certainly it was a tactic suggested by the success of the Pinkerton campaign against the Irish anthracite miners in Pennsylvania, where members of a secret order (the Molly Maguires) were convicted of dynamite murders—justifiably, if we dare at this distance

to weigh the conflicting evidence. The object of all these trials, whether just
or not, was to break the union and reassert the right of ownership to set
wages and hours. For the late–nineteenth-century fact was that the cost of
labor made the big difference in how much money a plant could make—not
necessarily for the stockholders, but for itself, for its own expansion.

Industrial labor was unwilling, in America as elsewhere, to make this
sacrifice willingly. Indeed, why should they for the sake of a company in
which they had no egotistic or financial investment? On the contrary, they
hated and feared their foremen, managers, and employers. The doctrinaire
anarchists, and the more anarchic anarchists of the IWW—"The working
class and the employing class have nothing in common"—and the early
American socialists may have used the terminology of Bukharin, of
Proudhon—"All property is robbery"—and of that extraordinary piece of
rhetoric, the *Communist Manifesto* of Marx and Engels. But the deep emotion that American radicals expressed was the same emotion as that of the ordinary miner or puddler or sewing machine operator. Why, then, did all of
these utopian creeds, which enraptured the imagination of a very large but
inherently incalculable majority of American workmen, always and regularly
fail?

One reason, it is obvious, is that all utopias, by their very nature, are ex-
tensions to infinity of the lines of human desire. One might move in that direction, but no society would ever get there. The fantasy of a golden age,
past or present or future, was, and still is so recurrent and so universal, that
it must be, in the true sense, a religious desire. It may be found in the pathetic Ghost Dance of the Plains Indians toward the end of the nineteenth
century. It was advertised by sincere frauds like Carl Browne and by common martyrs like Joe Hill, who wrote IWW poems to Salvation Army
hymns, and repeated the curiously thrilling slogan of all sufferers—"Don't
waste time in mourning. Organize!"—and was executed for a robbery and
murder that was never proven, nor quite disproven, either. And utopian fantasy was evident in the trials of gifted and magnetic leaders like Debs and
Haywood.

The Calvary story for each of these two took a different, if typical turn.
Haywood was arrested, tried, and freed by the jury. He was re-arrested for
violation of the intentionally vague wartime espionage act and then convicted. But he skipped bail and spent the rest of his life in Russia, leaving his
friends to pay some $300,000 in penalty.

Eugene Debs emerged from his six months in jail in 1894, a self-con-
vinced socialist. After the formal dissolution of his union, he advanced a proposal to resettle the unemployed—there were at least two million that year,
1896—in a giant utopian cooperative somewhere in the West. This was read
by the American press as another "communistic scheme." Three such colonies, manned by Pullman ex-employees, were set up in Kansas, Louisiana,
and South Carolina. They were all failures. Debs gave an address in Chicago

after his release: ". . . I am not here to bemoan my lot. In my vocabulary there are no wails of despondency or despair. However gloomy the future may appear to others, I have an abiding faith in the ultimate triumph of the right. My heart responds to the sentiments of the poet who says:

> 'Swing back to-day, O prison gate,
> O winds, stream out the stripes and stars,
> O men, once more in high debate
> Denounce injunction rule and czars.
> By Freedom's travial pangs we swear
> That slavery's chains we will not wear . . .' "[94]

Debs ran on a socialist platform in four successive presidential elections. The record is itself a fairly good index of the influence of utopian ideas in this country: In 1900, he got 96,000 votes; in 1904, he got 402,000 votes; in 1908, it was 420,000; and in 1912, 901,000. But in that year, he and his party suffered a moral disaster. They backed a union official, John McNamara and his brother James, who had been arrested on a charge of dynamiting a factory and the building of the then anti-union *Los Angeles Times* at 1:00 A.M. on October 1 two years before. Twenty persons had been killed. Clarence Darrow defended the brothers at their trial, and even Gompers said the arrests were "a capitalist conspiracy in league with the corrupting influences of detective agencies." But halfway through the proceedings, the McNamara brothers changed their minds and pleaded guilty. The issue of labor violence split apart the Socialist Party. Nevertheless, Debs remained a heroic figure to large sections of American popular opinion.

"There could be no more fitting place to note the service of this gifted man Debs, not alone to the imprisoned men, that was but an incident in the life of this knight-errant of humanity. All who come after him will be his debtors. From the great strike of the American Railway Union, in 1894, to the present, his voice and pen have been devoted to the oppressed . . .

"More than any other man capitalism fears Eugene V. Debs; more fully than any other he holds the hearts of the toilers. Their dumb agony finds speech through his lips. Their bowed and broken bodies grow tall and fair in his presence. The dreams of the ages flower in the love of that lofty soul.

"James Whitcomb Riley spoke in music for thousands when he said: 'God was feeling mighty good when he made Gene Debs.' "[95]

Debs got a ten-year jail sentence in 1918 for publicly denouncing the numerous arrests for sedition. While in federal jail, he ran for President in 1920 and got 919,000 votes. But his health was weakened, and when President Harding commuted his sentence in 1921, he was an old, sick man, and died five years later.

The Socialist Party he had founded became minute and inconsequential. Why? One reason was the hatred and fear of radical labor by a growing class of businessmen, well-to-do farmers, bank employees, clerks, foremen, engineers, technicians of all sorts, doctors, dentists, and small merchants. These were at odds with "the tramps," the landless, jobless or half-jobless and consequently utopian sort of workmen—the loggers, harvest hands, and miners, the temporary help for temporary jobs, more and more of whom joined the IWW. The songs of that characteristically American organization had a corn-fed ring:

> Long-haired preachers come out every night,
> Try to tell you what's wrong and what's right;
> But when asked how 'bout something to eat
> They will answer with voices so sweet:
> *Chorus:*
> You will eat, bye and bye,
> In that glorious land above the sky;
> Work and pray, live on hay,
> You'll get pie in the sky when you die.[96]

Yet, in 1905, when the IWW was founded by a conference of socilaists like Debs, militants like the one-eyed, pock-marked Big Bill Heywood, the naive labor missionary Mother Jones, and a Catholic priest, Father Thomas Hagerty, they issued a manifesto that was utterly sober and even pessimistic, and which analyzed the new, late–nineteenth-century into early–twentieth-century relationship of men to their jobs: "The worker, wholly separated from the land and the tools, with his skill of craftsmenship rendered useless, is sunk in the uniform mass of wage slaves. . . . Laborers are no longer classified by diffrences in trade skill, but the employer assigns them according to the machines to which they are attached . . .[97] This manifesto called for an industrial union that would burst open craft boundaries. But the public image of the IWW was far different—an unshaven bum with a pistol in his pocket and a bundle of dynamite in his handkerchief sack. And, to a curious extent, perhaps influenced by this very distortion and persuaded often enough by Pinkerton operatives, the IWW man tried to live up to rhetorical violence. And if this was but an old American tradition of the tough, honest, big-fisted individual, he was soon outgunned by another American tradition—the respectable mob of vigilantes.

10

In a larger sense, all these utopian ideas failed to win power in America because they were inherently too good to be true. The IWW promised exactly what it despised—pie in the sky. The hope of heaven, whether Southern Baptist, New England Episcopalian, or Midwest Catholic, has the disadvantage that one has to die in order to enter its blinding gates. But anarchy demands heaven on earth and when, after a decent interval of bloodshed and persecution, it still refuses to appear, the vision fades and withers into an old office and a brave bi-monthly bulletin.

Industrialization has its own iron logic. Any degree of expansion takes money, and rapid expansion takes lots of money. The most traditional, the most convenient, the most rapid way to get this extra money is, and has always been, to take it out of the cost of the workmen. The ten- and twelve-hour day; the wage scale of the late-nineteenth century, just sufficient to feed a workman through youth and early middle age; the systematic cheating in company stores; the reluctance to protect the arms, hands, legs, eyes and lives of workmen by safety devices that would certainly slow down production—all of these measures of the fifty years between 1865 and 1915 served to build up cash and credit and reserves to expand and expand again and yet again. Every society—whether Maoist and Chinese, or Leninist and Russian, or simply imperial and Iranian, or South African and fascist—can scarcely build the heavy foundation of an industrial pyramid at all, and certainly cannot build it rapidly, unless it gets a sufficiently high percentage of profit to reinvest. And that profit has got to come from the underpaid labor of its builders.

The issues were, as they still are, complex and ironic. For example, better wages are paid during rapid armament, although this armament will serve to kill, in increasing masses, the sons of these same workmen. So the main deception remains. Ideology of one country or another is merely the flavor. The substance is the aggrandizment, inevitable and even thrilling and not entirely immoral, of any modern industrial nation.

9

The Secrets of the Ordinary

O N SUNDAY, JULY 12, 1885, a partly deaf widower wrote in his vacation diary: "Awakened at 5.15 AM. My eyes were embarrassed by the sunbeams— turned my back to them and tried to take another dip into oblivion—suc- ceeded—awakened at 7 A.M. thought of Mina Daisy and Mamma G—— put all 3 in my mental kaledescope to obtain a new combination a La Galton. Took Mina as a basis, tried to improve her beauty by discarding and adding certain features borrowed from Daisy and Mamma G a sort of Raphaelized beauty got into it too deep, mind flew away and I went to sleep again. Awakened at 815 AM. Powerful itching of my head, lots of white dry dan- druff—what is this d——mnable material, Perhaps its the dust from the dry literary matter I've crowded into my noddle lately Its nomadic gets all over my coat, must read about it in the Encyclopedia. Smoking too much makes me nervous—must Passo (?) my natural tendency to acquire such habits— holding heavy cigar constantly in my mouth has deformed my upper lip, it has a sort of Havanna curl. Arose at 9 oclock came down stairs expecting twas too late for breakfast—twas'nt. couldn't eat much, nerves of stomach too nicotinny. The roots of tobacco plants must go clear through to hell. Satans principal agent Dyspepsia must have charge of this branch of the vegitable kingdom.—It has just occured to me that the grain may digest certain por- tions of food, say the etherrial part as well as the stomach—perhaps dandruff is the excreta of the mind—the quantity of this material being directly pro- portional to the amount of reading one indulges in. A book on German meta- physics would thus easily ruin a dress suit . . . I think freckles on the skin are due to some salt of Iron, sunlight brings them out by reducing them from high to low state of oxidation—perhaps with a powerful magnet applied for some time, and then with proper chemicals these mud holes of beauty might be removed."[1]

These wry notes were written by thirty-eight-year-old Thomas Alva Edison, who was rather slowly falling in love with a handsome, solidly built young lady named Mina Miller, the daughter of Lewis Miller, inventor of the Buckeye Reaper. Appropriately: "I taught the lady of my heart the Morse Code, and when she could send and receive we got along much better than we could have with spoken words by tapping our remarks to one another on our hands. Presently I asked her thus in Morse Code, if she would marry me. The word 'Yes' is an easy one to send by telegraphic signals, and she sent it . . ."[2]

Marvelous details. But why should they be relevant to these essays on America? Because it is the hidden argument of this book that the history of America—its vain and unavoidable Civil War; the rapid subsequent building of its temple out of gold, iron, and coal; the bitter, logical, and violent defeats of its laboring class, both native and foreign; the truth of all these majestic developments—is the result of millions of personal vectors, each of them a series of human lives. These small events, day by day, add up to a history that goes beyond, deepens, and often contradicts, conventional history. Finally, it is the irony of this contradiction—that a human life is more trivial, yet morally more important than any national event, however grand—that is particularly American:

"I had a soldier in my company by the name of Lipscomb who was noted for his wit and ready, prompt replies. He lost his right hand in the charge at Gettysburg and was disabled for active service. Being at home after the surrender of Lee's army whenever the federal troops came by Burkeville, where he lived, Lipscomb would go in among them and get up an argument and pretend to get mad and abuse the Yankees. No one every hurt him as he weighed only about 90 pounds and had only one hand. He was considered a sort of privileged character and allowed to go where he pleased and talk with perfect freedom.

"One day a lot of officers got off the cars at Burkeville and loafed around on the platform smoking for half an hour. Lipscomb went in among them and commenced to abuse Yankees as was his custom. For some time no one noticed him but after a while a proud looking lieutenant thinking he would silence Lipscomb said 'Mr., can you tell me what you fought for?' 'Yes,' said Lipscomb. 'I fought for eleven dollars a month. What did you fight for?' The officer replied, 'Well I fought for principle.' Then Lipscomb (looking surprised) said, 'I always thought both sides were right—fighting for what they wanted most. I lacked money and you [lacked] principle. Let's shake hands.' This caused a tremendous burst of laughter among the officers and the Col. slapped Lipscomb on the shoulder and said, 'Young man you will take something with me on that.' Then he had to take something with several others and they tried to persuade him to go along with them . . ."[3]

That was in late 1865. Did the American character change in the course of the next fifty years? Sadly, yes. And not just because the aspect of America had changed. City and countryside looked a lot different in 1917 than in 1865, though most of the changes were superficial. The dazzling succession of American inventions were none of them profound, but were simply devices to tempt the consumer. Basic movers like the steam locomotive were the invention of the Englishman Stevenson, as early as 1816. The basic theory of the electric dynamo and the electric motor was the creation of another Englishman, Clerk Maxwell. The first practical gas engine was built in 1860 by a Frenchman, Etienne Lenoir, and a superior one was designed by a German, Nicolaus Otto, in 1877. Most American inventions of the late-nineteenth century, however, were more amusements than necessities.

Everyone with a barn and a hacksaw might be an inventor. Even Abraham Lincoln applied for a patent in 1849 for Buoying Vessels Over Shoals, an "improved manner of combining buoyant chambers with steamboats or other vessels." The stream of these devices included not only the Improved Boot Tree (1874), the Combined Stepladder and Ironing Table (1879), the Paper Collar Machine (1872), the Improved Cherrystoner (1886), the improved velocipede, the improved roller skate, the improved oil can, and the wholly new and revolutionary Convertible Bedroom-Piano (1866), but also devices like the Gatling machine gun, which were meant, unkindly perhaps, for the general consumer.

And the consumer population—those people able to buy objects beyond potatoes, pork, "hard coal," kerosene, and shoes—was growing at a wonderful rate. Not that they were all making so much money in real earnings. For the industrial worker (in 1914 dollars as standard), wages came to $457 per year in 1860 and only rose to $573 in 1900. And if we deduct losses for time unemployed, the average yearly earnings even for 1900 was actually only $445; in 1910, $546 a year; and even in 1919, only $662.[4] But there was a large and increasing number of middle-class professionals with a lot more money to spare. Precise numbers were not recorded before 1890. At that time, though, public schoolteachers earned only $256 a year, ministers earned $794, and clerks $848. In 1905 a postal carrier or clerk made $935, a federal executive department employee $1,072, and a college professor made $1,100 a year.

An average professor's wife, like any other, had a lot of genteel complaints about the stringency of such a budget: "We pay eighteen dollars ($18) a month for this poorly built, eight small-roomed house, its three lots and barn made of piano boxes and other odds and ends of lumber. We could not hope to rent a better built house, merely a larger one, for more money, unless we were willing to go over forty dollars.

"The cow and the coal repose in our barn, and each has about equal space in its luxurious proportions. That cow is a big saving of money, but it adds to our labor, for we make our own butter, but we must have it to help those proverbial 'ends.' There is plenty of prairie south and east of us for pasturage. . . .

". . . With all this straining to live comes a wish from the President and Trustees of the college that we mingle more in town society; that it will be a good advertisement for the college to be well represented everywhere. Who can afford the evening dress to go? Or the evening's sewing left undone? Who can return invitations? Who has the strength—and this is at the highest premium—who has the strength to spare? . . ."[5]

Her complaints about her annual budget are fascinating in their implications. If she had such trouble with $1,100 a year, how about the public schoolteacher in 1905 living on $392 a year—which was actually less than a farm laborer, who got $302 a year plus a bed and meals. Then how was it possible to buy victrolas, cameras, and telephones? One bought them anyway, even at the cost of necessities, because they became socially important. And they were socially important because America, in this period between wars, was an aggrandizing society, voracious for novelty, committed to the dogma that life was lived in order to be improved. It was a curiously adolescent society, full of objective desires and pulsating with the energy to get them satisfied.

Remember that the novelties so imaginatively invented to satisfy consumer impulses and which became common and then universal, were never huge or expensive, but small, cheap, and produced in great quantity. One could live quite decently without the electric light bulb, the phone, roll film, and the movies. But life was a lot more fun if you had them.

Advances in nineteenth-century transportation, like the elevator, the Pullman, the electric streetcar, and the airplane, were actually inexpensive because they were collectively shared and collectively bought. The era of huge, profound, basic non-consumer inventions was in the past, though it would recur again with the dissection of the atom.

A peculiar exception to this analysis—and theories are not proved if they have no exception—was the automobile. The shift from horse to engine is, in the close relationships of daily life, very real and important. Autos have names, but they are the manufacturers' names. Ten million cars were all named Ford. But a horse was singular, and singularly named, and so much a member of the family that it even fought back when it chose:

"Morrow was very badly hurt and still in bed. Called Paul Tracy. Got his leg broken. Horse kicked him . . .

"Wed. Sept. 30 Day rather warm. East wind. Usual school. Fair on and a good crowd. School goes on. Elbert Rice thrown out of buggy last night and bruised somewhat. Does not seem to know just what happened. Mrs. W. A. Stone was thrown from buggy Sunday evening, ran into telephone pole. Has heart trouble also."[6]

A horse was alive, responded to pain or petting, had sex or was castrated, and if female, could be bred and give birth. It was born and grew and ate and farted in front of the human driver, and became old or ill, and had to be shot, whereupon it fell, bled, quivered in its last spasms, and by next year left a monument of ribs like huge human bones to bleach in the wooded lot. It was the ancient association of owner and working beast, of man, and sub-man. Tricked a little by the old emotions, one can have affection for a car. But to give it a lump of sugar would be, to say the least, poisonous, and one accident to a car puts it in bad grace. Nor have I ever seen a child mourn the day that the old auto was traded in for a better.

Henry Ford was not, as almost no one knows, the inventor of the automobile. The very word was French. Ford was the inventor only of the Ford, a vehicle engineered so that it could be mass-produced. In 1900, only a fifth of all automobiles had gasoline engines; the other four-fifths were driven by steam or by battery. Ford beat the competition by producing, in the moving assembly line, a single, durable, reliable model with interchangeable parts.

By the beginning of World War I in Europe, Ford was making 250,000 Model-T cars a year—a triumph of business engineering for the farm boy who had built a quadricycle in 1896. By 1925, he was making well over a million automobiles, many of which cost only $260. But that was still one-fifth the annual salary of a mill worker or a public schoolteacher. What most of the late–nineteenth-century inventions did was to change, superficially, if one likes to call it that, the quality of daily life. In that sense, they were essentially democratic. And so, to the point of caricature, were the inventors. If Edison had the American sense of self-deprecating humor, Ford had the other national trait—humor that loved nasty practical jokes. He once put wooden croutons in the soup of his guest, Harvey Firestone.

The cleverest inventor of consumer novelties was certainly Thomas Edison. As we have seen, he was not at all the secretive, malformed genius of folklore, but began his career in a way that was thoroughly and characteristically American in its mixture of brightness and naivete. His first laboratory was a corner of a baggage car on a Midwest railway, where he had a job selling candy and newspapers. He was twelve years old. When he was sixteen, though he had suffered the almost total loss of his hearing, he got a job as a telegrapher. When he was thirty, he developed the phonograph. It would play both band and operatic music as well as comic monologues, which were recorded by inscribing a sheet of tin foil wrapped around a thick cylinder. The first model was patented in 1877, but Edison worked until 1890 to get a machine that was not only audible, but cheap enough for millions to buy. By 1912, it cost $7.50. Edison, meantime, had acquired a laboratory and factory that employed 150 men, and in 1876, he owned an even larger plant in a small town in New Jersey, along with two other auxiliary factories: "My laboratory will soon be completed—The dimensions are one building 250 ft long 50 wide & 3 stories 4 other bldgs 25 x 100 one story high all of brick I will have the best equipped & largest Laboratory extant, and the facilities incomparably superior to any other for rapid & cheap development of an invention, & working it up into Commercial shape with models patterns & special machinery—In fact there is no similar institution in Existence We do our own castings forgings Can build anything from a ladys watch to a locomotive . . ."[7]

Edison had some, but by no means profound or academic, knowledge of scientific theory. He himself said that when he needed mathematics, he hired a mathematician. What Edison had were two particular abilities. The first, in his own words, "I know how to steal." His second ability was a nonverbal, non-symbolic, non-mathematical grasp of the mechanical world. Allied to this was another and equally important trait: an intuitive grasp of what the average person didn't yet know he needed but would need very desperately as soon as you told him about it. His inventions came because there was a place for them. The principles had long been known, though little applied. Electric light was already in use in some cities, but the lamps were based on the creation of light by a powerful electric arc between two rods. It had been known since 1654 that an electric current passed through a partly evacuated glass bulb would give a fine display, but it had always been simply an expensive Victorian toy. Edison had wanted to make a lamp that could be used by the millions—a typical combination of a scientific idea and a sales product. Characteristically, he tried carbon for the filament—the same material used in the arc light. But the form had to be thin and spun out, yet rigid. He even tried carbonizing ordinary cotton thread. When that didn't work too well, he got a Newark textile mill to spin special thread for him. This thread of carbon hung between two copper terminals and, fixed in a glass bulb which then had the air pumped out of it, was Edison's invention. But he didn't get one that would last long enough till October 19, 1897. His assistant Francis Jehl wrote, from affectionate memory in 1930:

"I have but to close my eyes to see once more the picture of our patient, painstaking, keenly observing chief carrying on his endless experiments, and at the same time educating and directing us. We never thought him wrong, whatever leading scientists said. Our quest never seemed vain or foolish.

"I see him tap carefully on the bulb with sensitive fingers as he watches for spots or irregularities in the carbon. If its condition appears good he proceeds even more carefully. If it does not, he is not greatly worried. I have never seen a man so cool when great stakes were at odds.

"After the lamp, good or bad, has finished its test he breaks it open and takes it to the microscope to study the filaments, seeking the reason for the failure of the slender black threadlike substance."[8]

Edison's production of the motion picture camera had many technical precedents, and indeed, what is most interesting is how little he had to do with its invention. It would have been impossible without the use of celluloid—it required a fifty-foot roll—and this plastic, one of the first synthetics, was invented by the brothers Hyatt in 1870. The phonograph had been a device for making money as well as music, which was perfectly natural, but profits were limited because only a few machines had been made. One put a coin into a public machine to hear a particular cylinder, and Edison felt there would be a greater market by supplying sketches that would move along with the music. Such animation, in the simple form of flipping pages, was a common toy. Edison gave the problem over to his assistant, W. K. Dickson, who worked on it for years, until, in 1889, he built a combination device that Edison could sell. But even when it had been patented, he never paid much attention to it. It was just one more department of his sprawling business.

Since 1839, another foreign idea—to fix an inverted image, greatly diminished, of what is seen through a glass lens upon a photo-sensitive plate—had been seized with delight by Americans of every class. As early as 1849, a handbook was printed for making photographs by the method of the Frenchmen Niepce and Daguerre, and the alternative method of the Englishman Talbot. The author, though, is an American patriot, ". . . an American gentleman—James M. Wattles Esq.—who as early as 1828—and it will be seen, by what I have already stated, that this is about the same date of M. Niepce's discovery—had his attention attracted to the subject of Photography, or as he termed it 'Solar picture drawing,' while taking landscape views by means of the camera-obscura. When we reflect upon all the circumstances connected with his experiments, the great disadvantages under which he labored, and his extreme youthfulness, we cannot but feel a national pride—yet wonder—that a mere yankee boy, surrounded by the deepest forests, hundreds of miles from the populous portion of our country, without the necessary materials, or resources for procuring them, should by the force of his natural genius make a discovery, and put it in practical use, to accomplish which, the most learned philosophers of Europe, with every requisite apparatus, and a profound knowledge of chemistry—spent years of toil to accomplish. How much more latent talent may now be slumbering from the very same cause which kept Mr. Wattles from publicly revealing his discoveries, viz; want of encouragement—ridicule!"[9]

The metallic image of the daguerreotype had the interesting disadvantage that it could not be replicated. It was both the "positive" and the "negative," depending upon how you tilted it. But aesthetically it was so perfect a method that I, for one, have never seen a daguerreotype that was not beautiful by its very nature. However, it was obviously useless for copies, and the talbotype, with its paper negative, lacked the infinitely fine detail of the daguerreotype. So these two inventions were superceded by two other English inventions: one by Herschel, who developed the wet-glass plate; the other by Dr. Maddox, who invented the dry plate, because, being in medical practice, he had an aversion to the ether used in the earlier process.

By developing these ideas, an American, George Eastman, erected a great fortune. In 1877, he'd been a bank clerk at $1,400 a year. Then he bought a big wet plate camera and a store of the necessary chemicals. "An accident that Eastman encountered shortly after taking up his hobby may have been responsible for his interest in dry plates. On his first trip away from home with his photographic outfit, the bottle containing the silver bath (the silver nitrate solution used to sensitize the collodion plates) leaked out and stained most of the clothes in the trunk in which they were all packed. Imagine the effect of this catastrophe on a young man who always considered carefully before spending money, and who as carefully recorded every cent that he expended. It was enough to make most beginners give up in disgust. At this time he read in an English photographic journal of experiments in gelatin dry plates . . ."[10] He began to make and sell such dry plates after banking hours, but gave up his clerkship and built a factory in 1883.

The next year, he greatly improved a method of producing flexible film that could be wound on rolls, which had been suggested by an Englishman, Melhuish, way back in 1854. Talbot, of course, used a flexible negative too, but it was made of paper and could never be as icy sharp as a daguerreotype, and Eastman's early methods had exactly the same problem. "When we started out with our scheme of film photography we expected that everybody that used glass plates would take up films, but we found that the number that did it was relatively small and that in order to make a large business we would have to reach the general public."[11] He never solved it, but sidestepped the problem by devising a simple, fairly cheap ($25) camera, loaded with a spool of paper negative sufficient for a hundred exposures, which had to be sent to his plant in Rochester for development and printing. The transparent, flexible roll for use in this Kodak was not invented by George Eastman, but by a Newark, New Jersey, minister, Hannibal Goodwin. He retired at sixty-five, and applied for a patent in 1887, but didn't get one till 1899. The decision was fought by Eastman who had been making the same flexible, transparent roll film since 1889, two years after Goodwin filed his patent application. It was manufactured, as Goodwin also specified, out of nitrocellulose. The court action was not resolved till 1914, when George Eastman settled by paying $5 million in cash to the Goodwin estate, for the Reverend had died, meantime, fourteen years before.

Ethics and profits aside, there was no doubt that the Kodak and its roll film changed, not the matter of the nineteenth century, but its consciousness. The photographic image became a new and original and highly forceful mode of art—not of books and museums, but the art of daily life:

"Oh dear this celestial mud bath has made another revolution and no photograph yet received from the Chataquain Parragon of Perfection, How much longer will Hope dance on my intellect Miss Igoe told me of a picture she had taken on a rock at Panama NY. There were several others in the group, interpolated so as to dilute the effect of Mina's beauty, as she stated the picture was taken *on a rock* I immediately brought my scientific imagination to work to ascertain how the artist could have flowed collodion over a rock and put so many people inside his camera. Miss Igoe kindly corrected her explanation by stating that a picture was taken by a camera of a group on a rock, thus my mind was brought back from a suspicion of her verbal integrity to a belief in the honesty of her narrative."[12] This arch anecdote was from the diary entry of July 19, 1885, written by Thomas Alva Edison.

2

Mobile, often separated by hundreds or thousands of miles from family and friends, Americans took daguerreotypes and tintypes and ambrotypes by the hundreds of thousands to enclose in their letters back home. No drawing

or painting had the force of such photographs, which even if extensively re-
touched, convey the sensation of a living person, or of the dead as well,
because they were often photographed in their open coffins. These bits of
paper or metal were a fresh kind of human experience, one that might or
might not follow the old graphic rules of chiaroscuro and composition, one
that for a long time was not colored like the real world or even like painting
or painted sculpture. But still it gave forth, through its very infinity of detail,
the unique smell of reality. It was a rectangular and singularly lucid window
to the world. Other arts were bound to suffer in comparison, and the history
of other mass media is contemporary proof of this fact, though the effect was
delayed by at least a generation, a common phenomenon in cultural change.

The photograph scarcely needs to be read or learned. It is instant and
universal. These qualities gave to the moving picture, however strained and
absurd its story, that same sensation of life being instantly lived and instantly
comprehended. The spectator did not actively move around this new kind of
visual art. Even his eyes need not circle and return as they would with a
painting, or snake across and down as they would do with a book. The viewer
was passive, fixed, hypnotized all the more strongly because he faced, in a
hypnagogic darkness, a bright and flickering screen. The audience was thus
drawn into the apparently realist world of the film, in which he had no part,
and which he could not change.

The close-up in cinema was a psychological invention, not really a technical one, because even in live theatre one's attention focuses on one powerful and significant detail, as it does in the simultaneous confusions of sound:
the person speaking, the person addressed, the killer or the victim, or a double detail of both. The famous close-up of the pistol pointing at the audience,
which was said to have caused consternation in its first audiences, was a psychological equivalent of one's area of attention if the same thing were done
from the stage.

So there were plenty of artful predecessors to the photographic medium. One was the more and more extensive use of realistic sets in the
American theater. And even more, of realistic disasters—the fire, the thun-
derstorm, the bridge exploding between the hero and the heroine—all
ingeniously produced on stage. Another precedent was the illustration of
books by photographs rather than drawings. This applied to novels and verse
as well, or to the chimaera of both together, like the extremely popular nar-
ratives of Ella Wheeler Wilcox at the turn of the century:

> I sat and sewed and sang some tender tune,
> Oh, beauteous was that morn in early June!
> Mellow with sunlight . . .[13]

And at the head of the page was the sunlight in a photograph of pine trees
and a lake. There were seventy photographs for this novel, the landscapes
taken by one photographer, the men and women by another, who was ob-

viously a specialist in human tableaux. A man embraces a woman before that essential furniture of romance, the piano, to accompany the text:

> Dear Roy! I know my words seem very strange;
> But I love one I cannot hope to wed.
> A river rolls between us, dark and deep.
> To cross it—were to stain with blood my hand.[14]

There was an even more notable one of a woman dying in a brass bed, giving up her baby, and by implication, her husband as well, to a lady painter who had once loved him. The photograph is certainly more convincing, with its real people and real clothes, than the letter that summoned this heartbreaking abnegation:

> My darling! I am dying. Come to me.
> Love, which so long the growing truth concealed,
> Stands pale within its shadow. O, my sweet!
> This heart of mine grows fainter with each beat—
> Dying with very weight of bliss. O, come!
> And take the legacy I leave to you,
> Before these lips forevermore are dumb.
> In life or death, Yours, Helen Dangerfield.[15]

Dying she might be, but was still strong enough to speak four pages of rhymed verse. We recognize here the old, irrepressible plots of democratic culture, stories which can be found in popular plays, novels, songs, and chromos—and quite naturally, in the first movies, and then in hundreds of subsequent ones, flourishing into our own sophisticated time. Such stories are a continuous and recurring narrative. They form parts of the same epic, in which the players simply change names. Because, whatever we would love to think, people can and do deal with the ephemera and the subtleties of emotion in their own lives, but they prefer their guided dreams to be melodramatic.

Sex and illness are the two main staples of mass entertainment. The third is success, with its attendant demons, work and money. This is, very broadly speaking, the masculine aspect of American nineteenth-century culture—not so much the realities of this culture, but its illusions. In the early twentieth century, its dominant artistic form was the silent western. Neither romantic sex nor romantic illness played much part in these dramas. Instead there was fortune and villainy, with male competition symbolized by the half hidden phallic pistol and the archetypal phallic horse. Added to this ideal of the lonely entrepreneur was the Protestant notion of the sinner finding Christ. Here was a summary of *The Gunfighter* with William S. Hart: "Twenty entries in a gruesome little notebook briefly recorded the slaying record of Cliff Hudspeth, the Killer . . . Yet [he] felt no qualms over these killings. Each of the dead men was either a gun-bully or ruffian who well deserved his fate . . . His conscience did not bother him until . . . Cliff slew

'Cactus' Fuller, the Mexican [raiders'] right hand man . . . That day Norma, the little milliner from the East came into Cliff's life and in fierce words of condemnation castigated 'the Killer' for his murder. The Killer saw red when this little slip of womanhood lashed him. With an oath he reached down from his saddle, flung the little feminine thing across his saddle, and galloped madly to his retreat in the mountains . . . But the girl discovered the gold in Cliff's nature. And the man was awakened by her words to bitter self recrimination and agony. He locked her up in a room and sought to drown the memory of her words in raw whiskey. The ghosts of 20 men he had slain passed before him. For the first time in his hardened life, since he had parted with his mother, Cliff responded to tenderness. And when he laid down his life for Norma after accounting for El Salvador, the human wolf, his soul had been redeemed by the little woman from the East."[16] Here was the half-bad man turning, by an act of courage, wholly good, and not merely good, but comfortable to small town society.

All the plots of such movies are exceedingly rich in cultural implication, as one can judge from the titles alone:

The Scourge of the Desert
A Knight of the Trails
His Life the Stake or The Conversion of Frosty Blake
Hell's Hinges[17]

A 1916 film, *The Return of Draw Egan,* was described as "a combination of chained lightning, hell, and quick shooting." This film was directed by Hart, and was shot in twenty-six days at a cost of $13,307.65. Hart got $875—three and a half weeks at $250 a week—about what a schoolteacher in 1916 earned in six months.[18] By the time he made *Two Gun Man,* he was earning $15,000 a week. But the American mill worker or backwoods farmer could see this film for anywhere from five to twenty-five cents. A child would see it over and over again, if the first viewing was too painfully anxious. And while popular drama of an earlier time, folklore in particular, often took a tragic road, the drama of the latter half of the nineteenth century in America would settle for nothing less than home, health, and happiness.

The early silents were not all crude. Nor were the Chaplin comedies the only examples of subtlety or complexity. Chaplin plots were outrageously sentimental, simple, and compact with the cliches of popular tears. But while these were the main drive of a story, the beauties of gesture and humor and character were in the details, the instants rather than the hours. In this respect, the rawest western had, and still has, a special interest—precisely how a man rides his horse, or how a woman smiles, the compelling interest of the moving human face seen as close as a baby sees its mother. There are no such infinities in any other art but the photographic and the cinematic.

The change from the broad gesture of the stage to the subtlety, for example, of Greta Garbo's lowered eyelash, was slowly acquired by the actors and actresses of the early twentieth century. They carried their rhetoric of movement into the studio, where it took decades to realize its absurdity. It changed less by the operation of public taste than by imitation of the enormously popular western hero. William S. Hart had played Messina on the stage, with the famous Modjeska, and was forty years old when he made his first movie. His long and noble upper lip was very suited to imperturbability. In any case, the western hero, by his very nature, showed emotion through the filter of a noble and monotonous face, the sort one can still see in traffic or riot police. This impassive ethical style fit beautifully, not with our lives, but with our illusions.

Drama, by the early twentieth century, was in one of those declines that seem inevitable to the evolution of any sort of art or society—as if they grew more and more rigid in form, hardening into shapes that were once, but then no longer, exciting. We can see the shift if we examine the actual experience of an ordinary actor. His name was George Berrell, and he was part of a touring company called the James Post Musical Comedy Company:

"*April 10* . . . Received telegram from Sim Allen, offering me $30. per week, for 'characters', and stage direction. Wired acceptance, saying I would leave here upon receipt of fare. A bird in the hand is worth a whole flock in the bush . . ."[19] He had one trait characteristic of all actors, a critical eye for someone else's performance: ". . . Owing to ill health, Evelyn Selbine will retire from the Bentley Stock Co. at Long Beach. Her health may be poor, but her acting is still worse. . . ."[20] The other common characteristic of actors was their chronic lack of money: "To-night I made my appearance and with the Rosabelle Leslie Stock Co. at the Pavillion Theatre, Elysian Grove. *The Senator's Daughter* was the play in which I appeared as 'Hon. Socrates Clay' a part I had played before. My teeth bothered me not a little, and I dispensed with the lower set entirely. The attendance was very light—the share of each member of the Company being only ninety-five cents . . ."[21]

The movies were an established novelty, even in 1909: ". . . [T]o the People's Theatre, and saw an exhibition of moving pictures. "Through Death Valley" and a trip over the Tonopah and Tidewater R.R., given free of charge to advertise 20 Mule team Borax, and the railroad; found it very interesting . . ."[22] But this novelty was edging out live drama by combined performances: "This week the attraction at the Arizona-Dome is 'Roberto, in the Great Milk Can Mystery', in addition to moving pictures, and Miss Hamilton, in illustrated songs . . . There was an excellent house, and the sketch which ran thirty-two minutes made a hit . . . To-night just before the performance began, while the picture operator was regulating his machine, a film suddenly ignited from a spark and in a very few minutes the little structure from which the machine is operated was totally destroyed, together with several reels of films inflicting a loss of several hundred dollars. The machine was not damaged, to any great extent, however, and motion pictures were shown to-night as usual."[23]

An interesting if inconclusive example of how historical tides affect human desires is in the diary of another, more complicated and metropolitan actor. He too complained about money:

"*August 17, 1904*   My winter is settled . . . part of Carduros, a noble and agent of the Inquisition—the heavy . . . One act and had a good death scene. I was only too glad to accept his terms . . . The same salary as last year for a smaller part cannot be called a setback."[24]

He was, at times, quite frank about his own abilities: "Never played so abominably." But—

"*Cleveland, December 12*   . . . Had a number of my photos framed for Christmas gifts."[25] And, most extraordinary of all, he was sometimes generous toward better men: "David Warfield is a great artist. Simple—magnetic—pathetic. He had the hearts of his audience in his hand and played upon their heartstrings at will. There was not a dry eye in the house . . . New Yorkers don't like to cry. They prefer to grin and haw haw so that the crowded houses are eloquent to the man's power . . ."[26]

He was feeling better, perhaps:

"*Christmas, 1904*   This has been a happy day for me . . . Three years ago I was with 'The Beauty and The Beast,' a musical comedy, on $15 per week—struggling to keep my hold on Percy [his son] and accepting a home for him and me from these dear friends . . . Christmas before last . . . my boy gone—health breaking and sick at heart . . . Still lonely beyond words to express, but gaining in health . . . At this rate—two more successful seasons will put me out of debt—square with the world and a free man—ready once more to recognize a God of Love. This is all too good to last. I am certain Providence does not intend prosperity or peace for me—mine must be a life of suffering—pain—strife—loneliness and eventual defeat—in the eyes of the world. To fight for success on noble lines and to win failure—what an attractive vista open before me. However—I shall live for the present and for myself—the only way to succeed in this world, God or no God. Look out for yourself and the world will respect you and pay you the tribute of success— You can be a decent Christian into the bargain. Live for others and you will be left in the lurch . . ."[27] But theatrical disaster was, as he feared, not far off. He was in a play with the famous English actress, Mrs. Campbell: "Last evening as she was getting into her carriage for the theatre, Mrs. Campbell slipped and fractured her knee cap and had to be taken to the hospital. As she had Pinki Panki Poo in one arm and a book and muff in the other she could not catch herself."[28]

At last, he tried to get work in film:

"*April 8th, [1914]*   No work at V. Slept until 2:30. Threatening. Saw Evangeline by the Canadian Bioscope Company. Good staging but very poor photography and the story not at all clear. . ."[29]

Even when he got work, it was not entirely pleasant:

"*July 2*   Had awful day in the Tangle, finishing up 'The Winksome Widow.' We all got 'drowned'—seven principals, five police, two firemen, and three feet of water. Bear in tub and a monkey on the piano. . ."[30]

". . . *Tuesday, August 11*   Chad Fisher cameraman killed by lightning. Harry Lombard standing by him and having his hand on Chad's shoulder—was fearfully hurt—burned on arms and legs—others demoralized."[31]

There was still some live theatre:

"*February 4, 1915*   Saw Marie Pickford in 'Mistress Will' at the Strand. She is much overrated and the stage management was very faulty."[32]

But the money was in film—more than he had ever earned on stage. This was perfectly logical, because movies were, in an economic and even in a cultural sense, the industrialization of live drama, and not the best of it, either:

"*April 6*   . . . Saw Hazel Dawn in 'Niobe' presented by David Frohman's 'Famous Players Film Company' . . . Niobe turned to stone and revived, after 3,000 years, by a coil of wire, in the home of the art dealer—while his family is at the theatre—and so on—all a dream."[33] Movies were invented, like Edison's talking doll, electric bulb and phonograph, not as a free exploration by the restless human mind, but as a novel way of making a lot of money, some of which went to the actors and technicians:

"*Wednesday, August 12*   . . . to see Mr. G. E. Brulatour of the World Film Company about a possible job. Present salary $150—automatic increase $10 every two months.

"*February 15, 1915*   Called to see Julius Stern of Universal by appointment at 10:30 sharp. Kept waiting for 20 minutes, then gate man informed me his secretary would attend to me. I informed gently but firmly that the young lady would not attend to me and departed . . . Went up to Edison's plant—Mr. Plympton most courteous . . . A delightful visit . . . Charming individual offices. The entire atmosphere breathes organization."[34]

The same year, he had an actor's comments on one of the most famous pictures ever made:

"*June 22, 1915*   Saw the Birth of a Nation. Splendid. Griffith does a lot of faking—but very cleverly. He also falls down in giving the sense of power in his handling of troops. They are all scattered—no charging line. Women are poorly selected. The acting is not equal to the directing. The geography is poor. Dr. Cameron's house—on a plantation—would not front on the dusty street of this little town—within 10 feet of the front fence."[35] And on November 12, he saw *The Birth of a Nation* a second time: "A triumph of fakery. Griffith has not been worthy of his opportunity—notwithstanding that some scenes are splendidly handled."[36]

How did this film—one-sided, schematic, even false in its pretense at history, and with acting so ludicrously postured—have so strong an effect on our grasp of the tragic Reconstruction? One good reason, I suspect, is that the film did not contradict, but simply and boldly reinforced the contemporary, and still current, entanglement of racial misconceptions—on both sides, and everywhere in between. This too has generally been a characteristic of popular culture—that it sharply divides good from bad. And America, by the sheer weight of its history from the Civil War onward, was a populist, rather than merely democratic society. Its ideal men were boyish enterpreneurs like Edison and Ford, and some a good deal worse. And its culture, by its very mass nature, was condemned to be easy and sentimental. There were no Hamlets, King Lears, Falstaffs or Macbeths in the American silent film, and all the cineastes in the world cannot invent one adult masterpiece among them. The best that such films achieved was an adolescent intensity, which in Keaton, Chaplin, and Laurel and Hardy, had a wild, sad wit derived from the ancient dumbshow of mime and puppetry.

3

A different, stranger, more exact, more poetic, and therefore perhaps a truer sort of history lies fossilized in nineteenth-century diaries, particularly those of American children. Here, for example, was a spring day near Fort Sill, Oklahoma:

"*Tuesday April 23, 1878*   The wind blows hard from the north. A cool day we have some fire in the stove. Pinquodle is sitting near the stove. Poco has his back toward the stove. I hear the wind blowing now."[37]

Such was the entry of an Indian boy in a white man's school. It does not relate events, the race from the future back into the past, but records the very present, the stillness at the heart of things:

"*Wednesday May 1, 1878*   Very windy today wind blows hard from the south. Heap Kiowa and Comanche Indians today. They have been long time sit down at St. Augustine in Florida now they have come back to Indian territory four years sit down in Florida . . .

"*Wednesday May 15, [1878]* . . . It may rain or it may not rain. I see some clouds and I hear the wind blowing. George Jackson cooks the meat and gravy and coffee for boys and girls. . . .

"*Wednesday May 22, [1878]*   One Indian boy standing on the north door. He has a bow and arrow in his right hand. Now the boy is gone away. For dinner we had red meat gravy peaches and coffee . . .

"*Monday June 17, [1878]*   Warm weather now boys and girls heap swim in the water. Fish live in the water. A fish will soon die out on the ground. A fish has no feet. A fish has scales on its body. A dog has hair on its body. A sheep has wool. A wild cat has fur. A bird has feathers. Indians like to have eagles feathers. Eagles fly high up in the air. Men cannot fly very high."[38]

All children must come to terms with what is imposed on them, whether they are red or white, rich or poor. An eleven-year-old girl named Eulalie Matthews sailed to Europe late in 1896 with her parents, four sisters

Three child laborers: oyster shuckers in Maggioni Canning Company, Port Royal, South Carolina, February, 1911.

Photograph by Lewis W. Hine. Library of Congress

and brothers, and four maids. She saved a sample dinner menu from the
Grand Hotel Victoria, in Sorrento:

Oxtail Soup
Soup de Mer Sauce Ecrevisses
Filet de Boueuf Parisienne
Supreme de Poulet aux Truffles
Haricots verts sautes
Faisans rotis
Salade
Plumpudding
Gateaux
Dessert[39]

A year later, Eulalie began her diary with an entry of September 29, 1897,
which was a good sample of her life in New York City:

"*October 11, 1897*   Went to school for the first time . . . I lost my silver
pencil holder. I am going to be in class 5A. Momma called for me early then
we went to Madame Thurm. We looked at some dresses but didn't get any.
Then we had lunch at the Waldorf and walked down to O'Nealls. I got a
lovely pair of dancing shoes and then went to Miss Kevlin and had my hands
and feet seen to. When we got home I had a lot of lessons to learn. I had a
milk punch."[40]

The disasters were real enough:

"*February 24*, [*1898*] . . . I had all wrong in arithmetic. . .

"*Monday, May 9, 1898*   I was sick last night . . . Momma gave me $2
for taking some castor oil."[41]

She had her duties. One was to wash and iron her own handkerchiefs,
and she learns every day how to grow up rich:

"*September 22,1898*   Today is my birthday and I got a $25 check from
Momma, a box of candy from Miss Smith and in the afternoon a sweet little
silver sealing wax pot from Mrs. Flynn. "*Sunday, December 25* [*1898*]   Got
up at about 7 o'clock and opened my stocking. I got three pieces of Dutch
silver from Momma and Grandma, a windmill, a mandolin and a little sleigh.
A set of little leather box books for odds and ends. Packs of cards in black
leather with silver cornered case. Silver gilt needle case from Miss Smith.
Two bottles with silver all over them from Momma and Mrs. Yznaga. Pin
cushion from Alfred P. Sewing box with initials from Josie, quilt basket filled
with candy lined with blue silk and a beautiful black leather book for my
photos with G. E. M. in the corner from Poppa, a present from Fraulein and
a $5 gold piece from Mom."[42]

She certainly noticed the Spanish-American War: "Went down in the
cars . . . to see the soldiers land from the transport Manitoba. I got two
bullets and one button. . ."[43]

"*February 23*, [*1898*] . . . Poppa gave me a Cuban silver dollar.

Coal mine "breaker boys" employed in Ewen Breaker of Pennsylvania Coal Company, South Pittston, Pennsylvania, January, 1911.

Photograph by Lewis W. Hine. Library of Congress

"*Saturday, April 23, [1898]*   War with Spain begun. . . .

"*May 24, [1898]*   . . . Momma called for me and we went down to see the soldiers going to war. . . .

"*May 27, [1898]*   . . . I put a large American flag over my bed.

"*January 30, 1899*   . . . Went down with Gwenn to see the coming home of the 69th Regiment. . .

"*Sunday, February 12, [1899]*   . . . I had ice cream for lunch in the form of soldiers. . ."[44]

It was a nice, brief, heroic war: "*Saturday, April 29, 1899*   Miss Kevlin came in and did my hands and feet. Had a music lesson . . . Helped decorate the table for the 'Rough Riders' luncheon. . .

"*December 1, 1899*   . . . We saw the whole procession. It was lovely! Roosevelt passed on horseback. . ."[45]

Her comments on life grew noticeably sharper:

"*June 23, [1899]*   . . . Went to see Buffalo Bill—It was grand and we had fine seats. The people in back of us were well dressed but spoke slang all the time, chewed gum and ate peanuts. . .

"*Sunday, August 6, 1899*   I went to our church . . . Cardinal Gibbons preached. There was a Bishop there who took snuff all the time and then would pull out an old common red handkerchief and blow his nose dreadfully hard. . .

"*Wednesday, August 9, 1899*   . . . I have taken such a dislike to Kit Welman, I can't think why. Perhaps it's because of his chewing tobacco."[46]

The world of Eulalie Matthews, chock full of silver presents, first class travel, German tutoresses, dancing school and colored sashes, was separated by more than time, for example, from the life of a boy in Galsburg, Illinois, in 1868. The two lived in extraordinarily different cultures, and the artifacts were correspondingly different, even if both were, nominally anyway, American. Ed Dunn, age thirteen, son of a grocer ("Tea, Coffee, Sugar, Butter, Eggs, etc., #9 Prairie Street) put out a weekly pen and ink newspaper he called the *Dunnville Journal*. This world was chock full of dogs with surnames, birds of several colors, fires in the brush, walnut trees, a harvest of ripe pears, lightning, a drowning in the Mississippi, two-dollar robbers, and domestic problems: "Your correspondent saw a runaway boy yesterday. His stepfather chased him through Main Street. He caught him in front of Willoughby's and Grant's Office. He cried like a loon."[47]

And visiting relatives: "Thursday night the occupants of the Dunn Hotel were awakened from their slumbers by loud and terrific shrieks proceeding from the room of that personage known as Aunt Columbia which proved to be the same enjoying a nightmare."[48]

And accidents: "A man was killed at Frost's Foundry last Thursday by the bursting of an emery wheel."[49]

And violent crime: "Policeman Pollock arrested a drunken man yesterday . . . He pulled him by the hair of his head, (he having no hat on) through

Main Street. The man was determined not to go into the lockup. He was howling hideously . . . A man was arrested today for stealing a sack of flour from a farmer's wagon."[50]

But there were outright murders: "Terrible Murder . . . Joe H. Dunn Assassin . . . Victim . . One of the Hen family . . . Mrs. Hen was quietly sitting in a bushel basket, when the villain, Joe H. Dunn seized her by the hind legs and cut off her head. When she was perfectly cold and dead she was ducked in hot water and her feathers pulled off by the handful. Mrs. Hen's cries were heard for some distance around, but no one came to the rescue."[51]

And domestic dramas: "Something startling has happened in this vicinity. A man cooly said goodbye to his family and walked out of the house to take the cars for Michigan where he intends taking up his abode with his first wife's children which cause he avers he is driven to by his untamed shrew who is his second wife. The gossips have been busy all day, most of them siding with him, and admiring his spunk. He didn't take another woman with him. His daughter and son said O, Father, don't go, but it was of no use."[52]

And then there was that common small town disaster: "The Great Fire at the Union Hotel. . . . . Last Tuesday afternoon the Union Hotel was found to be on fire and so quick did the news spread that before the bells began to ring a large crowd had collected. Then there was a great rush for buckets at the store, dozens going at a time. There was a good deal of excitement in getting out goods from the hotel when it was found to be going for good. The first thing the editor saw come out was the Turkish cook who ran down the street with his trunk as fast as he could. Next came a servant girl in her stocking feet with her clothes &c. running across the Square. Some one threw a trunk out of an upper window which smashed to pieces on the sidewalk. Some men ran downstairs with bedding &c. in their arms while one man threw a spittoon out of a third story window which was picked up uninjured and brought to the store for safety. Mrs. Belden's canary bird was saved and brought to the store. After the fire when she found it was safe, she rejoiced over it almost as much as though it had been a child. It kept the clerks busy pouring water on the roof and awnings of the store as there was some danger of their catching fire. But the wind was in the other direction and blew the firebrands away from us. Nearly every bucket in the store was in use and we lost many of them. One man was killed and several others badly burned at the fire. Henders building also took fire and burned to the ground."[53]

In all this three-year journal, 1868–71, a classic picture of nineteenth-century America shines through with proof on every page: the joy of flowers, fruits, and seasons; the quirks of animals and visitors; eggs discovered in unexpected places; the drama of fire engines; the pungent pleasures of the circus and the menagerie; the touring midgets and the greased pig on the Fourth of July. But there were hints of other matters, of a lower, darker

America: "Mr. Price, with several other members of the Legislature, visited the state penitentiary last week. They found a little orphan boy, eleven years of age, there from Chicago. His term is for one year, his crime being theft; he was guilty only of keeping watch while others acted. Mr. Price talked with him quite a while. The little fellow cried piteously and begged of him to get him away as he wanted to see his mamma. They are now interceding with the Governor to release him, being satisfied that he would be a better boy to return home now than to remain there a year when perhaps he would feel indifferent and reckless about it. . ."[54]

For the growing industrial society of nineteenth-century America was faced with yet another dilemma. The moral dominance of its rural and small town culture made a Christian virtue of putting children to work. Certainly no farm could support a family that did not—all of it—do labor of some sort. This necessity carried over into the economics of industrial life, and where it was at all possible, children were employed. This custom benefited with families and companies. The children working in mines, and in paper, textile, glass, and canning factories, contributed all their earnings to their families, and their wages were at so low a scale that it was very profitable for industry to use them:

"A labor commissioner of North Carolina reported that there are two hundred and sixty-one cotton mills in that State, in which nearly forty thousand people are employed, including nearly eight thousand children. The average daily wage of the men is fifty-seven cents, of the women thirty-nine cents, of the children twenty-two cents. The commissioner goes on to say: 'I have talked with a little boy of seven years who worked for forty nights in Alabama, and with another child who, at six years of age, had been on the night-shift eleven months. Little boys turned out at two o'clock in the morning, afraid to go home, would beg a clerk in the mill for permission to lie down on the office floor. In one city mill in the South, a doctor said he had amputated the fingers of more than one hundred children, mangled in the mill machinery, and that a horrible form of dropsy occurs frequently among the overworked children.' "[55]

In 1900, there were about two million children at work, all under fourteen. What were their working experience? In a report as late as 1914:

"The glare of the furnaces is like some giant burning glass upon the small boys, who sit over molds in a temperature of 100 degrees, turning out ten bottles a minute, or else run back and forth with trays. The hours are cruelly long; the day-shift of one week is the night-shift of the next; and always, in addition to the glare and swelter, there are the myriad particles of glass dust that fill the air . . .

"In the cannery the day-shift and the night-shift are one and the same. At midnight the family reels home; and at 4–30 in the morning, the children still drunk with sleep, the family trudges back to take up a new day of drudgery. Mere tots snip beans at a cent a pound; six-year-olds husk corn at three cents a bushel; and eight-year-old girls 'cap' cans.

"An interesting occupation that! When the cans are filled with syrup or brine, a conveyer carries them from the automatic filler to the capping machine; and, as these cans swirl by, it is the duty of the eight-year-olds to drop on the metal caps that are to be soldered. Forty a minute for nine hours a day!"[56]

Housing for cannery workers was a far cry from the gardens and towns of Ohio:

"Whether New Jersey, New York, Delaware or the Gulf Coast States, there is the same emphasis on squalor. Rude barracks, rough sheds, old box cars, ruined carriage houses—anything seems to be regarded as 'good enough' for the canning families. Delaware, however, holds the record with a chicken coop converted into a dwelling for seventeen children and five adults.

"This, by way of illustration, from the report of New York's commissioner of labor on canneries: 'The surrounding grounds were frequently littered with filth, while the shanties and dormitories were so thoroughly congested that at times families of from six to ten members were compelled to live, sleep, and eat in a single room.' "[57]

Mother Jones, compassionate and optimistic, nevertheless saw these child workers with clear eyes and unrelenting pen:

"Little girls and boys, barefooted, walked up and down between the endless rows of spindles, reaching thin little hands into the machinery to repair snapped threads. They crawled under machinery to oil it. They replaced spindles all day long, all day long; night through, night through. Tiny babies of six years old with faces of sixty did an eight-hour shift for ten cents a day. If they fell asleep, cold water was dashed in their faces, and the voice of the manager yelled above the ceaseless racket and whir of the machines.

"Toddling chaps of four years old were brought to the mills to 'help' the older sister or brother of ten years but their labor was not paid.

"The machines, built in the north, were built low for the hands of little children.

"At five-thirty in the morning, long lines of little grey children came out of the early dawn into the factory, into the maddening noise, into the lint filled rooms. Outside the birds sang and the blue sky shone. At the lunch half-hour, the children would fall to sleep over their lunch of cornbread and fat pork. They would lie on the bare floor and sleep. Sleep was their recreation, their release, as play is to the free child. The boss would come along and shake them awake . . .

"I got to know the life of the breaker boys. The coal was hoisted to a cupola where it was ground. It then came rattling down in chutes, beside which, ladder-wise, sat little breaker boys whose job it was to pick out the slate from the coal as the black rivers flowed by. Ladders and ladders of little boys sat in the gloom of the breakers, the dust from the coal swirling continuously up in their faces. To see the slate they must bend over their task. Their shoulders were round. Their chests narrow.

"A breaker boss watched the boys. He had a long stick to strike the knuckles of any lad seen neglecting his work. The fingers of the little boys bled, bled on to the coal. Their nails were out to the quick.

"A labor certificate was easy to get. All one had to do was to swear to a notary for twenty-five cents that the child was the required age.

"The breaker boys were not Little Lord Fauntleroys. Small chaps smoked and chewed and swore. They did men's work and they had men's ways, men's vices and men's pleasures. They fought and spit tobacco and told stories out on the culm piles of a Sunday. They joined the breaker boys' union and beat up scabs. They refused to let their little brothers and sisters go to school if the children of scabs went.

"In many mines I met the trapper boys. Little chaps who open the door for the mule when it comes in for the coal and who close the door after the mule has gone out. Runners and helpers about the mine. Lads who will become miners; who will never know anything of this beautiful world, of the great wide sea, of the clean prairies, of the snow capped mountains of the vast West. Lads born in the coal, reared and buried in the coal. And his one hope, his one protection—the union.

"I met a little trapper boy one day. He was so small that his dinner bucket dragged on the ground.

" 'How old are you, lad?' I asked him.

" 'Twelve,' he growled as he spat tobacco on the ground.

" 'Say son,' I said, 'I'm Mother Jones. You know me, don't you? I know you told the mine foreman you were twelve, but what did you tell the union?'

"He looked at me with keen, sage eyes. Life had taught him suspicion and caution.

" 'Oh, the union's different. I'm ten come Christmas.'

" 'Why don't you go to school?'

" 'Gee,' he said—though it was really something stronger—'I ain't lost no leg!' He looked proudly at his little legs."[58]

These seem the children of another country than the one described by the Indian school boy, the rich little girl from metropolitan New York, and the young journalist of Galesburg, Ohio. Yet in their small lives we glimpse, from another and more intimate angle, the strains under the spreading structure of nineteenth-century America.

4

The human appetites are old, powerful, and unshakable, yet precisely because of their tenacity, they are easily altered—food, liquid, and sex. So fundamental are their clusters of habits and so dim and masterful in the currents of the human soul, that they are, quite naturally, not merely associated, but actually confused with one another. Remembering these caveats, perhaps we can disentangle them, simply to expose and examine, not to judge. Food, far more than it does today, differed in the nineteenth century as to economic class.

Among the aristocracy of this country, for example the rich landowners of the pre-Civil War South, food was a form of interior decoration: " . . . the supper was a consolation; *pate de foie gras, salade, biscuit glace* and *champagne frappe.*"[59] Protein was the chief part of the diet. "Before the war shut us in, Mr. Preston sent to the lakes for his salmon, to Mississippi for his venison, to England for his mutton and grouse. But the best dish at all of these houses is what the Spanish call 'the hearty welcome.' Thackeray says at every American table he was first served with 'grilled hostess.' At the head of the table sat a person fiery-faced, anxious, nervous, inwardly murmuring like Falstaff 'would it were night, Hal, and all were well.'

"At Mulberry, the house is always filled to overflowing, and one day is curiously like another. People are coming and going, carriages driving up or driving off. It has the air of a watering place where one does not pay, and where there are no strangers. At Christmas, the china closet gives up its treasures. The glass, china, silver, fine linen reserved for grand occasions comes forth. But as for the dinner itself, it is only a matter of great quantity; more turkey, more mutton, more partridge, more fish—and more solemn stiffness."[60]

But among working people in the late-nineteenth and early-twentieth centuries, starches, carbohydrates and fatty proteins took precedence in the family budget. Total calories were obviously what was wanted, and the provision for food was amazingly similar whether the family was Italian or Scotch. Here was the basic provision bought by a Swedish homesteader:

	Cost
Cornmeal, 25 pounds	$0.47
Flour, 100 pounds	2.00
Lard, 10 pounds	1.00
Butter, 10 pounds	1.80
Codfish, 25 pounds	2.25
Ham, 12 pounds	1.20
Potatoes, 120 pounds	$1.40
Rice, 25 pounds	2.15
Coffee, 10 pounds	2.75
Bacon, 30 pounds	1.50
Herrings, 200	1.75
Molasses, 2 gallons	.60

And his normal breakfast was corn meal mush,[61] herrings, bacon, and coffee. But he planted not only potatoes, corn, and wheat, but also turnips, carrots, onions, melons, and pumpkins. There were rarely green vegetables or salads in his diet. That was just as true for a typical Anglo household in the steel town of Homestead, Pennsylvania, in 1910. Here were two typical days:

"MONDAY. *Breakfast:* Oat-meal and milk, eggs and bacon, bread, butter, jelly, coffee.   *Dinner:* Soup, bread, fruit.   *Supper:* Meat, beans, potatoes, fruit, red beets, pickles.

"TUESDAY. *Breakfast:* Chocolate, eggs, bread, butter, and jelly.
Dinner: Spinach, potatoes, pickles, warmed over meat, fruit, bread, butter.
Supper: Meat, sweet potatoes, carrots, beans, tomatoes, tea, bread,
butter and fruit."[62]

It's a high calorie diet, a necessity for men working long hours at hot,
hard jobs: "In mill-town economics, the dinner pail must be reckoned with
as part of the table, and a bill of fare must be read with that in mind. I was
struck with the pains often taken with the 'mister's' bucket. The women used
to carry hot lunches to the mill, but they are not now allowed inside without
a pass. Most of the men, as they are not given regular time for eating, snatch
a bite between tasks, though some, whose work permits, stop for a leisurely
meal. I even heard of men who took steaks to cook on the hot plates about
the machines. But they usually rely on the cold meal, and the women take
great pains to make it appetizing, especially by adding preserves in a little
cup in a corner of the bucket. They try to give the man what he likes the
most, apparently half from pity at the cold food and hard work that fall to his
lot."[63]

The food budget of a thrifty family differed as to whether "the mister"
was working a whole week, or a half week, which was the case during the
depression of 1907–08. On full pay, the family spent $5.11; on half pay, $3.84.
In neither case were any green vegetables bought. The money was spent on
meat, beans, cheese, eggs, butter, flour, and sugar. The astonishing thing is
that, even in hard times, there was no severe malnutrition of the sort that is
common in the rural communities, say, of India or Africa.

But one of the most stubborn difficulties which the wife had to face,
generally without any social weapons at her disposal, was the amount spent
by men on alcohol. This drug is, of course, an ancient palliative. It is probably concurrent with, and as old as, the rise of agriculture, because it is the
natural fermentation by-product of yeast feeding upon wet grain. Hunting
and gathering societies had similar remedies for pain and fatigue and
boredom—the psychopotent mushrooms and other wild herbs. America was
no exception to the need for narcotics, whether alcohol or something more
complex. In spite of our sophistication, we still think of the United States as a
utopian society, a place where people made a new beginning. Certainly they
did, but they brought their bodies with them. It is said—there are no figures
to prove it—that the average male American of the eighteenth century drank
a pint of whiskey a day. In fact, no statistics can be found till 1917 to show
how much of the budget went for beer and whiskey. But in Homestead:
"[There are] over 50 [saloons], eight being in a single block on Eighth Avenue next the mill entrance. A Homesteader summed up the situation in this
way: "We have at least 65 saloons, 10 wholesale liquor stores, a number of

beer agents, innumerable 'speakeasies,' and a dozen or more drug stores,"—and this in a community of 25,000."[64]

There were also a fair number of whorehouses, and this indeed was typical of America, certainly in the broad period we have been discussing. Though small towns and large cities had different patterns of culture which would diverge more and more as the twentieth century grew older, they had this very much in common—as common, indeed, as sex itself. The pattern of love for money was reinforced over and over in this country by events that took men, and young men especially, away from their natural contacts. They were moved by the various gold stampedes, by the railroad expansion into wild and empty country, and by the Civil War itself. Even more important, and each reinforcing the other, was the strong tendency of Americans to change jobs, change habitation, change sexual partners, and change their luck—not always for the better. To these lonely, rootless men, whether native or immigrant, alcohol and whores were the great consolations of life. Here was a contemporary description of a place where both (and this was generally the case) could be bought:

"At Tomales there are several houses, but the only one where we could get 'accommodations' was a very low Irish groggery, kept by a 'lady.' The place was filled with the Irish potato diggers, all as lively as the poorest whiskey could make them. One Irishman had just made some two hundred dollars by a contract for digging, and was celebrating the event, freely treating—in fact, he was just at the culmination of a three days' spree. The 'rooms' of the house were far from private, the beds not highly inviting, and the customers twice as many as the accommodations. Drunkenness, singing, fighting, and the usual noise of Irish sprees were kept up through the night. Much to my disgust I had neither 'bowie' nor 'Colt' along, so could not command the exemption from meddling which those companions would have insured. Now, I don't mind the discomforts of the *field*, of sleeping on the ground, of diet, dust, lizards, snakes, ants, tarantulas, etc., but from drunken Irishmen, from Irish groggeries, from 'ladies' of that description, 'Good Lord, deliver us!' "[65]

That was California. They were more genteel in Nevada:

"For those who enjoyed the company of women, there were the hurdy-gurdy houses. They had a number of girls, not necessarily of bad character, who would dance with a man. In return, after each number he would lead her to the bar and she could choose whether he should buy her a drink or give her its money value, two bits. By consistently shunning the liquor, a girl could make a good living.

"Much less innocent were the women of the town, for whom the law set apart a distinctive quarter located near the Chinese section. Here were 'two rows of white cabins with gaudily-furnished rooms, at whose uncurtained windows the inmates sat, spider-like, waiting for flies.' They dressed as close to the Paris mode as did anybody in New York City. In their rooms, so glamorous in appearance to a man straight from the mines, they enforced a strict, punctilious code of behavior; no matter how tough a male prided himself on being elsewhere, here he must be a gentleman."[66]

And in the Black Hills, lately wrested from the Sioux by simply disregarding the solemn 1868 treaty, such pleasures were doubled by combining them with those of the drama, for example, at the Gem Theatre in Deadwood:

". . . It secured some of the best traveling companies available and was the first to persuade the Sioux Indians to stage their war, squaw, and scalp dances for the entertainment of the palefaces. Tarnishing the Gem's reputation considerably was the regular sequel to each performance: the girls who had been performing on stage now devoted themselves, for pay, to the pleasure of the male audience. Each dance—and there was informal dancing after performances—ended with the caller's saying, 'All promenade to the bar and make room for the ladies.' At the end of any drink the man might go away with the girl. The last dance was 'The Hack-Driver's Quadrille.' During the prosperous years, the Gem took in five thousand dollars on an ordinary night and sometimes as much as ten. For scores of girls, many of whom were quite innocent upon arrival, this perhaps meant suicide, but much more likely it simply foreshadowed drifting into a bad life. Little attention was paid to this at the time, but many years later a county official inspecting the undertaker's records of the 1880s was appalled at the number of girls who had taken their own lives but had been listed in the local newspapers as victims of pneumonia or mountain fever. The only one of them to defy Al Swearengen [the proprietor of the 'Gem'] was a singer named Inez Sexton; given the alternative of rustling the boxes or shooting herself, she walked penniless out of the theater, took a hotel room, and told the owner her story. He spread it, the church people arranged a musical to benefit her, and with the proceeds she left the Black Hills forever.

"A step down from the Gem was the red light district, the so-called bad lands, where the police never interfered after six in the evening . . ."[67]

Nell Kimball's memoirs of New Orleans were exact and graphic:

"When I opened my house on Basin Street in the early '80's you could still find people who said they remembered those wild rivermen when the flatboats were used as cribs for the hookshops and the hookers lived, slept, ate, and boozed on the waterfront by that section of town where the flatboats looked on Tchoupitoulas Street. The Swamp began on Girod Street, some blocks from the river by the Protestant Cemetery at Cypress and South Liberty streets. The Swamp was the favorite of the flatboat men, that and Gallatin Street, the toughest area ever in New Orleans.

"Old-timers talking to me would have tears on their faces when they got to the charm of The Swamp. Ten to twelve people a week were done in there, and nobody gave a damn—or called the cops. The city didn't bother to make anything of it. The cops never came into The Swamp; it was a kind of unwritten law, if the vice didn't leak out into the hinchy, respectable part of the town. Girod Street, it didn't have no more law than any Western town before the marshalls came in, and it was fighting with your teeth, handy-andy [blackjack], hogleg [pistol], or chiv [knife], your only friends in The Swamp.

"The Swamp was a baker's dozen of blocks but real solid with whore houses, hot-sheet hotels (rented by the hour), gambling joints, and dance halls where the girls carried chivs in their garters and their tits flopped out of their dresses and the Johns [customers] got a dry rub standing up. The places stank from manure, privies, and the black mud street. The shacks were just old river barges broken up and used as lumber with the cypress planks raw-sawed.

"A red lantern or even a curtain was the decoration, a board was a bar. An old hustler that worked all The Swamp in those days, peddling it, told me the price for a woman; a snort of corn whiskey and a kip [bed] for the night was one or two picayune [six cents was the value of a picayune]. Some men were given mickeys, rolled, sandbagged, and even killed and dropped into the river . . .

"Talking with old madams who remember the yellow jack comings, they all said there were men and women who when they felt they might die threw themselves into fornication, just not able to get enough of it. The hookers were as bad as the customers, and those who couldn't go out of town or weren't permitted to leave, got drunk as pissants and entertained trade with or without payment. Till the madams had to put the whip to them or have the house bully give them a beating so they'd conduct themselves more like they were whores and not somebody giving it away in a doorway. It was a fearful time the madams would tell me over a gin fizz. In the midst of an epidemic the open cathouses could hardly handle the business, men just aching to get their ashes hauled, staying on all night. A lot just living in the houses, feeling if they had to take the deep six [death in a grave] they'd just as leave be found in bed with a whore and doing what a man seems to want more than anything else when he feels Ol' Scratch is at his heels . . .

"There is something crazy about the sex thing between men and women when things aren't normal. Polite as you try to make it and neat as you keep your place, and police your girls not to be sassy or lippy—come fire, war, ep-idemics, and it's like a mink farm. Don't think it's just the riff-raff, the sporting gentry or pete men [safeblowers, aristocrats of the underworld]. The best people in town come sneaking in at night, or bold as brass through the front door, often bringing their own brandy and cigars. It certainly is an itch that doesn't spare any class.

"You can say you never saw better people any place in town. I had put in a lot of Venice glass over the gas jets and drapes of blood-red velvet reaching to the floor and had eight girls I had picked out myself, some from as far as San Francisco, and two high yellows I called Spanish . . ."[68]

"Helter Skelter" chute at Luna Amusement Park, Coney Island, New York.

Library of Congress

One must remember that this is the account of an employer, not an employee:

"I never had no truck with the idea whores had hearts of gold, and I never turned a girl down because she was rabbity and jumpy, what they later called neurotic. They made the best whores sometimes. If a madam can't handle girls, she's better out of the business. The girls make or break a house, and they need a solid hand. You had to watch out for Lesbians among them, and while I didn't mind the girls doing a bit of chumming and doubling up, if I found a dildoe, I knew it had gone too far. Girls that become libertines with each other don't satisfy the Johns because they are involved with themselves . . .

"I'd punish the girls with fines, and if they got real out of line I'd have Harry work them over, but not bruise them. This may sound mean and cruel, I suppose, but they were often wild girls, a bit batty upstairs, who could do harm if they went off the deep end. And once a house gets a reputation as having girls who don't act right with the customers you might just as well close up and turn out the red light in the front of the place and throw away the key.

"I paid the girls one third of what they earned and never held back, and I didn't shark them with interest on loans I made them, or get them on drugs or have them mulcted by fancy men like some houses did. I never cottoned to the sweet daddies that attached themselves to a girl's earnings.

"The girls got their money and they could do what they wanted with it. They were charged for meals, linen, room, and if they weren't fall-down drunks, I threw in the likker free. A drunk is no good as a whore. You can't hide her breath, and she doesn't do her work in style. Hookers are mean but sentimental. They cry over dogs, kittens, kids, novels, sad songs. I never cared much for a girl who came to work in a house because it was fun for her. There was a screw loose somewheres. I remember a Jew girl from a good family who was the wildest thing in the act ever to hit Basin Street. She lasted two months, tried to kill a John with a chair, and hung herself that night in the attic.

"I never knew many whores to hold on to any money. But there was a half-Indian girl from Oklahoma who went back and married a farm boy who became a big oil man and later a U.S. congressman . . .

"I never counted the take till the next day—I was that bushed—but soaked my feet in hot water and one of the maids would rub my neck while I got out of my corset and into bed with a cup of hot milk and nutmeg. I was a poor sleeper as I got older, and sometimes I'd take one of the maids to bed with me and we'd just talk lazy, gab with a night-light burning, talk about the Johns, the family life the maid came from, and when the girl saw I was real woozy she'd get out of bed and I'd cork off and have a sleep until ten or eleven in the morning when I'd hear the girls coming downstairs, or Harry moving around with the big watchdog we kept by the stable, or outside testing shutters, and I'd come awake, and then it was goodbye Charlie to sleep."[69]

To what degree were the whorehouses, so universal in America between 1860 and 1917—I don't mean to imply that the situation has changed since then—the natural result of a Christian classification of sex, before or outside marriage, as a sin? Again, there is no firm evidence, and I believe one's intuition can be easily mistaken on this emotional question. In any case, the desire for deep excitement, combined with the pleasures of drama in one's life, all the while knowing it is pretense, would be sufficient in a commercial culture to support the thousands upon thousands of brothels. I hardly need add that this limited drama, these pleasures, this purchased freedom—was only for men. For women, even in marriage, the threat of another pregnancy was real; they could not afford fantasy. From the scant evidence, the common method of birth control was withdrawal, just at the man's climax, by the husband or lover. If they were clumsy or indifferent, the union never gave their wives much beyond a sense of, maybe, warmth and comfort.

Anthony Comstock, one of those curious paranoids who often do persuasively well in human society, was the author of an 1868 statute forbidding all sorts of immoral objects—books and paintings included—and by 1873, got the government into his game, via the pliable regulations of the postal service. He boasted he had destroyed in his lifetime 160 tons of nasty material, though what its gross weight had to do with its gross immorality is difficult, at this distance, to understand. One witness of his campaign was more specific: "Was present at Park Street Church Vestry . . . heard the speech of Comstock, in which he gave an account in detail of the vendors of obscenity in pictures, mechanical appliances and their various means of introducing them to youths of both sexes . . . articles of abortion and self abuse. After explaining quite minutely the details of this traffic . . ."[70]

Talking one way and doing another is considered hypocrisy, but that is too easy a word. The double standard of act and word applied to men as well as to women. It was the only way people were able to brake their runaway sexual energies in a statistically, as well as historically, young society. Of course, it led to absurdities, especially in the complex society of the South: "Bad books are not allowed house room except in the library and under lock and key, the key in the Master's pocket; but bad women, if they are not white and serve in a menial capacity, may swarm the house unmolested. The ostrich game is thought a Christian act. These women are no more regarded as a dangerous contingent than canary birds would be."[71]

Another possibility would have been freedom combined with comprehension, passion with responsibility, but America, in its wasteful, furious adolescence, was not yet ready for such wisdom, if ever it would be. In 1890, Governor Theodore Roosevelt, the clean, young, rugged, outdoor American, conscious of his superiority to the corruption of old Europe, took the occasion of the banning of The Kreutzer Sonata, to declare that Tolstoy was "a moral and physical pervert." William S. Hart could have said it no better.

This, too, was a necessary hypocrisy, for neither cultures nor persons like to see the full truth about themselves. The brothels were located on streets parallel to the main business avenues, and in a larger sense, coexisted

Fifth Avenue, 57th to 59th Streets, 1897–1899.

Photograph by Percy Byron. Museum of the City of New York

with family clusters. Of these, some families were certainly permanent and self-enriching, but a great many, in late–nineteenth-century America, were fixed only in name, with the husband taking "the cars" to find fortune in yet another state or occupation, with the boys going off as soon as they could get a job, and the daughters marrying young because they had managed to get pregnant. Certainly that was true in the mill town where I was born.

Before the Civil War, before industrialization and immigration, courtship for the well-to-do was a little less abrupt, although what we read here may be a matter of form rather than substance:

My dearest Miss Brewer,

I have tried in vain to make up my mind to leave Boston, without disclosing to you what I now write, (although you may have seen as I hope you have) that I loved you! Do not think that this is any sudden fancy of mind, far from it, I have loved and respected you since the first time I saw you . . . May I hope that you will give me a favorable answer, and at all events you may forgive the above, which although it may appear silly to one, who does not return my affection, may for the contrary reason, find favour with you, to whom it is addressed by one who feels the sincerest affection for you although he had not the courage to speak it out, tremblingly awaits your answer—will you return my love and allow me to ask your hand of your Parents?

Ever yours[72]

For all this, it's hard to believe there was not, before this letter was written, at the very least some genteel kissing. It was certainly true of the adolescents in upper-middle-class New York:

"*Sunday, July 9, 1899* . . . Went for a little walk on the road with Henny and Baba to meet Cor and then all came up to my room and courted as Baba expresses it. Baba sat on Guy's lap and kissed him all the time. She was dressed in my Japanese costume and looked very pretty. Cornelia then followed her example. We ate lots of candy and Cor and I wrote our names on Guy's hat. Baba was to sleep with us and the three of us got into one bed. Cor got angry because we wouldn't speak to her and began to cry . . .

"I am stealing Dudley's heart from Helen. I danced with him a lot today. His number is 692 Park Avenue and his last name is Leland.

"At lunch I only had my wrapper on and when Dr. Elliot came I jumped into the closet thinking he would go upstairs. Instead of that he sat at the table ate fruit and then he wanted a glass of soda so Millie went to get a glass out of the closet I was in but I held the door and she could not get in.

"*March 12, 1902*   A new rule is that any Spence girl seen walking with a boy even her brother will be asked to leave the school."[73]

And here was the opinion of a Southern woman in 1862:

"The beautiful Jewess, Rachel Lyons, was here today. She flattered Paul Hayne so audaciously, and he threw back the ball. She is daft about Mr. Chestnut, but Miriam Cohen says she has not learned his hours yet, since so far she has always called to see me when he was away from home. She gave Paul Hayne the benefit of her philosophy. 'Married or single, all men are alike to me.' She could only marry one of her own faith. She asked me what I understood by the word 'flirtation,' and answered her own question. 'A mere pretense of "love-making"; a semblance of love, not the reality. As soon as love itself was waked, it was no longer a flirtation. Is kissing legitimate in a flirtation? Some girls say you cannot keep a man off and on, as it is necessary to do in a flirtation, unless you let him kiss you. Indeed, he will kiss you!' Here Mem Cohen's face assumed such a look of amazement and disgust that

Miss Lyons brought herself up shortly. 'I think such freedoms horrid. I never let men kiss me!' . . .[74]

"It is an odd thing. In all my life how many persons have I seen in love? Not a half-dozen, and yet I am a tolerably close observer, a faithful watcher of men and manners. Society has been for me only an enlarged field for character study. Flirtation is the business of society. That is playing at love-making; it begins in vanity, it ends in vanity. . . . It is a pleasant but very foolish game—and so to bed."[75]

And again: "Another scandal: A father forbade his daughter's marriage. There was a party at the house. He saw something which made him consent at once, and joy go with her! Oh, what could it be that he saw? Yes, stern parent dozing in the piazza, which was not lighted, saw the forbidden man sitting by a window, his back turned to the piazza. Lightly his daughter tiptoed out; she daintily raised the red hair from the back of that stout, freckled neck and kissed it. "If things have gone that far, let her marry!" swore the father."[76]

But there were certain professional men who were sneakier:

". . . She was ill, had a bad sore throat; and she lay on the sofa, wrapped in a cashmere shawl and muffled in laces about the face and neck. Our surgeon dropped on his knees by her side. 'What is that for?' said the Captain, standing up brusquely. 'I mean to try auscultation, percussion, etc., to see if her lungs are affected.' 'Come now, that sort of thing won't do!' 'Miss Sally,' said Dr. Darby, 'This sort of thing is done everyday. It is strictly professional. I must rest my head against your chest. It is absolutely necessary for a medical diagnosis.' 'No you don't,' said the Captain. 'If I had a sore throat, you would drag me to the window, make me stretch my mouth from ear to ear, put a tablespoon down my throat until I choked, make me stick out my tongue, and then order me a nasty gargle. Or more probably you would barely touch my pulse and say, "Oh, nothing's the matter with you." Auscultation, and listening under shoulder blades, you keep for the women!' 'Nonsense! Miss Sally, let me put my head where I can hear you breathe!' The Captain cried: 'Sir! This furniture is rented. I believe it does not belong to Aunt Mary. But if you don't want to see a chair smashed over your head, take care not to move a peg nearer.'

"The surgeon got up, dusted his knees, and said: 'Everybody knows what a narrow-minded donkey you are.' The Captain received this compliment smilingly. 'You ought to have waited till I went out. The other fellow feels too like a fool, while that auscultation goes on under his very eyes.' "[77]

And there were other accounts, truthful I'm sure, that nevertheless sounded like cheap novels:

"I think it began with those beautiful, beautiful silk stockings that fit so nicely. I have been afraid to warm my feet on the fender ever since. You ought to hear him rave about my foot and ankle. Before that, he was so respectful; he kissed my hand to be sure, but that is nothing. Sometimes, when he kissed my hand, he said I was his queen, and what a grateful fellow he was that I liked him; and I was proud of that very respectful style he adopted.

"But as I stood by the fender warming my feet, he seized me 'round the waist and kissed my throat. When he saw how shocked I was, he was frightened and so humble, and so full of apologies. He said it was so soft and

1907 Renault coupe.

Photograph by Percy Byron. Museum of the City of New York

white, that throat of mine, he could not help it. It was all so sudden. I drew back, and told him I would go away, that I was offended. In a moment I felt a strong arm so tight around my waist I could not move. He said I should stay until I forgave his rash presumption, and he held me fast. I pretended to be in a rage. He said that after all, I had promised to marry him, and that made all the difference in the world; but I did not see it . . ."[78]

There was, of course, the impediment of the heavy, floor-length, ruffled and rustling costumes that women felt obliged to wear over their flexible steel corsetry. Yet the body was not all that hidden, particularly at dances, when Mary Chesnut noted that there was a generous exposure of "that which babies cry for." Nor was sex confined to courtship and marriage; extramarital love was as common in America as anywhere else. "It is only in books that men fall in love with their wives," wrote one amateur lady sociologist.

There are no tables in the Statistical Abstracts of the U.S. to suggest how much homosexuality was practiced in the late-nineteenth century. To judge from other repressive societies, I suspect it was neither more nor less than what was common in every other culture. But the pain and longing have been recorded for one individual anyway: "I long for friendship and love. Yet when I grow to know those who promise much to me in the way of soul communion I am disappointed for they fall so short of my expectations. Either I must worship a man or he must worship me. It seems impossible for me to meet anyone on an equal footing and say simply 'I love you.' . . . And sad my kissing . . . my empty fingertips."[79]

Under the muscular optimism of late–nineteenth-century America, continually renewed and reasserted by a succession of pioneers and immigrants, one glimpses a crisis of moral confusion. The violence of the rickety gold camps, Colorado mining police, and Homestead strikers, the violence of the urban poor, bursting out of their thick slums, were merely symptoms of the theatrical balance in American character between the brutal and the sentimental. Further, there were even more dark and private morbidities; in the letters, for example, of a New York investor and businessman:

Dear William Ward   January 29, 1883

Your letter has touched some chords that seldom vibrate by external influences—yes—I may even say that not for four and forty years have some of them been excited by any agency but my own. I was bereft of my Mother in 1839. [He was 29.] My relations with her were singularly like yours with your Mother. We were all the world to each other. It was some years before I could master my emotions if she were alluded to in my presence, although in private she was seldom out of my mind. In life we were inseparable, and in death I went with her to the brink of the grave, mourning most of all that I could not enter it with her and abide there. It was never 'a thing incredible' with me 'that God should raise the dead,' but my faith in the doctrine was intensified by the reflection that my Mother would live again. I was inspired with what I may call a love of that doctrine because it was fraught with such a consequence. I remember well the long night I spent in speculating upon that certain event. I even went the length of conceiving the mode and the incidence of the Resurrection. A much cherished idea of mine was that I would be buried not beside my Mother but that my coffin should rest upon hers, so that when the frail partition that separated us should crumble, my own dust would mingle with hers. Then, when the vivifying breath of God should reanimate the mass and each particle seek its fellow, it might happen that the Mother's arms would be reformed encircling her son and again clasp him to her bosom. Then too we might snatch a kiss in the twilight of the grave after the lamps of Time have gone out and before the beacons of Eternity were lighted . . . What a relation is that of Mother and Son![80]

5

There is, and was, something repellently attractive about sickness; the curiosity is unselfish—it applies to somebody else's illness almost as strongly as to one's own. There is, quite naturally, little said about such matters in standard histories. A microbe has to kill spectacularly in order to get more than a footnote. But in the erratic dramas of daily life, fever, infection, accident, and death were a constant punctuation:

"*March 26, 1885*   Today is the first warm day in many months, the winter has been particularly severe, many, many have died of pneumonia and kindred complaints, our mother-in-law, Mrs. Mary Ann Cooke, died of typhoid fever, after pneumonia, November 28, 1884."[81]

Cholera, too, was by no means uncommon in the late-nineteenth century, and so was rabies:

"*December 29, 1885*   The present craze is the mad dog craze. Dr. Pasteur of Paris some months ago discovered that inoculation would cure hydrophobia, and to prove his theory it does seem that every born dog has gone mad this cold weather so as to bite people and have them go across the ocean to M. Pasteur to be treated. Six children in one day two weeks ago were bit by one dog in Newark, New Jersey. Four of the children accompanied by one of the mothers were immediately sent over to Paris at the expense of Newark for treatment . . . All dogs are to be muzzled an unheard of thing in winter . . ."[82]

This disease, if caught in time, was painfully curable. Tuberculosis, typhoid, and diphtheria were not, so any cough or indisposition gave anxiety. Opium was a common medicine for ailing intestines; certainly it slowed things down, and gave dreams more pleasant than did purgatives. On the other hand, there were medicines as late as 1915 that were even more dangerous: "Have been taking a tonic (arsenic and strychnine pills) this past week."[83]

Amateur advice was abundant and specific:

My dear Mary

As you are so far separated from us, I *feel* it my *duty*—to give you some of my advice—& *experience*—which I feel sure you will receive with candor—& in all kindness—

When I was first married—being one of the *youngest*—I was as ignorant as a child—about children—and all those things that is so *very important* for them to know—I was very *careless—reached* over my head—put up *curtains*—& did various things that injured me,—all from *ignorance*, and a want of some kind friend to tell me how to *do*—and *behave*—consequently with my first children—I suffered greatly from want of *knowledge.* My husband purchased a Medical book from which I ob-

Army officers and friends, Staten Island, New York, November 6, 1888. Woman in striped waist is the photographer, E. Alice Austen.

Photograph by E. Alice Austen. Staten Island Historical Society

tained very important information which I have not failed to give to my female friends. Unfortunately that book is now out of *print*—I gave away mine to a very dear friend in Philadelphia, whom is now dead—but experienced (she said) great benefit from the information she thus gained.

But dear Mary you are not as ignorant *now*—as the ladies were 50 years ago. But let me advise you to be *careful*—and not to reach over your head—take moderate ex-

ercise every day; keep the body in a *healthy state*—and if *medecin* [*sic*] is *needed*—
Always take Castor Oil—*that*—*relaxes* the skin—You *may* say that you dislike Oil—
but never mind that—when it will do you so much more good—if you put wine—or
anything you like best, into the wine glass—rence [*sic*] the spoon first with wine
too—or whatever you take it in—then pour the oil *carefully* into the glass that has
some wine in it, & then put a little more wine on the *top* of the oil—Open your
mouth and swallow it down—and you will not *taste* it in the *least*—I hope that you do
not dislike oil as I do—for it is of *every importance*—that you keep your skin *soft* and
elastic—I wish you to use an oinment made of *beefs Marrow* & Mutton tallow, a little
more marrow than tallow—I should thin; & rub your bowels gently whenever you
feel *tight* and *uncomfortable*. It will perhaps be *less* exposing you to take cold, to rub
yourself carefully when going to bed—and to prevent you from feeling a *chill*, this
cold season—it will be best to rub you at the same time, with cologne or spirits of any
kind, that you like best—that will warm—& keep off *chills*—

I will, with great pleasure, dear Mary, make you a little jar of this ointment—if
you will tell me how I can get it to you.

But it is very simple—& made without any trouble—only I *know* you dislike to
be *fussing*—but do not mind a little trouble—the marrow is the worst to get—but
Mutton, every family has,—just simmer a little together—strain it, add any pleasant
flavor to it that you like best—marrow alone is very penetrating and good—God bless
you & yours

Truly your affectionate Grandmother A B[84]

Nor were the medical amateurs much more effective, in spite of the testimony—second hand as it always is—of a lady in New York City in 1899:

"Last Saturday evening Mrs. Elain from Americus, Georgia, came on to
New York. She deals largely with some of the New York merchants—has a
large Milennium of Fancy Stores. Is an exceedingly pleasant and well informed lady; looks like Martha Washington figure and face. Spoke of an old
man near their home who could positively cure cancer. Had in many cases.
He put a tiny plaster on the surface of the spot where cancer is supposed to
be. In a few days he puts on a mush poultice—when the whole cancer with
all its roots, drops out—new flesh fills in and the edges of the skin unite in
time. Twelve years ago half his face was gone or rather, eaten away by cancer, when in trying many things he hit upon the right one. Is an uneducated
man, but seems to work wonders. Poor people he cures for nothing. Rich
ones only takes what pays his expenses and time when handling. Mrs. Elain
knows four or five cases herself that he has cured. One of the lady who
thought she had one the size of a 'hickory nut'—which when out proved to
be as large as a cup and he found three other places in her face, where she
had cancer and she did not know anything about it."[85]

The fact of death was mollified by ceremony. It was naturally different
for different times and cultures, but had two invariables mingled together:
fear and mourning. It's a good proof, whether we are Baptist or Sunnite or
Zen or Catholic, how little real faith we have, finally, in a second chance at
life. For the stroke of death brings to all of us yet surviving a strong and sor-

rowful anger. We cannot forgive the universe for its deception. But we go on, anyway, softening our basic grief with ritual music, words, and decorations. By the late-nineteenth century, these had acquired an opulence, not for everyone, but for a good many, that was close to ludicrous. Tourists sought out the crowded monuments to our fear and love of the dead. A certain Mrs. Hall, on a trip to New York City in 1879, visited Macy's Emporium, Altman's, a sermon on tenement houses, Henry Ward Beecher, the Central Park Zoo, and the Greenwood Cemetery: ". . . Our driver seemed to have his knowledge of the principal places and etc., all 'cut and dried', and rattle it like an auctioneer. He seemed to be very familiar with the names, dates of deaths, and etc. of all Actors, Actresses, Suicides, Murderers, and etc. etc. Doubtless he supposed tragic endings would be the most interesting topics for his viewers . . .

"Among the most beautiful of all the monuments is one erected to Miss Charlotte Canda, who fell out of a carriage coming home from a party on her 17th birthday . . . The monument cost $30,000 . . . Abram Pasburgh has a monument surrounded by bayonets . . . A lady has a monument to her five dogs . . . Another fine (one of the most costly monuments in the country) . . . is erected . . . to a 'Soda Water Man'. His daughter's bust in marble is on the top. His son George below his wife is sitting in a chair and he himself is lying full length on a couch or bed . . . 'Boss Tweed' has a little monument compared to the others . . ."[86]

As opulent as these marbles were the deaths in nineteenth-century fiction:

> But lo! the bridegroom with no further warning
> Came for her at the dawning of the day
> She heard his voice, and smiled, and passed away
> Without a struggle.[87]

This sweet resignation, as everyone really knew, did not correspond to physical reality. It deceived few, because death was a constant and insistent visitor, and not necessarily met with grace on either side, as another nineteenth-century poet records:

> Is Heaven a physician?
>   They say that He can heal;
> But medicine posthumous
>   Is unavailable.
>
> Is Heaven an exchequer?
>   They speak of what we owe;
> But that negotiation
>   I'm not a party to.[88]

Nor was the late-nineteenth century lacking in another universal phenomenon—self-murder:

"*July 19th*   Maj. Thompson committed suicide at 6 A.M. by shooting himself through the heart, with a 44 caliber Colts revolver. He had been suffering for some days with disease of the kidneys, attended with great pain, and was I suppose unable to bear it longer. Poor Tompy, he was a gentle, genial man. A thorough gentleman, and his death has cast a gloom over the entire camp. He was buried at 6.30 P.M. All the officers and men of this command attending. Genl. Gibbon made a fine, appropriate remark. Maguire read the service. Very warm again today."[89]

Whitman, who saw everything, made note of this, too: "As I cross the Delaware, one of the deck-hands, F. R., tells me how a woman jump'd overboard and was drown'd a couple of hours since. It happen'd in mid-channel—she leap'd from the forward part of the boat, which went over her. He saw her rise on the other side in the swift running water, throw her arms and closed hands high up, (white hands and bare forearms in the moonlight like a flash,) and then she sank."[90]

6

Most journals of any sort were not kept by workmen, sharecroppers, or child laborers, and only rarely by clerks and housewives. When they were, the writer was hardly aware that industrialized America, built with such incredible haste, and hence at such excessive human cost, was turning away from its own ample borders, to begin the Americanization of the world. This was a process not necessarily bad, but not to be accomplished without the expense of blood. Among the accounts that reflect the history of our expansion, from below is the Philippine diary of the volunteer Captain J. Clifford Brown:

". . . You could hear the crashes of the volleys and the occasional boom of a field-piece. Every one I think would have been glad if the train, which stretched out over a quarter of a mile, had been attacked. Our danger of course was from raiders and marauding parties. It commenced to rain now and we came to a stream breast deep and very swift through which we plunged and halted, waiting for the train to close up. I thought they never would get the caribous through that stream. Every one of the beasts laid down in the water, and beatings nor bayonets could move him till he was ready. Such language! Frantic officers, stolid Chinos (as they call the Chinese), the natives solicitous lest their precious beasts be abused and twenty-five wet, tired, hungry and thoroughly exasperated soldiers. We crossed three such rivers and the same thing was repeated at each one. At one we had a new experience. It was very dark now. The 'point' suddenly challenged. Natives of course, two of them, loudly professing friendship. Spies I dare say, but orders are strict to treat all natives as friendly unless they are in uniform or have a rifle, so we let them go . . .

". . . we passed through two large inhabited villages, Bicetre Tanglela and Sapote . . . [the natives] were very humble and gave us bananas and cig-

Muskogee, Oklahoma, crowd greeting President Theodore Roosevelt, 1900, on election tour.

National Archives, Washington, D.C.

arettes, everywhere displaying the white flag. It commenced to rain and rained with tropical intensity, but we kept on . . . In one place where the water was waist deep a man laid down and said he had rather die than take another step. He was dragged along. Men began to throw away ammunition, so a short halt, the first, was called and I washed the sand out of my shoes . . ."[91]

The special American irony of the matter is that the war was urged for moral reasons: the oppression of the Cuban guerrillas by Spain. "Blood on our doorstep." And the leader of the Rough Riders was that great, stout equestrian, Teddy Roosevelt. It was a populist expedition, in the sense earlier described—combining moral reform with national fervor. It must be remembered, however, that the U.S. Army was fighting, not the tyrannical Spaniards any more, but the very Philippino insurgents who had revolted against Spain. "He was armed with an old Remington, the 'pull' of which was so strong as to make it impossible to shoot straight, one of the long knives or 'bolos' and a dark lantern. He expected to be shot every moment and the guard were handling and laughing at his equipment, saying 'boom, boom, poco tempo,' which means shot presently. He was a young fellow and stood it rather well, though you could see tears roll down his cheeks. He was turned over to the provost and will be put at work. Any one at home who believes these people capable of governing themselves has only to come out and he will be sadly disillusioned . . ."[92]

It is this kindly contempt for anyone beside one's familiar color, and particularly for those whose skin had rather more melanin than common, that was a psychological platform for all our late–nineteenth-century armed expeditions, whatever their undoubted economic benefit. It sent our soldiers to China, Korea, to Haiti, to Mexico, and eventually, to France.

Although Wilson had been elected in 1916 on a platform of peace, he felt compelled by circumstances whose momentous force possibly he himself could not realize. On April 3, 1917, he summoned a joint session of both houses of Congress plus the Supreme Court, and after citing German submarine warfare, he concluded: "There is one choice we cannot make, we are incapable of making: we will not choose the path of submission and suffer the most sacred rights of our Nation and our people to be ignored or violated."[93] *The New York Times* report of that day described the universal joy that followed: "At the word 'submission', Chief Justice White dropped the big soft hat he had been holding, raised his hands high in the air, and brought them together with a heartfelt bang; and House, Senate, and galleries followed him with a roar like a storm."[94]

It remains to balance this account as we have begun—from below—by quoting one small consequence of the Chief Justice's enthusiasm, and not a particularly frightening one. There are plenty of such entries available to anyone morbidly interested in World War I. It seemed more cheerful to end this series of studies, on the shifting pattern of American life between two wars, on a more musical note:

"*August 15, 1918*   As we sat there at the gun, 'Fritz' launched a gas attack on a neighboring town. The shells passed directly in front of our position, and if I live to be a thousand I'll never forget the sound of them. There must have been literally thousands of them, each one singing its own little chromatic song, the ensemble like the sound of a thousand violins, each humming its own ascending and descending scale—you cannot imagine the weird effect they create, as their voices cross and crisscross, giving the queerest discords, with an occasional note of perfect harmony . . ."[95]

Sources

1. Looking Backward: A Note in Warning

1. Mary Boykin Chesnut, *A Diary from Dixie*, ed. Ben Ames Williams (Boston: Houghton Mifflin and Co., 1950), p. 268; entry of July 12, 1862.
2. George Ward Nichols, *The Story of the Great March from the Diary of a Staff Officer* (New York: Harper and Brothers, 1865), pp. 89–91.
3. *Reminiscences and Experiences of a Union Soldier of the 79th New York Regiment, July 1861–April 1862*, New York Public Library, MSS and Archives Division, Astor, Lenox, and Tilden Foundations.

2. Whites Like Insects Too Many to Kill

1. Major General Granville M. Dodge, *How We Built the Union Pacific Railroad* (U.S. Senate Document No. 447 [Washington, D.C., 1910]).
2. *Ibid.*
3. Contemporary account by engineer W. F. Murphy, quoted in Nellie Snyder Yost, "The Wedding of the Rails," in *Trails of the Iron Horse*, ed. Don Russell (New York: Doubleday, 1975).
4. George E. Hyde, *Red Cloud's Folk* (Norman, Oklahoma: University of Oklahoma Press, 1937), p. 174.
5. Charles A. Eastman, *Indian Boyhood* (New York: Dover. Reprint of publication by McClure, Phillips, and Co., 1902), pp. 239–40.
6. Mrs. Helen Sargent, "Incidents in the Life of Norris Griggs," *Annals of Wyoming*, Vol. 25, No. 1, (January, 1953).
7. *Ibid.*
8. Robert A. Lowie, *Primitive Society* (New York, 1927).
9. George Bird Grinnell, *Cheyenne Indians, Their History and Ways of Life* (New Haven, 1923).
10. Bernard Mishkin, *Rank and Warfare among the Plains Indians* (University of Washington Press, 1940).
11. Senate Report No. 156, quoted in Dee Brown, *Bury My Heart at Wounded Knee* (New York: Holt, Rinehart, and Winston, 1971), pp. 53, 74.
12. Robert Bent quoted in Brown, *ibid.*, pp. 73, 96.
13. Lieutenant James Cernor, quoted in Brown, *ibid.*, p. 53.
14. Chief Smohalla (Wanapum), *14th Annual Report of the Bureau of American Ethnology* (1896), II, pp. 720—21.
15. E. S. Ricker's interview with American Horse, quoted in James C. Olson, *Red Cloud and the Sioux Problem* (Lincoln, Nebraska: University of Nebraska Press, 1965). *See also* Nebraska State Historical Society, Ricker MSS, Tablet 15.
16. Annual report of Colonel Henry E. Maynadier, Commander at Fort Laramie, to D. N. Cooley, Commissioner of Indian Affairs, 1866, quoted in Olson, *ibid.*
17. *Indian Heroes and Great Chieftains* (Boston: Little, Brown and Co., 1918), p. 102.
18. Contemporary account by S. H. Fairchild of Almo, Kansas, in "The Eleventh Kansas Regiment at Platte Bridge," quoted in George Bird Grinnell, *The Fighting Cheyenne* (Norman,

Oklahoma: University of Oklahoma Press, 1955. Reprint of publication by Charles Sribner, 1915), pp. 228–29.

19. *Ibid.*, pp. 237—38.
20. *Ibid.*
21. *Ibid.*
22. Ralph K. Andrist, *The Long Death* (New York: Collier, 1964).
23. Senate Executive Document No. 39, quoted in Brown, *op. cit.*, p. 66.
24. *Omaha Weekly Herald*, June 10, 1868, quoted in Brown, *op. cit.*
25. Senate Document No. 452, quoted in Olson, *op. cit.*, p. 341. *See also* Article 1 of Treaty of 1868 in *Indian Affairs, Laws and Treaties* (57th Congress, 1st Session), II, pp. 998–1007.
26. George E. Hyde, *Spotted Tail's Folk* (Norman, Oklahoma: University of Oklahoma Press, 1961), p. 173.
27. *Ibid.*, p. 174.
28. *Ibid.*, p. 175.
29. Olson, *op. cit.*, p. 102.
30. Report of Ely Parker to General Ulysses Grant, Senate Executive Document No. 13 (40th Congress, 1st Session), pp. 42–47.
31. Olson, *op. cit.*, pp. 104–05.
32. Quoted from "Transcript of Interviewers with Red Cloud in Washington, June 3 and 7, 1870," National Archives, NARS, RG 75.
33. From National Archives, NARS, RG 98, TR, Department of the Platte.
34. *Ibid.*
35. *Ibid.*
36. Hyde, *Red Cloud's Folk* (Norman, Oklahoma: University of Oklahoma Press, 1937).
37. Hyde, *Spotted Tail's Folk* (Norman, Oklahoma: University of Oklahoma Press, 1961).
38. Treaty of 1868, quoted in Olson, *op. cit.*
39. Senate Executive Document No. 39 (41st Congress, 3rd Session).
40. *New York Times*, June 12, 1870.
41. *Ibid.*
42. *Ibid.*, June 14, 1870.
43. *Ibid.*, June 15, 1870.
44. *Ibid.*, June 17, 1870.
45. President Andrew Johnson's message to Congress, 1867.
46. Gabriel Renville, a chief of the Sisseton tribe of South Dakota, quoted in George C. Allonsen, "An Interesting Account of the Historic Indian Reservation," *Sisseton Courier*, July 2, 1942.
47. Quoted by Brown, *op. cit.*, p. 183. But Olson, *op. cit.* has a different version, quoted from a report of First Lieutenant William Quintin to First Lieutenant M. C. Sanbourne, Post Adjutant, Fort Shaw, May, 1871, NARS, RG 75, Montana Superintendency: "Red Cloud returned to his people with wonderful stories of what he had seen and heard while visiting the Great Father at Washington. Red Cloud saw too much. The Indians say that these things cannot be; that the white people must have bad Medicine over Red Cloud's eyes to make him see everyting and anything that they pleased, and so Red Cloud lost his influence."
48. Quoted in Christopher Davis, *The North American Indian* (Feltham, Middlesex, England: Hamlyn Publication Group).

3. A Long Track to China

1. *New York Journal of Commerce*, September 17, 1864.
2. Reverend Moses Hoge, letter to his daughter Bessie, 1868 (?), Alderman Library, University of Virginia.
3. Elisha P. Douglass, *The Coming of Age of American Business*, (University of North Carolina Press, 1971).
4. Emerson D. Fite, *Social and Industrial Conditions in the North during the Civil War* (Williamstown, Mass: Corner House Publications, 1976).
5. Henry Thoreau, *Walden* (Libra Publishers, 1960), p. 74.
6. William R. Russell, letter to his mother, March 29, 1868, Library of Congress MSS Division.
7. *The Lynn* [Massachusetts] *Reporter*, February 28, 1863, quoted in Fite, *op. cit.*
8. Russell, letter to his mother, December 7, 1861, Library of Congress MSS Division.

9. Major General Granville M. Dodge, *How We Built the Union Pacific Railroad* (U.S. Senate Document No. 447 [Washington, D.C., 1910]).
10. *Ibid.*
11. William A. Bell, *New Tracks in America* (London, 1869), II, pp. 253–55, quoted in Martin Ridge and Ray A. Billington, eds., *America's Frontier Story* (New York: Holt, Rinehart, and Winston, 1969).
12. William H. Brewer, Professor of Agriculture, 1860–64, *Up and Down California* [a journal] (University of California Press, 1966).
13. Russell, letter to his mother, May 18, 1865, *loc. cit.*
14. Resolution adopted by a group of journalists on a Union Pacific press excursion in October, 1866, quoted in Lynn Rhodes Mayer and Kenneth E. Vose, *Makin' Tracks* (New York: Praeger, 1975), pp. 66–67.
15. From *The Boston Journal*, 1868, quoted in *Ibid.*, p. 86.
16. Craig Buck, "In Spite of a Fence," *Westways*, June, 1976, p. 44.
17. Dodge, *op. cit.*
18. Todhunter Ballard, "Building the Impossible," in Don Russell, ed., *Trails of the Iron Horse* (New York: Doubleday, 1975).
19. Samuel B. Reed, letter to his wife, July 30, 1877, quoted in Mayer and Vose, *op. cit.*, p. 102.
20. Testimony before Joint Congressional Committee, October, 1876, printed in *Report on Chinese Immigration*, quoted in George F. Seward, *Chinese Immigration in its Social and Economical Aspect* (New York: Scribners, 1881).
21. From a report in a San Francisco newspaper (Alta, California) May 1 and 3, 1869, quoted in Richard Reinhardt, ed., *Workin' on the Railroad* (New York: Weathervane Books [Crown], 1970).
22. Mayer and Vose, *op. cit.*, pp. 124–25.
23. *Ibid.*, p. 133.
24. Dodge, *op. cit.*
25. *Ibid.*
26. Reinhardt, *op. cit.*, pp. 45–6.
27. Martin F. Schmitt and Dee Brown, *The Settler's West* (New York: Bonanza Books, 1955).
28. Charles N. Harger, "Cattle Trails of the Prairies," *Scribner's Magazine*, XI (June, 1892), pp. 738–41, quoted in Ridge and Billington, *op. cit.*
29. Walt Whitman, "Specimen Days," printed in *Walt Whitman, The Death Bed Edition* (1892).
30. Robert A. Fremont, ed., *Favorite Songs of the Nineties* (New York: Dover, 1973), p. 152.

4. The Fires At Pittsburgh

1. *Historical Statistics of the United States* (U.S. Department of Commerce, House Document No. 93–78, Part 2 [93rd Congress, 1st Session] Series Q 321–328), p. 731.
2. *Ibid.*, Series Q 398–409, p. 740.
3. Richard Reinhardt, ed., *Workin' on the Railroad* (New York: Weathervane Books [Crown], 1970), pp. 274–75.
4. Bernard Asbell, "A Man Ain't Nothin' But a Man," *American Heritage*, Vol. 14, No. 6, (October, 1963).
5. Herbert Hamblen, *The General Manager's Story* (MacMillan, 1898), quoted in Reinhardt, *op. cit.*, p. 84.
6. *Ibid.*, pp. 86–7.
7. *Ibid.*
8. *Ibid.*
9. Quoted in *The Railroad Era* (Cambridge, Mass.: American Education Publications [Graduate School of Education, Harvard University], 1967).
10. Reinhardt, *op. cit.*, p. 130.
11. *Ibid.*, pp. 133–36.
12. Samuel Gompers, *Seventy Years of Life and Labor* (New York: E. P. Dutton, 1927), I.
13. *Ibid.*
14. *Ibid.*
15. J. A. Dacus, *Annals of the Great Strikes* (New York: Arno Press, 1969. Reprint of work originally published in 1878), p. 27.

16. Ibid., p. 29.
17. Ibid., p. 30.
18. Ibid., pp. 32–3.
19. Ibid., pp. 22–3.
20. Ibid., p. 51.
21. Ibid., p. 20–1.
22. Ibid., p. 43.
23. Ibid., p. 47–8.
24. Ibid., p. 49–50.
25. Ibid., p. 60.
26. Ibid., p. 61.
27. Ibid., p. 66.
28. Ibid., p. 85–6.
29. Ibid., p. 67.
30. Ibid., p. 71–2.
31. Ibid., p. 95.
32. *Humboldt Register and Working Mens Advocate*, Unionville, Nevada, May 15, 1869, quoted in Richard E. Lingenfelter, *The Hard Rock Miners* (University of California Press, 1974).
33. Dacus, *op. cit.*, p. 102–3.
34. Ibid., p. 103–4.
35. Ibid., p. 106–7.
36. Ibid., p. 106–7.
37. Ibid., p. 121.
38. Ibid., p. 124.
39. Ibid., p. 94–5.
40. Susan J. Kleinberg, "Technology and Women's Work: The Lives of Working Class Women in Pittsburgh, 1870–1900," *Labor History*, Vol. 17, No. 1 (Winter, 1976); based on an article in the *American Glass Review*, December 12, 1877.
41. Dacus, *op. cit.*, pp. 139–40.
42. Ibid., p. 141.
43. Ibid., p. 146.
44. Ibid., p. 253.
45. Ibid., p. 208.
46. Ibid., pp. 255–56.
47. Ibid., Ibid. p. 363.

5. Dig Up and Bury Again

1.–27. All quotes from John W. Grannis, Book and Diary ("Bought this Book of Woolworth & Moffat in Denver City Colorado Territory May 1st 1863"), Montana Historical Society, Helena, Montana.
28. Christopher Columbus, letter to his friend Sanchez, 1493.
29. E. Gould Buffum, *Six Months in the Gold Mines* (Ward Ritchie Press, 1959), pp. 54–5.
30. Vardis Fisher and O. L. Holmes, *Gold Rushes and Mining Camps* (Caldwell, Idaho: Caxton Printers), p. 51.
31. Libeus Barney, *Letters of the Pikes Peak Gold Rush* (San Jose, Ca.: The Talsiman Press), pp. 23–25.
32. Lucille McDonald and Werner Lenggenhager, *The Look of Old Time Washington* (Superior Publishing Co.), p. 53.
33. T. H. Watkins, *Gold and Silver in the West*, p. 51–2.
34. Ibid.
35. William S. Greever, *The Bonanza West* (Norman, Oklahoma: University of Oklahoma Press, 1963), pp. 97–8.
36. Dee Brown, *Bury My Heart at Wounded Knee* (New York: Holt, Rinehart, and Winston, 1971), p. 265.
37. Watkins, *op. cit.*, p. 87.
38. Buffum, *op. cit.*, p. 64.
39. Howard C. Gardner, *In Pursuit of the Golden Dream* (Stoughton, Mass.: Western Hemisphere, 1970), pp. 81–2.

40. Barney, *op. cit.*, p. 40.
41. Fisher and Holmes, *op. cit.*, pp. 211–12.
42. *Ibid.*, p. 402.
43. William H. Brewer, Professor of Agriculture, 1860–64, *Up and Down California* [a journal] (University of California Press, 1966), pp. 555–56.
44. Correspondence of John Taylor Hall, New York Public Library, MSS and Archives Division.
45. Brewer, *op. cit.*, p. 440.

6. The Bottom of the Pyramid

1. Diary of Benjamin Franklin Jones, Archives of Industrial Society, University of Pittsburgh Libraries.
2. *Ibid.*, entry of May 24, 1875.
3. *Ibid.*, entry of June 2, 1873.
4. Thomas L. Lloyd, *History of the Jones and Laughlin Steel Corp.*, Archives of Industrial Society, University of Pittsburgh Libraries, December 1, 1938, p. 4.
5. Jones and Laughlin Steel Corporation, *Pioneer in Steel Progress—A Brief History of Jones and Laughlin*, in Archives *loc. cit.*
6. Lloyd, *op. cit.*
7.–30. Jones diary, *op. cit.*
31. John A. Fitch, *The Steel Workers* (New York: Arno Press, 1969. Reprint of original book by Russell Sage Foundation, 1910), p. 200.
32. *Ibid.*, p. 218–19.
33. *Ibid.*, p. 33–4.
34. *Ibid.*, p. 241.
35. *Ibid.*, p. 64–6.
36. *Ibid.* pp. 195–96, 198–99.
37. Willis L. King, "Address Delivered at Dedication of the B. F. Jones Memorial Library, Aliquippa, Pennsylvania, February 1, 1929," in Archives, *loc. cit.*
38. Lloyd, *op. cit.*
39.–53. William R. Russell, letters to his mother, Library of Congress MSS Division.
54. Vice-President Colfax's speech, July 4, 1870, quoted in Walt Whitman, *Democratic Vistas* [Notes] (September, 1870).
55. *Historical Statistics of the United States* (U.S. Department of Commerce, Series M 205–220), p. 600.
56. *Ibid.*, Series M 93–106, p. 590.
57. Leon Stein and Philip Taft, eds., *Workers Speak: Self Portraits* (New York: Arno Press, 1971. Reprinted from the original publication by Hamilton Holt in the weekly *Independent* between 1902 and 1906), pp. 16–19.
58. *Ibid.*
59. *Historical Statistics of the United States* (U.S. Department of Commerce, Series P 318–374), p. 701.
60. *Ibid.*
61. *Ibid.*, Series L 113–121, p. 542.
62. Father Andrew M. Prouty, Archdiocese of Seattle, "Logging with Steam in the Pacific Northwest" (Master's thesis, University of Washington, 1973), p. viii–xiv.
63. *Ibid.*, p. xvi.
64. *Ibid.*, pp. 150–51.
65. Fitch, *op. cit.*, p. 201*et seq.*
66. *Historical Statistics of the United States* (U.S. Department of Commerce, Series P 1–12), p. 666.
67. *Ibid.* Figures reckoned by dividing total production in dollars by the population of the workforce.
68. *Ibid.*
69. Merl E. Reed, "The Augusta Textile Mills and the Strike of 1886," *Labor History*, Vol. 14, No. 2 (Spring, 1973), p. 230.
70. *Labor and Capital, Investigation of the Senate Committee on Education and Labor*, 1885, III, p. 452.
71. "A Collar Starcher's Story," (August 10, 1905) in Stein and Taft, eds. *op. cit.*, pp. 78–79.

72. "The Story of a Sweatshop Girl," (September 25, 1902), *ibid.*
73. James Swisher, *How I Know, or, Sixteen Years Eventful Experience* (Cincinnati, Ohio: Published by author, 1881).
74.–77. Len F. Carroll, Diary, Archives of the Oklahoma Historical Society.
78. Isaac Phillips Roberts, *Autobiography of a Farm Boy* (Cornell University Press, 1946. Originally published in 1916).
79. Richard Ringer, Diary, Department of MSS and University Archives, Cornell University, Ithaca, New York.
80. "One Farmer's Wife," (February 9, 1905) in Stein and Taft, eds., *op. cit.*
81. Nancy Holeman, Diary, Western History MSS Collection, University of Missouri.

7. A Storm of Strangers

1. *Historical Statistics of the United States* (U.S. Department of Commerce, Series C 89–119), p. 105 *et. seq.*
2. Michael Ebner, "Deserting the Poor," *Labor History*, Vol. 12, No. 4 (Fall, 1971).
3. Mary Boykin Chesnut, *A Diary from Dixie*, ed. Ben Ames Williams (Boston: Houghton Mifflin and Co.,⁀), p. 270.
4. *Historical Statistics of the United States* (U.S. Department of Commerce, Series C 89–119).
5. Chesnut, *op. cit.*, pp. 542–44.
6. Allis R. Wolfe, "Letters of a Lowell Mill Girl and Friends," *Labor History*, Vol. 17, No. 1 (Winter, 1976), from the MSS. in the Harriet Hanson Robinson Collection, Schlesinger Library, Radcliff College, Cambridge, Mass.
7. William Cohn, *A Pictorial History of American Labor* (New York: Crown Publishers, 1972), p. 54.
8. *Ibid.*, pp. 54–6.
9. Herbert G. Gutman, "Five Letters of Immigrant Workers from Scotland to the U.S.," *Labor History*, Vol. 9, No. 3 (Fall, 1968). These letters were originally published in the weekly *Glasgow* [Scotland] *Sentinel*, October 6 and November 13, 1869.
10. *Ibid.*
11. *Ibid.*
12.–22. J. C. Kuner, "Memoirs of J. C. Kuner," unpublished, dictated by Kuner from May 17 to July 29, 1897, trans. C. E. Mead. Now in the possession of Kuner's great-great-granddaughter, Mrs. Margaret McDowd Leiser.
23. *Historical Statistics of the United States* (U.S. Department of Commerce, Series M 205–220).
24. Stephen Thernstrom, *The Other Bostonians* (Cambridge, Mass.: Harvard University Press, 1973), p. 139.
25. Victor Wolfgang von Hagen, *The Germanic People in America* (Norman, Oklahoma: University of Oklahoma Press, 1976), pp. 334–35.
26. Mary K. Simkhovitch, *City Workers World* (New York: MacMillan, 1917).
27.–33. Agnes M., "The True Life of a Nurse Girl," (September 24, 1903), in Leon Stein and Philip Taft, eds. *Workers Speak: Self Portraits* (New York: Arno Press, 1971), pp. 99–104.
34. Christian Jensen, *An American Saga* (Boston: Little, Brown and Co., 1927).
35. *Ibid.*
36.–40. Axel Jarlson, "A Swedish Emigrant's Story," (January 8, 1903), Stein and Taft, eds., *op. cit.*, pp. 88–92.
41. *Historical Statistics of the United States* (U.S. Department of Commerce, Series M 205–220).
42. Jacob Riis, *How the Other Half Lives* (Scribners, 1890).
43. *Historical Statistics of the United States, op. cit.*
44. J. Walter Coleman, *Molly Maguire Riots* (Richmond, Virginia: Richmond, Garrett, and Massie, 1936), p. 20.
45. Joel Tyler Headly, *The Great Riots of New York* (New York: Dover, 1971. Originally published by E. B. Treat, New York, 1873), pp. 146–49.
46. *Ibid.*, p. 304.
47.–49. "The Story of an Irish Cook," (March 30, 1905), Stein and Taft, eds., *op. cit.*
50. Jacob Riis, Papers, Library of Congress MSS Division.
51. Lester S. Levy, ed., *Flashes of Merriment* (University of Oklahoma Press, 1971), pp. 126, 140.

52. "The Story of an Irish Cook," *loc. cit.*

53. John Taylor Hall, letter to his friend William Ward, April 8, 1876, New York Public Library Archives and MSS Division.

54. New York Public Library, William Williams Collection, Item 47X539 (1).

55. Simkhovitch, *op. cit.*, pp. 14–16, 77, 122, 131.

56. *Ibid.*

57.–65. "Biography of a Bootblack," (December 4, 1902), Stein and Taft, eds., *op. cit.*

66. Ernest Boehm, letter to William Williams, Commissioner of Immigration (n.d.), New York Public Library, William Williams Collection.

67. Lee Chew, "Biography of a Chinaman," (February 19, 1903), Stein and Taft, eds., *op. cit.*

68. Antanas Kaztauskis, "From Lithuania to the Chicago Stock Yards," (August 4, 1904), Stein and Taft eds., *op. cit.*

69. Chew, *op. cit.*

70. *Ibid.*

71. Kaztauskis, *op. cit.*

72. *Ibid.*

73. Chew, *op. cit.*

74. Kaztauskis, *op. cit.*

75. *Ibid.*

76. Chew, *op. cit.*

77. Kaztauskis, *op. cit.*

78. Chew, *op. cit.*

79. Kaztauskis, *op. cit.*

80.–82. *Ibid.*

83.–93. Kazuo Ito, *Issei: A History of Japanese Immigrants in North America* (Seattle: Executive Committee for the Publication of Issei, 1973).

94.–109. Mrs. Ethel Ginsberg, tape in possession of the author, recorded May 9, 1976.

110. Ito, *op. cit.*

111.–113. Ginsberg, *op. cit.*

114. Ito, *op. cit.*

115.–117. Ginsberg, *op. cit.*

118. Stein and Taft, eds. *op cit.*, pp. 6–7.

119.–121. Ginsberg, *op. cit.*

8. If You Don't Come in Sunday Don't Come in Monday

1. Ray Stannard Baker, *The Tourney*, [Chicago], 1894.

2. Baker, *Chicago Record*, March 16, 1894.

3. Baker, *The Tourney*, 1894.

4. "The Prayer Answered," 1894, a throwaway sheet, Library of Congress MSS Division.

5. Baker, *The Chicago Record*, March 14, 1894.

6. *Ibid.*, March 15, 1894.

7. Baker, Papers, Library of Congress Archives and MSS Division.

8. Baker, *The Chicago Record*, March 18, 1894.

9. *Ibid.*, March 22, 1894.

10. *Ibid.*, March 22, 1894.

11. *Ibid.*, March 23, 1894.

12. *Ibid.*, March 27, 1894.

13. *Ibid.*, March 24, 1894.

14. *Ibid.*, March 29, 1894.

15. *Ibid.*, March 27, 1894.

16. *Ibid.*, March 28, 1894.

17. *Ibid.*, March 29, 1894.

18. *Ibid.*, March 30, 1894.

19. *Ibid.*, March 25, 1894.

20. *Ibid.*, March 25, 1894.

21. *Ibid.*, April 3, 1894.

22. *Ibid.*, April 8, 1894.

23. *Ibid.*, April 15, 1894.

24. *Ibid.*, April 15, 1894.

25. *Ibid.*, April 18, 1894.
26. *Ibid.*, April 30, 1894.
27.–31. *Ibid.*, May, 1894.
32. *Ibid.*, May 2, 1894.
33. Emma F. Langdon, *The Cripple Creek Strike* (New York: Arno Press. Originally published by Great Western Publishing Co., Denver, Colorado, 1904).
34. *Rocky Mountain News,* March 5, 1903.
35. Franklin E. Coyne, *The Development of the Cooperage Industry in the United States* (Chicago: Lumber Buyers' Publishing Co., 1940), quoted in Herbert G. Gutman, *Work, Culture and Society in Industrializing America* (New York: Random House).
36. Frederick W. Taylor, Hearings Before the Special Committee of the House of Representatives to Investigate the Taylor and Other Systems of Shop Management, 1912.
37. Richard L. Ehrlich, "Immigrant Strike Breaking Activity," *Labor History,* Vol. 15, No. 4 (Fall, 1974), p. 553.
38. Emma F. Langdon, *op. cit.* p. 118.
39. *Ibid.*, pp. 78–9.
40. *Autobiography of Mother Jones* (Chicago: Charles Kerr and Co., 1927), pp. 69–70.
41. Emma F. Langdon, *op. cit.*, p. 95.
42.–56. *Ibid.*, pp. 95, 50, 106, 104–42, 282, 212, 285, 453, 385, 327, 280–82, 352–53, 316–19, 320 (testimony of Arthur Parker, "While Lying on a Hospital Cot"), 422, 423–24, and 345.
57. John A. Fitch, *The Steel Workers* (New York: Arno Press, 1969. Reprint of original book by Russell Sage Foundation, 1910), pp. 239–40.
58. Merl E. Reed, "The Augusta Textile Mills and the Strike of 1886," *Labor History,* Vol. 14, No. 2 (Spring, 1973), p. 234.
59. Arthur G. Burgoyne, *Homestead* (Pittsburgh, 1894).
60. Harvey Wish, "The Pullman Strike: A Study in Industrial Warfare," *Journal of the Illinois State Historical Society,* Vol. 32, No. 3 (September, 1939).
61. *Ibid.*, p. 294.
62. *Ibid.*, p. 295.
63. *Ibid.*, p. 298.
64. *Ibid.*, p. 299.
65. *Ibid.*, pp. 301–07.
66. Graham Adams, Jr., *The Age of Industrial Violence, 1910–15* (Columbia University Press, 1960), p. 133.
67. *Ibid.*, p. 149.
68. Brigadier General John Chase, "Report of the Commanding General of the Colorado National Guard," April 6, 1914, reprinted in *The Ludlow Massacre* (New York: Arno Press), pp. 12–13.
69. *Ibid.*, p. 14.
70. *Ibid.*, p. 27.
71. *Ibid.*, pp. 28–29.
72. *Ibid.*, pp. 33–34.
73. *Ibid.*, p. 45.
74. George P. West, "Report on the Colorado Strike," for the U.S. Commission on Industrial Relations, Washington, D.C., 1915, reprinted as part of *The Ludlow Massacre* (New York: Arno Press), p. 129.
75. *Ibid.*, p. 130–31.
76. Graham Adams, Jr., *op. cit.*, pp. 162–64.
77. *Historical Statistics of the United States* (U.S. Department of Commerce, Series P 1–67), II, pp. 666–80.
78. *Ibid.*, Series D 927–969, I, pp. 176–78.
79. *Ibid.*, Series D 913–926, I, pp. 175–76.
80. *Ibid.*, Series D 765–778, I, pp. 168.
81. John A. Fitch, *op. cit.*, p. 18.
82. *Ibid.*, p. 232.
83. Mrs. Gertrude B. Hunt in *The Bethlehem Globe* (February 11, 1910), quoted in Robert Hessen, "Bethelehem Steel Strike of 1910," *Labor History,* Vol. 15, No. 1 (Winter, 1974).
84. Margaret F. Byington, *Homestead: The Households of a Mill Town* (New York: Arno Press. Originally published by Russell Sage Foundation, 1910).

85. From the manuscript of the constitution of The Miners Union of Gold Hill, Nevada, in the Special Collection, University of Nevada Library, quoted in Richard E. Lingenfelter, *The Hard Rock Miners* (University of California Press, 1974).

86. *A Brief History of the American Labor Movement* (U.S. Department of Labor, Bulletin 1000 [Washington, D.C., 1970]), p. 15.

87. Samuel Gompers, letter books, Library of Congress MSS Division, quoted in Philip S. Foner, "Samuel Gompers to Frederick Engels: A Letter," *Labor History*, Vol. 11, No. 2 (Spring, 1970).

88. *Chicago Tribune*, May 5, 1886.

89. Samuel Fielden, address to the court, printed in full in *The Accused and the Accusers* (New York: Arno Press. Originally published by the Socialistic Publishing Society, Chicago, 1887).

90. *Ibid.*, address of Albert R. Parson, p. 91.

91. *Ibid.*, address of Michel Schwab, p. 27–8.

92. *Ibid.*, address of Albert R. Parsons, p. 160.

93. *Ibid.*, address of Albert R. Parsons, p. 118.

94. "Liberty, A Speech by Eugene V. Debs, Delivered on November 22, 1895," printed in full in *The Pullman Strike* (New York: Arno Press, 1969. Originally published by E. V. Debs Company, Terre Haute, Indiana).

95. Emma F. Langdon, *op. cit.* pp. 487–88.

96. Joe Hill, "The Preacher and the Slave," reprinted in *The I.W.W. Anthology*.

97. *Proceedings of the First Convention of the I.W.W.* (New York, 1905).

9. The Secrets of the Ordinary

1. Thomas A. Edison, Diary, original in the Edison Archives, Edison National Historical Site, West Orange, New Jersey, p. 27–28.

2. *Ibid.*, pp. 17–18.

3. Captain Henry T. Owen (Pickett's Division), "Reminiscences of the War," MSS from the Virginia State Library, Richmond, Virginia.

4. *Historical Statistics of the United States* (U.S. Department of Commerce, Series M 205–220).

5. "A College Professor's Wife," (November 30, 1905), in Leon Stein and Philip Taft, eds. *Workers Speak: Self Portraits* (New York: Arno Press, 1971).

6. Doctor Boon, Diary, Idaho State Library, MSS Archives, 1914–16.

7. Thomas A. Edison, *op. cit.*

8. Franis Jehl, *Menlo Park Reminiscences* (1930), quoted in George E. Davidson, *Beehives of Invention* (National Park Service History Series).

9. Henry H. Snelling, *The History and Practice of the Art of Photography* (New York, 1849. Reprinted by Morgan and Morgan).

10. Robert Taft, *Photography and the American Scene* (New York: Dover. Originally printed by MacMillan, 1938).

11. *Ibid.* Quoting George Eastman's testimony in the case of Goodwin Film and Camera Company versus Eastman Kodak.

12. Thomas A. Edison, *op. cit.*, p. 34.

13.–15. Ella Wheeler Wilcox, *Maurine* [a verse romance with photographs] (W. B. Conkey & Co., 1901).

16.–18. Summary of *The Gunfighter* by Monte M. Katterjohn, Library of Congress MSS Division, William S. Hart Collection.

19.–23. George Berrell, Diary, Archives, Arizona Historical Society Library.

24.–36. L. Rogers Lytton (born Oscar Legare Rogers), Diary, New York Public Library, Archives and MSS Division, Astor, Lenox, and Tilden Foundations.

37. Anonymous, journal of an Indian boy at school in Fort Sill, Oklahoma, MSS and Archives Division, Rutgers University Library, New Brunswick, New Jersey.

38. *Ibid.*

39.–46. Miss Eulalie Matthews, Diary, New York Public Library, MSS and Archives Division, Astor, Lenox, and Tilden Foundations, courtesy of her daughter, Mrs. Eulalie Ashmore Scull.

47.–54. From *The Dunnville Journal*, a family newspaper put out by eleven-year-old Edwin M. Dunn, Library Archives, Knox College, Galesburg Hill, Illinois.

55. Edwin Markham, Benjamin B. Lindsey, and George Creel, *Children in Bondage* (New York: Arno Press. Originally published by Hearst's International Library, 1914), pp. 46–7.
56. *Ibid.*, p. 28.
57. *Ibid.*, p. 30.
58. Emma F. Langdon, *The Cripple Creek Strike* (New York: Arno Press. Originally published by Great Western Publishing Co., Denver, Colorado, 1904).
59. Mary Boykin Chesnut, *A Diary from Dixie*, ed. Ben Ames Williams (Boston: Houghton Mifflin and Co., 1950), p. 32.
60. *Ibid.*, p. 228.
61. Stein and Taft, eds., *op. cit.*, p. 90.
62. Margaret F. Byington, *Homestead: The Households of a Mill Town* (New York: Arno Press. Originally published by Russell Sage Foundation, 1910), p. 63.
63ı. *Ibid.*, p. 64.
64. *Ibid.*, pp. 27–28.
65. William H. Brewer, Professor of Agriculture, 1860–64, *Up and Down California* [a journal] (University of California Press, 1966), p. 348.
66. William S. Greever, *The Bonanza West* (University of Oklahoma Press, 1963) pp. 139–40.
67. *Ibid.*, pp. 319–20.
68.–69. Autobiography of Nell Kimball, quoted in Stephen Longstreet's *Sportin' House*, Sherbourne Press, 1965.
70. John March, letter concerning Comstock's speech at the Park Street Church, Boston, March 28, 1877, in the Comstock File, New York Public Library, MSS and Archives Division, Astor, Lenox, and Tilden Foundations.
71. Chesnut, *op. cit.*, p. 44.
72. Letter to Mary Brewer from her future husband, George Henry Penniman, private collection of Mary Millard, Aspen, Colorado.
73. Miss Eulalie Matthews, *op. cit.*
74. Chesnut, *op. cit.*, p. 272.
75. *Ibid.*, p. 463.
76. *Ibid.*, p. 309.
77. *Ibid.*, pp. 312–13.
78. *Ibid.*, pp. 529–30.
79. Anonymous diary, Library of Congress MSS and Archives Division.
80. John Taylor Hall, Letter, New York Public Library Archives and MSS Division.
81. William and Harriet Waters, Diary, Archives and MSS Division, Rutgers University Library, Princeton.
82. *Ibid.*
83. L. Rogers Lytton, *op. cit.*, entry of August 29, 1915.
84. Letter to Mrs. Mary Penniman from her grandmother, Abigail Brewer, private collection of Mary Millard, Aspen, Colorado.
85. Mrs. Hall, diary of a trip to New York City, April 10, 1879, New York Public Library, MSS and Archives Division, Astor, Lenox, and Tilden Foundations.
86. *Ibid.*
87. Ella Wheeler Wilcox, *op. cit.*
88. Emily Dickinson, *Poems* [second series], ed. Thomas W. Higginson and Mabel L. Todd (Boston: Roberts Brothers, 1891). Poem written in 1873.
89. General Henry Freeman, Diary, Wyoming State Historical Research and Publications Division, Cheyenne, Wyoming.
90. Walt Whitman, *Specimen Days and Collect* (Philadelphia: Rees Welsh, 1882), entry of August 26, 1879.
91. *Diary and Letters of John Clifford Brown* (privately printed, 1899), Library of Congress.
92. *Ibid.*
93. *New York Times*, April 3, 1917.
94. *Ibid.*
95. *Diary and Letters of Sergeant Peyton Randolph Campbell* ([published privately] Buffalo, New York: Pratt and Lambert, 1919).